THE PORTABLE QUEEN

The
Portable
Queen

Elizabeth I
and the Politics
of Ceremony

MARY HILL COLE

UNIVERSITY OF MASSACHUSETTS PRESS

AMHERST

Copyright © 1999 by
University of Massachusetts Press
All rights reserved

Printed in the United States of America
LC 99-27676
ISBN 1-55849-214-3

Designed by Milenda Nan Ok Lee
Printed and bound by Sheridan Books

Library of Congress Cataloging-in-Publication Data

Cole, Mary Hill, 1957–
The portable queen : Elizabeth I and the politics of ceremony / Mary Hill Cole.
p.   cm.—(Massachusetts studies in early modern culture)
Includes bibliographical references (p.   ) and index.
ISBN 1-55849-214-3 (cloth : alk. paper)
1. Elizabeth I, Queen of England, 1533–1603.   2. Great Britain—Court and courtiers—
History—16th century.   3. Rites and ceremonies—England—History—16th
century.   4. Great Britain—Politics and government—1558–1603.   5. England—Social
life and customs—16th century.   6. Visits of state—England—History—16th
century.   7. Royal visitors—England—History—16th century.   8. Processions—
England—History—16th century.   9. Monarchy—England—History—16th
century.   I. Title.   II. Series.
DA356.C56 1999
942.05′5′092—dc21   99-27676
                                                                                              CIP

British Library Cataloguing in Publication data are available.

For my parents, Howson and Elizabeth Cole

Roam and you will confound adversaries,
sit and they will confound you.

Clifford Geertz, "Centers, Kings, and Charisma"

CONTENTS

ACKNOWLEDGMENTS

As my own progress through the queen's progresses concludes, I am glad of the opportunity to thank publicly some of the people who have helped me along the way. I began this study under the supervision of Martin Havran, whose love of history, high standards, and concern for his students continue to inspire. In 1993 at a summer institute sponsored by the National Endowment for the Humanities at the Folger Shakespeare Library, Thomas Greene's discussions of Renaissance ceremonies and texts led to important refocusing. I would like to thank him, the NEH, Barbara Mowat, Lena Orlin, and all the members of our group for a transformative summer.

In shadowing the queen, I spent many satisfying hours in archives and libraries, where I was helped by the staffs of the Coventry, Essex, Norfolk, Suffolk, and Warwick Record Offices, the Public Record Office, Bodleian Library, British Library, Cambridge University Library, Institute of Historical Research, Lambeth Palace Library, Dr. Williams's Library, Virginia Historical Society, and Alderman Library, University of Virginia. I especially appreciate the efficient and gracious aid from the Reading Room staff of the Folger Shakespeare Library. In particular, I would like to thank Betsy Walsh for her advice and timely suggestion of the jacket illustration.

My manuscript has been in good hands at the University of Massachusetts Press, a contact I owe to David Sacks. Arthur Kinney, editor of the series, advised and kept me informed at each stage. It has been a pleasure to work with Bruce Wilcox, Carol Betsch, Pamela Wilkinson, Ella Kusnetz, Catlin Murphy, and Barbara Palmer. Thanks also to the University of Delaware Press for permission to reprint parts of chapter 5 from Doug Rutledge, ed., *Ceremony and Text in the Renaissance* (1996), 84–100; and the Bodleian Library and the Public Record Office for permission to use the material in the appendixes.

Teaching at a small liberal arts college has many joys, but the leisure to research during the academic year is not one of them. I am grateful, therefore, for the commitment to sabbaticals of Cynthia Tyson, president of Mary Baldwin College, and James Lott, dean of the college. Without that crucial time, I still would be inching my way through a rough draft. Institutional support provided by the Menk Award and college grants for summer research have facilitated my travels to archives. Lydia Petersson helped in preparing grant applications, Charlene Plunkett filled my interlibrary loan requests, it seemed by return mail, and Eric Jones more than once solved my computer and printing problems.

To the readers who have critiqued different stages of this study, I owe a large debt of gratitude. Ralph Cohen read every draft, always urging me to greater clarity of logic and felicity of language; I cannot imagine completing this work without him. Malcolm Smuts and Susan Frye made extensive comments on the entire manuscript that helped me hone the argument and strengthen my organization. I also appreciate the responses of Everett Crosby, Nicholas Edsall, Cindy Kierner, Kate Cohen, Judy Klein, Marlena Hobson, and Anne McGovern.

Hospitality and friendships have colored here both life and text. In London, Major Dick and Mrs. Fatima Richards welcomed me into their family, and the neighborliness of John and Lisa Neikirk, Judy and Ralph Cohen, Tom Berger, and Robin and Harry Atwood led me to stay longer sometimes than I should have. Generous colleagues who shared their expertise include Martha Evans, Carrie Douglass, Gary Gibbs, Ken Keller, Kate Franzén, Sarah O'Connor, Jim Schiffer, Lex Renda, and Ken Fincham. And for their conviviality and prodding, my warm thanks to Kathy Jennings, Judy Klein, Anne McGovern, Cindy Kierner, Helen Poindexter, Paul Borzelleca, and Marlena Hobson.

The encouragement from my parents, from Howie, Lisa, Shane, and Brett Cole, and from Amy, Sady, Kate, Judy, and Ralph Cohen cheered me during the course of this project. And to my students, first at the University of Virginia, then Wilson College, and now at Mary Baldwin, I thank you for the challenges, the creativity, and the growth that we have shared in studying history together.

M. H. C.

THE PORTABLE QUEEN

The Counties of
ENGLAND

MILES

0   20   40   60   80

SCOTLAND

NORTHUMBERLAND

CUMBERLAND   DURHAM

WESTMORLAND

ENGLAND

YORKSHIRE

LANCASHIRE

CHESHIRE   DERBY   NOTTINGHAM   LINCOLN

WALES

STAFFORD

SHROPSHIRE   LEICESTER   RUTLAND

NORFOLK

WORCESTER   WARWICK   NORTHAMPTON   HUNTINGDON

HEREFORD   BEDFORD   CAMBRIDGE   SUFFOLK

MONMOUTH   GLOUCESTER   OXFORD   BUCKINGHAM   HERTFORD   ESSEX

MIDDLESEX

LONDON

WILTSHIRE   BERKSHIRE   SURREY   KENT

SOMERSET   HAMPSHIRE   SUSSEX

DEVON   DORSET

CORNWALL

ONE

Introduction

Every spring and summer of her 44 years as queen, Elizabeth I insisted that her court go with her on "progress," a series of royal visits to towns and aristocratic homes in southern England. Between 1558 and 1603, her visits to over 400 individual and civic hosts provided the only direct contact most people had with a monarch who made popularity a cornerstone of her reign. These visits gave the queen a public stage on which to present herself as the people's sovereign and to interact with her subjects in a calculated attempt to keep their support. While all Renaissance monarchs of necessity traveled, the progresses of Elizabeth were both emblematic of her rule and intrinsic to her ability to govern. These visits provided the settings in which Elizabeth crafted her royal authority. In their expression of her role as sovereign queen, the progresses reflected the strengths and limitations of Elizabeth's personal monarchy.

The progresses of Elizabeth I reveal much about the queen's agenda, her priorities, and her character. During four decades, the queen committed her financial resources to the maintenance of the court on progress. That these funds came from a fiscally conservative monarch, not known for largesse, heightened the significance of this royal investment: in Elizabeth's judgment, the burdens of travel were worth its rewards. The heart of the progresses was the blend of politics, socializing, and ceremony that enabled the queen to accomplish royal business on the move while satisfying the needs of those courtiers, townspeople, and country residents who welcomed her into their communities. These groups, always changing in their membership and motives, pursued their own local and individual agendas within the larger national arena created by the traveling court now suddenly available to them. For hosts, royal visits became occasions to fan local pride and woo favors from their powerful, momentarily accessible guests. At the center of the crowd was a female sovereign who embraced the visit's turmoil and pageantry for the flexibility they offered. For the queen, these progresses satisfied her needs—personal and political—by creating ceremonially rich moments of dialogue that advanced royal goals and diminished ministerial interference. No wonder she kept moving.

Through her intentional wanderings, the queen made conscious choices about her destinations that reflected her perception of the political and diplomatic scene. Her progresses brought the queen into the homes of both her favorite courtiers and those in disgrace, such as the duke of Norfolk, for whom the private visit might erase past indiscretions and return them to favor. Trusted ministers and old friends had their privileged position marked by frequent or lavish royal visits. Elizabeth recognized that the power of her queenly presence and the symbolism attached to the crown made the progresses useful in matters related to her prerogative. The queen saw such issues—the succession, marriage, war, diplomacy, and religion—as properly belonging to her, and traveling provided occasions for her to communicate her views on these matters. Her military duty to defend the kingdom, which her fellow kings fulfilled in invasions, battles, and wars, Elizabeth carried out by crafting bellicose ceremonies that expressed England's power. Visiting ports such as Bristol, Southampton, Portsmouth, and Dover let her inspect the defenses in the fortified towns. These civic visits, with their martial pageants and mock battles, conveyed an impression of English military strength to foreign rulers. Standing on English soil, she fought her international battles.

In matters of religion as well as war, the progresses helped the queen exert her prerogative. In her travels, Elizabeth encouraged religious conformity by setting the correct example and then pressuring her subjects to abandon their resistance to the established church. The vestments controversy, for example, drew the queen to the two universities, where her presence brought the scholars, at least temporarily, into outward conformity. One of her steps against unlicensed preaching involved visits to Bristol and Canterbury so that the wayward people could see their religious governor in all her royal splendor and thereafter mend their ways. Bolder methods characterized her visit to Ipswich, where the angry queen issued a ringing denunciation of women residing on the cathedral grounds and demanded obedience to her injunctions to vacate. But she proved willing to tolerate occasional Puritan activity when the controversy threatened the local stability. In East Anglia in 1578, for example, her concern for religious conformity yielded to her concern for harmony, and she turned the religious issue into a political one that she could finesse. By publicly rewarding her conformist hosts, no matter how marginal or nominal their obedience, and by reversing the anti-Puritan policies of the bishop, the queen recognized that peace in the counties was worth some increased Puritan activity. Even recusant hosts entertained the queen, as Elizabeth chose to validate their loyalty and by example to draw them into conformity with her national church. Her progresses reminded observers and participants of the ceremonial authority of the queen in matters of religion.

Thus, in a variety of ways Elizabeth made her progresses part of a government that existed as an extension of her royal authority. Beyond the matters of royal prerogative, her travels brought the people into contact—visual, physical, or indirect—with their monarch in an overt solicitation of their support. Her public entertainments, speeches in welcoming towns, and open travel through the countryside allowed people to form an impression of Elizabeth as accessible and successful. As propaganda, the progresses fostered an appealing image of the queen that won her the goodwill so necessary to her longevity and success as a monarch. This image was often more important than the reality: the demonstrable popularity of Elizabeth, the sense that she had a secure tenure, carried her through the rough spells that came more frequently in her later years. Her popularity implied a consensus, real or imaginary, which in turn created a base of support for the last Tudor.

The extensive participation of her hosts in the progresses indicated how central to her rule was this interaction with hundreds of her subjects. Increased access to the queen enabled hosts to solicit favors and enhance their local prestige through such occasions of hospitality. In her later years, as her ministers and household grew reluctant to suffer the inconvenience of travel and dissatisfied courtiers and hosts looked with self-interest toward the arrival of the next monarch, willingness to entertain the queen waned, but Elizabeth still could make a progress if she chose. Compared to hosts in the 1570s, later reluctant hosts had become more vocal about their feelings, but the queen always had hosts ready to open their doors as she made her last long journeys in the 1590s. The tradition of hospitality and the opportunity for rewards created a general willingness among hosts to entertain the queen, who continued through her reign to see progresses as central to her government and to her dominance of the court.

The progresses enabled Elizabeth to learn about local concerns and offered her subjects opportunities to solicit the queen. The civic visits in particular brought the queen face to face with petitioners who voiced grievances to their sovereign. Local officials asked the queen for help in strengthening the civic economy, especially the harbors, markets, and industries, as well as in adjudicating local disputes. A royal visit fed civic pride and, her hosts hoped, civic prosperity. The energetic receptions from the towns matched the queen's pleasure in visiting those communities so important to her governance.

Because so many willing hosts participated in the progresses, the financial burden they assumed for a visit must not have been prohibitive. The queen did not leave a stream of destitute hosts in her wake. Although civic and private hosts incurred expenses for food and entertainment, the royal household paid a substantial share of the costs for provisions, accommodations, and transportation. The progresses cost the queen more than living in royal palaces near London. Had Elizabeth wanted to save money, she would not have increased her travel but instead would have abandoned it. She never did, and this very commitment to travel, despite its expense and inconvenience to the royal household, reveals the value she placed upon progresses year after year.

Taken as a whole, her progresses offer some commentary upon the nature and strength of the monarchy in sixteenth-century England. Far from being unpleasant and inefficient rambles by an avaricious queen through her inhospitable realm, her travels gave Elizabeth moments of self-display and interaction with her subjects that became intrinsic to her rule. The cooperation between the legions of people involved in the progresses—household officers, private hosts, civic leaders, and servants—outweighed the complaints and difficulties of royal travel. The considerable organization and cost sharing by hosts and guests made the progresses possible. It was the overt cooperation of so many hosts that maintained the institution of her progresses during her long reign.

If her hosts usually supported the progresses, the royal household and financial ministers did not. Because her ministers had to cope with the added expense and inefficiency of her travels that generated extra work for them, concerted opposition to the progresses came more from within the government than from her hosts. The more, for example, Lord Burghley struggled to find money from household funds to pay for the queen's travels, the more assiduously he tried to persuade her to abandon them. He was joined in this attempt by Sir Francis Walsingham, who rarely went on what he considered wasteful progresses that distracted the queen from business. Elizabeth ignored much of this discontent because the progresses facilitated her ability to govern and enhanced her royal image; she clearly thought them worth the investment. The criticisms of the system of feeding the court, however, coming as they did from local people whose goodwill she intended to foster through her visits, at last had an impact on the queen and led to her gradual financial change from a system of purveyance to one of composition. Since the success of the progresses depended, in part, upon the public response to a royal visit, the queen took care to reform an unpopular method of supplying her court. Elizabeth cultivated her popularity by traveling; if she alienated some people by those very visits, then she would have nullified a major advantage of the progresses.

This study, then, places the progresses in the sixteenth-century world of politics and images, where the queen and her hosts exchanged ceremonial messages that advanced their own agendas. People who entertained the queen sought favors or turned that access itself into a statement about their status and reputation in the locality. For Elizabeth, going on progress reiterated her central position in the country and in the court. The constant disruption of court life inherent in her progresses generated a climate of chaos, I would suggest, whose effect was to keep the queen at the center of everyone's attention, as courtiers and hosts focused on welcoming, entertaining, and petitioning her. Elizabeth's travels inconvenienced every member of the court and hurt her treasury, but as queen she found power in the turmoil of an itinerant court and in a ceremonial dialogue with her subjects.

When I began this project, I seemed to be caught in the slip between history and literature. Literary scholars studied the progresses, for the most part, in order to concentrate on the dramatic entertainments, while historians looked at a few special visits and pageants to describe court life and the cult of Elizabeth. While both groups might briefly generalize about progresses in a larger biographical, political, or literary analysis, neither viewed the full picture of royal travel—from the symbolic to the mundane—and its impact on and reflection of the government.

The starting points for all scholars of Elizabethan progresses are two compendia published a hundred years apart: John Nichols's *Progresses and Public Processions of Queen Elizabeth* (1823) and E. K. Chambers's *Elizabethan Stage* (1923). Nichols collected and printed documents that related to the queen's four decades of travel. He included government correspondence, accounts, civic records, speeches, and family papers in his chronological reenactment of her progresses. Chambers drew from primary sources to compile a detailed itinerary of the queen's movements and a list of the plays staged before her. Despite occasional errors, together they provide a structural map of Elizabeth's travels and ceremonies.

To many scholars of Elizabethan political life, a lavish royal visit denoted Elizabeth's power as queen and the cult that developed around her. In his royal biography, John Neale linked her travels to the popularity that Elizabeth nurtured.[2] Her visits to favored courtiers and welcoming towns fostered her subjects' love and showed the quick-witted queen to advantage. The imagery of these pageants, as well as miniatures and portraits, revealed the queen in an artistic communication with her subjects that Roy Strong has analyzed in several thematic studies of political symbolism.[3] Their works show a manipulative, charming woman who controlled others through her wit and mastery of royal state ceremonies. They admire an Elizabeth who used the media of her age to shape her subjects' perceptions of their Virgin Queen and triumphant Gloriana.

A less court-oriented view emerged in the work of scholars interested in the exchange of messages between sovereigns and subjects. They turned to the pageantry of royal entries to explore competing political agendas and the maintenance of royal authority. In *Spectacle, Pageantry, and Early Tudor Policy,* Sydney Anglo found in the shows for Henry VII and Henry VIII messages of loyalty to the new conqueror, instructions on good governance, and Tudor mythmaking. David Bergeron extended such an approach to the civic entertainments that Londoners staged for Elizabeth and the Stuart kings to mark their coronation entry into the city.[3] While their ideas on the political use of public ceremony apply to progresses in general, neither author studies the extensive travels of Elizabeth.

When modern scholars do write on the progresses themselves, they often focus on an aspect of travel, not its totality. For one progress in 1561, Miller Christy chronicled the queen's itinerary, her hosts, and their expenses.[4] Curt Breight used the famous Elvetham visit of 1591 to dissect the Earl of Hertford's ceremonial agenda that led to his return to favor.[5] In her excellent analysis of purveyance in the royal household, Allegra Woodworth explained the methods and costs of feeding the court.[6] Her emphasis on the economic underpinnings of royal travel, however, excludes the political and cultural impact of progresses. Despite its apparently comprehensive title, *Palaces & Progresses of Elizabeth I* by Ian Dunlop describes only the royal residences along the Thames and ignores civic visits, the impact of travel on the household and government, and the geographical extent of the queen's movements over four decades. The kaleidoscopic effect of such particular studies suggested to me the value of an institutional study of the relationship between the government and the progresses of Elizabeth.

A cultural approach to royal travel and ritual attracted historians in the 1980s and 1990s, many of whom embraced the concepts of symbolic anthropologists. The works of Victor Turner and Clifford Geertz, in particular, have influenced historians interested in a ruler's use of ritual, the social bonds within a community, and the public expression of hierarchies.[7] Turner's analysis of rites of passage and the phases of separation, liminality, and incorporation inform Lawrence Manley's work on the processions that defined the civic identity of London.[8] They also have shaped my understanding of the effects of royal entries on a community: in the course of her progresses, Elizabeth crossed many thresholds whose owners incorporated her into their new group of subjects. She also profited, in my view, from what Turner describes as an interplay between structure and antistructure, in which she regularly created disorder through travel and used that chaos to facilitate her ability to rule. Drawing more upon the literary allegories of her public processions, Geertz argues that Elizabeth became an emblem of messages to her viewers and so invested herself with charisma or sacred authority. In analyzing Tudor–Stuart royal entries into London, Malcolm Smuts moves away from Geertz's intellectual emphasis to focus on the "social and religious conventions deeply embedded within English culture," especially among the crowds of ordinary citizens, whose responses to royal processions also defined the concept of monarchy.[9] This attention to the realities of ritual for all levels of participants, which Smuts and Manley share, has marked my approach to Elizabeth's progresses as a political institution, economic force, and impetus to hospitality.

Recent studies of Elizabethan culture have drawn together threads of literature, ritual, perspective, and gender. In her edition of four texts of shows performed for the queen, Jean Wilson argues that Elizabeth, in her courtiers' eyes and through her meetings with fantastical wild men, acted as a "figure out of romance" for whom "[e]ach progress became a Quest."[10] Wilson's view of progresses as literary romance set in a host's "fairyland" destroyed by the rude royal visitor is not one that I share. The oddity of an unmarried female ruler of a male-centered society leads Louis Montrose to argue that Elizabeth's unique status ultimately strengthened that patriarchy.[11] To the extent that she cleared herself a space in the heart of her male court and government, I would suggest, Elizabeth reshaped gender boundaries for herself, if not for others. Two recent works explore the queen's images, their messages, and her attempt to control them. In *Gloriana's Face,* editors S. P. Cerasano and Marion Wynne-Davies see the queen's strong hand in the content and dissemination of certain royal portraits.[12] The struggle for control of her image is the subject of Susan Frye's persuasive analysis in *Elizabeth I: The Competition for Representation.* Frye sees the queen blending, refiguring, and redefining aspects of gender in a way that ultimately critiqued those common assumptions. The cultural emphasis in these later works complements the related issues of power and gender that I develop in a more historical context.

Political historians of Elizabeth's reign have joined this interdisciplinary conversation and used it in their own reassessments of the queen. In her evocative works, Carole Levin explores the queen's rhetoric and actions through which she twisted contemporary views on gender into a defense of her own female sovereignty.[13] Questioning whether Elizabeth controlled her own destiny in these matters, Susan Doran and Christopher Haigh see a queen dictated to by advisors and circumstance. Haigh follows Wallace MacCaffrey in criticizing the queen for indecision and reluctance to entrust others with military power beyond her sight. In Doran's explanation, court politics, not her own desire, accounted for Elizabeth's single status.[14] The queen wanted to get married, but as no suitor satisfied everyone at the same time, the reluctant Virgin Queen lost control of that most important and intimate aspect of her life. By removing gender from the discussion and positing a queen who suffered serial disappointments, however, Doran leaves us a passive, agentless Elizabeth at odds with my analysis. As we see through this study of royal travel, her characteristic of deferring decisions, seeking control, and governing among conflicting advisors enhanced the queen's authority. The pattern of travel that I see developing over her entire reign does support John Guy's work on the disappointment and difficulty with which Elizabeth ruled in her last decade.[15] Whether the focus is marriage, court life, royal prerogative, or the role of advisors, the strengths and weaknesses of Elizabeth's rule appeared also in her progresses and serve to illuminate her government as a whole.

Exploring the intersection of these political, cultural, economic, and civic issues was a major reason for my approach to Elizabethan progresses as an institution. Studying four decades of royal travel has allowed me to see patterns and raise issues not necessarily attached to a solitary visit, although at times the questions have piled up faster than their responses. Given the potentially large nature of the project, I did make several decisions that narrowed and shaped it. For the most part, I have concentrated on those trips Elizabeth made that took the court away from London, because that city had no peers at the time and visits within its environs demanded less of the court by way of preparation. This study is not a history of every ceremonial occasion in Elizabeth's reign, complete with a semiotic analysis of all her pageants, nor does every one of her hosts appear; instead, I have concentrated on some of the important visits, for which sources were available, and on smaller moments that speak to larger issues. In many cases regarding finance, the records do not necessarily give a full, accurate picture, and the correspondence between government officials does not always contain the evidence for which I searched. I hope, however, that my layered analysis of royal travel, with its attendant expectations, costs, and inconveniences, suggests how entwined were the strategies of the queen in shaping both her image and her government through the progresses.

The structure of this book reflects the perspectives of the participants in Elizabeth's progresses. After an overview in chapter 2 of the patterns of the queen's travels during four decades, I examine in chapter 3 the difficulties such movement presented to her court, household, and purse. The most sustained criticisms of her progresses came from within her own government, voiced by those who had to do the work and find the money to sustain the court's travels. Objections about the inefficiency, inconvenience, waste, and danger of royal progresses, some of them valid, suggested that Elizabeth had compelling reasons to travel that urged her to disregard the court Cassandras. What did she stand to gain, as a monarch and a queen, that made the expense and inconvenience of the progresses worthwhile?

8

The emphasis in chapter 4 is on the individual hosts who entertained the queen. By virtue of sharing the same accommodations and schedule for at least several days, these hosts gained access to the sources of power and patronage—the queen and her councilors—and could ask for favors. Whether or not Elizabeth granted their requests, her hosts wanted to have the opportunity to live for a brief time in that royal world: their reputations, and perhaps their purses, would be the better for it. Against this background of general hospitality stand out the rare cases in which a host did not want to participate in the progresses; such famous examples of reluctance prove the exception to the rule of willing hospitality. How these reluctant hosts expressed their displeasure and why they tried to avoid a royal visit depended upon the context of the occasion. Not surprisingly, their methods and reasons changed over the course of the queen's long reign in ways that echoed the vagaries of court life and her monarchy.

To complement the analysis of private hosts, chapter 5 focuses on the occasions when an entire town served as host to the queen. Corporate hospitality suggested a relation between the single civic entity and the many citizens whose efforts comprised the town's welcome of queen and court. Explored here are the types of entertainment, the financial burden, and the civic expectations of a royal visit. Civic leaders made public requests to Elizabeth on matters ranging from improvements in the town's infrastructure to economic aid to the arbitration of local grievances. All the towns proudly invoked their charters, issued by Elizabeth's predecessors, to argue for continued royal interest in their community even as they reemphasized a long-standing corporate identity. In ceremonies that included the socially prominent and the ordinary majority, civic hosts balanced their need for concrete favors with their pride in the town's reputation and accomplishments. They expressed these ideas in a "ceremonial dialogue" in which, through actions, words, clothes, and objects, both civic host and royal visitor participated. In visiting towns, Elizabeth cultivated her popularity and strengthened the bonds of civic and royal authority.

The nature of Elizabeth's authority and her monarchy as revealed through travel is the theme of chapter 6. Through manipulation of her presence and her absence, the queen engaged in personal diplomacy on matters of religion, foreign policy, and national defense. Elizabeth blended persuasion, threats, inclusion, and exclusion in her efforts to exert her prerogative powers. In displaying her image as queen around the southern part of England, she worked to validate the social and political hierarchies while shaping and protecting her established church. Through her progresses, Elizabeth cultivated the popularity that she claimed guided her rule. While her direct contact with citizens did enhance that relationship, her travels also at times endangered her person. The success she achieved, however, pointed to the limitations of her authority as well as to the symbolic power that a monarch, even a female one, could wield.

These ideas of access, patronage, hospitality, and royal authority go to the heart of the Elizabethan monarchy. But they suggest something else about the nature of the queen's relations with those people in her constantly changing orbit: the progresses provided another opportunity for Elizabeth to manipulate her environment. Her progresses, I would suggest, created a dislocating confusion that reminded courtiers, citizens, and hosts of the queen's centrality in their lives. Every day on the road began and ended with discussions of what the queen wanted: Did she intend to stick to her schedule? Would the weather allow her to hunt? Did she enjoy the ceremonies? Would she grant the request or favor? As a single woman in a sea of male courtiers eager to influence her, Elizabeth used the dislocation of travel to preserve her royal flexibility. Her travels were an important part of her efforts to fashion a public image that portrayed her as both king and queen, man and woman, God's chosen, a warrior and a judge. Through the chaos of the progresses, so frustrating to her ministers, came a disorderly structure that Elizabeth used to preserve her independence.

What did the progresses reveal about their prime mover, the queen? This intricate system of travel that mixed the work and play of ruling a kingdom has become associated with no English monarch more closely than with Elizabeth, and that bond remains strong through generations of writers on the court of the last Tudor. In part, the great entertainments, elaborate plays, and larger-than-life images place the progresses at the heart of the Elizabethan monarchy. But what also made them central to her ability to govern, as I will argue, was the space in which to maneuver that her travels created for the queen. She relied upon the whirlwind of travel, where intentional confusion required her courtiers and hosts, most of them male, to look again and again to the woman who ruled them for decisions that shaped the smallest moments in their days. Her insistence on travel over the objections of her court wrought on a daily basis royal power, the authority of a queen regnant.

Exerting this power through the chaos of her progresses was a strategy that served the queen well in other state matters. Elizabeth used that same method to avoid making risky political or military decisions that, by their selection of one option and rejection of another, would have restricted her. She preferred that the die never be cast. Both in policy and in progresses, Elizabeth used the strategy of delay to keep eyes focused on her. When faced with a crisis, Elizabeth never enjoyed making decisions and rarely judged with speed. For some analysts and in the eyes of the general public, Elizabeth has, therefore, become famous for her waffling. Her preferred manner of handling important matters was to stand back and watch, with the hope that the crisis would dissolve or resolve itself. After all, who besides God knew when an enemy might die, a battle would erupt between English rivals, a Scottish claimant to her throne might seek sanctuary in Elizabeth's very arms? This happy fortune followed the queen in many of her most critical moments, the most significant being the destruction of the Spanish Armada, blown by a "protestant wind" north of its intended English target to crash on the rocky Irish coast. Her strategy of waiting for decisions to become moot led to her refusal to name an heir, a risky policy that rightly troubled courtiers and parliamentarians but one that time ultimately validated as Elizabeth outlived her rivals. In all these ways then, the cautious queen turned an aspect of her own character into the modus vivendi of her government. So, too, did she change her mind about a destination on her progresses or decide to stay longer in one town and skip another. The court schedule meant only what she intended it to mean, and no more. But her strategy of waiting for things to come her way, as Fortune's wheel turned, kept her councilors on progress attentive to her littlest shifts and cognizant of who ruled the kingdom.

The communication inspired by the progresses gave Elizabeth a base of support, but as her travels became limited in her later years, so did the access to her court. The separate and confrontational groups that came to characterize Stuart England had their beginning partly in the royal isolation that grew out of the crises in the 1580s and 1590s and continued more intensely in the 1630s and 1640s. However, the era in the 1570s of lengthy progresses and royal contact with the provinces gave Elizabeth a popularity that often facilitated her government in her later years. But the high value she placed upon this popular support seemed misplaced at times to her Stuart successors. The progresses helped Elizabeth with two problems that both James I and Charles I faced, namely, popular support and the cultivation of consensus among the gentry and aristocracy. As she restricted her use of progresses, she also began to face more difficulties in these matters; the cult of Elizabeth grew stronger even as the object of veneration declined in her public's estimation. Perhaps in yet another way, therefore, the last Tudor monarch experienced problems that would trouble her successors. The difficulties of the 1590s did not yield to the solutions offered through the queen's progresses, nor did subsequent kings try to make progresses essential parts of their monarchy in the way that Elizabeth had done.

However, before foreign affairs, old age, and sadness at the deaths of so many friends contributed to the decline of her great progresses, Elizabeth had profited from the "stamina, a sense of duty, and a belief that it was worth while to travel great distances and live a public life."[16] The movements of Elizabeth during her long reign provide a chronicle of her efforts, successes, and failures. Other English sovereigns had understood the benefits and pitfalls of royal travel. Most of these rulers, however, had not made the idea of travel central to their government in the way that Elizabeth had. The spectacle of her progresses fascinated her contemporaries, in part because Elizabeth had made the process of travel so representative of her government and of herself. In their reputation as great occasions of entertainment and ceremonial dialogue and in their demands, both financial and physical, placed upon the government and the people, the progresses of Elizabeth represented the same strengths and weaknesses of the queen who so valued them.

TWO

Patterns of the Progresses

A ll English and European monarchs traveled around the kingdoms they claimed to rule. The necessity of motion came from long-standing realities of personal and dynastic health. Palaces needed airing and cleaning to remove waste from months of the court's continued presence. Rulers visited scattered royal castles and fortifications to coerce obedience from subjects in a time when royal authority depended upon such face to face meetings. In her need to move between royal palaces and visit the houses of her nobles, Elizabeth was no different from her medieval predecessors or other Renaissance princes. But this English queen so famous for her progresses was oddly provincial and limited in where she chose to travel. Even though Elizabeth spent much of her long reign packing and unpacking her luggage, she remained pointedly English in her destinations and never saw much of the kingdom she fought so consistently to defend. In this regard, she was not her father's daughter. Nor were her royal plans the same as his. Marriage and the succession, wars and defense, and international rivalries had a different significance for the Virgin Queen, who would not visit a foreign rival or lead troops abroad in war. Through their geography, ritual, participants, and timing, Elizabeth's progresses emphasized what was important to her as monarch: her popularity, public ceremony, a lively court, her own safety, and a caution that preserved her options.

ENGLISH AND EUROPEAN CONTEXTS

From the time of William the Conqueror, English monarchs had moved their courts through a realm that included, depending upon the year, parts of England, Scotland, Wales, and Ireland as well as large chunks of France. Medieval English kings went to fight on the continent and repent in the Holy Land, and, with the exceptions of Richard I and Richard II, they rarely found that foreign travel was detrimental to their effectiveness at home. During the hundred or so years before Elizabeth ascended the throne, her Lancastrian and Yorkist ancestors had used a continental exile to launch invasions of their homeland, and her own grandfather had grown up on Welsh and French soil. After landing at Milford Haven in Wales and winning his crown at Bosworth Field in 1485, Henry VII left his palaces around London for several progresses north. In 1486 he went into the heartland of Yorkist sympathy to assert his authority. Stopping in Cambridge, Lincoln, Nottingham, and York, Henry then suppressed a minor revolt in Worcester before heading to Hereford and Bristol. After this 4-month circuit, he reached London.[1] His later travels usually took him around the kingdom to hunt and sharpen his martial skills.[2] The major progress of the first Tudor reflected his need to subdue the unsettled kingdom.

Whether he went to fight or to celebrate, Henry VIII enjoyed traveling. On ceremonial visits around England, he led a retinue that often included his current wife, as they presided together over numerous civic welcomes and entertainments. Until his dissolution of the monasteries in the 1530s, Henry VIII frequently stayed at monasteries for their convenient lodgings and hunting.[3] His most famous ceremonial expedition was to join his French counterpart, Francis I, outside of Rouen in 1520, where they indulged in such elaborate displays of regal power that the meeting became known as the Field of the Cloth of Gold. Military adventures took Henry to France in 1513 and 1544, and despite physical problems his desire to travel remained unslaked. None of his children, however, left the island they ruled. His son and heir, Edward VI, lived in the marches of Wales before assuming the throne and staying around London. In fact, the abrogation of Edward's short progress to nearby Guildford in 1552 drew the praise of the duke of Northumberland, in whose opinion it was "superfluous . . . in these troublesome days."[4] In her youth, Mary Tudor also lived in the Welsh border region and enjoyed accompanying her father on progress in 1526. As queen, she went to Winchester for her marriage to Philip of Spain in 1554, after which the royal couple made an almost private progress to crown residences at Basing, Windsor, and Richmond before reaching London. Her movements around the countryside decreased when her marriage proved unpopular, and also her ill health caused Mary to remain at Richmond, Hampton Court, and St. James's.[5] In either case, the "middle Tudors" had such comparatively short reigns that it is not fair to compare their movements to those of their father or sister who enjoyed decades of power. In her journeys, therefore, Elizabeth combined her father's enthusiasm for travel and her siblings' narrower geographical experience to create the public rituals known as Elizabethan progresses.

In this spectrum of monarchs, Elizabeth's English-bound life was unusual. Her Stuart successors all had more experience in foreign lands than did Elizabeth. Before coming to rule England, James I had governed Scotland and had crossed the sea to Oslo, where he rescued his stranded bride, Anne, and toured Denmark before returning home six months later. As king of England, James returned to Scotland in 1617. His son and heir, Charles I, proved a reluctant, even shy, traveler when in England, but he went to Spain to seek a bride in 1623 and had his coronation in Edinburgh in 1633.[6] The same military reasons that led Oliver Cromwell to travel the island and cross to Ireland impelled Charles II to journey into Scotland and France, before returning home as the restored monarch determined never to go on his travels again. The pattern of foreign travel continued with the successful invasion from Holland of William III and Mary II, William's campaigns in Ireland and on the continent against the French, and the shuttling between Hanover and England that occupied the first Hanoverian rulers of Britain.

Her geographical single-mindedness set Elizabeth apart from many European rulers as well. Italian aristocrats became diplomatic pioneers because they spent so much energy traveling between the courts of the Sforzas, Borgias, Medicis, and Viscontis, even as they dealt with the northern invaders from France and the Holy Roman Empire who brought their armies into the peninsula.[7] The French kings, Charles VIII and Francis I, invaded the regions bordering their realm, and after his capture at Pavia, Francis I resided in gracious imprisonment in Spain for more than a year. Catherine de Medici left Florence and Rome to live in France, first as queen, then as queen mother, and kept her court constantly in motion as she traveled to the extremities of her kingdom. Matrimonial bonds induced Philip II occasionally to visit his wife in England, and dynastic claims took him to Brussels, until the palatial haven of the Escorial became his residence in later years. But the ruler who chalked up the most time on the road and at sea had to have been Charles V, king of Spain and Holy Roman emperor, who traveled to supervise his far-flung empire. Until his retirement in 1556, the Hapsburg ruler resided in Burgundy, Spain, and German lands in an attempt to keep his empire intact. He also visited Henry VIII in England. Charles saw proportionally more of his realm than did Elizabeth, who ruled a much smaller, physically united kingdom.

While these monarchs traveled in varying degrees, all of them except Elizabeth left their kingdoms. It is significant that she never once abandoned the familiarity of her native land for new experiences in a foreign country. Elizabeth had linguistic skills that would have made her comfortable in most European courts, she enjoyed the public ceremonies that her foreign hosts would have staged, and her courtiers and guards would have provided her with the impressive retinue needed to uphold England's honor. At times the danger to Elizabeth, as the strongest Protestant queen, of visiting her Catholic enemies would have closed those courts to her. But she could have considered the Celtic parts of her kingdom, the Protestant Low Countries, and Scandinavia. By staying in England—southern England at that—Elizabeth did not experience a change of cultures, architecture, cuisine, and topography, nor did the queen feel the disorientation of being in a land she did not govern. Instead, she remained within the safest parts of her own realm. At a foreign court she would have been only one of the centers of attention. Perhaps she hesitated to have comparisons drawn or to lose control of her physical space when others set the schedule. After all, she had entertained foreign visitors and therefore knew that they yielded to the wishes of their royal host. While even one trip abroad would have shaped her conception of the world, the risks must have outweighed curiosity or political benefit.

What also might account for Elizabeth's decision not to leave England, apart from the dangers of travel and England's loss of continental empire by 1558, was the different military role that she assumed as a queen. English rulers, before and after William the Conqueror, had claimed the loyalty of their thegns and barons through the king's ability as a warrior to protect his subjects. Although as monarch she had the duty to defend the country, a responsibility that led some kings eagerly into foreign wars, no one expected the queen to accompany English troops on land or sea in their battles against the French, Scots, Irish, and Spanish. That general view of women rulers eschewing combat was, in fact, what lent such impact to the actions of Queen Matilda in the eleventh century, and Queen Margaret of Anjou and Joan of Arc in the fifteenth century; it also infused Elizabeth's visit (or stories of the visit) to her troops at Tilbury with great symbolic power.[8] In addition to gender, Elizabeth had reasons not to leave the country based on her own definition of herself and her monarchy: she was the native daughter of two English parents, she bore the features and coloring of her increasingly popular father, and her ability to govern relied upon her English subjects' goodwill. By casting herself in these ways as a homegrown English ruler, Elizabeth perhaps removed a political reason for traveling abroad.

What Elizabethan progresses had in common with those of other Renaissance rulers was the infusion of ceremony and pageantry. Some of the era's most elaborate displays occurred at the courts of Charles V and Henry II, who used their great wealth to create memorable royal entries.[9] In an overwhelming show of royal power, the procession of Henry II into Rouen in 1551 included 50 Norman knights, horse-drawn chariots for the figures of Fame, Religion, Majesty, Virtue, and Good Fortune; 57 armored men representing the historical kings of France, musicians, military and regional groups parading en masse; 6 elephants and a band of slaves and captives, all of whom moved through a Roman Arch of Triumph. The occasion included a separate entry for his wife, Catherine de Medici, public shows at other arches, and an elaborate river triumph with mock battles, boats, and mermen with tridents riding fish.[10] This entry followed a similarly flamboyant one that Henry II had made into Paris in 1549, and together they suggested how richly staged were these events of continental royal power.

On a lesser scale, most English monarchs marked important public occasions with shows staged by civic guilds and officials or arranged by royal servants. In a tradition traced to the accession of Richard II in 1377, the citizens of London staged a civic triumph before or after the monarch's coronation.[11] Using classical allusions and allegorical figures, the civic ceremonies offered a model of good government that the monarch both should and would provide. Whenever the ruler visited a town of any size, its citizens marked the royal entry with street ceremonies whose pageantry addressed political, dynastic, and local issues. When Henry VI entered London in 1432, the pageantry included street dramas with the allegorical figures of Nature, Grace, Fortune, Mercy, Truth, and Clemency, as well as the city's sword-wielding champion. Emphasizing the king's English and Lancastrian background, the pageantry offered advice on good governance to a king who had more symbolic authority than military strength.[12] Having seized the crown from Henry VI in 1461, Edward IV found his royal entry into Bristol that year was full of appropriate symbolism. A giant gave him the keys to the town, and he met St. George and, significantly, William the Conqueror.[13] In a similar vein, the town of York's dynastic sympathies welcomed Richard III and Queen Anne when they brought their son to be invested as duke of York in July 1483. Under the leadership of town recorder Miles Metcalfe, civic leaders created impressive shows and gave a generous gift of money to the king, with whom many northerners were already familiar.[14] The civic pageantry on Henry VII's progresses reflected the delicate political situation arising from his capture of the crown in battle. His visits to York in 1486 and 1487 required the town to proclaim its loyalty to the new king, which it did through shows extolling civic ties to the preceding six King Henrys. Generous use of the Tudor rose, petitions to the intercessory powers of the Virgin for mercy, pageants about peace, and presentation of the keys to the city were all dramatic strategies for reconciliation between town and king.[15]

More lavish and internationally inspired than that of Henry Tudor's court, the pageantry of Henry VIII highlighted his stellar qualities as a Renaissance prince. The entertainments on his first progress in 1510 were full of music, hunting, tournaments, and wrestling.[16] On his visit with Catherine of Aragon to Coventry, Henry was entertained with three pageants and a display of the nine orders of angels. Pageants accompanied the visit of Emperor Charles V to London in 1522 and the coronation of Anne Boleyn in 1533.[17] Such travel accompanied by civic ceremonies continued until the king in his old age grew irritable and put an end to the public festivities. In the brief reigns of his son and elder daughter, the machinery of ceremony had fewer opportunities to operate. The coronation entry of Edward VI in February 1547 was a ramshackle affair. Civic officials dusted off the pageant used a hundred years earlier for 10-year-old Henry VI, when another child had followed his popular father to the throne. Edward VI "made such speed" through the London streets that some spectacles were omitted, but he did hear speeches from the Liberal Arts, a phoenix and two lions, and from four children representing Royalty, Justice, Truth, and Mercy.[18] With the exception of Christmas shows in 1552, his reign had few ceremonial moments. Those for his sister Mary Tudor came at her coronation in 1553, with pageants at Cornhill and Cheapside, and at the arrival in 1554 of her husband, Philip II, who was entertained with a show of Great Philips in history: Philip of Macedon, the Roman Emperor, Philip the Good of Burgundy, and Philip the Bold of Burgundy.[19] After this nuptial show, however, the absence of her husband, her illness, and religious turmoil meant that Mary's court was rarely festive.

In this broader context, the progresses of Elizabeth I represented a blend of old and new. Her travels placed her in the mainstream of Renaissance rulers who communicated with their subjects through an array of symbols and pageants imbued with civic, royal, and local messages. London officials used her coronation entry to offer Elizabeth instruction in how to rule by displaying virtues and vices, Tudor roses, the English Bible, and steadfast Deborah of the Old Testament. It was a call for peace, unity, and royal responsibility.[20] She also was following the example of her English predecessors by traveling around the kingdom in order to rule it. But she differed from them in the range, frequency, and design of her travels. Compared to her Tudor family, Elizabeth proved more committed to regular summer progresses, while she was less eager to journey the great distances covered by the first Tudors and continental rulers. The ceremonies on her progresses were not as extravagant as some French or Imperial ones, but they consistently served a more essential function in her government than in those of the other Tudors. What distinguished the progresses of Elizabeth I was their intrinsic role in her monarchy; they were like an endlessly repeated coronation, the tool without which she could not or would not rule. Her progresses enabled her to exchange messages with her subjects, and, despite the expense, she readily embraced the chaos they created as a means of reaffirming her own authority as queen. Her travels inspired and spread the images of royal sacred governance embodied in a female ruler even as the dislocation of her court reminded everyone in its orbit who was at its center.

FACTORS OF NATURE

The queen and her court changed residences during the year according to festival cycles, weather patterns, outbreaks of disease, and royal desire. In the late fall, with dropping temperatures and the advent of Christmas, the court remained around the London area to celebrate Christmas and the New Year in the relative comfort of royal palaces. Through the winter and early spring, rough road conditions and demands of Parliament, if in session, encouraged the queen to restrict her movements between her London and river palaces. With Easter and St. George's Day celebrations concluded as better weather arrived in the late spring, Elizabeth took a series of short forays to nobles' palaces and her hunting lodges in the counties surrounding London. Summer heat and cessation of Parliament heralded the season for progresses, when from the early summer through late fall the court could expect to move away from London through the countryside until the cool, darker November days urged the queen back to the city.

Linked to such seasonal rhythms of travel was the queen's constant effort to avoid disease and plague. In the hot, fetid summer months, Elizabeth followed the pattern set by her predecessors of leaving London, where sickness easily spread, for freshly aired houses in the countryside. In the summer of 1570, for example, the queen moved from Osterley (3 days) to Denham (2 days) to Chenies (26 days) to Pendley (3 days) to Toddington (2 days) before ending the trip at Rycote (4 days) and Reading (4 days).[21] As the water grew foul, the gardrobes full, and local supplies of food dwindled at each residence, Elizabeth moved her court.

Queen and courtiers used travel to steer clear of the most common deadly diseases. Elizabeth's unpleasant memories of her illness at Hampton Court banished her from that palace for five years. There, in 1562, she had contracted the smallpox that jeopardized her life, seriously enough that she tried to have the council declare Robert Dudley protector in the event of her death. While nursing the queen back to health, Lady Mary Sidney became so disfigured from the disease that her husband abandoned her. Sir Henry Sidney callously blamed the destruction of his marital happiness on Mary Sidney's appearance: "I found her as fowle a ladie as the smale poxe coulde make her which she did take by contynuall attendance of her matie most precious person (sicke of the same disease); the skarres of which (to her resolute discomfort ever synse hath don and doth remayne in her face, so as she lyveth solitarilie *sicut nucticorax in domicilio suo,* more to my charge then if we had boorded together as we did before that evill accident happened."[22] After such harm to her friend, to her favorite courtier (the horrified council refused to accept Dudley as protector), and to herself, Elizabeth did not soon venture back to the scene of so much pain. Upon her first return to Hampton Court in 1567, the Spanish ambassador noted the queen's unease. Elizabeth, he wrote, "does not like the house, and would never go to it only that she does not wish it to fall into decay. Since she was ill of small-pox she has been much afraid of the place."[23] To the queen, place and event were entwined. And given the scarring and mortality rates from smallpox, Elizabeth's respect for the disease was prudent. As a public figure, a vain woman, and a player on the international marriage market, the queen needed to protect herself.

Worse than smallpox was the plague. In 1563 London faced a major outbreak of plague brought by soldiers returning from the Low Countries. John Stow estimated that the city and its liberties lost 23,660 souls to the plague from January to December 1563.[24] For fear of infecting the queen, Robert Dudley isolated himself at Bagshot and wrote to apologize to Elizabeth for his absence. Elizabeth stayed at Windsor while her councilors arranged to move the law courts that "cannot be kept at london for the grt perell that will fall therof." In a November letter to the lords-in-council at Windsor, the marquis of Winchester advised that the Exchequer remain at Syon "and that will kepe the quenes matie from hampton court and richmount.", After recommending other options, such as Oatlands, Eltham, Woodstock, and Farnham, the marquis concluded: "And of all this matter provide first for the quene, that the term the eschequer nor the comissioners sittinge be not ny to her grace by cause the resort to them [the courts] wilbe from all places in the realme wherof may grow perell."[25] The queen's safety dictated that she not be exposed to potentially infected travelers who had business with the royal courts and government. She, therefore, must lodge at a distance.

On many occasions the queen fled from outbreaks of plague. To avoid it in 1564, Elizabeth put an early end to her progress to Cambridge. Spanish ambassador Guzman de Silva explained that "the places she was to stay at are unhealthy . . . [and] she is much in fear of falling ill." De Silva attributed the anxieties of the heretic queen to a general fear for her safety, given "the prophecies that are current about her short life," but Elizabeth was right to be careful.[26] When outbreaks of smallpox occurred in Worcester, Elizabeth delayed her visit in 1575.[27] News of plague in August 1581 forced Elizabeth to cancel a visit to Mortlake and stay at Oatlands and Windsor "without makyng any speciall progress."[28] During her most special progress escorting the duc d'Alençon from England in 1582, the queen was warned of six houses afflicted by plague in Dover, "whearupon I thinke yt not so convenient for her matie to coom hither." Instead of stopping at Canterbury, as Charles, Lord Howard, had suggested, however, Elizabeth continued to the port town with her disappointed suitor.[29] The high mortality, especially in London, from the sweating sickness during the summer of 1583 again ensured that the queen "would not reside long so near London."[30] By the end of May she had gone to visit Burghley at Theobalds before heading for her Surrey palaces of Nonsuch and Oatlands. The death of a servant in the Windsor keep in 1593 caused the queen to leave a week later for Hampton Court.[31] That same year, as the plague continued, Thomas Phelippes noted that the queen and court "kepeth in out places, a great part of the household being cutt of" from London.[32] Fear of deadly diseases that threatened everyone, regardless of rank, motivated some royal travel.

Reasons of health also constricted the queen's movements. A painful ulcer on her leg forced Elizabeth, while still in her mid-thirties, to ride in a coach instead of on horseback during the 1570 progress into Berkshire. Still in pain, she altered her itinerary so that she could linger at Chenies with the earl of Bedford for two weeks.[33] She delayed traveling because of illness in 1596, returning to London early on her Accession Day.[34] A more severe attack slowed her down in 1599, during the preparations for an imminent Spanish attack. Elizabeth "hath appointed a progresse into Surrey, Hampshyre, Wilshyre, Glocester, and Barkshyre, and many dayes sett for her first remove from Greenwich, as among many others, this present day, but still it hath been differred, and so againe it is thought it will. Some suppose it is by occasion of the newes of this fleete, but rather as I have heard some courtyers relate, it is an indysposition of her matie bodye, now growen in yeares and unable to endure travle."[35] In her old age, Elizabeth had to slow down. When bad weather deterred courtiers from extensive travel in August 1602, the queen relinquished her plans for a last progress to Bristol. Rather than force a reluctant retinue to travel across the island, she stayed instead in nearby Middlesex and Buckinghamshire.[36] Three months later, the court went to Richmond, "where the Quene findes her self so well that she will not easilie remove."[37] On 5 November, she was still at Richmond. The changed itinerary of 1602 reflected the queen's growing infirmity. In her youth, Elizabeth would have ignored the grumblings of her courtiers, but physical ailments at last forced her to be more sedentary than she wished. In her sixties, she talked of great travels more than she experienced them.

DEFINITION AND FREQUENCY

The seasonal and salutary nature of the queen's travels resulted in much motion but not always in an official progress. Royal progresses comprised those lengthy trips away from London that required, over a number of days or weeks, a series of hosts in several counties to provide hospitality for an itinerant court. Based upon this definition, Elizabeth had a total of 23 progresses in her 44-year reign, beginning with a tour of Kent and Surrey in 1559 and continuing until her last circuit of the home counties in 1602.[38] These progresses typically began in July and ended in September, averaging between 48 and 52 days in length and containing an average of 23 visits, usually lasting 2 days. Exceptions to these patterns arose, for example, when a winter progress was necessary to usher the duc d'Alençon out of the kingdom in February 1582. She also had a much longer progress than usual when the 1575 one began in late May, sustained itself over 139 days, and ended in early October. Nonetheless, the essential characteristics of her progresses held true over the long haul and bear noting. The length of a visit was relatively short, in essence two days and the intervening night, which made a royal visit manageable for her hosts in terms of preparations, entertainment, and expense. Although her closest courtiers, such as William Cecil and Robert Dudley, occasionally had the queen in their houses for longer than a week, such a lengthy and inconvenient visit was not the norm. Besides fostering hospitality through their brevity, these short visits in progresses of roughly 7 weeks required the queen to have many changes of hosts, houses, or both. The number of visits within a single progress ranged from a low of 6 in 1567, when the trip lasted 11 days, to a high of 44 visits each in two progresses: once in the longest progress of 1575, which was not surprising given that it lasted almost 20 weeks, and again in 1592, when Elizabeth went into Wiltshire and Gloucestershire for 8 weeks. The queen expected her progresses, these numbers suggest, to bring her into the houses and lives of many different people, whose individual, brief moments of hospitality collectively enabled Elizabeth to have a life on the road.

The queen's 23 progresses were the most extensive travels of her reign but hardly the only ones. When not on progress or at her own palaces, Elizabeth visited people who lived within a day's travel from London. In 1580, for example, she visited Sir Francis Carew in June at his Surrey estate of Beddington, went in July to see the earl of Lincoln at Pyrford, and found Dr. John Dee twice at Mortlake in September and October. Throughout her reign, Elizabeth often visited people living near or in London, with whom she dined and spent an evening or even several days, before leaving for one of her own river palaces between Greenwich and Windsor. On such visits the royal household officers faced few challenges and little expense, because provisions were close at hand and not as many people needed lodgings. These "local" visits, therefore, offered entertainment to Elizabeth without the burdens, or expectations, attached to progresses. These numerous visits made singly or in a cluster differed from progresses because, while important, they did not have the same impact on court life, finances, and policy, nor did they necessarily generate the ceremonial structures found in progresses to distant counties and towns. The difference was one of scale and, therefore, significance. Thus, in some of the charts and averages discussed in this chapter, progresses per se appear separated from individual "visits" and "visits in the greater London area." These single visits do figure in the later analysis of hospitality, access to the queen, and royal manipulation of the court, because these concerns transcend specific destination and distance from London; here, however, in assessing the dimensions of royal progresses as a series of visits linked by pressures of geography, accommodation, provision, and expense, the single visits would skew the findings about progresses. So while all progresses contain individual visits, not all individual visits form a progress.

GEOGRAPHY

For a queen who liked to travel, Elizabeth was not adventurous in her choice of destination. Her caution in military, political, religious, and marital matters also characterized her progresses, as she never traveled to the areas most removed from direct royal authority. She governed a country divided into 53 counties, yet she visited only 25 of them. The entire region of Wales remained a mystery to her, nor did she reach the extremities of her kingdom—to the southwest in Cornwall and Devon; to the north in Yorkshire, Cheshire, Lancashire, Durham, Westmorland, Cumberland, and Northumberland. Her farthest ventures north were to the middle region of the island: Sempringham, Lincolnshire, and Ellenhall, Staffordshire, represented her most northerly visits, and other "northern" points included Coventry, Kenilworth, and Warwick. To the west, she reached Gloucester, Bath, and Bristol, while her southwestern itineraries ended around Salisbury, Wiltshire, and Portsmouth and Southampton in Hampshire. Moving from London in the other direction, the queen went northeast into East Anglia all the way to Norwich and traveled southeast through Kent to reach Canterbury and the shores of Dover and Rye. A line connecting Norwich, Stafford, Bristol, Southampton, and Dover, therefore, circumscribed roughly the distance and direction from London that Elizabeth traveled. She did not risk going into areas known for their rugged terrain, Celtic heritage, or Catholic sympathies. Instead of using progresses to bring order to troubled regions, the queen in her progresses validated royal authority and social stability where it already existed. Elizabeth traveled as she ruled—with fanfare, caution, and care for the preservation of royal authority and royal life.

Such an area of travel meant that the queen often stayed within the secure region of the Thames valley and London. Although her itineraries could take the queen on lengthy trips for weeks at a time, her progresses often occurred in a 40-mile radius, with London as the center of a lopsided sphere. On ten progresses, Elizabeth remained within 40 miles of London. Destinations a short distance from London included Reading, Cambridge, Oxford, and Canterbury (40–60 miles). She traveled 40 to 80 miles from London on eight of her progresses. Progresses of a medium range went to Stamford, Coventry, Warwick, Salisbury, Winchester, Southampton, Portsmouth, Dover, and Ipswich (70–100 miles). She strayed 90 to 130 miles from London only five times in her life. The farthest from London she traveled was to Staffordshire, Lincolnshire, Bristol, Gloucester, Bath, Norwich, and Worcester (110–30 miles). These longer trips (50–130 miles distant) occurred in only 13 years of her 44-year reign: in another 21 years of visits the queen did not leave the home counties around London. For much of her peripatetic life, therefore, Elizabeth remained within some 40 miles of London. She did not reach out for new audiences as much as she used the progresses to emphasize her royal presence in the wealthier, more populated, and stable areas of her kingdom.

Within this region of her progresses, certain counties proved more popular with Elizabeth than others. She spent many days each year in London and in her royal palaces along the river in Middlesex, Berkshire, Surrey, and Kent. Excluding these short trips around London, the itineraries of her progresses most often included visits in the counties of Essex, Kent, Hampshire, and Surrey, accessible and populous areas where many of her nobles had houses. Based upon the number of royal visits within a county, hosts in these four shires most often received the traveling court, while only one or two hosts in the distant counties of Leicestershire, Rutland, and Somerset ever participated in the progresses. Not surprisingly, the queen made more visits in those counties close to London.

Another way of analyzing the court's travels is to see how many times a county figured in the itinerary of all the queen's 23 progresses. Surrey proved the most popular and convenient, according to the 12 different trips Elizabeth made there, often as she began or ended a progress, followed closely by Hertfordshire with its combination of houses and hunting parks that drew the queen on 11 trips. For progresses northwest from London, Oxfordshire and Buckinghamshire each welcomed the queen on nine trips;

on eight trips she went east into Essex or west into Berkshire, and she headed southwest through Hampshire seven times. The counties she explored least often (excluding the ones she never saw) were Leicestershire, Lincolnshire, Norfolk, Rutland, Somerset, Staffordshire, and Worcestershire, each of which figured in progresses only once and represented the limits of her travel. Although some of her most famous entertainments occurred on the longer westward journeys, which increased their prominence, these progresses were unusual. Because the queen wanted to see the more secure parts of her kingdom, her travels kept her relatively close to London.

While the queen might have come infrequently to a county, once there she stayed with many people. The accessible county of Kent figured in only three progress itineraries, but on those three occasions the queen made a total of 58 visits within its borders, the second highest number for any county. The most visits within a county happened in Essex, where the queen made 67 stops during her eight progresses, but her twelve trips into Surrey resulted in a comparatively small number of visits, 49, illustrating its convenience as a place of passage to other areas. In the counties at the edge of her area of progresses that were not royal gateways to more distant reaches, the queen lingered to visit. In both Norfolk and Staffordshire, which she visited once, she made nine stops on the progress; her three journeys in Gloucestershire yielded a total of 23 visits, nearly twice the number of visits than in closer Sussex, where she traveled on two progresses for 12 visits. Determining the queen's favorite destinations or the ones she most visited, therefore, requires a distinction between royal trips into the county and royal visits within the county. Although these rankings shift a bit, her patterns of movement show that Elizabeth spent much of her progresses within the borders of Essex, Kent, Hampshire, Surrey, Hertfordshire, Buckinghamshire, Oxfordshire, and Berkshire, counties that all surrounded the heartland of royal palaces in Middlesex and contained much of the population Elizabeth governed.

HOSTS

On progresses Elizabeth stayed with her subjects in their country houses or town dwellings, as well as in some of her own royal residences scattered around the countryside, but her preference for residing with her subjects was one of the distinguishing features of her progresses. Unlike her father, who accumulated royal residences through his own building projects and confiscation of church lands, Elizabeth built very little and failed to maintain all the residences that she inherited. According to the records of the

King's Works, many royal houses fell into ruin during the later sixteenth century, a state of decay attributable in part to the queen's reluctance to commit funds to their repair.[39] This erosion of royal residences perhaps encouraged Elizabeth to stay with her subjects, but equally significant in this decision was her interest in combining travel with politics, statecraft, and governance through the opportunities of meeting people. While her successor James I preferred hunting to public spectacles on progress and lived in royal houses and hunting lodges, Elizabeth chose to make her travels into more public occasions by staying in her subjects' houses.

It is possible, but difficult, to generalize about the hosts who entertained Elizabeth on progress. The number of hosts during her progresses reached about 320, while the number of hosts whom she visited around the London area was about 140; since some hosts belong to both groups, a total of about 420 different people opened their homes to the queen. My caution about these figures comes from the difficulty in determining names and identities of some hosts, the vagueness of sources, and the impossibility of knowing the queen's location on every day of her reign. Because the problems inherent in such tasks as ranking hosts according to their economic and social status seemed even to outweigh possible benefits, I have not attempted to do it. But with these caveats in mind, some analysis of the group of hosts is possible.

Not surprisingly, many progresses included houses that belonged to members of her court and government. Throughout her reign, Elizabeth made 147 visits to 39 different privy councilors, although the two men closest to her, William Cecil and Robert Dudley, received a disproportionately large number of visits, 20 to Cecil and 23 to Dudley. Of the members of her first Privy Council, the queen visited about half of them (11 of 20); of the 40 men later named to the council, 26 of them at some point entertained the queen; most of her Privy Council in 1586 would have had a royal visit (14 of 19); by 1597, when the council had shrunk to 11, Elizabeth visited 9 of them; and in 1601, 9 of the 13 councilors had participated in a progress or entertained the queen in the greater London area.[40] Of all her 60 privy councilors over the course of her reign, therefore, the queen visited 39, almost two thirds of them.[41] She naturally also visited many hosts who held positions at court and in the county and who were members of Parliament. Almost 200 hosts (or their close family) had served as justices of the peace, sheriffs, or members of the House of Commons. Of this group, some 90 were also officers at court and in the royal government.[42] Such a concentration of royal visits among these men reflected the nature of court dynamics. Many courtiers and privy councilors with large houses close to London, and perhaps farther away along a progress route, would expect by virtue of their political status to entertain the queen. Such visits from the court fostered the conduct of royal business, as Elizabeth relied upon a cooperative network of officers (a "royal affinity") to run the government.[43] It would have been odd had the queen not visited many of her close advisors.

Several other groups of hosts, ecclesiastical and female, figured in the progresses and reshape our assumptions about the queen's attitudes. Elizabeth had proven reluctant to include the clergy in her Privy Council and had denounced the practice of clerical marriage inherited from the Edwardian church, but she did make a small number of visits to some of her bishops, usually at their diocesan residences. She paid one visit each to the bishops of Salisbury, Norwich, and Ely and went twice to the bishops of Worcester and London, but her favorite clerics to visit were Robert Horne, bishop of Winchester (5 visits), Thomas Cooper, bishop of Winchester (5 visits), Matthew Parker, archbishop of Canterbury (8 visits), and above all, John Whitgift, archbishop of Canterbury (12 visits). Some of her preferences were obviously related to geography, convenience, and policy. In 1578, when she visited Norwich as the town was embroiled in religious controversy, the queen naturally turned for accommodations to the bishop of Norwich. A similar situation occurred when she went to Worcestershire and to the house of its bishop. She also found ecclesiastical houses around Salisbury, Winchester, and Farnham helpful in breaking her journeys. But more than convenience affected her contacts with the three archbishops of Canterbury of her reign, as policy and personality brought her into the residences of two and kept her out of the third. The demands of organizing the church in the 1560s and overseeing the changes in the 1570s, if nothing else, led the queen to visit Matthew Parker in Croydon, Lambeth, and Canterbury, while the disputes with Edmund Grindal about prophesyings and reform that led to his sequestration gave the queen little reason to cross his doorstep. Matters changed with the translation of John Whitgift, who as her last archbishop of Canterbury received the queen at Lambeth and Croydon. Elizabeth's good working relationship with Whitgift, whom she called her "Black Husband," and his presence on the Privy Council inclined the queen to visit Whitgift as she had Parker. Royal visits to these clergy, however, were relatively few when considered in the context of her 44-year reign: ecclesiastical hosts accounted for only 38 of her royal visits during progresses and on brief trips close to London. So while Elizabeth included individual clerics in the political aspects of her progresses, as a group they did not form a large segment of her progress hosts.

Balanced against these clerical hosts was a group characterized by Catholic sympathy or recusancy. Elizabeth visited some 38 hosts with Catholic leanings or whose close family members held those beliefs.[44] Progresses in the 1570s accounted for most of the visits (14), followed by those in the 1590s (11), 1560s (9), 1600s (2), and 1580s (2). The progress of 1591, the first one after the Armada's defeat in 1588, took the queen into five Catholic-affiliated homes in Sussex and Hampshire, the largest number in any single year. Her willingness to seek accommodations with these suspect hosts suggests that Elizabeth sought religious inclusion, to a degree, in her travels. Loyalty to the crown, good service in the government, and personal friendship were reasons for the queen to bring her court into Catholic households. The pope might have excommunicated her and the king of Spain might have waged war against her, but Elizabeth knew the value of subjects who favored both the old religion and their Tudor queen.

Another small but noticeable subset of hosts were the women who entertained the queen. The names of 40 female hosts, without the accompanying name of a husband, appear in the sources from which these lists were compiled. I have assumed that, given past and present conventions, many wives of male hosts participated in the progresses even though their names did not receive separate notice, while the reverse was not necessarily true: women serving as primary hosts probably had no husband in the background because his name would have registered in the sources. An example is the case of the queen's two visits to Ingatestone Hall, the Essex home of Sir William Petre and his wife, Anne, Lady Petre. On the first occasion in July 1561, Chambers names Sir William Petre as host, but we know from studies of the visit that Lady Petre prepared their residence and helped entertain the queen. When Elizabeth returned to Ingatestone in September 1579, seven years after Sir William's death, the host of record is Lady Petre.[45] To judge from this and other examples, during the progresses many women shared the duties of hospitality with their husbands, and a smaller number of women, some of them widows, acted independently as hosts to the queen.

Elizabeth visited these female hosts at steady intervals throughout the course of her reign, with no apparent consolidation of visits in one era, and they figure in 17 of her 23 progresses.[46] In the course of her progresses and short visits around the London area, the queen made a total of 49 visits to specifically designated female hosts, most often in Middlesex (11), Surrey (6), London (5), and Essex (5). That these counties frequently received the itinerant court suggests the queen did not travel in new directions to stay with women but instead blended these visits into the general pattern of her trips. In fact, as with Lady Petre, some women first entertained the queen with their husbands and then later as widows, and nine received two visits from the queen. Most of the female hosts (32 out of 40) were noblewomen, some of whose husbands had served as privy councilors, or women whose husbands were knights. Such characteristics might suggest that the queen returned to familiar houses regardless of whether her hosts were a couple or a widow, but it is also possible that through her progresses

Elizabeth maintained her friendships with these women and recognized their status in the local community.

Familial ties also led the queen to visit her relations, most of whom had titles and duties in the government that overlapped their personal bonds with Elizabeth. The queen made trips to visit cousins, nephews, and relations by marriage on the Boleyn side, who included Sir Richard Sackville; Henry Carey, Lord Hunsdon; George Carey, 2nd Lord Hunsdon; Sir Francis Knollys; Sir William Knollys; and Thomas, Lord Delawarr. Few hosts on her paternal side, however, drew the queen to their houses, partly because Tudor infertility and executions had culled their numbers, but also because of overwhelming political difficulties. Although she planned to visit her Scottish cousin in 1562, the meeting with Mary Stuart never occurred. Elizabeth preferred to keep a punitive distance from the Grey cousins descended from the marriage of her father's sister, Mary Tudor, with Charles Brandon, duke of Suffolk. Only toward the end of her reign did she relent by allowing the widowed husband of Catherine Grey, the earl of Hertford, to stage a magnificent entertainment for her in 1591 at Elvetham. In these visits to relatives, Elizabeth embraced her maternal side both as hosts and members of her government, while she kept more distance from the few problematic paternal survivors of dynastic conflict.

Bonds of friendship, as well as the business of governing, drew the queen to the homes of her favorite courtiers and officials. The enduring relationship that generated more progress visits than any other was her friendship with William Cecil, Lord Burghley. Whether serving as her principal secretary, privy councilor, master of the wards, or lord treasurer, Burghley maintained close contact with the queen from 1558 until his death in 1598. Their mutual esteem and national responsibilities drew them together. Burghley often traveled with the court on progress and entertained Elizabeth at his several houses in and outside London. Elizabeth dined at his Savoy house in Westminster in 1561 and stayed at his Greyfriars house in Stamford, Lincolnshire, in 1566. Most frequently she visited Burghley at Theobalds, his estate in Hertfordshire.[47] From her first visit there in 1564 until her last call in 1597, Theobalds and its owner occupied the prime place of importance in Elizabeth's travels as they did in her government.

The frequency of her visits and her constant claims upon Burghley's time virtually turned Theobalds into another royal palace, even though the actual transference had to wait until James I and Burghley's son Robert Cecil exchanged the family estate for the royal Hatfield House. Like James I, Elizabeth decided that Theobalds offered too much convenience to the monarch to remain in private use. It lay only 12 miles from London in a community of homes owned by government officials such as Sir Thomas Smith, Sir Anthony Cooke, and Sir Nicholas Bacon. The magnificent building, with its turrets and beautiful fireplaces, offered much comfort to a royal visitor.[48] Indeed, Burghley used Theobalds, at the queen's request, for entertaining foreign visitors, such as the Scottish ambassador, in quasi-royal splendor.[49] In addition to the grandeur and location of the house, Theobalds drew its royal visitor so frequently because of her desire to placate its owner. Elizabeth wanted Burghley with her more than he felt able to attend, what with his familial and manorial responsibilities. Staying at Theobalds, the queen believed, would allow Burghley to advise her and tend to his estate as well. She made Theobalds the site of an important reconciliation in 1587. The queen had ostracized Burghley for his role in securing the death warrant for Mary Stuart in February 1587. After four months she restored him to favor during her visit to Theobalds in June.[50] When Burghley refused to join the itinerant queen, as happened in 1596, Elizabeth felt the loss. Much to her disgust, the "froward old fool," in the queen's words, stayed from court to take the physic. To while away the spring, made dull with neither Burghley nor the earl of Essex in attendance, Elizabeth "had a desire to make [a progress], to consume the Lent, and so be at Greenwich eight days before the solemn feast." As Sir Anthony Standen wrote to Anthony Bacon from the court at Richmond: "I judge it will be resolved; for she seems to be weary of Surrey, and would over into Middlesex, from hence to Osterley, Highgate, and Hackney."[51] Two years later, in his final illness, the queen stayed by Burghley's side to care for him. This friendship of four decades dominated Elizabethan politics and certainly influenced the location of the court.

The other favorite host of the queen was Robert Dudley, earl of Leicester, whose charms and friendship occupied Elizabeth from 1558 until his death in 1588. In 1578 she visited Wanstead, Leicester's home in Essex, returning there three times in 1579, again in 1581, and another time in 1582. She also enjoyed entertainments at his London house.[52] When Leicester needed the medicinal Buxton waters in 1576, Elizabeth organized her progress so that he could take the cure.[53] A "feigned illness," in the view of Spanish ambassador Mendoza, drew Elizabeth to Wanstead for 2 days in 1579 to supervise Leicester's recovery. A similar errand of mercy found Elizabeth at Leicester's bedside at Wanstead in May of 1588, only a few months before his death in September.[54] But the house most associated with Elizabeth and Robert Dudley was the Warwickshire estate of Kenilworth, granted to him in 1563 and extensively improved in the 1570s.[55] The queen stayed with him at Kenilworth in 1566, 1572, and 1575. Leicester kept "two great tables of the Queen's Majestys pictures" at Kenilworth and seriously wooed her in its sylvan privacy.[56] His grand entertainment in 1575 has come to signify all that was extravagant and ceremonial about the progresses. In his hubris, Leicester gloated to Burghley, himself a fine host, that the queen "never cam to place in her lyfe she lyked better . . . or comendeth more" than Kenilworth.[57] As the man who inspired the strongest affection in Elizabeth, Leicester naturally claimed the same for his residence.

But the queen's concern for public opinion, which vilified Leicester, made her cautious about these visits. Her feelings for Dudley had become common knowledge both in and out of court by the time his wife, Amy Robsart, fell to her death in 1560. In the next few years Elizabeth realized how difficult for her a Dudley marriage would be. Probably in order to quell the rumors about Amy Robsart's mysterious death, Elizabeth avoided Kenilworth for three years after granting it to Leicester. Her attachment to him, however, remained as she continued to accept his hospitality both in London and in Warwickshire. Her later visits to Kenilworth in the 1570s occurred amidst negotiations for her own marriage with the duc d'Alençon. Leicester tried to argue through George Gascoigne's pageantry that the queen should marry him instead, but Elizabeth held firm. When she no longer considered him a suitor and even when he had remarried, the queen continued to visit her favorite earl.

Leicester's stepson, Robert Devereux, earl of Essex, exerted a strong influence upon the queen's progresses in her later years, as Elizabeth wanted both to keep an eye on the headstrong courtier and to enjoy his company. As commander of English forces to aid the French in August 1591, Essex was sailing from Portsmouth, near to the southern coastal counties where Elizabeth had planned her progress for proximity to him and speedy reception of foreign news. In July she had Lord Chamberlain Hunsdon organize her itinerary and accommodations in Sussex, where she stayed with Sir William More at Loseley and Lord Montague at Cowdray.[58] After a leisurely trip through Surrey and Sussex that took most of August, Elizabeth and a large retinue reached Portsmouth.[59] During September, when she hoped to have Essex return for a visit, Elizabeth remained in the south, staying in Winchester and enjoying the lavish hospitality of the earl of Hertford at Elvetham. These arrangements, however, did not have their desired end. Neither Essex nor the French king, Henry IV, whom she had also invited, crossed the Channel to visit Elizabeth: Essex did not come home until his recall in early January 1592, and King Henry never arrived.[60] Although her attempt to combine friendship, foreign policy, and travel failed in this instance, the affections of the queen played a significant role in determining her itineraries.

Special times of celebration or trouble drew the queen to the side of her friends. She attended many weddings in London that united members of her court, her favorites, and the aristocracy. In 1600 she attended the wedding of Anne Russell and Henry, Lord Herbert, in Blackfriars. Coming from the river in "a curious chaire," Elizabeth dined with the wedding

guests there and saw a masque before retiring to her lodgings at Lord Cobham's.[61] She also offered her support in less happy moments. In 1573, Sir
Christopher Hatton suffered from kidney pains, causing some to despair
of his recovery. Gilbert Talbot reported in May that "the Queen goeth almost every day to see how he doth." Hatton regained his health and credited the queen's affection with the recovery of "your Lidds."[62] When the
servant of another close advisor, Archbishop of Canterbury John Whitgift,
killed a man, Elizabeth went to the distraught prelate to offer her sympathy. According to John Chamberlain, "the archbishop takes yt so grevously
that the Quene her self was faine to come and comfort him at Lambeth."[63]
The short trip to Lambeth took little of Elizabeth's time but revealed her
priorities. She also intervened in quarrels between her favorites and
through her presence coerced them into politeness. In December 1588,
the jealous rivalry between Sir Walter Raleigh and the earl of Essex finally
embroiled the queen. Elizabeth traveled from Greenwich to Richmond
"to pacify a quarrel between her two favorites" and secured a truce.[64] This
blend of motives—personal, political, and diplomatic—characterized
both the queen's progresses and her monarchy.

TOWNS

Complementing the individual hosts who entertained the queen in their
country or town houses were the citizens of provincial towns who collectively acted as host to the itinerant queen and her court. A total of 83 civic
visits occurred in 20 of her 23 progresses, a steadiness that suggests towns
regularly participated in 4 decades of progresses. The three progresses without visits to towns were in 1567, 1597, and 1602, years in which the queen
had relatively short journeys through Surrey, Essex, Middlesex, and
Buckinghamshire, and they thus represent limitations of time rather than
royal aversion. Elizabeth visited over 50 towns of varying sizes, from local
market towns to the bustling regional centers where large numbers of
people mingled. By far the most populous city was London, in whose center and environs the queen spent much time, but she also visited the next
largest towns of Norwich in 1578 and Bristol in 1574. Other significant
provincial towns receiving a royal visit included Bath, Bury St. Edmonds,
Cambridge, Canterbury, Chichester, Coventry, Gloucester, Hertford, Ipswich, Northampton, Oxford, Reading, Salisbury, St. Albans, Stamford,
Thetford, Warwick, Winchester, and Worcester. The queen made a point
of visiting 13 of the 16 cathedral towns in the archdiocese of Canterbury,
and she inspected the large ports and small harbors in Dover, Folkestone,
Harwich, Portsmouth, Rochester, Rye, Sandwich, Southampton, Win-

chelsea, and Woolwich. The queen's accommodations in towns ranged from public inns to her own royal residences, converted monastic buildings, and private dwellings owned by leading civic officials, but where she stayed in some towns remains unknown. A combination of residences in and close to town sometimes housed Elizabeth, as in the case of her 1572 progress to Warwick, where she stayed in town at Warwick Castle with the earl of Warwick, at nearby Kenilworth with Robert Dudley, and on the outskirts in Warwick Priory with Thomas Fisher. For a queen who traveled to meet many of her subjects, royal visits to the market towns, major ports, small villages, and provincial centers of the southern part of her kingdom proved an invaluable tool for Elizabeth in constructing her relations with the court and citizenry.

OVERALL PATTERNS

The patterns that Elizabeth established in her 44 years of royal travel mirrored her priorities as queen, her relations with courtiers and citizens, and the attitudes of hundreds of people who opened their doors to her. This cadre of hosts offers powerful testimony to the willingness of many subjects to entertain the queen and to Elizabeth's commitment to maintaining her monarchy through travel. The direction of her travels shows a queen cautious in not wanting to go too far from London while still committed to staying with her subjects. She moved most easily around the populated, wealthy areas of the southeast, and she ventured west and north in order to visit favored courtiers and provincial towns, but Elizabeth did not use her progresses to reach out to subjects living in isolated areas where risks to her throne or established church might threaten.

This aversion to political and physical risk appears in a chronological view of her progresses. In the years immediately after her accession, Elizabeth tentatively explored her kingdom, first in the nearby areas of Middlesex, Kent, Surrey, Hampshire, and Essex, and then with confidence in the more distant counties of Suffolk, Hertfordshire, Cambridgeshire, Northamptonshire, Leicestershire, Lincolnshire, Rutland, Warwick, and Oxfordshire. During the northern tensions of 1569, however, she remained around London before heading south on progress into Hampshire. In the aftermath of rebellion, the next year's itinerary kept her mostly in Buckinghamshire and Bedfordshire, while in 1571 she had only a brief progress in Essex and Hertfordshire. Her increased experience as queen, the familiarity of imprisoning Mary Stuart, and the accomplishment of reorganizing the church were all perhaps reasons why Elizabeth confidently embarked on the long, elaborate, memorable progresses of the 1570s that have come to represent them all. From 1572 to 1578 (with the exception of 1577), the queen went relatively far afield for months at a time into Kent, Warwick, Staffordshire, Worcestershire, Gloucestershire, Somerset, Wiltshire, Suffolk, and Norfolk, where many pageants and ceremonies reiterated her popularity and symbolic significance. This explosion of travel contracted, however, in the plots and tensions of the 1580s, when Elizabeth had no progress (except for her journey in Kent with Alençon) and remained with friends close to London or in her own castles along the Thames. Elizabeth withdrew into the geographical and political safety of a restricted world after the execution of Mary Stuart in 1587 and the defeat of Philip II's Spanish Armada in 1588. Her quasi isolation ended when she resumed traveling south and west on long progresses into Sussex, Hampshire, Wiltshire, Gloucestershire, Oxfordshire, and Buckinghamshire in 1591 and 1592. But these two trips were the last ones that shared the breadth and pageantry of those in the 1570s, as increasing age and fewer close friends, many of whom had died between 1588 and 1591, gradually forced Elizabeth to limit her travels. She did have good progresses in counties near London in 1597 and 1601, but her last progress for two weeks in 1602 showed a queen fighting to keep up the habits of a lifetime more than anything else.

Elizabeth's motives in traveling were a blend of personal and political concerns that reflected the nature of her monarchy. Her progresses enabled the queen to consolidate her image and popularity, to strengthen royal authority in towns, to display herself and her court in public ceremonies, and to nourish social ties with the gentry and aristocracy. But these political aspects of royal travel cohabited with personal ones. In her choice of destinations, Elizabeth kept herself safe from plague, revolt, and invasion, and she favored certain regions and hosts while slighting others. Such a combination of motives reflected the personal monarchy of the sixteenth century. The queen's ability to rule had its foundation in the obedience of her people, high and low, and their recognition of her authority as God's agent and Henry VIII's daughter. Given the nature of such personal monarchy, the progresses both contributed to and constituted the government of Elizabeth. Through direct contact with her subjects during the progresses, Elizabeth cemented the relationship with her people that was the core of her monarchy.

THREE

The Challenge of Royal Travel

H ad each progress been put to a vote, the Elizabethan court would never have moved beyond the royal palaces on the Thames. From nobles to laundresses, the queen was virtually alone in enjoying such official journeys. Government officials had to keep the political machinery running as they themselves trotted away from London. Courtiers had to abandon their estates and families, sharing domestic decisions and news through tardy letters and pretending in front of Elizabeth to enjoy their life on the road. As the earl of Arundel wrote to Robert Dudley in 1560, "Theye that shall atend the quenes majestie in the progresse shall swer from the hyest to the lowest to find solft wayes, how hard soever they fynde theyr loging & fare."[1] Those servants responsible for "lodging and fare" found their household tasks complicated by the daily packing and unloading. Harbingers and purveyors had to produce, as if by magic, beds and foodstuffs in challenging circumstances. This sustained resistance to the progresses came from the Tudor officials most responsible for carrying out royal policies. While the lowly clerks did not complain directly to Elizabeth, her leading ministers certainly did. These statesmen believed that the progresses impeded the daily governance of England. And they were right. Given the complicated tasks and household expense for any progress, the impact of travel on her court was significant.

But in travel, as in so many other areas of government, Elizabeth resisted the pressure of her advisors and did what she wanted. She used criteria other than efficiency and simplicity to judge the worth of progresses. She realized the importance of contact with her hosts and of the public ceremonies that reinforced her royal authority. Elizabeth also found that the turmoil of her travels had the effect of focusing the court's eyes on the monarch at its center. The structure of a typical progress, from the planning to the fulfillment, revealed a complex system of organization that existed in the midst of managed chaos. Despite the universal unpopularity of the progresses within the royal government and household, the queen insisted on the travels that through their uncertainty reminded the court of her own centrality as monarch. The chaos of her progresses satisfied Elizabeth's desire to be a stable base in that changing world.

THE BUSINESS OF GOVERNING

Progresses forced Elizabeth and her officials to conduct royal business while uprooting themselves every few days. No matter where the court was, the government needed to continue its operations in a timely and sustained manner with an involved queen. When such things suited her, Elizabeth was assiduous about paying attention to business. On progress the queen issued proclamations, corresponded with ambassadors abroad, signed commissions, and convened the Privy Council on a regular basis.[2] The records of the Privy Council attest both to the mobility and the productivity of the government during its travels. Usually the Privy Council traveled with Elizabeth and met wherever she was staying, either in a royal palace or at the house of a private host. When the queen was in Essex in 1579, for example, the Privy Council's meetings matched her destinations: Greenwich, Wanstead, Havering, New Hall, and Giddy Hall.[3] The earl of Bedford received the council at Chenies five times in 1570, and Burghley convened eight sessions at Theobalds in 1575.[4] The council met more frequently at those royal palaces outside of bustling London. Between 1570 and 1575, Westminster and Star Chamber held the council 67 times and 17 times, respectively, but the slightly distant palaces proved more popular: the council met at Greenwich 100 times, Hampton Court 81 times, Richmond on 27 occasions, and Windsor 17 times.[5] On progress the council rarely met more than once at any residence unless it was the home of a privy councilor who presumably would expect such busman's holidays.

Although Elizabeth and the Privy Council traveled together, they frequently lodged apart. Because the principal secretary headed the council in the queen's absence, this separation allowed government business still to proceed. The council, for example, continued its session at Hampton Court when Elizabeth left there for Greenwich after the 1594 scandal about her physician, Dr. Lopez.[6] Councilors would take a temporary leave from the progress for personal or business reasons, which effectively separated the queen from the council. As the progress continued toward the next stopping place, the council might remain in its session and catch up with the queen later. Elizabeth and the Privy Council moved together as two planets orbiting one another: the presence of one generally indicated the proximity—nearer or farther—of the other.

On progress the queen had her ministers and advisors at hand, and the court kept apprised of news by special posts. The presence of the lord treasurer, principal secretary, lord chamberlain, and other court officials meant that the councils of state and the administration of the household, such as the Board of Green Cloth, had their members assembled and available for meetings. Wherever the queen traveled, the master of the posts arranged for the series of horses and riders who carried messages to the court. The Privy Council set standards of time for the posts. During the summer months when Elizabeth often was away from London, the posts had to cover seven miles an hour; that speed meant news from London reached Berwick in 42 hours. Between September and March, when progresses were shorter and roads deteriorated with the weather, the posts slowed to five miles an hour (60 hours between London and Berwick).[7] Extra posts linked the court to the established network of messengers during progresses and kept the government current with foreign news. The duties of government mingled with the pleasures of hospitality.

Many participants and petitioners nonetheless viewed the progresses as a time of confusion, sloth, and self-indulgence. Members of the government who remained in London complained that their letters were ignored and their actions circumscribed by the queen's absence. Others moving with the court cast a jaundiced eye on the festivities that they believed distracted the queen from her real business of governing. Writing to Mr. Herbert from Lichfield in July 1575, Sir Francis Walsingham bemoaned his enforced participation in a peripatetic frolic that offended his Puritan sensibilities: "we are altogether given to banquettinge and pastime takinge pleasure sometime notwithstandinge to heare of the continuance of others trouble, as the onelie foundacon of our quiett." A month later at Stafford, Walsingham complained to Burghley that he heard little news, "being lodged as I am far of from the coorte, and having no great dysposytyon to repeyre thither but drawen by especyall occasyon." He disliked the ceremonies and rituals of the visiting court that to him distracted the queen from attending to serious matters. By the next year Walsingham was fed up with, in his view, the wasteful attendance on progress. All he wanted, he wrote, was "to be quyte of the place I serve in, which is subiect unto so many thwartes and harde speches ase none that serve the with a good mynde can take any comforte to supplye the same."[8] Fortunately, his foreign embassies would remove him from the court he found so hedonistic and short-sighted, but his criticisms spoke for others. For those such as Walsingham who wanted to direct the court's agenda, the celebratory atmosphere of the court did create difficulties.

Other government officials echoed Walsingham's complaint that the court on progress ignored its responsibilities. The turmoil of travel could affect the important task of defending the realm, according to frustrated officers in the 1590s. When Sir Thomas Shirley in September 1592 had mustered troops upon royal order to use against Spain, he did not have time to consult the queen about his next course of action. "The coort beynge so farr from hence," he wrote to Burghley, he was isolated and leaderless.[9] Shirley was informing Burghley that he had decided on his own to send the troops ahead to Southampton and meet them there; he trusted that the queen would accept his judgment. A year later, Sir Simon Musgrave was trying to find gunpowder and munitions needed for the royal defenses in Berwick and Newcastle. He asked for the queen's approval of his actions in a last-minute request "because the Quenes matie was goinge in progresse" and thus would be out of Musgrave's reach, while Burghley would be "dalie & howerlie imployed in hir highnes affayres."[10] Officers seeking immediate decisions from Elizabeth sometimes found themselves forced back on their own initiative.

Elizabeth encouraged and took advantage of such confusion to maintain an independent course of action and justify her cautious indecision. She saw an opportunity to keep her officials off balance and to defer decisions by inconveniencing her petitioners. But the efficacy of such royal manipulations was little comfort to those not privy to them. When Sir Thomas Smith wanted the queen to sign a commission for the council in the north in 1572, she refused because Burghley was not with her at Winchester to offer advice. To no avail did Smith remind her that the commission had already passed through Burghley's hands and, therefore, had his approval. The frustrated Smith wrote Burghley that "I do well perceive hir highnes is disposed to signe no thyng except your ldship be here."[11] Her own ministers were not the only ones whom Elizabeth dodged while on progress. During the fall of 1581, Ambassador Bernardino de Mendoza had spent days trying to see Elizabeth in order to deliver his message from Philip II of Spain. The queen, however, chose to shut her doors to Mendoza on the advice of Sir Christopher Hatton and the earl of Leicester. While Mendoza searched for a way to gain a royal audience, Elizabeth remained nicely outside his grasp by continuing to hunt at Nonsuch. The discouraged Mendoza wrote to Philip that "it was difficult for me to attend to your Majesty's interests here under such circumstances as these," but he was hoping for better luck once the queen moved to Richmond.[12] At least he knew where she was going and how to reach her. The Dutch ambassador Noel de Caron knew neither when he sought an audience with Elizabeth in 1591. Caron brought with him a resolution from the States General that required discussion with the queen, who was then on progress through Surrey, Sussex, and Hampshire. The ambassador hoped to intercept her, but unfortunately none of his people knew what road the travelers were following or where the court was going.[13] Without itinerary or destination, Caron was

stymied. Before they could begin their errands, courtiers and foreign ambassadors on official business found themselves hunting for the court.

Once petitioners had intercepted the court, some remained pessimistic
that their pleas would get a hearing during a progress. For every person
who gained access to the traveling queen, there were other suitors with
tales of hardship and rejection. William Tresham delayed pressing his suit
with the queen or approaching his intercessor, John Herbert, the second
secretary to the Privy Council, "for that I did understand that her Matie
was in progresse, a tyme very unfitt for negotiation."[14] When Bishop Tunstall of Durham learned of an upcoming progress while he was with Elizabeth at Hampton Court in 1559, he delayed petitioning the queen on behalf of Sir Thomas Parry. Tunstall explained to Parry that the preparations
for traveling had tainted the atmosphere for discussion: "in Removinge I
do knowe the tyme not to be convenyent to make any sute unto her matie
shall come to some staye."[15] Gilbert Talbot, who sought in 1589 to present
a petition to the queen during her visit at Barn Elms, held the same opinion as Tunstall. Talbot worried that Elizabeth would not answer him because, "whilst she is there, nothing may be moved but matter of delyghte
and to content her, which is the only cause of her going thither."[16] His
letter to Walsingham, owner of Barn Elms, was part of Talbot's strategy to
gain access to the queen through her host. Maybe John Harington, godson
to the queen, had the best approach. When he wanted to find Elizabeth in
a giving vein and cheerful mood, he tried to see her first thing in the morning: "I must go in an earlie hour, before her Highnesse hathe speciale matters broughte up to council on. I muste go before the breakfastinge covers
are placede," stand bare-headed outside her chamber, and ask for a later
appointment when she emerged from the chamber.[17] While the progresses
gave some people more access to the queen, they also could complicate the
channels through which petitioners communicated. The more the queen
moved, some petitioners believed, the less likelihood they had of obtaining
any, much less a favorable, response.

Progresses complicated the business affairs of the travelers as well as
those of the government. They had to neglect their private business, leaving creditors or delicate negotiations hanging, in order to follow the queen.
When a gentleman pensioner, bound by his office to attend the traveling
court, could not defend his interests at a hearing on *inquisitions post mor-
tem,* the Privy Council charged the commission to deal properly with the
case in his absence.[18] He was fortunate in having that official support. Others took advantage of their enforced attendance on the mobile court to
dodge obligations. Courtiers could, as the queen did, avoid tiresome petitions without offense by invoking the excuse of going on progress. Robert

Bouth explained to his cousin Williamson of Sawlye, Derbyshire, that "My Lo. cannot do any thing about the letter of atturny which you sent upp now, bycause of much othr urgent busyness. he wayteth this morning up-pon the Quene in progress: it might therfore of necessity be differred untill he come into the cowntry."[19] One person's inconvenience was another's evasion, but regardless of motive, everyone who had business at court knew that it might suffer during the progress season.

Progresses thus complicated the business of governing, a situation that frustrated courtiers but apparently satisfied the queen. Although the Privy Council and ministers worked while accompanying the queen, their Her-culean efforts could not compensate for time lost to travel. The queen, however, did attend to some political and diplomatic affairs on progress. The court always was in contact via posts with its most important servants, the queen read her correspondence, and she ruled. Given that she traveled so intensely for months at a time, Elizabeth could hardly abandon the kingdom to govern itself or suspend governmental activities while on prog-ress: of necessity she worked.

Unlike her officers, however, Elizabeth viewed the business of govern-ment and of travel as one. Moving with her court through the kingdom was, to her, essential to being a popular, successful monarch. By intention-ally denying access to some, Elizabeth sought to avoid entanglements with the "outside" world of ambassadors and petitioners. By dislocating the court, the progresses upset some normal avenues of patronage while creat-ing new ones in the communities visited by the queen. Everyone recog-nized that the progresses complicated life at court in numerous ways, but the turmoil that troubled her councilors typified the queen's approach to government. Elizabeth found the chaos of her progresses useful, as it shielded her from certain political, marital, and diplomatic decisions that she characteristically tried to avoid.

BED, BOARD, AND TRANSPORTATION

The mundane aspects of travel—food, beds, transport—posed the hardest challenge to members of the royal household on whose efforts the queen's and court's comfort depended. Before every progress, the household staff plunged into frenzied preparation for a royal visit. The lord chamberlain drew up an itinerary of that summer's travels, called the gestes, which in-dicated the order and approximate dates of Elizabeth's arrivals and de-partures. This preliminary schedule, however, often changed according to royal whim or weather. Of her plans for the Christmas holiday in 1565, Francis Alen wrote to the earl of Shrewsbury that "next week it is thought

[Elizabeth] will remove; not, as it was first intended, to Greenwich, but to Windsor." But by the close of his letter, Alen had to amend the earlier plan: "now there is no removing at all" because the queen would stay at Westminster.[20] Such alterations were irritatingly common.

With the hosts and route determined, the officers of the queen's household then organized the retinue of people, equipment, and animals. Courtiers, administrators, councilors, and foreign ambassadors joined the queen's ladies and gentlemen of the privy chamber, maids of honor, captain of the guard, grooms of the privy chamber, and court physicians in the progresses. The wives of these officials and some prominent clergy on occasion would come. When the queen went to Croydon in May 1574, the court provided lodgings and meals for 14 nobles and courtiers, as well as members of the royal household. In Worcester in 1575, Elizabeth was attended by 14 noblemen and royal officers, 6 bishops, and 10 ladies of honor. A larger retinue went with her to visit Lord Burghley at Theobalds in 1583. The busy host found rooms for a score of nobles, as well as grooms of the privy chamber, officers of the cellar and pantry, cooks, clerk of the kitchen, squires of the body, gentlemen ushers, groom porter, servants to the lords, and gentlewomen of the bedchamber.[21] This large group of travelers required planning, energy, and many supplies for their journey.

The largest entourage undoubtedly would have gone with the queen to York in 1562, had she actually met Mary Stuart there. Before the progress collapsed under the weight of foreign affairs, Elizabeth had drawn up plans for accommodating an English retinue designed to impress her Scottish cousin. Listed in the train were 10 lords and 4 court officers, 9 of whom brought their wives, and 184 servants accompanying them. The marquis of Northampton had 20 servants, the earls were allotted 18 each, the lords 14, and the court officers 8 each. At York, 16 ladies would lodge with the English court and have the provision of horses and beds. The duchess of Somerset commanded 20 horses and seven beds, while "every knight's wife" made do with 4 horses and one bed. Another 18 noblewomen would join Elizabeth before her interview with Mary. With the duke of Norfolk and 27 nobles in attendance, Elizabeth's entrance would have been complete.[22] Had the visit ever occurred, the queen would have lodged and fed at least 223 people.

Court officials needed an array of subordinates to conduct the business of the itinerant government. Secretaries, armed with their seals and ledgers, kept up a steady flow of correspondence, while clerks tried to monitor the receipts and expenses in their department. The most important of these departments was the Board of the Green Cloth, under whose jurisdiction came the suppliers of food, drink, bedding, and sundries to the royal household. Sitting on the Board of Green Cloth were the lord steward, the treasurer of the household, the comptroller of the household, the cofferer of the household, clerks of the green cloth, and clerks comptroller, many of whom were on progress by virtue of their other functions.[23] The secretariat brought along its seals, wax, inks, nibs, parchment, paper, and desks. These government servants composed the bureaucracy that enabled the queen to travel without going on vacation.

Largest in number were the servants, numbering over 300, including 70 in the kitchen alone.[24] The departments primarily responsible for feeding, housing, and moving the queen's retinue were the household, especially the household belowstairs and the Board of Green Cloth. The household belowstairs divided its functions into purchasing, preparing, and distributing supplies to the royal household. The level of organization was truly impressive. In charge of buying supplies were departments that included the bakehouse (grain), the cellar (wine), the buttery (beer and ale), the spicery (spices and fruits), the acatry (meat, fish, salt), the poultry (lamb, fowl, butter, eggs), the scullery (charcoal), the woodyard (wood and rushes), and the cart takers. Preparation of food involved the kitchen (general tasks), the boilinghouse (meats), the scaldinghouse (poultry), the baking house (breads), and the pastry (baked meats). Foods and supplies were stored and distributed through the larder (meats and fish), the pantry (bread), the chandlery (candles), the wafery (wafers), the confectionary (fruits), and the laundry (linens).[25] Feeding, housing, and moving the queen's retinue required the services of the clerk of the market, gentlemen ushers, grooms of the chamber, yeomen waiters, yeomen of the mail, yeomen of the flagons, a sergeant at arms and marshal, officers of the spicery, officers of the buttery, officers of the cellary, clerk of the kitchen, warden of the beds, harbingers, surveyor of the ways, porters, messengers, footmen, cooks and boilers, laundresses, and carters. Proper royal pageantry depended on the contributions of the sword bearer, trumpeters, musicians of the viols, other musicians, and heralds-at-arms.[26] Each of these household departments had its staff, most of whom worked for the court as it traveled (see Appendix). During a progress, therefore, Elizabeth would have a retinue that ranged in number from 30 people, for a brief trip, to some 350 people for a major journey.

Before Elizabeth reached each destination, her court officers had to prepare for her arrival.[27] The royal advance team typically consisted of an ordinary gentleman usher of the chamber, one yeoman usher, three yeomen of the chamber, two grooms of the chamber, two grooms of the wardrobe, and one groom porter.[28] The gentlemen ushers and harbingers began to answer the pragmatic questions of travel: Where would people sleep? How many rooms were available? In what condition were the rooms and bedclothes? Were new structures needed? Where would the tents go? Was there pasture for the horses? Where would they store supplies until the queen arrived?

These tasks, known as "apparreling," fell to the harbingers. In the 1580s to mid-1590s, the men in charge were Simon Bowyer, Richard Brackenbury, Anthony Wingfield, Richard Coningsby, and Thomas Conway.[29] At each royal destination, they unlocked the house and unbolted the doors and windows to give the whole house a good airing. The harbingers checked that the bedrooms had chairs, beds, carpets, and hangings, and they freshened the bedclothes. After noting the supplies of charcoal and fagots for fires in bedrooms and kitchens, they catalogued any foodstuffs stored in the cellars. They then tallied how many sleeping quarters to construct: while tents would do for the household staff, more illustrious guests required their own rooms, which the harbingers arranged to facilitate socializing, preserve modesty, and separate enemies. Hosts collaborated with the court representatives in creating a sleeping chart for those entitled to housing at court. With the court's arrival, harbingers handed out the billets, or tickets, that gave authorized people a set number of rooms and beds. Ushers found rooms in the main house and grounds for courtiers, while harbingers handled the large numbers of people "outside" the court staying at nearby inns and private homes.

Feeding these travelers cost much money and demanded intense organization. To know who had the privilege of eating and residing at court, on progress or in London, the Elizabethan household relied upon two books: the Bouche of Court and the Book of the Diet. Between them, these two compendia listed the name or position of every person within the court who could claim room and board at the queen's expense.[30] In a precise culinary hierarchy that mirrored the social pecking order, courtiers by virtue of their office received specific allotments of food and rooms. All the major household officers received messes or portions of meat for each meal at court. They included the lord steward, the lord chamberlain, the treasurer of the household, the comptroller of the household, the secretary, the master of the horse, and the vice-chamberlain. The queen, her ladies of the privy chamber, and other female servants filled 23 places at dinner, and the male officers of the household numbered 21 at meals. For them, the Book of the Diet apportioned 48 dishes of meat.[31] These figures indicate the minimum amount of food—and by extension, the expense—that the Diet required on a daily basis. The two books limited the number of guests and servants at court, recognized fish days, avoided expensive delicacies, and required communal dining. Such attempts at regulation, however, met with little success as courtiers ignored the dietary restrictions. They ordered different, costlier foods from the kitchen; they ate at private tables in their rooms, a habit that wasted many dishes; and they invaded the kitchen and cellar for unauthorized feasts. Elizabeth also broke the rules, especially concerning fish days, and failed to prevent systemic pilferage.[32] Some rules in the Bouche and Diet were most honored in the breach.

The court consumed prodigious quantities and varieties of food. According to the Book of the Diet, one large table, seven yards long and one yard wide, should hold a feast of items as set down in the monthly household rules. In August, there should be 1 swan, 19 capons, 4 pullets, 3 chickens, 2 bitterns, 2 herons, 2 ducklings, 2 gulls, 18 bunnies, 16 pigeons, 8 mews, 4 brewes, 4 godwits, 4 partridges, 12 quails, 40 lambs, 4 teals, 12 coarse pullets, and 8 coarse chickens. In the winter months, pheasants, lapwings, larks, and geese appeared.[33] A sample of the annual supply of food to the court in 1589 included: 13,260 lambs; 2,752 dozens of different kinds of poultry; 60,000 pounds of butter; 4,200,000 eggs; and 4,000 bunches of onions and scallions. A few years later, the acatry was supplying 1,240 oxen, 8,200 sheep, 2,330 veals (or young sheep), 760 young cows, 310 pigs, 53 boars, and 560 sides of bacon. To wash down the meal, from the buttery came 600,000 gallons of beer and ale, and 200–300 tuns of wine. The sumptuous feasts at court reflected an almost methodical attempt to consume every species within a category of food: Why have just a chicken when one could eat swans, turkeys, geese, herons, pheasants, partridges, woodcocks, lapwings, plovers, mallards, pigeons, gulls, larks, quail, ducklings, or shore birds? Choices of fish included "pike, carp, tench, bream, eel, perch, dace, roach, barbel, gudgeon, flounder, knobber, shrimp, and oysters," as well as cod, salmon, and dried fish.[34] This shopping list would have challenged the most diligent of purveyors.

A look at the monthly provisions for the queen's table from only two departments, the acatry and the poultry, suggests that the court's arrival must have depopulated the wildlife in surrounding counties to supply it. In his household book, William Cholmley listed the edible inventory needed to cover the queen's large table. According to his records, diners selected their menu, depending on the time of year, from offerings of: swans, geese, capons, pullets, chickens, heron, ducklings, gulls, rabbits, bunnies, coneys, pigeons, partridges, pheasants, plovers, lapwings, quail, larks, woodcocks, lambs, mallards, teals, and Kentish hens. The quantities of meats and fowls varied according to the season. Peak times were from April through July and November through January. When the court had many entertainments during the progress season in early spring and midsummer and calendar festivals during the extended Christmas season, the number of dishes rose. The drop in quantity reflected the falling demand during the quiet of the Lenten months and the harvest time.[35] Cholmley's account indicated the court required less meat during August and September, part of the progress months, a slight decline probably reflecting contributions from hosts and more freshly slaughtered beef and mutton. Fish would not have replaced meat on the diet, except during part of Lent, because of the difficulties in providing fresh fish and the widespread disregard of the "fish days," which Elizabeth had decreed for both court and country.[36] Fish ponds at three royal manors could not satisfy the court's demands, nor always could purveyance. When Dorothy Gamage sent supplies to her husband John for the court at Hadnam, she could offer only salt fish, not fresh, to Elizabeth. She explained that "as for fresse fishe, there is none to be geven in the river."[37] Provincial suppliers, such as the Gamages, could not provide for the queen what they did not have themselves. The inventories of food and the organization to procure it show how the government worked to keep the hungry court fed at all times.

To wash down their feast, members of the court consumed enormous quantities of beer, ale, and wine. Although Elizabeth was not a deep drinker, she was certainly the exception in an age known for its love of alcohol. One historian estimated that Swedes in the sixteenth century consumed 40 times more beer per person than was consumed in the mid-twentieth century.[38] Discounting the greater variety of drinks available now and the unhygienic water then, the explanation of such consumption mostly lies in the need for calories and the strong spices that flavored many foods and the heavy doses of salt used to preserve meats, fish, and butter in the days before refrigeration. The household carried its own beer from London because the abstemious queen preferred light ale to strong beer. Purveyors would lay in huge supplies before the queen's arrival. To ensure against pilfering the royal stock, double padlocks secured the cellar: one key returned with the purveyor to court, and the other remained with the keeper of the place.[39] In case the transported beer ran out, household officers issued licenses to local people for supplementary alehouses. Such licenses authorized persons to operate alehouses only during the time of the court's presence, after which the license expired. These temporary tapsters could not sell beer, ale, or bread in altered or lesser measures; they had to obey the price lists set by the clerk of the market; nor could they engage in dicing, gaming, and other illegal activities such as prostitution.[40] Thus, the queen's officers ensured that the traveling court had plenty to drink.

As Elizabeth moved through the countryside, her supplies both preceded and followed her court. Although shoddy roads made water transport the most efficient way to move goods in sixteenth-century England, most of the household goods were hauled in carts on the progresses. Whenever possible, the itineraries took advantage of convenient waterways, and barges afforded the queen easy access around London and her palaces in the Thames valley. But travel over land in carriages and on horseback was inevitable since many progress houses lay some distance from the rivers. Elizabeth consequently relied upon her surveyor of the ways to map out the best route between houses and upon her builder to provide sturdy coaches, litters, and wagons for the overland travel.[41]

The complexity of moving the court, as well as the number of people involved, was staggering. The queen and nobility traveled in carriages pulled by six horses capable, according to William Harrison, of moving 400 pounds. Horses also pulled the hundreds of carts laden with supplies. Elizabeth had 128 to 152 horses for her own use, and her master of the horse supervised a stable of 230 to 270 double horses and hackneys, a number that grew in times of progresses. Harrison disapprovingly noted that replacing packhorses with carts to move the court "causeth the trains of our princes in their progresses to show far less than those of the kings of other nations."[42] Despite Harrison's equine preference, the sight of hundreds of carts, horses, and bedecked nobility stretched along dusty English roads offered no small dose of pageantry and spectacle.

Members of the retinue had carts assigned by the lord steward according to their function, status, and position at court. First in priority were the household departments: 13 carts for the jewel coffers; 10 for the wardrobe of the bedchamber; 10 for the kitchen; 8 for the robes; 5 for the larder. The other offices each used one cart. According to a 1589 list drawn up by the lord steward, these departments required a total of 169 carts.[43] An additional 79 carts went to the household officers, privy councilors, ladies of the court, and other departments. Each important person usually had one cart, swelling the number to some 248 carts for that progress. Since other carts augmented this orderly assignment, the queen often led a caravan of over 300 carts around the countryside.

PURVEYANCE AND ITS PROBLEMS

The difficult task of gathering supplies for the itinerant court was the job of court officials called purveyors. The medieval system of purveyance as it operated in the sixteenth century was the right of the crown to force subjects to sell goods at discount.[44] Purveyors reported to the queen's clerk of the market, who determined whether the town's supplies were wholesome for the royal table, set the prices for all goods purchased on progress for the court (an attempt to prevent false inflation in those sellers' markets), and enforced the use of standard weights and measurements.[45] The chief purveyors for each department, appointed by the Board of Green Cloth in the household, chose their own deputies. Purveyors had a commission authorizing them to secure goods for only six months within a specific county. By 1589, 56 purveyors and their 111 deputies held 111 commissions that took them into the counties. Carrying his commission, petty cash for purchases under 40 shillings, and tallies for more expensive items, the purveyor entered a market town and arranged with the constables for the delivery of the requested supplies from outlying regions. If he preferred instead to deal directly with farmers, the purveyor could go to an estate and purchase supplies from the owner without incurring additional costs for transport of the goods to the market town. Or the purveyor could select foods for sale at the market stalls and from carts on the highways and take immediate possession of the items.

The system of purveyance caused problems in the localities and within the government that only worsened with Elizabeth's continual progresses. In particular, the strains on an outdated method of finance and marketing highlighted the weaknesses of the widely unpopular purveyance system. Criticism of purveyance within the government and in localities helped to usher in the next, briefly acceptable, system of composition, in which the county negotiated a contract with the government to deliver specific quantities of food at designated times. The change from purveyance to composition occurred, in part, because of the stresses to the system and the royal household created by the queen's progresses.

The unrelenting demand for food led purveyors to use unpopular and at times dishonest shortcuts to supply the ravenous court. Direct purchase aroused the most protest because unscrupulous purveyors could easily cheat the vendors by underpricing the goods and escaping the cost of transportation. What seemed fair at the time could later turn into a financial loss for the sellers. The two parties reached a sale price either by using the standard set by the clerk of the market or by haggling, and they exchanged receipts instead of money to close the deal. The swindling or saving, depending on one's point of view, came during the process of reimbursement. The sellers took their receipts to the constable, who forwarded them to the justice of the peace, who sent them to the Board of Green Cloth for comparison with the purveyors' tallies. Only then would the sellers receive their final payment. After having extended the government what amounted to a credit for the goods thus far, the sellers faced the danger that the board would disallow the amount on the receipt as excessive and arbitrarily reduce it. From the government's perspective, such an action checked possible collusion between the purveyor and sellers, who could inflate the price and pocket the difference. But for the sellers, reducing the money owed them meant that they had sold their wares at a loss.

Another offense common to purveyors was purchasing goods for the queen's table but then reselling them at market and keeping the money.[46] In a series of attempts to regulate this process, statutes from 1275 to 1555 stipulated that purveyors could buy food only for the royal family, had to show their commissions to vendors and obtain their approval, must set prices jointly with four local people, must submit to semiannual audits and obey the orders from the local bailiff and constable. Despite the legal safeguards to ensure fairness, however, abuses still occurred. Purveyors remained one of the most hated representatives of Elizabethan government, but hated or not, they were essential to the progresses.

Purveyors also ran into local resistance when they tried to provide carts and horses to move the court. According to the rules laid down by the Board of Green Cloth, purveyors known as cart takers had to assemble carriages and horses within a 12-mile radius of the departure point of the progress; they had to give the high constable of the hundred a list of all carts taken; and they could use the equipment for only 16 miles or one day's journey. Outlying regions had to pay a ten shilling tax for each cart taken within the 12-mile radius in order to share the burden of the queen's removes.[47] Sometimes the carts remained loaded through the night in order to be ready for a sudden change of plans. With only 12 hours' notice to assemble and load several hundred carts, frantic cart takers would break the rules in order to meet a royal deadline. They often used any available vehicle regardless of its place of origin. Although owners of the carts received a rental fee of two pence per mile, some doubted their loan of carts would be profitable. Those who feared they would never retrieve their goods or who had their own work to finish bought their way out of the purveyance by paying a fee. Others preferred not to show up with their chattels at the scheduled time. The transportation system of royal progresses gave purveyors irritating powers with little regulation, while forcing the cart owners to comply or face fines and imprisonment. These subjects must have had conflicting responses, therefore, to the news that the queen intended a progress near their villages.

Many of the abuses under purveyance occurred because the system did not block unscrupulous purveyors from skimming profits and embezzling funds. In an attempt to curb abuses and enforce the laws, the government tried and punished corrupt purveyors. The Privy Council periodically ordered justices of the peace to investigate purveyors in their localities. These enquiries led to the prosecution of accused purveyors in the county's quarter sessions and occasionally in the prerogative courts of the household, the commission for household causes and the Board of Green Cloth acting in its judicial capacity.[48] Corrupt purveyors committed a variety of abuses. For buying smelt in the queen's name and reselling them to fishwives at a profit, a purveyor was pilloried with a collar of smelt around his neck.[49] Purveyor William Seward was indicted for extortion of goods and money at the Essex assizes in 1569, found guilty, and fined four shillings. A grand jury presented Edward Bryan, alias Wilson, for using the queen's commission to take two chickens at 8d. from Anne Wyatt and seven chickens at 2s. 4d. from others, which he then sold to Owen Paxson for his personal profit. Thomas Sheriffe was acquitted of similar charges in 1583 at the Witham assizes; William Barton was convicted there of extortion and allowed benefit of clergy.[50] At Rochester in 1586, deputy purveyor William Dundre faced a charge of embezzlement over six hens. At Hertford that year deputy purveyor William Sharpe failed to answer a count of extortion also involving chickens.[51] Two servants of purveyor Walter Kyppynge were indicted at Southwark in 1587 for conversion, the crime of buying goods for the queen and reselling them for personal profit. They were accused of converting a bunch of wooden spokes, but they escaped with a pardon for their offense.[52] No such mercy saved deputy purveyor Edward Sharpe, who confessed in 1591 at Chelmsford to converting chickens and who was sentenced to hang for it.[53] The sums involved in these cases came to only a few shillings, but the continued abuses were generating much local anger that might extend to the court itself. Thus, by the 1590s Elizabeth had determined to appease public outrage by striking down some of the corrupt purveyors. She and her ministers felt threatened by rising household costs, due in part to the progresses, and by an increasingly vocal demand for reform from Parliament that she tried to silence by litigation against the purveyors.

While the government prosecuted corrupt purveyors, the counties tried to bar them from entering their territories at all. If the county or town could get an exemption from the government, that exemption would free the area from all obligations to supply the royal table. Frequently visited territories, such as Havering and Eye in Essex, and the forests and towns near royal residences in Berkshire and Surrey, easily received exemptions from the Board of Green Cloth. The counties of Northumberland, Cumberland, and Westmorland, which bore the cost of defending the Scottish border and never received a visit from Elizabeth, escaped the purveyors as well. Special interest groups also received exemptions: purveyors could not trouble the scholars at Oxford and Cambridge or the household servants or certain privileged towns.[54] During Elizabeth's reign, the town of Colchester tried unsuccessfully to guard its exemption, granted by Edward IV, but its petitions and prosecution of offenders failed to hold back the encroaching purveyors. The county of Essex, however, fared better: it secured an exemption from providing carriages for the queen's progresses from Greenwich, Hackney, St. James's, Westminster, and the suburbs, because the distances were too great.[55] Localities prized exemptions that freed them from future liability, but the government issued them with the greatest reluctance and fought to revoke some already issued. The queen, after all, had to eat. When counties could not gain an exemption, they tried to trade their obligations for less onerous duties or substitute the required items. The sheep and storks from Huntingdonshire were too small, according to the purveyors, so the county's justices of the peace applied to change their quota from sheep to poultry. Sometimes money was easier to find than the specific commodities requested for the queen's table. In Dorset, the 120-mile journey to market ruined local cattle, so the county paid a monetary fee instead of producing ragged cattle. A similarly logical swap occurred in Sussex over the cost of carting wood.[56] Given the difficulties with purveyance, some localities sought a practical solution that fit their individual circumstances without attempting to change the entire unwieldy system.

Although no one believed purveyance was working well, the queen refused to try to fix the system until near the end of her reign. According to the queen, centuries of historical precedents had made purveyance a part of the royal prerogative, and she would not diminish by any reform her authority in that area. The current rules established by a 1555 statute, requiring receipts, regional oversight, and orders not in arcane Latin but in common English, were sufficient for her. But many members of Parliament felt otherwise. During three decades of discussions, Parliament repeatedly called for reform and tried to modify the system of purveyance. The queen and her ministers, however, construed those parliamentary actions as an attempt to limit the monarch's power to command supplies and, by extension, as an attack on the royal prerogative.[57] The bills to reform purveyance, therefore, died in the first two parliaments for lack of the queen's assent. The struggle continued through the 1571 session and again in 1581. With Sir Walter Mildmay's backing, the Commons in 1587 introduced and passed a bill limiting purveyance and punishing illegal purveyors with a £20 fine. However, in defense of the prerogative, Elizabeth again refused her assent.[58] Because the crown's right to secure supplies under the prerogative blended so closely with purveyance, the recognized abuses of purveyors drew no additional statutory punishment after the one of 1555. Widespread agreement about the nature of the problem did not bring about unified solutions.

The major crisis in the battle over purveyance came in 1589. The abuses of purveyors supplying troops against the Armada had irritated a Parliament already sensitive to the problem after three decades of royal progresses. Elizabeth at last agreed to create a royal commission to seek reform in 1589. She felt unable to ignore the irate members any longer, but she refused to accept a bill against purveyors. In a typical strategy of delay, the queen hoped that the commission would air grievances without proposing statutory changes harmful to her prerogative.[59] With the parliamentary commission and the new emphasis on composition, the royal household sought to move away from purveyance and secure its supplies increasingly from composition agreements that did not affect the royal prerogative.

Composition set contracts between the court and the counties for supplies at a fixed reduced price. Justices of the peace known as undertakers enforced the contracts. The success of composition hinged upon the cooperation of the undertakers who bought and sent supplies to the court and then levied charges upon the community. The composition agreements listed the quantity and cost of the supplies owed by each county. Kent, for example, had to deliver six score of fat wethers between 25 July and 30 September to Greenwich for the royal household; a separate contract called for 20 storks from the county. The total cost of the composition agreements for each county reached large proportions. According to a list of 1593, Essex owed £717 3s. 4d. in composition fees, Lincolnshire £666 13s. 4d., Leicestershire £488, Somerset £433 6s. 8d., Bedfordshire £323 13s. 4d., and Warwickshire £321 13s. 4d. The sum owed by these and five other counties amounted to £8,429 18s. 4d.[60] By agreeing to negotiated terms, the counties that compounded were not liable for any purveyance of those goods. Composition allowed Elizabeth to maintain her prerogative rights and the counties to escape the hated purveyors. Once Elizabeth appreciated the savings to her household from composition, she gave more support to Burghley's efforts and Parliament's initiative.

Although purveyance for the royal household decreased as Burghley pressed for more composition agreements, it still remained a necessary method of supplying the court on progress. Despite the composition agreements, purveyors could still enter a county during any progress if the court traveled within 20 miles of the border. That so many counties near the court in London eagerly compounded indicated the universal unpopularity of the purveyors. Distant counties innocent of purveyors had little incentive to compound and received much governmental pressure before capitulating.[61] But the counties that saw Elizabeth often on progress had no doubt that composition was the better policy. Purveyors and progresses went together, in the common view, and the eagerness to escape the burden of purveyance reflected the localities' unpleasant contact with the traveling court. The hosts wanted the queen without the purveyors, and Elizabeth wanted the supplies and progresses without the ill feelings from purveyance. Composition greatly eased the tension so that the remaining uses of purveyance seemed more reasonable.

In the last decade of Elizabeth's reign, the worsening financial state of the crown sparked a flurry of activity in the household. Burghley continued to press for more composition agreements as the economy lurched from one crisis to the next. The war with Spain demanded higher taxes that brought decreasing yields; the war closed continental markets to the

English; dearth and plague disrupted domestic markets; and the German principalities expelled the Merchant Adventurers in 1597.[62] In 1591 the lords in commission for household causes investigated more complaints about purveyors and supported again the changes to composition. Through Burghley's vigorous use of compounding, the commission had succeeded in bringing all the counties into the composition system by 1597. When Elizabeth became queen in 1558, her court had received its supplies through purveyance; by the time of her death in 1603, virtually all supplies came to the household under composition agreements. Such extensive use of composition by 1597 had reduced household costs by £19,000 per year, although Elizabeth did not realize such a windfall: her refusal to limit her retinue negated some of Burghley's tidy savings.[63] The value of composition, nonetheless, was apparent. The progresses facilitated this change by demonstrating the inadequacies of purveyance to supply a large, mobile, and loosely structured court.

COSTS TO THE QUEEN'S HOUSEHOLD

At the heart of all these issues—attendance on progress, bed and board, supplies—lay the matter of money. The challenge of travel for the royal household was a financial one. The queen spent more on the diet, on transportation, on supplies, and on accommodations when the court traveled than when she remained in the London area. The more Elizabeth changed her itinerary, once it had been established, the greater the costs were of coordinating the preparations for her arrival and stay. As Elizabeth's lord treasurer, Burghley struggled to convince the queen that she could not afford her progresses. Despite the lord treasurer's detailed lists of royal expenses and strongly worded memoranda, however, the queen refused to stay home. Torn between her desires to govern frugally and to travel widely, Elizabeth chose the progresses that supported her monarchy, her popularity, and her ability to govern.

Although hosts spent their own money on royal hospitality, Elizabeth paid for a large share of her court's expenses from royal household funds. Preparing for the royal retinue, buying and transporting the food, building the accommodations, arranging the ceremonies, purchasing gifts, staging the entertainments, and extending full hospitality had their price, and the cost was great. Because Elizabeth hated to spend money on armies, foreign rebels, courtiers' rewards, or artistic patronage, historians for some time have seen the same pattern in her progresses. Writers from David Hume to Wallace MacCaffrey depict a stingy queen who sponged off her hosts to save her own treasury, making her progresses "a great oppression on the nobility" and "a free holiday at her subjects' expense." David Howarth perpetuates this interpretation of royal rapacity by asserting that Elizabeth "conducted her progresses on the basis of eating her courtiers out of house and home." The financial demands of feeding, housing, and supplying the court, itself the size of a hamlet, therefore overwhelmed the town or noble foolish enough to entertain the queen. According to Conrad Russell, "gentlemen who wanted favour had to entertain the queen more lavishly than the gentleman before, and when she left the minimum present for a man who did not want to be suspected of plotting rebellion was £100." When she arrived the hosts were flush, but at her departure they had not two groats to rub together. With all the expenses shouldered by her hosts, in Lawrence Stone's view, Elizabeth supposedly "was more or less living free."[64]

Contemporary evidence, however, does not entirely support this harsh balance sheet in which the queen, in theory, bankrupted her nobility. The financial records do not offer a complete picture of the expenses and revenues of the Elizabethan household, nor does a confusing system of recording payments clear a path for us to follow the money. Thus, the anarchy in extant accounts makes it difficult to separate payments from the queen and her hosts.[65] Nonetheless, a financial overview of the progresses is possible by including all the tasks involved in moving the court, with their costs and the party responsible for payment. This breakdown of financial responsibilities leads to a different picture of the funding of the progresses, one in which the queen's expenditures proved large and sustained. Elizabeth and her court were not aristocratic vultures picking at a host's manorial carcass: in truth, they were special guests bringing a potluck dinner to their host.

Expectations of hospitality kept the royal expenses high. By the sixteenth century, courtiers had abandoned the shared public tables, characteristic of medieval court hospitality, for private dining away from the community. This growing privacy continued into the next century and ultimately undermined the value of communal hospitality. John Evelyn noted the passing of this custom in 1663, when he "dined at the Comptroller's with the Earl of Oxford and Mr. Ashburnham. It was said it should be the last of the public diets or tables at Court, it being determined to put down the old hospitality."[66] Undoubtedly one of the reasons for putting down the old hospitality was the expense of maintaining its corrupted version under Elizabeth.

The queen bore the financial burden of supporting her court whether she was staying in London or traveling across country. All who were listed in the Bouche of Court and the Book of the Diet received food and beds courtesy of the queen. According to the observant French ambassador De

Maisse, Elizabeth "has also the charge of her Court, which she pays almost wholly, the Lords of her Household being entertained at her charge. She bears the charges of all her officers and those of her Council from term to term without any lack, so that her expense is very great."[67] The number of courtiers, ministers, servants, and laborers in the progress retinue could range from several dozen to several hundred on any given trip, and they expected to receive wages, food, and shelter during their time at court. Because the royal household included scores of servants and government officials, the expenses incurred by Elizabeth were substantial.

The organization of the queen's household caused her expenses to remain high in London and to soar on progress. The household belowstairs was the most expensive and important department of the court because it supplied food to all the people and departments at court. The lists of people and rules in the Book of the Diet and the Bouche of Court suggested that this burden was large and resistant to cost-cutting measures.[68] The large numbers of people dependent upon the royal hospitality meant that an itinerant court saved the queen little money. Wherever the court was, her household coffers paid for much of its food.

Expenses for food from purveyance always exceeded the household budget. The duplication of dishes on separate tables, the wasted food, and the special meals destroyed any possible savings from the diet and bouche rules. According to the diet book drawn up in 1573 but "never put into practice," the annual cost of feeding the queen and her household should have amounted to £15,793. The actual cost was £21,004, an increase of some £5,300, which reflected the expense of extra dishes and higher prices.[69] In 1576 all dishes of meat for the household should have cost £15,441; instead, they totaled £21,096. The entire household of 118 people cost £21,639 to feed that year.[70] Four years later, an estimate of the diet's cost again revealed the optimism of those reformers seeking to limit the expenses of the household to £15,330. By 1578 the daily cost of Elizabeth's breakfast, dinner, and supper on a flesh day (meat, not fish) totaled £8 17s. 5d., putting her meals alone at a cost of £3,223 19s. 8d. for that year.[71] Yet another reform attempt in 1589 found that the cost of feeding the household in December while the court was at Richmond and Greenwich averaged £40 a day. The seasonal feasts at Christmas and New Year's elevated some of the figures.[72] The fact that this daily figure is less than in 1573, when it would have been about £57, indicated the earlier long progresses cost more due to waste and additional personnel around the queen. The stationary court in the winter of 1589 consumed less than it had during the lengthy, ceremonial, and lavish travels of the 1570s.

These moneys were more than reformers like Burghley and even Elizabeth wished to pay for household provisions, but in perspective they seem reasonable enough. The personal diet of Henry VIII in 1546 cost about £18 per week, whereas that of Elizabeth in 1575 cost her £29 2s. 11d. a week.[73] The queen's light appetite, however, was not the source of the problem. Her courtiers and servants had the wasteful, expensive eating habits, but she could not diminish her retinue without losing the pageantry created by her progresses. Since the progresses drew crowds to court, where they dined at royal expense, the queen in reality could not save money by traveling. And her household officers never considered going on progress as a way to lighten royal expenses.

For duties specifically related to the progresses, the queen's servants in the household received daily wages and collected fees. As builder of all the queen's conveyances in 1573, Walter Rypyn received a daily fee of 1s., amounting to £18 5s. annually, in addition to his livery. The yeoman cart taker received a fee of 100s. annually in addition to a daily wage of 2s. while provisioning carts. The grooms received 4 marks annually plus 2s. per day. The Board of Green Cloth paid out 2d. per mile to the owners of carts borrowed for the court's use. The master of the horse saw to the management of the royal stable, and expenses for hay alone reached £1,090 for the long progress to Warwickshire in 1575.[74] An account of "incidental expenses" for 1589 reveals that the carriage of provisions and supplies had cost the queen £1,368 that year, when she had done little traveling and remained mostly at Richmond, Oatlands, Nonsuch, and Hampton Court.[75] With longer progresses, the queen could expect to pay much more for the transportation of her court.

She also paid for special posts that supplemented the regular network of communication.[76] The four special posts during the progress to Norwich in 1578 involved eight riders from Bristol to "Marliborow" who received a total of 88s. for 43 days' service. Special messengers attended Elizabeth on progress, and they received 2s. 8d. a day in 1564, according to the treasurer of the Exchequer.[77] F. C. Dietz estimated the annual expense of the posts to be £4,000 toward the end of Elizabeth's reign, and part of these costs reflected the additional expense of the progresses.[78] Her decision to go on progress entailed extra costs across the board, and the special posts constituted a vital, recurring expense to her household every time she traveled.

In addition to wages and posts were the fees for harbingers. Financial records of these duties filled the account books of Sir Thomas Heneage as treasurer of the chamber. Heneage also recorded the queen's itinerary, members of her retinue, and payments made to household servants. He recorded the costs incurred by the harbingers for preparing the progress residences. They received wages as gentlemen ushers for work lasting from two to eight days at each place. In the three years for which there are surviving accounts, the charges for appareling amounted to £262 from Michaelmas 1581–82; £114 from Michaelmas 1585–86; and £54 from November 1593 to September 1594.[79] These sums, admittedly "little," as F. C. Dietz notes, nevertheless contribute to the larger picture of the costs of even shorter progresses during that period. None of them, however, reflects what must have been the higher costs of the lengthier, elaborate progresses of other years: Essex in 1561; Warwickshire in 1572 and 1575; Gloucestershire in 1574 and 1592; Worcestershire in 1575; Norfolk in 1578; and Southampton in 1591.[80] What explained the high appareling cost in 1581–82 was the ceremonial escort that Elizabeth provided for the duc d'Alençon as he left London for Canterbury and France. She saw him off in high style with 100 gentlemen and 300 servants in his honor.[81] The lower appareling costs in the other years came when the queen was staying closer to London and traveling less widely or with less ceremony, as was true in 1585 and 1586. Later, between 1593 and 1594, Elizabeth visited private homes at Wimbledon, Osterley, Theobalds, Highgate, and Friern Barnet in the greater London area. The lower costs reflected the advantage of proximity to London and a smaller court. The inflation from the 1570s to the early 1590s would not markedly distort the comparison of these costs, which for the longer progresses would have neared or exceeded £300. These appareling costs formed part of the progress expenses which the queen paid.

In addition to readying the houses on her progress, the queen had the expense of maintaining her own palaces and houses throughout the year. Signs of her frugality appeared in the decay of many royal houses and in her refusal to erect new buildings. While Elizabeth loved ritual and pageantry, she seemed to have little desire to commemorate herself in stone and masonry, and what buildings she had she neglected.[82] William Paulet, marquis of Winchester, surveyed the queen's houses in June 1559. In all of them he recommended major repairs before Elizabeth could use them. The terraces and wharf at Hampton Court had decayed, the chapel roof at Windsor was a shambles, the gallery at Richmond might soon collapse, the wall of the great chamber at Westminster was weak, St. James's had rotten water pipes, Somerset House and the Tower had structural weaknesses, Greenwich and Enfield required new outbuildings, and without new tiles and guttering New Hall would decay. Paulet advised razing Amp-thill for the salvage of its stone, glass, and iron. Of the 25 structures Winchester inspected, only Havering at Bower, which had been "well repared by Anthony Cooke," passed his critical view.[83] The queen's itinerary would determine when Paulet could begin the repairs in her absence.

Although Elizabeth built no new palaces for herself, she did spend money to keep her existing houses habitable. The progresses exposed inadequacies in the royal buildings, and the financial records of their repairs trailed behind the itinerant court. From Havering to Enfield to Hatfield, until her progress ended at Windsor, in 1568 the queen paid for alterations and repairs that cost a total of £744. Her Hampshire progress the next year likewise led to repairs of £180. The short progress through the home counties in 1570 cost the queen £161 in repairs. The renovations and preparations included such items as new doors and tables, roof tiles, wooden floors, stables, additional stairs, glass, ceiling plaster, and everywhere new locks to reduce the chronic pilfering.[84] The upkeep of these royal houses, even with the queen's economical attitude about bricks and stone, escalated by the end of her reign. The charges compiled in December 1594 for repairs to royal estates in the county of Kent alone amounted to £5,736, with more than £3,100 spent on Eltham.[85] Although the discomforts of old age no doubt urged Elizabeth to some of these repairs, the "neglected state of her royal houses at her death testified to her priorities which placed governmental and household needs ahead of architectural splendor."[86] Her sporadic efforts to preserve these structures against the forces of nature only resulted in the great decay of many principal houses and palaces. Two years later, in 1596, a warrant for funds to keep up the major palaces in and near London noted their poor condition, while limiting the total annual repairs to £4,000 for the entire group.[87] Her travels required her to use her own residences and, when the court had moved on to the next palace, highlighted the need for repairs.

It still remains difficult, however, to arrive at an estimate of the total costs of the progresses. The figures are frustrating in their ability to hint at solid answers while questioning those solutions by their very fragmentary nature. Some accounts do exist for one of Queen Mary's trips during her first peaceful summer in 1553. On her progress that lasted from 12 June to 18 August, the court paid allowances to the knights at arms, the heralds, and the pursuivants amounting to £212 16s.[88] That figure would not include the meals, lodgings, and posts at additional cost to her. As a comparison, we have some records of the progress of her half-sister Elizabeth into Essex and Suffolk in 1561. Thomas Weldon, the cofferer of the household, kept a tally of the daily charges incurred during the new queen's second progress of any length. During her 76-day progress, Elizabeth visited, among others, Sir William Petre at Ingatestone, Lord and Lady Rich at Lees Priory, Sir Ralph Sadler at Standon, and the towns of Colchester, Harwich, Hertford, and Ipswich. Weldon recorded the expenses in a calendar listing the location of the queen, the dates of her visit, and the cost at each place to the court. The court's expenses at these places varied from £83 to £146 per day. The total cost for the progress amounted to £8,540, for which the court paid an average of £112 a day, according to Weldon's reports.[89] By contrast, the most expensive visit was proposed, but never achieved, with Mary Stuart in 1562. The Privy Council estimated costs at £40,000. In light of "ye chargees of the iornaye with ye accidents," Sir William Cecil expected, correctly as it turned out but for other reasons, that the progress would not occur.[90] As Elizabeth's progresses continued into the next decade and beyond, the expenses of royal travel fluctuated but never vanished.

HOUSEHOLD REFORM

When Elizabeth was enjoying some of her most extensive and entertaining visits during the 1570s, the costs of her travels were beginning to concern the ministers of her government and household. They worried about the household expenses that increased each year, but in particular the costs of the progresses drew the analytic eyes of Burghley. As lord treasurer, principal secretary, and close advisor to the queen, Burghley was in a good position to look for departments that needed reform. By nature as well, he disliked what he perceived as extravagance in the queen and the government. In a series of memoranda stretching over 40 years of service to Elizabeth, Burghley made lists and detailed charts outlining ways to fix the government or solve any political problem. During the 1570s, and later as well, Burghley analyzed the operations of the royal household in an effort to lower its expenditures.

One apparently easy suggestion to reduce the costs of the progresses proposed that the queen not change her itinerary once it was set. Reorganizing the accommodations, stocking again the houses with supplies of bedding and food, and moving the supplies yet again involved servants at the crown's expense and required additional purchases of perishables. These continual changes in her itinerary ruined the best efforts of harbingers, purveyors, and cart takers to apparel the progress houses. A reasonable suggestion was made "yt the daies appointed for removes in tyme of hir mate progresses maie be as lytle chaunged as neded shall be, and the alteracons of plans avoyded as nere as maie be conveniently, for by the contrary great losses do follow." Without shifts in the political and personal landscape that led the queen to rework her travel plans, the household could save a good sum of money. In Burghley's jaundiced view, however, there was little chance that such a spontaneous queen would stick to the original routine. His sardonic comment told the story of other futile attempts to lower the costs of royal travel: "a good order if it may be kept."[91] Of course, it was not.

After 15 years of participating in the progresses, Burghley decided to codify his observations of the financial arrangements supporting them. Basing his account on the progress of 1573 in Kent and Sussex, he drew up an itemized list of the extra expenses created by the queen's decision to go on progress. The lord treasurer would present two financial statements comparing an itinerant and a stationary court, and the balance sheet, he hoped, would persuade the queen to adopt more fiscally conservative views. He titled the comparison, "an estimate of increases of chardgies in the time of progresses [which] should not be if her majtie remeyined at her standing [houses] within xx myles of London." Not surprisingly, Burghley found that most departments in the household incurred extra expenses when the court was on progress. The bakehouse spent 1d. more for each loaf of bread baked on progress; the scullery required boards, bricks, loam, and nails to build temporary kitchens; and the stable paid 1d. more for hay and 6s. 8d. more for oats than when the queen was at one of her standing houses. Most of the charges reflected the transportation of supplies to upcoming houses on the queen's route and the wages of harbingers and laborers for provisions. The carriage of supplies cost time and money. The progresses placed burdens unequally throughout the household departments. The largest increases in costs were in the spicery, the buttery, and cellar, followed in descending order by the stable, the scullery, the poultry, the bakery, the kitchen, and the acatry. The spicery, with its imported luxuries of dried fruits and the spices that provided some flavor in cooking, spent £306 more when on progress. The buttery and cellar faced increased costs amounting to £294 because of the awkwardness of carrying the tuns of beer, ale, and wine to all the queen's houses. The stable needed £229 more to feed the 140 horses in the queen's train. Burghley estimated the total increase of charges to the queen's household as she traveled in nearby Surrey, Kent, and Sussex to be £1,018 for that year.[92] Thus, Elizabeth might spend at least an additional £1,000 each summer for the opportunity to leave the London area. As the distance away from the city increased and the length of the route increased, the queen's household would incur larger expenses. By her lord treasurer's account, the progresses certainly placed a financial burden on the government.

Three years later, Burghley tried to use these findings to reform the household and save money. Having determined that the progresses did increase household costs, he naturally wanted to enforce reforms from his analysis of 1573. In July 1576, Burghley drew up a list of "reformations to be made to diminish the great expenses of the Queen's household." In it he found much wrong with the disorderly and inefficient dining arrangements. He criticized the multitude of tables that wasted costly foods, suggesting a return to communal dining and provisioning. During progresses, the great tables should be kept "either within the court, or as nere as maie be together, so that their allowances maie be had every meale out of the howse, or else brought to one certain place, for many howses make double and triple expenses for the tyme." If the court was feeding the retinue, then he wanted the members of the retinue to follow the rules set down in the Diet. Duplication of functions occurred between groups within and without the court: "lodgings of the whyte staves and others that be appointed ordinarie tables without the corte in the tyme of progresses doth cause double expenses of beer, ale, and wyne, and other allowancies." Strictly following the Book of the Diet all year, instead of the mere 50 days currently given to it, would further decrease the queen's expenses.[93]

The most powerful criticism from Burghley, echoed by others, was that the length of her progresses caused the costs to rise. The more days that Elizabeth moved from palace to house to town without being near London, the more of her own money she spent funding those travels. Anthony Crane served as cofferer and saw for himself that not all progresses were equally expensive. As he looked for ways to cut costs, he considered "the increase of chardges in the tyme of a longe progreasse."[94] Burghley gave reality to Crane's assessment with a figure: £2,000. He calculated that Elizabeth could save that sizable sum of money by not going on long travels. "If her matie hade not so long continenewed her prograce," Burghley advised, "her mate chardgis had not bene as much as it was by two Thousand pounds."[95] This figure came from his analysis of the royal expenses incurred during seven weeks of travel during the 1576 progress through Essex, Hertfordshire, Buckinghamshire, Berkshire, and Surrey. Elizabeth had made about 34 stops during that progress, and she had stayed in counties near London. It is probable that her earlier, longer journeys to Bristol, Warwick, Coventry, Worcester, and Stamford cost even more than the several thousand pounds' increase. In Burghley's opinion, the savings would climb when the queen limited these long trips, but he would wage that fruitless campaign for another 20 years.

A year later Burghley continued to press for reform, but he changed the terms of the debate. In 1577 he drew up a set of articles limiting the household expenses of the queen to £40,000 per annum. If Elizabeth stayed within the £40,000 budget each year and reformed her household to save £2,000 (a significant 5 percent of her household budget), then her lord treasurer would have accomplished his goal and the queen would have more money. That approach was not new. The 1577 articles covered the usual ground in suggesting stricter adherence to the Book of the Diet and Bouche of Court and stricter limitations on personnel allowed at court. But in a departure from his past analyses, Burghley recommended a change that created the appearance of saving while enabling the queen to adhere to her budget. With one brief sentence, the strongest voice for fiscal reform proposed a political solution. Burghley seemed to recognize at last the impossibility of persuading Elizabeth to agree with him: she would never restrict her progresses merely to save money. So instead of fixing the system, he took the path of least resistance by proposing to skew the figures. Burghley suggested that the government change what charges were included in the household budget. If the queen could not limit her expenses to the £40,000 range, then the lord treasurer offered to transfer the progress expenses to another category that would not accrue to that total household limit. In Burghley's words, "it may please hir matie not to accompt the surchardge of progresse within the compas of £40,000 but to be allowed otherwise."[96] He hoped that by eliminating the extra costs of the progresses, which could reach £2,000 a year, he could lower the household expenses to within the prescribed limits. Because progresses increased the cost of maintaining the court, the lord treasurer looked for ways to hide and mitigate their harmful effects on the ledgers.

In order for the court to travel as much as it did, the queen had to decide that the progresses were worth the great effort, aggravation, and cost to her government. The queen's wanderings were constant (in an annual sense), organized, directed, and intentional, and they enabled Elizabeth to craft a personal monarchy based on her royal image and prerogative. Through the progresses, Elizabeth created an accessible court and fostered the patronage and petition that characterized the court until her last decade. In her commitment to the progresses, regardless of their expense, Elizabeth expressed the importance to her monarchy of the ceremonial dialogue that came from royal travel.

In addition to the public benefits from royal travel, the progresses offered Elizabeth the opportunity to retain her influence over the dozens of her courtiers and councilors, many of whom held different opinions about what royal policy should be, and all of whom had to live with the anomaly of a woman ordained by God to rule their kingdom. As queen, she held the constitutional cards full of sacred authority, but she was one against many. Courtiers used their own powers of patronage and proximity to the monarch to maneuver for their own and their families' advancement. Councilors sympathetic to Calvinist or Catholic views sought to influence the queen and shape policy. The issues of the age, from war against Scotland, Spain, France, and Ireland, alliances with Dutch Protestant rebels and Huguenots, and the fate of Mary Stuart, to the selection of a royal husband and the settlement of the succession, all divided the English court. But such different voices gave the queen additional flexibility in seeing her options while alone retaining the power to decide. On her progresses, as in matters of marriage and succession, Elizabeth overrode ministerial dissent and chose her own course.

This cacophony extended to the progresses. Even though hundreds of people participated in the progresses, the queen was happily flourishing at the center of that chaos. The court moved or stayed, according to her word; some towns she entered, others she chose to pass; all her movements engendered crowds and entertainments focused on her presence. The face before the crowds, of course, was that of a woman, their queen, the daughter of Henry VIII, who was reminding her hosts of the stability of her queenly rule through her kingly actions. While engaging in an important dialogue through ceremony with her subjects, Elizabeth could maintain some freedom of maneuver in this turmoil that her courtiers so disliked. By going on progress with all the expense and difficulty, the queen could dodge decisions, delay commitments, and preserve her royal power. And unlike in other areas of her government—rewards, military support, fiscal reform—Elizabeth was willing to pay for the benefits that came to her from the much criticized, expensive, chaotic progresses.

FOUR

Private Hosts

N o other aspect of her government was more important to Elizabeth than maintaining her popularity. As a way of fostering loyalty, obedience, and support for her monarchy, the progresses proved invaluable. Travel was a mechanism that created access to the queen, giving her direct contact with a large group of prominent subjects and displaying her royal image in a ceremonial framework that validated both hosts and sovereign. Such face-to-face dealings formed the basis of court life, patronage, and especially Elizabeth's royal authority. Through her visits, Elizabeth expressed a style of personal monarchy that depended upon direct contact with people important in their locality as well as at court. Indeed, her hosts included aristocratic friends, members of her Privy Council, members of Parliament, clergy, and even supposed Catholics—the very groups on whose loyalty and political participation her government, and her monarchy, depended. These individual hosts sought access to the queen and courtiers in her entourage. Through such contacts were matches made, grants conferred, and patronage extended. Her repeated progresses, in effect, expanded the membership of her court, as a changing group of hosts rotated into and out of the sovereign's path. The benefits of such access kept many hosts willing to entertain the queen for the better part of four decades. But as patronage and politics changed in those years, some hosts grew reluctant to spend the money for and endure the turmoil of a royal visit. As Elizabeth flourished, they either tactfully opened their doors or asked for a raincheck; as she aged, rewards dwindled, and costs rose, they became direct in their denial of hospitality. Her monarchy survived the difficult 1590s, but prominent members of the political community began to envision a time without the queen. The popularity of progresses with her hosts mirrored the vitality of Elizabeth's government.

HOSPITALITY AND ITS COSTS

Hospitality in the sixteenth century stemmed from a combination of motives: the religious impulse toward charity, the social desire to form close relationships, the competition of impressing neighbors, and the political ambition to gain power and advance at court. All of these motives shaped the Elizabethan progresses. At mealtimes on the country estates, traveling nobles and their retainers—often between 40 and 60 people—filled the great halls and dined at the host's expense. Surplus food went to household servants and the poor at the gates. Having a reputation as a generous host bespoke a certain level of wealth, honor, and social prominence. The earl of Southampton kept a large household of "at least a hundred well-mounted gentlemen and yeomen," whose presence drew attention to the master who commanded and paid for their services.[1] Henry, Lord Berkeley, and Katherine, Lady Berkeley, rode to hunt with such a large retinue of liveried servants that they became famous as people able to entertain well. Their talented cooks fed the frequent guests, and Berkeley gave food to the poor three times a week. Such impressive manor houses required visitors to appreciate them. Thus, nobles involved in court life expected to entertain both their neighbors and their sovereign. Most of Elizabeth's hosts would have echoed the sentiments of Burghley about the nature of their hospitality: "God send me my harts desyre, which is without regard of cost to have hir maty see my good will in my service, and all other to fynd no lack of good chere."[2] Public and private motives, therefore, intertwined to generate the hospitality that enabled Elizabeth to spend so much time in the homes of her subjects.

Displaying one's status through fine clothes, jewels, servants, buildings, horses, and extravagance was not merely boasting: it showed one's place in the community. In a society where sumptuary laws dictated a relationship between social status and apparel, the gauge to measure hospitality was that of propriety. Each host should offer the guest what was appropriate in the context of the host's status. Wealthy owners of great houses faced a more lavish, expensive standard of hospitality than did members of the gentry. Certain elements of hospitality always appeared—food, accommodations, public shows, and gifts—but the gentry offered them on a lesser scale than that of noble hosts.[3] On the progresses, many social conventions and distinctions remained.

The extraordinary nature of a royal visit, however, strained the customary rules of hospitality that governed visits between social equals. By custom, hosts shared lodgings, meals, and shows with their guest; this display of friendship also underlined the host's social standing and resources. In return, the visitor graciously accepted the hospitality. Both parties expected to reciprocate, an attitude that encouraged hospitality. Hosts justified their expenses of entertaining as partial protection against future trouble, an attitude Alan Macfarlane terms "an investment" in social relationships.[4] This interdependence also existed as "neighborliness," where friends gave and received aid as part of the mutual obligations that strengthened the members of the "moral community."[5] But when the host and guest differed markedly in status, as occurred during the progresses, bonds of deference and patronage, not neighborliness, instead defined the etiquette of the visit. The customary role of hospitality changed in the face of political reality.

When Elizabeth visited in a subject's house, she entered into a situation of social and economic comfort that usually she had made possible. The queen became both guest and host, while her hosts became almost guests in their own homes. In William Harrison's words, "every nobleman's house is her palace, where she continueth during pleasure and till she return again to some of her own."[6] There was much truth in that statement. The fine buildings and the resources to erect them often had come into the host's control by a royal grant. Through grants or monopolies, keeperships of royal palaces, lands, and offices, the queen had given hosts the same fortunes that were paying for her visit, and she expected their public acknowledgment of her temporary gift. Elizabeth took Robert Dudley to task when he forgot to recognize her royal ownership of his borrowed estate Kenilworth during the queen's visit in 1575.[7] A few hosts recognized the incongruity of the situation and used it to emphasize their attachment to Elizabeth. Burghley and Hatton played with the ritual of hospitality by figuratively bestowing their impressive houses upon the visiting queen. They offered the conceit that their houses were built only for Elizabeth's amusement and, as such, they belonged to her. Neither man, however, moved out and handed her the keys. While the kind words flattered Elizabeth, the purpose of the symbolic gift was to suggest the loyalty, financial strength, and political aspirations of the already privileged hosts.

This blend of altruism and ambition added to the awareness that entertaining Elizabeth could bring tangible favors to her hosts. To those subjects who bestirred themselves on her behalf, entertaining the queen on progress might put Elizabeth, in some small way, in their debt. Meeting with Elizabeth and conversing at length gave her hosts a prized opportunity to ask for favors. For the brief time of a visit, the queen's daily schedule and her host's coincided in a way impossible at the court in London, where the structure of court life worked to protect the queen's privacy. In her royal palaces, suitors negotiated their passage through a series of chambers before gaining audience with the queen, but these restrictions eased for those who entertained the queen on progress. When she lodged in their rooms, the hosts of the traveling court found their path to the queen was a smoother one; even a brief overnight visit gave the hosts the opportunity to discuss private matters with the queen. After all, it could take only a wisely chosen moment to ask Elizabeth for favors and rewards. Whether the hosts actually received their favors or only saw their suits deflected, the impetus for extending their hospitality remained. On this dual basis of social obligation and self-interest, the Elizabethan progresses flourished.

Because hospitality varied according to the hosts' social stature and goals, some privileged hosts naturally offered Elizabeth the most spectacular receptions. A few wealthy hosts sought to please Elizabeth through a flamboyant gesture, preferably one that confounded the laws of time and nature. When Elizabeth visited Sir Thomas Gresham at Osterley during her 1576 spring progress, she arrived at a well-tended, spacious house. As they toured the grounds, the queen commented in passing that the large courtyard "would appear more handsome if divided by a wall in the middle."[8] To her accommodating host, this royal suggestion became a plan of action. While the queen finished the day's activities and went to sleep, Gresham sent to London for workmen who came to Osterley and overnight constructed the desired wall. Upon rising the next morning, Elizabeth discovered that her words had been translated into masonry. From a bit of energy, money, and enthusiasm, Gresham created a lovely moment for his queen that also reflected well on her host. A similar creativity colored the visit of Elizabeth to Sir Francis Carew in 1600. In anticipation of the queen's arrival in August, Carew set out to dazzle her with his ability to manipulate nature itself. In his famous gardens at Beddington, Surrey, Carew covered one of his cherry trees to block out the sun and retard the fruit's ripening. When Elizabeth dined with Carew, therefore, she found before her the beautiful fresh fruit that elsewhere was out of season. The wizardry of her host had turned the seasonal clock back, in effect making time stand still, so that his royal guest might have a delicacy at his table.[9] Elizabeth enjoyed these metamorphoses of stone and fruit presented by her clever hosts, whose flair and panache honored their sovereign and fed their own reputations. These grace notes of hospitality suggest how some imaginative hosts responded to a royal visit.

In their efforts to impress Elizabeth, other important hosts moved beyond fruit and walls to fashion entire houses for the queen's use. The country houses of Theobalds and Holdenby owed their origin, in part, to the desire of established courtiers to have private dwellings grandiose enough to entertain Elizabeth. Lord Burghley, a frequent host as well as reluctant traveler, began construction of Theobalds in Hertfordshire as a country estate large enough for the queen and close enough to London for an easy ride into the city. By inviting the queen to stay with him, Burghley could attend to his estate's business, make political requests, and keep current with government affairs. In March 1583, he had invited Elizabeth to Theobalds. Vice-Chamberlain Christopher Hatton replied that the queen intended to come during Easter week and that she "acceptithie in most gracius and good kind parts, the offer of your l[ordship's] howse."[10] Elizabeth could always count on the hospitality of her chief minister.

The architectural achievement of Burghley inspired Sir Christopher Hatton, who also wanted to entertain the queen on a regular basis. After getting advice from Burghley on the matter of houses, Hatton constructed Holdenby in Northamptonshire "in direct observation of your [Burghley's] house and plot at Tyball's."[11] Hatton called Holdenby a "shrine" dedicated to Elizabeth, "that holy saint," and consecrated it to her entertainment—even though she never stayed there. From the start, both Hatton and Burghley intended their houses to serve as lodgings for the queen whenever she chose to visit. Writing to Hatton in 1579, Burghley reflected on their architectural efforts to further their political careers, and his assessment of their investment in the two estates was practical: "God send us both long to enjoy Her, for whom we both meant to exceed our purses in these."[12] That wish was more or less granted: Hatton welcomed Elizabeth several times to his London house before his death in 1591. Burghley died in 1598, after years of having the queen at his several residences. Lest Elizabeth overlook this sacrifice, Hatton conveyed these words to Sir Thomas Heneage, with the request that Heneage "acquaint her Highness herewith." These "most pretentious private mansions," Theobalds and Holdenby, embodied the aspirations of two eminent courtiers who saw compelling advantages in playing host to their monarch and who risked the financial expense for the rewards of office and patronage from an itinerant queen.[13]

Few imitated Burghley and Hatton in their architectural tributes to Elizabeth, partly because of the great expense and partly because such heavy investment was not necessary. The key requirement of a host was the willingness to participate in the progresses, whether the guest was Elizabeth or someone in her retinue. The news of a progress drew aggressively eager invitations from prospective hosts who lived near the intended route and who used the opportunity to angle for a visit from the queen. If the queen lodged elsewhere, hosts could still share in the progress by housing members of the court, whose large numbers dictated that they stay separately from the queen at nearby houses. The occasion of a progress encouraged hosts to attend to the needs of important courtiers traveling with the queen, which they did by inviting nobles to share their hospitality. In August 1601, the queen planned a visit to Richard Bancroft, bishop of London, at his Fulham residence in Middlesex. When Thomas Lowe of Putney heard the news, he offered his "poor" house to other travelers attending the queen. Writing to Michael Hickes in the Cecil household, Lowe wanted Sir Robert Cecil to know that he was welcome to stay with Lowe during the queen's visit to the bishop of London.[14] Lowe knew that the bishop's house could not hold all of the court, and he would welcome a visit from the queen's secretary of state. Cecil also received an invitation during that same progress to stay near the queen with a different host. In 1601 the court ventured into Berkshire near the Wiltshire border, where Sir John Popham invited Cecil to stay with him at Littlecot. Using the rhetoric of hospitality that emphasized generosity and modesty in a host, Popham combined words of welcome with disclaimers about his inferior accommodations. Cecil and his party should "make the best of what they shall find here, and to take all in good part; otherwise I fear me I shall be utterly ashamed."[15] As both host and guest knew, however, the best of what Cecil would find at Littlecot would be quite fine indeed. Sir John's words reflected the attitude appropriate to a host who had the reputation as "the greatest Howse-keeper in England" and who "kept a table like a prince."[16] By worrying that his famous hospitality would not be up to the standards of Cecil, Popham flattered himself and his guest. In the end, however, these politenesses amounted to nothing because the court did not travel near Littlecot; the progress went westward only as far as Aldermaston, some 14 miles distant from Littlecot, before turning south into Hampshire.[17] Although a change in the royal itinerary dropped Littlecot from the progress, Popham's offer of hospitality remained, nonetheless, as a testimony to the eagerness of hosts to participate in the queen's travels.

With so much at stake for her hosts from a royal visit, it is understandable that some of the hosts became anxious at the prospect of entertaining their sovereign. Elizabeth accepted hospitality in the spirit it was offered, but her expectation of appropriate hospitality did not always reassure nervous hosts. Michael Hickes, patronage secretary to Lord Burghley, had invited Elizabeth to stay at Ruckholt, his house in Essex, during her progress in August 1597. Hickes had asked for help from his friend and fellow secretary, Henry Maynard, in arranging with Lord Chamberlain Hunsdon the details of her stay—rooms, meals, supplies. Hickes worried about suitable accommodations at his small house, which "had noe convenient place to entertaine sum of hir Maties necessary servants." With his experience in these logistical matters, the lord chamberlain advised Hickes to keep things simple and not to overspend for the visit. Hunsdon suggested, in fact, that the anxious owner could "leave the howse to the Quene" and retreat from the situation. As for a gift, Hunsdon thought that Mrs. Hickes might give the queen a present of "sum fine wastcoate, or fine ruffe, or like thinge, which . . . would be acceptablie taken as if it weare of great price."[18] The advice from the lord chamberlain came from his understanding of the levels of hospitality that varied from host to host. What was appropriate for one was excess for another. Despite this advance reassurance, Hickes was disappointed in his own efforts and felt the queen's visit had gone poorly for him. When "the resplendence of her Majesty's royal presence and princely aspect did on a sudden so daunt all my senses and dazzle mine eyes," Hickes's prepared speech of welcome died on his lips. Once Elizabeth stood on his steps, the unfortunate host claimed that "I had use neither of speech nor memory." [19] Elizabeth had bereft him of all words, but Hickes hoped that his good intentions spoke to her through his hospitality.

The insecurity of some nervous hosts caused them to appear inhospitable. When these hosts muttered about Elizabeth's comfort and denigrated their own estates, they often were seeking guidance from others on how to entertain her. Even seasoned courtiers, such as Lord Keeper Sir Nicholas Bacon, felt the pressure of a royal visit. While he comfortably welcomed petitioners who streamed into his Hertfordshire estate of Gorhambury, the center of the lord keeper's ecclesiastical patronage system, entertaining the queen was another matter. Upon word that Elizabeth intended her first visit to Gorhambury in 1572, Bacon sought advice from another host on that progress, his friend Lord Burghley. Bacon hoped that Burghley knew the precise dates of the queen's visit and could advise him about royal hospitality. Placing himself in Burghley's hands, he claimed that "no man is more rawe in suche a matter then my selfe," and that he "wold gladly take that cours that myght best pleas her Matie which I knowe not how better to understond then by your help." [20] Bacon's solicitation of advice, whether spurred by genuine worry or grounded in typical court rhetoric, yielded happy results as Elizabeth would return to Gorhambury three times in the next five years. In this instance, the lord keeper's concern reflected not a wish to avoid the progress but a strong sense that he should participate appropriately in it.

The same matters troubled Thomas Sackville, Lord Buckhurst, before Elizabeth's visit to Lewes in July 1577. Buckhurst also worried that his preparations and accommodations would prove inadequate for his exalted guest. Seeking help at court from Lord Chamberlain Sussex, Buckhurst wanted to know the dates and length of the queen's stay so that he could lay in enough supplies. He feared that, because "the time of provision is so short," other hosts in nearby counties (Kent, Surrey, and Sussex) would have already commandeered the best supplies, thereby forcing Buckhurst to send to distant Flanders for his. Above all, he worried that her lodgings might seem shabby and so pressured Sussex to delay her visit for the year required to renovate the house. Should he not escape his hostly fate, however, Buckhurst philosophically proposed to do the best he could: "I can but besech of God that the hous do not mislike her; that is my cheif care: the rest shalbe performed with that good hart as I am sure yt wilbe accepted." [21] In the midst of his planning and despite his concern, Buckhurst knew that his "good hart" would determine the success of Elizabeth's visit. Had he but known that plague would prevent the queen's progress into

Kent and force her to bypass Lewes, the anxious host could have relaxed.[22] Lacking that crystal ball, however, he organized for the anticipated arrival of the traveling court. By wisely writing to the household officer in charge of lodgings on the progress, focusing on the issue of the queen's comfort, and appealing to her goodwill, Buckhurst had sounded the right chords. He hinged his reluctance only upon his fear of disappointing the queen.

Quality of housing again was the sticking point with the earl of Leicester, when Elizabeth planned a visit to Wanstead in 1578. He worried that the empty and unadorned house, which she already disliked, would displease her: "I fear that little liking to it she had before will through too, too many more faults, breed her less love hereafter."[23] With so many choices, the queen had little reason to lodge in an uncomfortable house. Neither did the visit accomplish anything for the worried absent host, as Leicester himself noted. In his anxiety, however, Leicester confused the unpleasant event with the issue of hospitality. While Wanstead was the site for his secret marriage with Lettice Knollys two months after this visit, and it remained a house that Elizabeth preferred to keep a distant memory, the house itself was not the most important part of Leicester's hospitality. His success as a host came from his efforts to please the queen, whose presence and courtesy, in turn, rendered the house acceptable. The tensions during this particular stay indicated that sometimes a host was right to be nervous about a royal visit, but the reasons often had little to do with the host's ability to entertain well. Sometimes hospitality could not smooth all waters.

When hosts attached such importance to entertaining the queen, a change in the itinerary disappointed hosts who dropped off the progress route. The queen's good friend, Lady Norris, expected Elizabeth to stay with her at Rycot during the short 1582 progress. Instead of traveling west into Oxfordshire, however, the queen went south to Surrey and stayed at Nonsuch, at Beddington with Sir Francis Carew, and at Pyrford with the earl of Lincoln. Lady Norris blamed this change of plans on Leicester and Hatton who, she presumed, had persuaded Elizabeth not to travel on the poor roads leading to her house. For some reason, Leicester decided to explain the situation to Lady Norris in person. He compounded the problem by showing up at Rycot on the date originally scheduled for the queen's arrival, whereupon he received the brunt of Lady Margaret's anger. "At my arrival," he wrote to Hatton, "I met with a piece of cold entertainment at the Lady's hands of the house here." Part of that coldness undoubtedly reflected the great preparations for Elizabeth that were just so much wasted money and effort. Leicester found that the erstwhile hosts "had put the house here in very good order to receive her Majesty." Since the Norrises believed he and Hatton "were the chief hinderers of her Majesty's coming hither, which they took more unkindly than there was cause indeed," Leicester found himself in an unpleasant bind of his own making. In addition to that tension, the late hour prevented his seeking other lodging than at Rycot, so he imposed himself on the disappointed hosts. Leicester tried to mollify Lady Norris with the rationalization that Elizabeth would have disliked Rycot at that time of year when "you should find it winter already," but that obvious tactic won him little credit. At last, Leicester sued for peace by offering Lady Norris his own accommodations when the queen went to Oatlands; at least she could have a visit with Elizabeth even though she was not the queen's host. He told Hatton to have Elizabeth smooth over the situation "or else have we more than half lost this lady." The anger at Leicester and Hatton revealed some of the factional maneuvering that colored court life under Elizabeth, as other courtiers, and not the queen, were blamed for unpopular decisions. Although the queen did not visit Rycot until 1592, the Norrises remained two of her closest friends and "a hearty noble couple . . . towards her Highness."[24] Their strenuous response to missing a royal visit suggested the real pleasure with which willing hosts extended their hospitality to the traveling queen.

Some hosts found the queen irritatingly reluctant to accept their offers of hospitality. Elizabeth did not visit everyone who invited her; she rode past the doors of some eager hosts, while her indecision prevented any visit at all to others. Despite the valiant efforts of Henry Percy, ninth earl of Northumberland, to welcome the queen at Petworth, Elizabeth passed by his family's Sussex estate in 1591. At issue could not have been his hospitality, for Percy had a fine reputation as a host who kept a table for 250 strangers. The lodgings were appropriate, and her route took the retinue close to Petworth. The house was near enough to Elizabeth's stops at Farnham and Bramshott for an easy visit, had she so chosen. Considering his eagerness to entertain the queen, Percy must have felt a stinging rebuke when Elizabeth chose to stay at Cowdray with Lord Montague, an estate no more than five miles from Petworth.[25] Her actions suggest that Elizabeth preferred not to lodge at the same house where Percy's father, the eighth earl, had reluctantly harbored Charles Paget as he plotted a Catholic invasion of England. Despite this pressing offer of hospitality, Percy did not receive the queen at his house.

These efforts to entertain Elizabeth, both intended and realized, underscored the importance of hospitality in Tudor politics and society. Hospitality allowed for the public display of relationships shaped by patronage, landholding, and royal authority, as the queen moved her court into hundreds of her subjects' houses. Just as people sought their fortune at the court in London, so they pursued it across the fields of southern England. These hosts valued the occasion of a royal visit to shine in their county, to participate in court life, and to impress their sovereign. When they lost or missed that opportunity, their disappointment matched the significance of the imagined occasion. Despite the challenge and expense of a royal visit, hosts wanted to claim that honor.

The privilege of hospitality came at a price to the queen's hosts, who opened their purses, as well as their estates, when Elizabeth appeared. Without the powers of taxation enjoyed by towns to spread the cost of a royal visit, individual or private hosts drew upon their own resources and contacts to provide for the royal retinue. Their fields, local markets, pantries, and kitchens yielded the foodstuffs with which hosts loaded their tables for the queen. Two characteristics of the progresses, however, assisted the hosts in caring for large numbers of people over several days. First was the understanding that the nature of the hospitality should reflect the host's abilities and status: lavish spending that might come naturally from a duke would seem inappropriate from a lesser person. Views of proper entertainment balanced the common ideas of "prudence, moderation, and good order" against extravagant hospitality.[26] The second aspect of royal visits helped hosts even more directly: the queen provided many of the supplies that fed the court during her visit. As we noted in the preceding chapter, court officers used purveyance to buy supplies for the queen and designated members of the court. But other expenses fell to the hosts as part of their hospitality. The financial cooperation between hosts and royal guest ensured that the ceremonies, petitions, diplomacy, political maneuvering, and dialogue of the progresses would continue.

The rules of hospitality dictated that certain costs of a royal visit, such as preparation, shelter, provisions, entertainment, and gifts, naturally belonged to the hosts. As owners of the house, they were responsible for any repairs or improvements to the manor. Some hosts decided to erect new structures, or they bought tents for temporary shelter. The buildings where the court lodged and dined needed airing, cleaning, and possibly repairing. All of these kinds of expenditures fell to the hosts, although the court sometimes contributed to the erection of temporary dining structures. Beyond the expense of dwellings, hosts on a progress expected to have large amounts of food and drink available to satisfy the hungry court and supplement the provisions brought by the travelers. Trips to the markets, special shopping, and numerous tasks of preparation occupied the hosts' servants as they equipped the estate for the royal visit. Whether hosts paid for the entertainment of the court is harder to discover. Usually they had paid servants or local musicians to provide songs and dances, and some hosts commissioned poems, orations, and pageants to play before the court. Elizabeth enjoyed special shows, for example, at Kenilworth, Wanstead, Elvetham, Quarendon, Cowdray, Bisham, and Harefield.[27] But nearby towns often contributed to the entertainment by producing a mock battle, shooting fireworks, or staging a play in conjunction with the shows offered by the hosts. Taken altogether, the expenses of hosts reflected their desire to provide both the necessities and the special delights that would enhance their reputation within their local community and that would cause Elizabeth to remember her visit well.

A primary duty of the hosts, for which they bore the cost, was preparing for the queen's arrival. Although gentlemen ushers and harbingers from the royal household assisted in these arrangements, hosts had the final responsibility for providing laborers and completing the tasks. The hosts also paid for additional food and provisions to supplement those brought in the progress caravan. When Lord Keeper Puckering prepared for a royal visit to Kew in 1594, he made a list of remembrances that showed the duties, and thus the expenses, for which he was responsible.[28] Puckering had to arrange a reception for the queen outside and then inside his house, purchase a present for her which he formally bestowed, and have a special gift for Elizabeth from Lady Puckering. He itemized the rewards he would offer as host to the numerous members of the royal household, a contingent that included the ladies of the bedchamber, the grooms of the privy chamber, the gentlemen ushers, the footmen, and guards. In the area of food, Puckering oversaw the diet for the lords, ladies, and footmen; the appointment of his own officers to serve the guests, as well as the order of servants carrying the meals; the proportion of diet and the service of silver and plate; and the banqueting provisions in addition to meats, breads, ales, wines, and basic foods. His house needed sweetening and airing, he needed to decide what quiet rooms would house the queen, and he organized the ceremonial attendance at her departure. In the middle of this laundry list of chores for the host, however, lay a telling reminder of the royal contribution to the party. Puckering noted the "purveyed diet for the Queen, wherein are to be used her own cooks." To the busy host faced with unusual expenses, every bit helped.

One expense of a progress visit that fell to the individual hosts was the gift. An intrinsically personal gesture, a gift could not be a shared expense between host and visiting queen. Although custom dictated that the host make a present to Elizabeth and members of her retinue, the host enjoyed considerable leeway in the choice, and thus the price, of these gifts. Popular presents for Elizabeth included clothing, gloves, books, plate, and especially the jewels that she so enjoyed wearing. She received a pair of golden spurs from Lady Style; a gown from Sir William More; jewels from Sir Edward Coke and Sir Arthur Gorges; and a gown made from cloth of gold and a jeweled hat from Julius Caesar.[29] The cost of the gifts varied widely because some hosts could afford only a small but tasteful present, while

others indulged in lavish offerings. Private hosts who were nobles and senior government officers usually spent about £100 on the queen's present,
although this figure was hardly mandatory. Lord North at Kirtling in 1578
gave Elizabeth a jewel worth £120, and Burghley presented her with a gown
costing £100. Lady Hickes presented the queen with a waistcoat. Sometimes the queen herself chose a gift from the furnishing of the house, and
the host was expected to agree with the selection. The earl of Nottingham
caused a stir by not presenting the queen with his gorgeous tapestries wo-
ven to commemorate the defeat of the Armada, when she had indicated
that she very much admired them.[30] He had instead an expensive dress to
give Elizabeth, but that appropriate gift lost its luster when the queen had
another preference.

In addition to presents for the queen, hosts also offered small remembrances to courtiers in the progress train and rewards to the servants. During the 1578 visit, Lord North spent £48 for gifts to attendant nobles and
gave another £41 to their servants. Sir William Petre of Ingatestone spent
£14 for gifts and rewards in 1561. Lord Keeper Egerton in 1602 offered £48
in rewards to attendants at Harefield.[31] While the costs of the gifts varied,
allowing thrifty hosts to regulate their expenses and wealthier hosts to
make grand gestures, the financial responsibility for them remained the
same. Paying for gifts that proclaimed open hospitality and recognition of
the visitors' social and political status was a function of acting as host during a progress visit.

A central part of most progress visits was the show or play staged before
the queen, but determining who footed the bill is difficult. In the towns,
such entertainments were created and financed by the guilds. At a private
estate, however, where the host might sponsor a troupe of players and the
visiting queen could sponsor shows by one of her courtier's companies, the
financial responsibility is hard to assign. Often the private hosts paid for
the shows. When the entertainment was of a volatile kind, such as the
fireworks at Kenilworth and Elvetham, hosts claimed the glory of providing the queen with a good show. As her hosts sought to benefit from
their hospitality, they ensured that the queen knew whom to thank for the
ceremonies.

As these costs varied from host to host, so the total amount changed as
the years passed into decades of Elizabethan rule. From the extant accounts, hosts on the earlier progresses managed to spend less money in
entertaining Elizabeth than her later hosts, a change that no doubt contributed to some growing reluctance to lodge the royal retinue. These higher
costs of the later progresses reflected the burden of inflation, the increased
extravagance of aristocratic hosts who sought special favors, and the com-

plexity of the progresses as they grew into another institution of Tudor government.

Annual repetition had turned the costly rituals of entertainment into a formal part of the progresses that were harder for the average host to ignore. During the 1561 progress into Essex and Suffolk, hosts spent modest sums for the queen's brief visits. Some hosts managed for an average daily cost of about £40. The earl of Oxford had Elizabeth at Hedingham from 14 to 19 August and spent £273 for the privilege of that visit of six days. For five days from 21 to 25 August, Lord Rich entertained the queen at Lees Priory at a cost of £389.[32] Fuller details come from the accounts kept by John Kyme, chief officer to Sir William Petre, during the queen's visit to Ingatestone for four days. Petre paid two harbingers 10s. for news of her intended visit; over £4 went toward Lady Petre's new curtains for the royal suite; another £3 8s. 2d. enabled carpenters to construct sheds to house some of the servants; a similar sum was paid for carriage of beer from London. Friends and tenants of Petre donated supplies that defrayed some of his expense. Even so, the total amounted to £136. About a third of this cost was for food, much of which came from the stores already at Ingatestone. Provisions from the estate cost £39 2s. 10d., expenditures amounted to £83 1s. 10 3/4d., and presents of victuals cost £14 5s. 6d. While the sum of £136 was a substantial amount, it covered the costs of entertaining the queen for four days, or £34 per diem.[33]

The amount of food may have been prodigious, but in light of Petre's considerable wealth, the total expense was not. In his income and expenses, Petre maintained a "satisfactory balance throughout the second half of his life," according to F. G. Emmison, and incurred no debt through his royal entertainment. His annual expenses for 1561, exclusive of those attached to Ingatestone (estimated at £400), were £2,610 during the time that he spent £136 for the progress visit. His income for the closest available year to the progress of 1561, that being three years later in 1564, amounted to £2,458 from rents, manor courts, timber sales, salaries, and fees.[34] Petre and other hosts on the 1561 progress stayed within their means by offering comfortable, appropriate, but staid hospitality. Certain arrangements of the figures can emphasize the seemingly high cost to the hosts of the progresses. Emmison concludes, for example, that the 1561 progress "must have cost the hosts about £2,500 in food and drink," a high figure suggestive of waste.[35] By looking at the entire progress, however, we can see what that sum included. Elizabeth traveled for 68 days and visited 18 private hosts, 2 towns, and 4 royal residences. Dividing that £2,500 among the 20 individual and civic hosts in an admittedly arbitrary manner results in her hosts spending £125 each, on average, in entertaining the queen. The figure would have fluctuated depending on her length of stay at each residence. The total expenses of £2,500 for a progress of 68 days breaks down to about £37 per day spent on royal travel. This comparison places the daily costs of each host and Elizabeth in perspective. When the average daily cost of a progress visit ran £34 for William Petre, £45 for the earl of Oxford, £77 for Lord Rich, and £100 for Elizabeth, the distribution of the shared costs highlights a little-known part of the progress picture. The queen spent considerable sums to go on progress, but her private hosts could entertain her at a moderate, acceptable expense.

During the more elaborate progresses of the 1570s, however, many hosts faced higher costs for their more lavish royal hospitality. From 18 to 22 May in 1577, Sir Nicholas Bacon spent £577 when the queen visited him at Gorhambury. In 1578, Lord North entertained the queen for three days at Kirtling for £762.[36] By the turn of the century, hosts spent much larger sums for a progress visit than did their counterparts in the 1560s. Whereas the daily costs of a progress for these hosts in the 1570s amounted to £155 for Bacon and £254 for North, Elizabeth's visit to Sir Thomas Egerton at Harefield for four days in 1602 cost him about £500 per diem. Egerton's total expenses of £2,084 reflected, in part, his gifts and rewards to servants to the tune of £115 19s. 2d.; another £1,225 12s. for provisions; and additional sums for presents, carriage of supplies, and construction.[37] The ordinary rise of inflation accounted for some of the increase from the 1561 progress, but more importantly, these hosts of the 1570s found themselves caught up in a competitive opulence that characterized these progresses. After the interruption in the 1580s of the queen's long, stately, and lavish journeys, her travels in the last decade of her reign dwindled to individual visits of a particular ornateness, such as her stays at Harefield and Elvetham, and shorter progresses overall. The queen continued to assume some of the financial burden of her progresses, but the hosts felt pressure, real or imagined, to provide equally lavish entertainment that would compare with, or outshine, that of other hosts. By the 1590s, the customs associated with royal visits grew more costly to hosts caught up in the tradition of providing gifts and festivities for the queen. Critics lamented the decline of hospitality throughout English society by the end of the sixteenth century, even as the cost of maintaining the old ways was rising.[38] The effects of this tradition and the inflation of the period increased the progress expenses for the hosts and also fed a growing reluctance to entertain the traveling queen.

The private host whose expensive hospitality received wide recognition, then and now, was William Cecil, Lord Burghley. Because he was one of the queen's closest advisors and a frequent host to her traveling court, Burghley's experience has come to be taken as representative of all progress

hosts. The idea, drawn from Burghley's anonymous biography and popu-
larized by Francis Peck, that Burghley entertained the queen on 12 occasions at a cost of £2,000 to £3,000 a visit should not become the standard
by which to assess the financial burden of the progress hosts.[39] These figures need reexamination from Burghley's perspective and also from the
perspective of other hosts. When Elizabeth stayed at Theobalds for two
weeks in 1565, Burghley spent £32 6s. 6d. for gifts and rewards; £110 10s.
5d. for provisions; and £198 5d. in ready money for unforeseen expenses.
This progress visit cost him not thousands of pounds but a respectable
£340 17s. 4d.[40] Most of the cost of provisions came from wine for the cellar
(£66 5s. 4d.) and meats for the kitchen (£158 16s. 8d.). For a four-day royal
visit in 1578, Burghley spent £337 7s. 5d. at a time when his household
expenses were approaching £2,000 a year.[41] His entertainment expenses in
the 1570s resembled those of Sir Nicholas Bacon and Lord North. After
another 15 years, however, Burghley found impossible the economy of his
1575 hospitality. When he entertained Elizabeth at Theobalds again in 1591,
her 11-day visit cost him £998 13s. 8d., with another £100 for the royal gift
of a gown.[42] These visits had neither the length nor the expense that Peck
states and others have assumed. Instead of long stays of three to six weeks,
Elizabeth actually spent several days to two weeks at Theobalds. Four of
her visits lasted only 1 day; three visits were for 11 to 14 days; and the other
six visits took 3 to 8 days. Instead of outrageous expenses of several thousand pounds per visit, Burghley kept costs within a modest range (for him)
of around £340 in the 1570s and £1,098 in 1591 (for a per diem expense of
£99). Since Burghley entertained Elizabeth 13 times at Theobalds and another 6 times at his other houses, the cumulative expense of his hospitality
appears to have been affordable to him. Because the royal household was
subsidizing some its own expenses through purveyance, for example, this
progress host could entertain the monarch without financial suicide.

The modest costs possible in entertaining the queen also held true for
other hosts and guests. When William Mingay, mayor of Norwich, gave a
dinner for the duke of Norfolk's party in 1561, the small payment of £1 17s.
9d. bought six kinds of fowl, three muttons, three veals, geese, eight stone
of beef, two gallons of wine, one quart sack, one quart malmsey, and two
quarts of other drink.[43] Similar items graced a table for diners in the Court
of Wards and Livery on 29 November 1600. The cost there came to £6 18s.
2d., with the most expensive single item, spices "to dresse the dynner,"
amounting to 12s.[44] Such reasonable costs support Alan Macfarlane's analysis of the hospitality bestowed by Ralph Josselin at Earls Colne, Essex.
During his 42 years in Essex, Josselin spent about £150 on dinners and gifts
for his family and neighbors.[45] The cost of elaborate hospitality might have
been rising during the sixteenth century, as individuals tried to outdo their

rivals, but the ability to open one's doors and larders to friends in a spirit of hospitality remained.

These expenses of prominent private hosts indicate that they could entertain the queen on progress in a socially appropriate yet economical manner. While their high station required some luxuries, nobles could choose which items merited the greater expense.[46] Their hospitality for Elizabeth on the progresses often cost them a reasonable sum, and the hosts' ability to finance a royal visit was necessary to continue the progresses. By the end of Elizabeth's long reign, however, the weight of tradition associated with the progresses had caused some hosts to spend larger amounts for the queen's visits than their predecessors had. When the hosts decided upon a lavish masque or banquet, their costs soared, but the queen's expectations suggested that they incurred some of this financial burden at their own behest. Ordinarily the private hosts could keep their expenses within an affordable range and still offer the hospitality appropriate both to their own abilities and to the importance of the royal guest. Because the queen and her host shared the cost of a visit and the host could flexibly offer a variety of appropriate entertainments, individual hosts could afford to welcome the queen into their houses.

REQUESTS AND PETITIONS

Hosts on progresses relied upon hospitality as they did on personal ties at court: both were a facet of the patronage system essential to Elizabethan government. These visits gave hosts access to the queen and personal contact with influential courtiers who might aid in their advancement. One of the major reasons to participate in the progresses, for both Elizabeth and her hosts, was the ability to cultivate key relationships through conversations and ceremonies. Having the queen in their houses gave hosts some control of the agenda and thus facilitated their requests for royal aid.

Such opportunities for royal access appealed even to so highly placed a courtier as Lord Burghley, who in his official capacity had more frequent contact with the queen than almost any other person. His attendance at court did not replace, in Burghley's view, his need to meet with the queen at his own houses. In 1583 he used the presence of the queen to sue for her forgiveness of his ungovernable son-in-law, the earl of Oxford. The young man had quarreled with Sir Philip Sidney on a tennis court in 1579 so violently as to invoke royal intervention. By secretly converting to, and then denouncing, Catholicism, he had lost many friends at court on both sides of the religious divide. In 1581 he spent several months in the Tower for his paternity of a son with Anne Vavasour. In 1582 Oxford had another vicious fight, this time with Thomas Knyvet of the privy chamber, that lingered afterward in a long feud between their supporters at court.[47] No wonder, then, that the queen was refusing to receive Oxford at court. Turning to his long-suffering father-in-law, Oxford sought redemption and Burghley helped him achieve it. Burghley persuaded Sir Walter Raleigh to plead Oxford's case to the queen and to present her with a letter from Burghley, which Raleigh did "to witness how desirous I am of your Lordship's favour and good opinion."[48] With this plan in motion, the grand finale came when Burghley orchestrated Oxford's return to grace by bringing together all the principals at Theobalds in 1583. The penitent offender, the aggrieved father-in-law, and the insulted queen met under the roof of a building that epitomized, more than any other, ministerial servitude to the monarch. With his use of hospitality and patronage, Burghley touched all the strings when playing for royal favor. For hosts who had a special suit to advance with the queen, the progresses offered an ideal opportunity to manipulate the royal visit for their own ends.

Burghley used the queen's visit to Theobalds in 1594 to seek another political favor. This time his request, conveyed through extensive pageantry, was for his son Robert Cecil. As his own failing health and advancing age now kept him frequently from court, Burghley wanted to ensure the prominence of Robert as a royal advisor. Burghley feared the rising star of the earl of Essex, who was building his own patronage network to rival that of the Cecils, so he determined to solidify the place of his son and, he hoped, successor at court. During her stay at Theobalds, he treated Elizabeth to a none-too-subtle masque on that theme. After introductory thanks for past favors, the "poor Hermit," played by Robert Cecil, reminded the queen of Burghley's merits and fragile health: "When his body being laden with yeares, oppressed with sicknes, having spent his strength for public service, desireth to be ridd of worldly cares, by ending his dayes; your Majestie, with a band of princelie kindness, even when he is most greviosly sicke, and lowest brought, holdes him back and ransometh him." Through her affection, he argued, the queen held the father hostage in the name of good government. But rescue was in sight. By popular report, the son of the wise father had earned general praises for his early achievements and could take on the elder's burden. The hermit-son then extolled the suitability of his real self, Robert Cecil, to carry on the father's duties: "seeing I heare it of all the Countrey folke I meet with, that your Majestie doth use him in your service, as in former tyme you have done his Father my Founder; and that although his expence and judgment be noe way comparable; yett, as the report goeth, he hath something in him like toe Child of such a Parent."[49] In other words, the queen could look to the father to see what the son would become; she could profit from the son's service as she had from the father's. As a host, Burghley used his control of the entertainment to project his request onto a dramatic character. The hermit became, in effect, an intermediary with the queen on Burghley's behalf; the role of the hermit, when acted by Robert Cecil, underlined the nature of the host's suit. Only by entertaining the queen at his house could Burghley have the sure opportunity to make the dramatic point about the transition of power from father to son. His hospitality both created and shaped the moments of communication.

Some requests came long after a royal visit. Petitioners hoped that their earlier participation in the progresses would induce Elizabeth to grant their requests. When Anne, Lady Lawrence, was summoned before the Court of Requests, she traveled from Hampshire to London only to find that the tribunal was absent. She asked Edmund Clerke to write on her behalf to Richard Oseley in January 1570, requesting that she be excused from further trips to London. She believed that her attorney could handle the matter without her. Clerke attested to Lady Lawrence's good character and then offered the decisive piece of testimony: "this last summer," the queen had stayed with Lady Lawrence at Soberton.[50] The queen's past visit and her own high position at court would, Lady Lawrence hoped, impress the clerks of the court and incline them to favor her petition.

A more serious problem induced Sir John Smythe to use the memory of a progress visit as he solicited a royal favor. Smythe's knowledge of military and legal matters led him to a public dispute over the government's power to send local troops abroad. He asserted that the queen could not fight her continental battles using men from county levies. For his temerity in questioning the queen's prerogative, Smythe earned a confinement in the Tower. The government's forceful response and his imprisonment persuaded Smythe to recant. In 1597 he pleaded with Burghley, in what the lord treasurer termed a "rayling letter," to ignore his dangerous speeches. Wine had muddled his mind, Smythe wrote, and he never intended to arouse the people of Essex against the levies. To bolster the temporary insanity defense, Smythe invoked a past act of loyalty and hospitality extended to the queen's court. His imprisonment in the Tower had almost undone his innocent wife, who had made Burghley "so wonderfull wellcome unto her and to her house when the Queene was last at Newhall."[51] By reminding Burghley of this past hospitality under the aegis of Elizabeth's progress, Smythe hoped to win a favorable reply. Using the memory of a royal visit to sue for mercy, however, did not erase his admitted guilt: despite his utter abasement, Smythe failed to secure his release until 1598, after a three-year imprisonment. These suits of Lady Lawrence and Sir John Smythe, nonetheless, suggest the direct connection between hospitality during a progress and a subsequent request from a host. After they were long over, the progresses gave hosts an entrée at court.

People who had not yet entertained the queen also used that possibility to ask for current rewards. Knowing that the queen tended to travel in an area encouraged local people to frame their requests within that context. Because the court's presence affected the local economy, some enterprising people saw an opportunity to link their personal interests with those of the itinerant queen. An unidentified man from Otford petitioned Lord Burghley about purchasing a house in 1596. The man sought permission from Burghley to buy a house used by the queen when she visited Otford. To encourage a favorable reply from the lord treasurer, the petitioner stressed the advantage from that sale to Elizabeth. Were he able to purchase the queen's old house, in need of repair, the man would build another "pretty howse where she may dine as she passeth by in some more fitt place."[52] The proposed buyer's plan cleverly recognized how unwilling Elizabeth was to spend money repairing her houses. By the sale, the queen would, in effect, trade an inferior dwelling for a fine one without spending any royal funds, and she would still have access to the new house whenever she wished. As the queen had visited Otford only twice in her reign, during 1559 and 1573, such an offer was at once practical, hospitable, and cautious.

A similarly self-interested concern appeared in a suit from Sir John Fortescue that united the queen's comfort on progress with Fortescue's dynastic security. His petition addressed the control of two offices that supported the family's holdings in Oxfordshire. Fortescue wanted the bailiwick and keepership of Whichwood Forest and Cornbury Park, which he had held since 1560, to remain in his family as a sign of royal favor and as "a quyetnes" to his heirs. Should these familial arguments prove insufficient, Fortescue linked his request to the future benefits Elizabeth would enjoy from upholding his claim on the offices. When the queen traveled in that region, there was no "other place for hir matie receyuing when it pleaseth hir to come into these parts but my house only."[53] Granting Fortescue's request would maintain his family in the county, where they could continue the hospitality that Elizabeth relied upon when she traveled in that area. Fortescue pointed out the common interests both he and Elizabeth had in preserving the status quo through a royal grant. The success of his suit would provide better accommodations for the queen on progress.

Whether the requests came before, during, or after a visit from Elizabeth, the petitions suggest how a variety of people counted upon the progresses for access to the queen. Traveling around the country made the queen accessible to different groups of expectant suitors. Whether they asked Elizabeth for lands, judicial exemptions, offices, fees, or her good opinion, these supplicants knew that the progresses brought special opportunities for them to have a dialogue with the queen. Although a careful look at the success of petitions shows no pattern of greater largesse when the queen traveled, the common assumption that the progresses opened access to the monarch helped sustain such travels. Former hosts, current hosts, future hosts, and their royal guest all understood how the importance of their meetings contributed to the better government of the country. Their communication occurred because it served the interests of all parties and because the role of hospitality in their society made such meetings possible. As it sparked other Elizabethan achievements, so the desire for private favors and public reputation sustained the progresses.

Some hosts managed to entertain the queen without even meeting her. On rare occasions Elizabeth and her court arrived at a house whose absent owner was attending to court matters elsewhere or being detained abroad. The dismay with which these absent hosts responded to the news of a missed royal visit reveals how desirable such participation in the progresses was. Part of their disappointment stemmed from a missed moment of hospitality: by their absence, such "step-hosts" lost some of the prestige involved in personally entertaining the royal retinue. But their disappointment also reflected a missed opportunity to solicit favors from Elizabeth, as they had to defer laying their requests before the queen until they had such access to her again.

This double concern appeared in Sir Thomas Smith's reaction to missing the arrival of Elizabeth in 1565. When the queen visited his "poor house at Ankerwick," Smith as the ambassador to France was struggling with his duties.[54] His hatred of the assignment in France permeated his correspondence, and he continually maneuvered to be recalled. He had antagonized the queen and her councilors by what they perceived as his diplomatic ineptitude in negotiating the Treaty of Troyes. Neither did he redeem himself by failing to secure the release of fellow ambassador Sir Nicholas Throckmorton, arrested and held by the French for ten months. From abroad, Smith tried with some difficulty to mend fences at home. He made a futile appeal to Throckmorton's supporter, Robert Dudley, to intercede both in the quarrel and with the queen. Couching his request in terms of Elizabeth's happiness, Smith asked that he be allowed to return to England so that he could meet the queen at his house. The news of Elizabeth's intended progress made him sigh with envy, as "he heartily wished to be among" the queen's retinue.[55] In a letter to Dudley, Smith bemoaned the bad timing that brought Elizabeth to his house when her orders mandated his absence. Knowing that the queen had enjoyed her stay there "recompenseth all," Smith wrote, but he still hoped she would return when he could welcome her in person. Underlying these genuine social regrets was

Smith's irritation at a missed opportunity for politicking, when he could have used his hospitality to soften the queen's obduracy. This approach, supplemented by other pleading letters, at last brought Smith home to England with royal approval in 1566. This fortunate conclusion to his service in France must have eased Smith's earlier distress at missing the queen's visit.

While some eager hosts wanted to give their all for their sovereign, none expected that their absence during a royal visit would amount to a sentence of death. The absent host with the most at stake was undoubtedly Thomas Howard, duke of Norfolk, who was about to lose his head on a charge of treason. While the duke was under arrest in the Tower for his involvement in the Ridolfi plot in 1572, the queen paid a visit to Norfolk's house. From his prison, Norfolk chafed at many things, including his inability to extend the proper welcome to the queen who herself had prevented his attendance. Of course he was pleading for his freedom and pledging his loyalty to the queen through these words, but his argument relied upon his duty of hospitality toward his monarch. The father couched his plea for his life in terms of concern for his child's ability to substitute as a proper host. Norfolk regretted that the queen "schuld goe to my boyes howse wher nether I schuld be readye accordyng to my bownden dewtye to receave her hyenesse nor yeat my boyes chyldysche age wyll make hyme suffycyent to supplye that offyce."[56] Perhaps she should have joined him in the Tower? By that point, no feast or gift Norfolk could offer would have convinced the queen to pardon him, and his execution followed closely that occasion. Whether the host wanted to avoid death or life in France, these absent hosts wanted to further their suits with the queen by entertaining her in their houses. Missing the queen's visit, for whatever reasons, deprived these hosts of that access that originally caused them to seek the queen's company during a progress.

These absent hosts could take comfort in the knowledge that at least Elizabeth had stayed in their house, which might count for something, but other people were disappointed because the progress completely bypassed them. For petitioners whose houses were not on the queen's itinerary, other options existed for soliciting favors: they could intercept Elizabeth on the road or lie in wait for her at someone else's house. In such ways nonhosts could take advantage of the general hospitality and moments of spontaneity that infused the queen's progresses. The spontaneity of travel that disturbed the routine of court business also made the queen more available to both hosts and people outside the court. From this dislocation came unorthodox occasions for surprising Elizabeth with requests. When the queen traveled toward Barn Elms in May 1589, she was heading toward more than just a visit with its owner, Sir Francis Walsingham. Awaiting her with petitions ready was another optimistic courtier, Lord Gilbert Talbot. Talbot apprised his father, the earl of Shrewsbury, of his hopes for aid from the queen: "I am appointed amongst the rest to attend on her Majesty at Barnellmes. I pray God my diligent attendance there may procure me a gracious answer in my suit at her return."[57] By his persistence, Talbot hoped to distinguish himself enough from the other members of the retinue so that Elizabeth would listen to, and grant, his request. On this occasion, Barn Elms had become a clearinghouse for petitions whose beneficiaries reached far beyond the person of its host and owner. With his hospitality, Walsingham performed an appreciated service for other courtiers seeking access to the queen.

Petitioners who were not in the queen's retinue hoped to meet her with their requests as she traveled between houses. As the court became a moving assembly of horses and carriages, it lost the palace walls that blocked outsiders from approaching the queen at its center. With different houses, new streets, constant crowds, and fluctuating courtiers, the progresses gave Elizabeth many chances to meet her subjects. Such travels also brought her into contact with people whom she might not have seen in London. One of these was the countess of Derby, who sought to regain the queen's favor with a royal audience. As a descendant of Mary Tudor and Charles Brandon, duke of Suffolk, the countess of Derby risked incurring the queen's displeasure by the very fact of her royal blood. She sought an opportunity to heal the breach during the summer progress of 1583 and enlisted the services of Sir Christopher Hatton as intermediary. The countess asked Hatton if he would help her "to present myself to the view of her Majesty at what time her Highness removed from her house of Sion to Oatlands."[58] By catching Elizabeth in the open or in the process of departing, the countess hoped that the queen would not again deny her an audience. The combination of a well-placed intermediary and good timing created the opportune moment for a subject to intercept the itinerant queen; indeed, the countess succeeded in regaining the queen's favor. The more open access to the queen during a progress meant that Elizabeth lost some of her privacy when she traveled, but petitioners such as the countess of Derby gained an opportunity in the process. People normally excluded from court might steal a moment of the queen's time when she journeyed away from protective buildings that limited access to her. Without being a progress host, the countess profited from the movements of the queen.

Another importuning petitioner adopted this strategy of interruption to place a request before Elizabeth. Valentine Lee sought royal redress of a grievance she had against her absent husband, Thomas, then in Ireland. During her husband's Irish campaigns with the earl of Essex, Valentine had heard nothing from him. He had abandoned her in England without supporters or money, and she was desperate for news of him. The separation was indeed a lengthy one: Lee was in Ireland by 1576, and he remained there until 1599. She had beseeched her husband for a reconciliation, or at least some financial support, in the hope that "this request is so small that it may be granted."[59] At the same time, Valentine must have anticipated his recalcitrance, because she informed Thomas of her next step should he remain silent. She would take her grievance to Elizabeth: "I hear that the Queen is this next week to go on progress, to whom I mean to appeal for justice if my reasonable request is refused." Her threat to appeal to the highest judge in the realm apparently did not impress Thomas, so she touched someone in Ireland closer to the delinquent. Valentine enclosed a copy of the above letter in one to the earl of Essex, asking Essex to intercede with Thomas on her behalf. Neither of her strategies, however, won Valentine the support she needed. Whether she spoke with Elizabeth is unclear, and the earl of Essex had other concerns. When Thomas Lee did return to England, he came not in response to his wife but as a dutiful follower of Essex. In any event, Valentine Lee did not have her husband's company long after his reappearance, because his support of the earl's uprising in 1601 cost him his life. Notwithstanding the ultimate failure of her strategy, her appeal to Elizabeth highlights the significance of the progresses to attentive citizens. When she needed assistance, Valentine saw the queen as her source of justice. She used the progress to intercept the queen and plead her cause. The unfortunate circumstances of Valentine Lee led her to seek justice from the queen who on progress might see a petitioner not likely to win access through the royal chambers at court in London. In their disruption, spontaneity, and chaos, the progresses created a window of opportunity for subjects, whether they were hosts or not, to bring petitions before the traveling monarch.

RELUCTANT HOSTS

Although self-interest and generosity induced many people to entertain the queen, there were a few hosts who should, at best, be called reluctant. They tried to avoid the traveling court, they pulled strings to have their houses ignored during a progress, and they even barred their doors to the queen. Because these colorful stories of resistance have been widely discussed in the literature, the image of unwilling hosts forced to entertain Elizabeth has come close to dominating the discussion of her progresses. Instead of seeing the series of willing hosts who used their hospitality to win favors and prestige, these analyses conclude that the progresses were composed of antagonistic hosts who could not escape a royal onslaught.[60]

This small part of the picture, with its genuinely reluctant hosts, should not, however, displace the widespread hospitality that characterized the progresses. The notoriety of an unwilling few served to highlight the customary hospitality of the majority of hosts.

The reluctant hosts during the period of the magnificent progresses of the 1570s adopted a different approach from those unwilling nobles during the shorter trips of the 1600s. By the 1570s, Elizabeth had survived religious turmoil, foreign threats, and domestic rebellion. Progress hosts of the earlier period saw a vigorous queen who had the power to make or undo their careers and fortunes; any hesitation or reluctance they felt about her visits required careful expression to keep both their independence and her favor. Although reluctant hosts of the 1570s worried about the expense of entertaining the queen, they adopted a diplomatic approach in seeking to avoid the progress route. The ploy adopted by these hosts was to make the comfort of the queen the primary goal of her visit and to worry, in varying degrees of sincerity, about their abilities to welcome her appropriately. By stressing how unworthy their poor houses were, reluctant hosts hoped to persuade the queen to look elsewhere for good accommodations. Their diplomatic attitudes played up their concern for her welfare. This politeness stemmed from the hosts' desire not to alienate a monarch whose health promised a long life and whose wrath was dreadful.

An outbreak of plague encouraged one reluctant host to seek an exemption from his duties of royal hospitality. Robert Horne, bishop of Winchester, tried to take advantage of the contagion near his house to encourage Elizabeth to travel elsewhere without directly refusing to entertain her. In 1569 Horne wrote to the earl of Leicester that the Hampshire area was unsafe for the queen, whose fear of sicknesses was well known. While his public concern appeared to be for the queen's safety, many people were saying privately that the bishop did not want to spend the necessary money for a royal visit. The common wisdom had decided that "the Bishop makes more of the matter than needeth to save his own charges."[61] His exaggeration of the danger did not, however, divert Elizabeth from his doorstep. Despite his reluctance, he played host to the queen at Farnham Castle in mid-August as part of her extended progress through the county. By masking his reluctance, he avoided insulting the queen; he also remained on the royal itinerary.

This conformist exterior served the earl of Bedford's purposes when he worried about receiving the queen in 1572. When Elizabeth decided to visit Woburn, the earl of Bedford expressed concern about the queen's lodgings. In a letter to Lord Burghley, Bedford regretted that he had not finished improving the accommodations for Elizabeth, but time would not permit it before her arrival. The elegant comfort of Woburn made this modesty

seem perfunctory; surely the queen could find shelter there amidst whatever construction was actually happening. Then Bedford went a step further. In an effort to control the royal visit and retain his authority as host,
Bedford asked Burghley to ensure that the queen's "tarieng be not above
two nights and a daye; for, for so long tyme do I prepare."[62] Rarely did a
host try to restrict Elizabeth so precisely, and even fewer made their intentions known at court. Bedford, however, was hesitant about participating
in the progress and fearful that the queen might place demands on his
hospitality that he could not fulfill. Instead of trying to avoid a visit, he
focused on exercising his rights as host. Having done his best to avoid an
indefinite stay, Bedford could extend a hearty welcome to Elizabeth and
then enjoy her punctual departure. Maintaining control of the visit became his goal as host.

Other reluctant hosts of the 1570s chose a familiar political route in persuading the queen not to visit them. Using their contacts at court, they
tried to have other, disinterested voices persuade Elizabeth to change her
plans. In 1576 Elizabeth was considering a visit to Loseley in Surrey, whose
owner, Sir William More, lacked the eagerness of a willing host. When
More realized that he faced a royal visit, he turned to a friend at court, Sir
Anthony Wingfield, an ordinary gentleman usher of the chamber, who
might have the queen's ear. More's strategy was to start a whispering campaign about the poor accommodations that the queen would have to suffer.
Wingfield passed the message to the lord chamberlain, telling him "what
few small rooms, and how unmeet your [i.e., More's] house was for the
Queen's Majesty," but the itinerary remained unchanged.[63] From that un-
helpful contact, the persistent Wingfield turned to Lady Clinton, a close
friend of the queen, who advised More himself to "come and declare unto
my Lord of Leicester your estate, that her Majesty might not come unto
your house." Because Elizabeth had a reputation for not listening to political requests from her female servants, Lady Clinton urged More to take his
suit to the persuasive and powerful Leicester. Perhaps also for that reason,
Wingfield seemed not to make use of More's daughter Elizabeth, who was
a lady-in-waiting to the queen. The issue of Loseley moved up a ladder
from a gentleman usher to the lord chamberlain, then to two royal favorites, Clinton and Leicester, without bringing any satisfaction to the petitioner. The "small rooms" at Loseley, rebuilt between 1562 and 1568, did at
last prove spacious enough for the queen, who visited them on at least four
occasions.[64] Although More did not succeed in avoiding a progress visit,
his efforts failed to tarnish his reputation as a host of "impeccable character." By conducting his campaign within the bounds of politeness, More
preserved his good relations with Elizabeth, the very person he sought to
avoid. His tactful attempts to avoid a progress recognized both the inevit-

ability of court travel as well as the inferiority of all subjects before the queen. The politic More kept both his reputation for hospitality and his high standing at court, even as he tried to shirk his role of host.

During the 1573 progress into Kent, Matthew Parker, archbishop of Canterbury, turned to a combination of court contacts and friendly alternatives to lead Elizabeth from his door. In the midst of these travel plans was a continuing discussion between queen and primate about a proclamation concerning religious conformity. The archbishop was pressing the queen to issue the order, and he certainly did not want his reluctant hospitality to derail the publication of such a religious policy.[65] In addition, Parker knew how valuable the queen's presence would be in encouraging the witnessing crowds to participate in sanctioned worship. He wanted the public vision of Elizabeth in her established church, which would promote religious obedience, more than he wanted to make an issue of her lodgings. Realizing that the visit to Canterbury was inevitable, Parker sent Elizabeth a discourse on Dover and the preface to William Lambarde's *Perambulation of Kent* to orient her to the locality, while he concentrated on the queen's public communion in Canterbury Cathedral.[66] But still hoping not to lodge her court at his Beakesbourne house, Parker broached the delicate subject to Lord Burghley in a letter that both invited and discouraged the queen's stay with him. According to the letter, Parker would gladly entertain the queen and, having no other counsel to follow, would do for her all that his predecessors had done; however, he had not been feeling well. He also offered his house for the "progresse tyme" to Burghley, Leicester, Hatton, and Sussex; however, "they saye myne house is of an eiull ayer, hanging upon the churche, and having no prospect to loke on the people, but yet I trust the convenience of the building woulde serve."[67] The unpleasant atmosphere and seclusion, Parker judged, would deter the queen from staying with him when she could stay, as he suggested, at her own fine palace of St. Augustine. Hoping to entice Burghley, and thus Elizabeth, with this alternative, Parker offered the four lords better lodging with several prebends. Mr. Bungey "would be glad to have yor L. in his lodging, where the frenche cardinal laye and his house is fayer and sufficient"; Mr. Lawse had a "convenient house"; and Mr. Peerson could offer a "fine house, most fitt." Parker's own entertainment of the queen would consist of a dinner at his house which Elizabeth could view from a private gallery overlooking the "bigger hall" for the nobles and other members of her retinue. Such episcopal hospitality would display the finer points of his house without requiring the queen to submit to its "eiull ayer."

Archbishop Parker refined the tactful strategy of Sir William More and ultimately had more success in altering the royal itinerary. While both

More and Parker emphasized their houses' faults that would discomfort the queen, Parker expanded the list to include important courtiers who also would suffer. More used his court connections to persuade the queen not to visit him, but Parker appealed as well to the self-interest of Burghley (and of Sussex, in a separate letter): as Burghley discussed the matter with Elizabeth, his advocacy would have a special eloquence as he spoke for his own comfort as well as the queen's. But the key to the archbishop's success lay in his understanding of how the court functioned. Because of their offices and proximity to the queen, Sussex and Burghley often oversaw the arrangements for the houses used on progresses. Since Elizabeth stayed with the local nobles and officials wherever she traveled, a royal visit to Canterbury would traditionally entail some time at the archbishop's house. If the prelate refused to house the court, then her officers had to find other accommodations, an irritating task when obvious lodgings already existed. Parker presented Burghley and Sussex not only with his reluctance but also with alternative, superior lodgings. The change of houses cost them no time because Parker had found the replacement himself, and all the people at court had to do was agree to the move. His strategy of praising other homes while denigrating his own worked. Burghley noted on the reverse of Parker's letter that it "adviseth how ye Qu. should bee entertained at ye church at Canterbury & invites her & her train to dinner," without mentioning lodging at Beakesbourne. When Elizabeth did visit Canterbury, she stayed at St. Augustine's from the third to the sixteenth of September.[68] Her birthday dinner, however, she reserved to spend with Archbishop Parker at his house just as he had promised.

These reluctant hosts of the 1570s showed that tampering with the queen's plans involved risks and subterfuge if the hosts were to keep the incident from becoming an embarrassment or a political liability. They drew attention to their solicitude for the queen's comfort, even as they suggested postponing the visit, and they relied upon networks of friendship and patronage. Instead of complaining in private, they spoke directly to the advisors close to the queen. If mere modesty and anxiety about the lodgings sparked their letters of supplication, then they judged correctly the situation at court. Such appeals established a sense of hostly obligation and royal superiority, as well as the idea of appropriate hospitality that sustained the progresses. If, however, the nervous hosts wanted to have their houses removed from the queen's itinerary, then their efforts failed. Such mild protestations had little impact on the court's route. But none of these hosts dared deny Elizabeth admission to his house. Their reluctance did not lead to a direct refusal of hospitality. They understood court politics and appreciated the queen's power, so they preferred to participate, whatever the cost or inconvenience, rather than offend the sovereign who had such control over their fortunes. Any inhospitable voices of the 1570s were hushed in the presence of the queen.

But during the later years of her reign, the voices of reluctant hosts grew louder and uglier as they warned Elizabeth away from their gates. The veneer of politeness slipped to reveal their blunt, confrontational refusals to entertain their sovereign. As prices rose and the possibility of royal reward faded, the reluctant hosts at the turn of the century saw little reason to engage in the ceremonial displays of an earlier, more prosperous era. As Elizabeth aged and the eventuality of a Scottish male successor grew, the popularity of her progresses declined. While the old motives for travel—politics, personal display, royal manipulation—continued to impel Elizabeth, some hosts found them less compelling. Concerns about reputation, hospitality, access to the monarch, and personal requests seemed, to these hosts, no longer addressed through progress visits. As Elizabeth kept more of her funds and honors to herself, thereby blocking many courtiers' ambitions, people recalculated the benefits of such hospitality. Despite the risks, the new math led some angry, disappointed hosts to withdraw from the progresses. The last years of her reign proved as difficult for the queen's progresses as they did in matters of her government.

The dread with which some later hosts viewed a visit from Elizabeth caused them to hide in the countryside in hopes of avoiding her eye. Thomas Arundell of Wardour Castle adopted the dual strategy of hiding and bribing a court official. In August 1600, Arundell solicited the goodwill of Sir Robert Cecil in helping him forestall a royal visit through the gift of a stag and part of the "fattest buck that I have ever seen." Arundell pleaded that "there may be no speech . . . from whence this venison comes, being unwilling to have Warder named in a progress time."[69] Since her progress route could change daily, Arundell feared an offhand remark about Wardour Castle might bring Elizabeth there for some hunting. With the present of venison, he sought Cecil's favor in avoiding a visit from Elizabeth and, in fact, managed that summer to remain inconspicuously beyond the bounds of the progress train.

No such restraint, however, marked the response of Sir Henry Lee to the news that Elizabeth wanted to visit him again. When he heard that the queen "threatens a progress" in June 1600, Lee wrote in a strident letter to his friend Sir Robert Cecil that the queen was not welcome at his house. In a catalogue of his grievances, Lee ticked off the queen's offenses: "my estate without my undoing cannot bear it, my continuance in her Court has been long, my charge great, my land sold and debts not small: how this will agree with the entertaining of such a Prince your wisdom can best judge." Blaming the queen for the poor state of his affairs, he would have entertained her "as oft beforetime, if my fortune answered my desire, or part of her Highness' many promises performed."[70] Such reasoning clearly showed the hosts' view of the progresses as a time of ceremonial bonding and patronage. Lee's bitterness reflected his failure to convert royal favor into high office and grants during the turnover in government in the 1590s, especially the Cecil–Essex contest over the patronage of the vice-chamberlainship. He therefore did not hesitate to break the patronage cycle of spending money on the queen in hopes of reward later. This "gentleman of a good estate, and a strong and valiant person," the Queen's Champion and guiding force behind the Accession Day tilts, the creator of the famed masque presented at Woodstock in 1575, and host to her at Ditchley in 1592, this same Sir Henry Lee refused the queen hospitality at his house a second time.[71] His blunt language in 1600 saved his purse from what he saw as the ravages of another fruitless royal visit. Through his outright refusal to undergo the inconvenience of entertaining the queen, Lee condemned the patronage system and the supposed political advantages of the progresses.

Lee's manner of refusing the queen, however, did not approach the rudeness with which Sir William Clark of Buckinghamshire treated Elizabeth in 1602. While a letter had conveyed Lee's rejection, Sir William behaved badly in public before the queen. When the court arrived at Burnham, Clark gave a public and obvious show of his unwilling hospitality. A firsthand account of the incident came from Henry Percy, ninth Earl of Northumberland, who traveled with the court on its short progress through Middlesex, Buckinghamshire, and Surrey. Writing from Burnham to Lord Cobham in London on 6 August 1602, Northumberland lamented that the court would stay until Monday with the inhospitable host. Clark had committed the sin of disdaining the social conventions of hospitality. According to Northumberland, Clark "nether gives mete nor monny to any of the progressers; the house her ma. hathe at commandement and his grasse the gards horses eate, he shafes and this is all." The only good news was that a dinner (and presumably proper entertainment) at a nearby estate would interrupt the ascetic offerings at Burnham: "To morrow wee goe to Sir Henry Gilfords to dinner, as yett is appointed, and soe backe againe."[72] Clark guarded every penny by eschewing the customary responsibilities of a progress host: he fed the court nothing, he gave no presents or rewards, he organized no hunts or masques. The court received the only two things the begrudging host could not easily deny—his house and his pastureland.

If Clark were going to abdicate his role as host, the least Northumberland could do was to publicize such insults abroad. Spreading the news of Clark's rudeness was one effective way of punishing him for the breach of hospitality. While the queen did not expect her hosts to go into debt to entertain her, she did demand that they adhere to the rules of hospitality requiring at least the appearance of hostly pleasure before the sovereign. Sir William Clark behaved badly on both accounts because no impressive entertainments covered his displeasure with the queen's visit and no warm hospitality masked his stingy reception. As he was neither generous nor pleasant, all Clark earned from this experience was general condemnation as a man "who so behaved himselfe that he pleased no body, but gave occasion to have his miserie [i.e., miserliness] and vanitie spread far and wide."[73] Clark's rudeness overshadowed that of Sir Henry Lee, who had snubbed Elizabeth from afar, when Clark allowed the queen to stay at Burnham and then treated her and the court shabbily.

In this later period of royal travel when reluctant hosts had grown bolder, one nobleman stood out even from this group for his blunt, public refusal to participate in the progresses. In 1601 Henry Clinton, earl of Lincoln, did not want to entertain Elizabeth, a sentiment, as we have seen, shared by others such as Sir Henry Lee and Sir William Clark. The earl of Lincoln, however, pursued a course of action that made these other reluctant hosts seem virtually companionable. While Elizabeth had a note of dismissal from Lee and suffered through the churlish reception from Clark, she received from the earl of Lincoln a physical insult in front of her court: the mention of her arrival at his house in Chelsea caused the earl to bolt the doors against her as he fled the area.[74] When the queen and her retinue, which included the Scottish ambassador, reached the earl's house on 30 April 1601, servants of the absent host blocked the royal party from entering the house and garden. According to the earl's enemies, the servants dared to behave in "so rude a fashion" only at their master's explicit instructions. Two members of the party, the earl of Nottingham and Sir Robert Cecil, defended the absent earl before an angry Elizabeth. Lincoln, they said, had readied the house for her visit but then had to leave precipitously. To mitigate his insult, Lincoln supposedly had left provisions with the promise to "make us your stewards for a dinner" at his cost. All this explanation was, however, a fiction. The idea of the dinner had come from Nottingham and Cecil, who informed Lincoln of his own hospitality by letter. In recognition of the earl's financial difficulties, they promised to "moderate expenses as if it were for ourselves." Not only was Lincoln an absent and reluctant host, but he was also a host by proxy. The newly scheduled dinner was acceptable to the queen because it would enable her to save face before the Scottish ambassador. With angry words, she swore "that he . . . that saw her kept out, may see her also let in."[75]

The earl of Lincoln's version of the incident explained why he fled London for his Lincolnshire home of Tattershall. He invoked the customary claim that his Chelsea house was unfit to provide hospitality for the queen, and he buttressed that line of defense with the additional excuse of having to attend to business at the assizes that day.[76] Those two reasons, he hoped, would explain to the fuming queen why he had abandoned his duties as host. Few people, however, seemed to have believed this obviously deceitful account. According to his son-in-law, Sir Arthur Gorges, Lincoln was well known for his irascible, unstable behavior: "his wickedness, misery, craft, repugnance to all humanity, and perfidious mine is not amongst the heathens to be matched. God bless me from him. To have his lands after his death, I would not be tied to observe him in his life."[77] The earl's retreat to Tattershall saved him from both his creditors and the queen, but such a common financial problem alone could not explain his obnoxious behavior. According to N. Fuidge, a more personal explanation accounts for his transparently odd actions, such as locking out the queen. She suggests that Lincoln could not have controlled himself because "by modern standards Lincoln would be adjudged insane, at least during the last years of his life."[78] His unusual tactics and bizarre actions should stand out as an "insane" exception to the typical behavior shown to the queen on progress.

The forceful reluctance of Sir Henry Lee, Sir William Clark, and the earl of Lincoln achieved mixed results. Bluntly refusing the queen access to a house did not always keep her out, nor did the host's rudeness necessarily drive her away. Such actions only earned those men the ill will of the queen and made them the target of court gossip. Those hesitant hosts of the 1570s who tried persuasion had about the same success in turning away the queen as their more forthright counterparts. Whether they appealed to the queen's comfort or relied upon friends at court for help, these polite hosts often ended up providing a roof for the queen and her court. Since neither rudeness nor maneuvering could guarantee the queen's absence, the best response for reluctant hosts was to exhaust all reasonable means of persuasion, even locating an alternative host, but then to accept the inevitable visit in time and with enough graciousness to reap the benefits of a royal visit.

However, by the turn of the century some hosts questioned the advantages of this access to Elizabeth. These men represented the extreme responses of unwilling hosts who felt the cost of a royal visit was not worth the price. But their financial concerns were also shared with other hosts less inclined to refuse the queen a welcome. The significance of these blunt rejections lies in their timing. By 1600 Elizabeth was in her sixties, Robert Cecil was corresponding with James VI in Scotland, and the succession question already appeared settled. Progress hosts unwilling to open their houses to the troublesome queen counted on the eventual change of monarch to erase their transgressions. They treated Elizabeth in her last five years as they never would have dared in her prime. Of course, no one knew when the queen would die, but her control in some areas was slipping. Although she continued to rule with vigor, as evidenced in her handling of Essex's uprising, she faced problems at court and in Parliament that held no easy solutions for a queen notoriously committed to upholding her prerogative. The more obviously reluctant hosts of this later period had no interest in access to the monarch, the main attraction of entertaining the queen, and they sought nothing from her. With that incentive lost, they dismissed the progresses as a sham in which they would not participate.

A larger shift in social expectations figured in the hosts' reactions to the later progresses of Elizabeth. Many voices during the last decade of her rule and well into the next century commented upon the declining importance of hospitality in English society. This trend also occurred in some towns, and the patterns of Elizabeth's progresses reveal a decline in the number of towns she visited during her later travels. The decline in civic hospitality, Felicity Heal argues, occurred as a product of changes in the ruling groups: as towns became "more introverted and oligarchic, we might conclude that one explanation for a decline in feasting was a diminishing need to impress or persuade a wide circle of burgesses."[79] A key aspect of both individual and civic entertainments was their public claim on large numbers of observers and participants. As entertaining developed into a more private occasion, the goal of fostering civic unity and communal pride faded. In government, theater, and royal entries, this change had important implications for the relationships between the ruled and their rulers, the hosts and their audiences. Such changing attitudes toward the public responsibilities associated with hospitality formed a larger social picture that also contained the increasing reluctance to entertain Elizabeth. Unwilling hosts disdainful of the honor formerly attached to a royal visit could ignore pressures from peers and neighbors to engage in costly, inconvenient hospitality. Without the broad base of social support for public ceremonies and hospitality, Elizabeth in her later years turned to a smaller group of friends and familiar nobles when she wanted to take to the road. That she still could enjoy progresses to Southampton, Portsmouth, and Gloucestershire suggests that while traditional English hospitality might be fading, it had not yet vanished.

This survey of the hospitality offered to Elizabeth should give a proper balance to the ubiquitous assertion that Elizabeth imposed herself on unwilling hosts during her progresses. In most cases, the queen wanted to visit her subjects, her subjects wanted the queen in their homes, and the hosts competed for the honor of a royal visit. This long history of hospitality continued, with some modifications, well into the last years of Elizabeth's reign, when she could still expect to be welcomed into the homes of her hosts. Elizabeth loved to travel on progress even in her later years, partly to visit old friends and partly to deny the advances of old age. Many of the courtiers who accompanied her grew tired of the discomfort of rough roads, makeshift beds, and constant packing. Some of them determined in 1602 that the queen should not drag them around on another Christmas progress between royal palaces. Instead, they planned a strategy to keep her close to London. During the two weeks before Christmas, these conspirators arranged for Elizabeth to dine with Sir Robert Cecil at the Savoy, the earl of Nottingham at Arundel House, Lord Thomas Howard at Charterhouse, and George Carey, Lord Hunsdon, at Blackfriars. This schedule limited her to London while distracting her from distant lures: "all is to entertain the time, and win her to stay here yf yt may be."[80] The court's plan worked: Elizabeth did not go to Windsor or her other nearby palaces. "These feastings have had theyre effect to stay the court here this Christmas," the courtiers congratulated themselves, "though most of the carriages were well onward on theyre way to Richmond." The conspiracy succeeded because its premise, that her nobles wanted the queen to visit them, had been true for her progresses in the past. Elizabeth readily believed in 1602 that these willing hosts desired her company because their behavior followed the pattern of responses to her 43 years of travel. Her "popularity" during the Christmas season of 1602 was part of the same hospitality she had encountered on almost all of her progresses, but now her hosts used invitations to influence where the queen would not go. Although the nobles created the plan because they disliked winter travel, more significantly, they organized festive entertainments that touched the old chords of conviviality in Elizabeth. In order not to go on a progress, the court created a "progress" at home.

The longevity of Elizabethan progresses reflected their significant place in royal government, court life, and local communities. The progresses offered a setting where the queen and her hosts could pursue matters of mutual importance. Both royal guest and private hosts depended upon such direct contact that came, even briefly, from living together. Through this hospitality, hosts cultivated their reputation at court and with neighbors; through their access to the queen, hosts petitioned for special favors and strengthened the ties of patronage. Elizabeth, too, valued these public moments that expanded the basis of her personal monarchy, a kind of government dependent upon large-scale pageantry and quiet conversation to bolster the queen's popularity. Through her progress visits, the queen carried out the business of governing as she expanded the number of people attached to her court and to her monarchy. Because of this symbiosis between sovereign and subjects, the progresses mirrored the vitality of the queen, her court, and her government. The most successful progresses came during the exciting days of the 1570s, in the glow of the religious settlement, suppression of the northern revolt, and containment of Mary Stuart. Who knew but what Elizabeth might even choose a husband and determine the succession? Later, the difficulties of the 1590s, a time of ineffectual war against Spain, conflicts between court rivals, deaths of cherished friends, bad harvests, and inflation, soured some hosts and caused the aging queen to retrench. Despite her best efforts and commitment, the familiar rewards of royal travel diminished. The hospitality on the progresses reflected the changing nature of Elizabethan politics.

FIVE

Civic Hosts

The queen's need to cultivate her popularity led Elizabeth to visit towns in the southern part of the island, where she could interact with more people at one time than was possible at a private house. She entered a variety of urban centers, from those with cathedrals and universities, large county markets, and bustling ports to fortified towns, sleepy harbors, and small villages on well-traveled roads. Civic visits formed an important part of Elizabeth's progresses: they occurred regularly in the progress itineraries, they allowed larger concentrations of the populace to see the monarch, and they provided a public arena for shaping royal and civic reputations. During these visits, civic officials and all residents of the town acted as the queen's hosts. With that power, they designed public ceremonies to present their communal history, local accomplishments, and, of course, requests that Elizabeth might grant. The citizens also shared the expense of hospitality. The significance of these occasions came from the layered messages exchanged between civic hosts and royal guest. This public dialogue focused on the participants' reputation at home and abroad and their role as members of the commonweal. For both towns and queen, these civic visits provided a valuable opportunity to advance civic, royal, and national agendas.

Townspeople on a progress exerted considerable effort to make the queen's visit a satisfying one. Guilds organized shows and pageants, people spruced up the façades of buildings, civic leaders prepared speeches and donned new gowns, the council chose gifts for the court, and the local authorities raised the money to pay for the ceremonies. From all the preparations, it was clear that towns on the progress route regarded the arrival of Elizabeth with optimism. Even more apparent was the queen's enthusiastic welcome from large towns as well as tiny villages of modest means. The towns did not display any corporate reluctance to entertain the queen, although on rare occasions a citizen might grumble at paying the assessment and refuse to participate in the civic welcome. Those dissenters, however, were few, at least according to the written sources, and the rest of the townspeople drowned out the note of discord with their communal, and apparently genuine, welcome. Such uniform civic hospitality reflected the corporation's relationship with the crown. The monarch granted economic and political privileges to the towns and codified them in town charters, which theoretically the ruler could revoke; the towns generated much of the trade and industry that kept England healthy within and linked to markets abroad. In addition, local governments were the most visible representatives of royal law for many people. The queen, therefore, needed to maintain civic respect for her laws, officials, and personal monarchy. The royal government depended upon vibrant, flourishing towns that, in turn, looked to the monarch for help in preserving their political and economic vitality. This relationship existed in the significant ceremonies that marked the meetings of civic leaders and visiting aristocrats and royalty. Through ceremonial references to their historic rights and past royal aid, towns magnified their current importance even as they pressed for new favors from the visiting queen. But beyond the tangible aid for which towns petitioned, civic hosts entertained Elizabeth because their public conversations created a ceremonial dialogue that validated the sense of community within the town and spread its civic reputation beyond the liberties.

COST OF CIVIC ENTERTAINMENT

Any town that received a royal visit incurred expenses from the occasion. In addition to the queen's contribution toward her own maintenance in the form of food, supplies, staff, and transportation, her civic hosts had to spend money from the town's treasury to extend a proper welcome to the visiting court. The amount of money varied, as it did with private hosts, according to the size and importance of the town. Smaller corporations could participate in the progresses without having to match the splendid celebrations of larger, wealthier towns because a sense of hospitality appropriate to each town governed the civic entertainments. This aspect of civic hospitality enabled Elizabeth to visit a variety of villages and towns without draining local treasuries. The civic funds spent for a royal visit subsidized ceremonies and exchanges between monarch and citizens that, the townspeople hoped, would bring glory and royal beneficence to the town for years to come. As town governments collected funds from their citizens to meet the cost of a royal visit, so these citizens acted in unison as the corporate host to the queen. Paying for a royal visit bound together the members of the local community, reaffirmed their obligations to the corporation, and enabled them to engage in the ceremonial dialogue with Elizabeth that lay at the heart of a civic progress.

The financial responsibilities of the civic host essentially focused on providing the ceremony needed during a progress. In general, the towns crafted a ceremonial welcome by investing in both temporary and long-term improvements. Expenses that yielded important but transient changes in the civic fabric included payments for painting, whitewashing, cleaning, and tidying those public areas in which the court would move. Such a civic facelift could not last but was important while it did. Likewise, the music, bells, orations, and performances paid for from town coffers created the ceremonial dialogue without surviving it. More permanent improvements generated by a royal visit ranged from repairing decayed structures, regilding coats of arms, and erecting crosses to purchasing new gowns for civic officials. These lasting improvements then became an investment that the town made in its own future. Civic hosts paid for another tangible part of the ceremony that, although concrete and therefore lasting, did not remain in the town: the gifts from civic host to courtly guests. The town leaders customarily presented a gift to the queen and lesser gifts to nobles in her retinue and officers of the royal household. The civic hosts hoped that these visual, tactile, financial, and even gustatory reminders of the occasion would incline the recipients to favor the town in any future dealings. Thus, through this combination of expenditures for evanescent and lasting aspects of the ceremony, civic hosts assumed part of the financial burden of a visit from the queen. They expected that the success of the visit would justify its cost.

The cost to towns from making temporary improvements before a royal visit was slight but yielded important results. Public maintenance was a priority because the procession of the queen through the town would show her all its warts and smiles. Towns erected platforms and scaffolding near the guildhall and market square for public ceremonies. In the open space, players performed, artisans displayed their skills, orators delivered speeches, and the mayor presented a gift to Elizabeth. The queen's visit created the need for these structures, and when she left they came down, all at civic expense. In other temporary improvements, laborers cleaned the streets, covered the dunghills, and spread reeds throughout the public areas. Butchers removed offal from public view, and hogs were herded to pens out of sight. A more unusual nuisance than swine worried the corporation of Lichfield before the queen arrived in 1575. The town paid five shillings to William Hollcroft "for kepynge Madde Richard when her Matie was here."[1] It is difficult to discover more about this intriguing comment on civic reputation, royal visits, and treatment of the insane. At the very least, the desire of Lichfield to prevent its royal guest from encountering one of its uncontrollable citizens linked "Madde Richard" and unruly swine as civic eyesores. In a more general sense, towns tried to conceal the messiness of daily life during royal visits. Although the residents enjoyed the benefit of a briefly clean town, the temporary costs were a minor drain on the civic treasury. The wages and materials for the cleaning amounted to only a few shillings, and the town put the financial burden for tidying houses on their owners. As a result, the temporary garnishings improved appearances without incurring great expense.

Another ceremonial expense borne by the towns was the hiring of musicians and bell ringers, whose skills helped to create the celebratory atmosphere appropriate to a royal visit. They announced the queen's arrival with music and pealing church bells, for which the bell ringers received a fee from the funds administered by the churchwarden. When Elizabeth passed through Chelmsford during her Essex progress in 1561, the churchwardens paid 6s. 8d. to their ringers and an additional 12d. for their drink. Smarden Church in Kent "laid out for the ringers when the quenes grace was here" the sum of 2s. 10d. in 1573. The ringers at Kingston-upon-Thames in 1600 welcomed the queen to nearby Norbiton, the home of George Evelyn.[2] When the town of Gloucester hosted her in 1574, the waits of Shrewsbury received 26s. 8d. for playing each morning. Portsmouth gave her martial music in 1569 with the sound of drums and flute.[3] After the music had faded, a speaker chosen by the town would make an oration of welcome, and occasionally the town treasury recompensed him. Following the oration, pageants by the guilds began on platforms erected near the town gates and guildhall. Military garrisons, like that at Sandwich, staged elaborate mock battles to impress Elizabeth. In addition to this civic entertainment, traveling players in company with the queen received small rewards from the town for providing private amusement when Elizabeth had withdrawn into her lodgings. Unlike the physical improvements, such entertainments were obviously of the fleeting moment. The costs were not investments in tangible benefits for the towns, but they did contribute to the civic reputation for hospitality that motivated such welcomes.

Other ceremonial preparations gave the towns benefits for years after the transitory occasion of a royal visit. Their costs, therefore, were less an expense than an investment in the corporation. The entire council might order new gowns and maces in honor of the queen and as a reflection of their own social and political standing. In fact, many towns did invest in new regalia with which to greet Elizabeth. The council of Southampton spent over £20 for new liveries before the progress in 1569. Worcester and other towns mended and regilded their maces and staves of office before carrying them in a procession before the queen. Every public monument received its share of attention. Stonemasons repaired the crosses in Warwick, laborers fixed walls and roofs, town gates received a fresh coat of paint, and inhabitants whitewashed their houses. The towns of Worcester, Northampton, and Bristol used the occasion to attach the royal arms to the gates and guildhalls.[4] Such repairs cost the towns or owners from a shilling to several pounds, but the money was not wasted. Not only would the improved buildings, bright gowns, and fashionable houses indicate civic prosperity to the queen, but they would also endure for the town's benefit in her absence. Regardless of a royal visit, these repairs would have been necessary. The arrival of the queen merely set a deadline for such repairs that later might evoke the memory of Elizabeth's presence.

The towns' permanent investments in new buildings, regalia, and repairs had some lasting civic benefits that mitigated, in part, their costs. Townspeople could see, at least, where their funds were going. But the gifts presented to the court, which of course the citizens never saw again, constituted the largest expense attached to a royal visit. Almost every sizable village and all the towns gave Elizabeth a present even if she only passed through the area without spending a night. A silver or gold cup was the customary gift that some towns then filled with coins. The size and cost of the cups varied, but the total, including the money, was rarely less than £15. Bailiff Dighton of Worcester gave Elizabeth a silver cup worth £10 17s. 2d. that was filled with £40 of coins.[5] The people of Cranbrook, Thetford, and Dover each presented her with a silver cup. From Faversham came a silver cup worth £27 2s. James Woodhall, the treasurer of Saffron Walden, visited Elizabeth when she was at nearby Audley End to offer her a silver double gilt cup with cover valued at £19 3s. The mayor of Cambridge gave a silver cup of £16 containing 40 angels. The people of Gloucester offered a double gilt cup costing £26 11s. 4d. with £40 of coins inside. Sandwich sent two jurats to London for a cup worth £100 for Elizabeth. The town of Yarmouth commissioned a silver cup worth £16 in the shape of a ship, evoking the town's leading industry. The lords of her retinue received it for her, as Elizabeth remained in Norwich when they visited the coastal town.[6]

Other towns preferred to forgo the expense of a cup and instead offer the queen a purse of money. Southampton and Lichfield each gave her £40. The town of Northampton spent £6 on a purse and filled it with £20. Mayor Thomas Kelke of Bristol presented a silk purse with £100 in gold inside. Canterbury enclosed £30 in a 16s. purse, and King's Lynn pledged 100 angels for a royal present. These gifts showed, the towns hoped, their pleasure at entertaining the queen as well as their ability to do so with appropriate civic generosity. If she appeared to miss the point, mayors such as Edmund Brownell did not hesitate to remind her. When accepting a gift from the people of Coventry, Elizabeth commended it, saying, "I have but few such for it was a ¢ li. [£100] of angels in gold." In response,

Brownell "answered very boldly 'if it like your grace it is a greate deale more . . . it is ye faithfull harts of all your true loveing subjects.' 'Wee thanke you, Mr Maior saide the Queene it is Indeed a greate deale more.'"[7]

Even as the towns bestowed generous gifts upon the queen, they remembered the courtiers and special friends who might work some good on the town's behalf. Courtiers with ties to the area and officers of the household received separate gifts from town officials in a gesture of goodwill and hospitality. The earl of Leicester received sugar loaves at Saffron Walden and two gallons of hippocras, a spiced wine, at Worcester. Lord Burghley accepted sugar loaves also at Saffron Walden, while citizens of Bristol gave him a gallon of claret, two gallons of sack, and a gigantic sugar loaf weighing 50 pounds. Sir James Croft, comptroller of the household, received a gilt tankard from the Worcester officials. The cost of these gifts ranged from 17s. 8d. for a sugar loaf (and upward of £3 for Burghley's large one), to about £6 for the Worcester tankard.[8] Wines, sugar loaves, gloves, and cups allowed the towns an inexpensive way to solicit favor and extend their hospitality.

More expensive were the rewards that towns customarily offered to the court servants traveling with the queen. These payments expressed both civic hospitality and an appreciation of the extra business brought into the local markets by the progresses. Civic leaders also hoped that the presents would win them favors from these court servants. A gift to the clerk of the market, who set local prices of provisions during the progress, for example, might result in reciprocal benefits to the town. The town of Southampton in 1569 gave 20s to the clerk of the market, the sergeant of arms, footmen, trumpeters, and musicians. Rewards of 5s went to the yeomen of the mail, yeomen of the bottles, and the queen's porters. The crier for the clerk of the market pocketed 2s. The rewards cost Southampton a total of £8 7s. Other civic hosts chose to spend more than Southampton in rewards to its guests. In 1573 Canterbury offered £14 11s. 10d. to the household officers, while Worcester scaled new heights during an elaborate entertainment in 1575, with its gifts amounting to £77 11s. 10d. for the visitors. One of the best enumerations of rewards comes from the queen's visit to Norwich in 1578 (see Appendix). Household officers from the clerk of the market and gentlemen ushers to the cooks and boilers merited some part of Norwich's bounty, as the rewards to members of the queen's retinue totaled £37.[9] Through these gifts and rewards so characteristic of Tudor public life, civic hosts participated in the ceremonial dialogue of the progresses.

The substantial cost of these gifts indicated how much the towns valued visits from Elizabeth and how seriously they cultivated royal favor and their own reputation. The towns spent most money on the queen's gift precisely because it became the best direct and tangible reminder of their provincial loyalty when the court returned to London. They hoped she would use the gilt cups and silk purses, along with the occasional pair of gloves, and remember their worthy town.[10] The purses of money probably meant more to Elizabeth, however, since royal funds always were insufficient for her needs.

Although civic funds paid for part of the royal visit, towns did not have to pay for other progress expenses. The towns did relatively little for Elizabeth as far as her lodgings and provisions were concerned. Whereas the royal household and chamber had the primary duty of housing and provisioning the court on progress, town records show little involvement of local officials in these functions. Neither did many towns have to prepare lodgings for Elizabeth, since she usually stayed with nearby nobles or in a private house within the town. On the occasions when Elizabeth did stay within the town liberties, the town seldom contributed to her maintenance at these private houses. In Sandwich, she stayed at Sir Roger Manwood's house, as had her father twice before.[11] In Coventry, she lodged in Whitefriars, a former monastery turned into a home for Sir John Hales. Sir John Young accommodated Elizabeth in "The Great House" during her visit to Bristol in 1574. During her longer visit to Warwick in 1572, the queen stayed with her host Ambrose Dudley in Warwick Castle, a domesticated fortress that dominated the town while remaining walled against it. Only in Ipswich were the bailiffs asked for financial help in readying the house of Mr. Withipoll for the queen's visit in 1561.[12] Most of the civic hosts prevailed upon local gentry and nobles to shelter the queen, and few towns defrayed those expenses. Thus unburdened of two expensive and taxing duties—feeding and housing the court—town officials could concentrate their energies and finances on arranging the ceremonial structure of Elizabeth's visit.

This breakdown of costs and financial responsibilities suggests that towns had flexibility in deciding how much to pay for their welcome of the queen. Since the towns paid for municipal improvements, preparations, entertainments, and gifts but relatively little for provisions and lodgings, they kept the expenses of a progress visit within reasonable limits. Although complete accounts are rare and extant records deluding in their brevity, the following list offers some figures that represent the approximate cost to the town of a royal visit.

1575	Worcester	£173
1573	Sandwich	£100 (gift only)
1569	Southampton	£90
1575	Lichfield	£78
1574	Gloucester	£75
1573	Canterbury	£45

1573	Faversham	£44
1571	Saffron Walden	£37
1563	Northampton	£26 (gift only)
1578	Saffron Walden	£21
1564	Cambridge	£16 (gift only)[13]

The range of total costs suggests that towns did not have to incur great expense in entertaining the queen. Some of the smaller towns managed for less than £50, which would not strain the resources of the community. Other than a modest gift for the queen, the expenses for preparation and repairs could cost the towns less than £10. For a town such as Warwick, which collected £86 19s. 2d. in total revenue and paid out £63 19s. 8d. from December 1565 to December 1566, a royal visit did not create large debts or harm the local economy.[14] The town of Saffron Walden invested £37 4s. 16d. in the queen's visit in 1571, when its annual receipts amounted to £83 2s. 3d. and annual expenses came to £68 10s. 10d. Somehow, the treasurer, James Woodhall, ended his term with a respectable surplus. By comparison, in a year without a royal visit, for example, from October 1575 to October 1576, the town had a surplus of £23 5s. 7d.[15] In the overall financial picture, Saffron Walden enjoyed a surplus of revenue over expenses both when the citizens entertained the queen and when they did not. At the other end of the spectrum, the towns of Worcester, Sandwich, and Southampton made extravagant occasions of the queen's visit. Their most costly expense was the beautiful cup filled with money that they presented to Elizabeth. In the context of sixteenth-century hospitality, these gifts reflected a civic awareness of what was appropriate for their individual community. Whether the presents were small or large, the gifts signified civic hospitality, loyalty, and communal solidarity to their royal guest. The standard against which the towns measured the quality of their progress entertainments was a relative one, appropriate to the distinctive history, economic status, and civic pride of each community.[16] Such an outlook allowed the towns to fund their civic welcome at a level within their corporation's ability to pay.

As they planned and cleaned, civic leaders also arranged the financing of the queen's visit. They began raising money and administering its expenditure in accordance with civic laws and customs. The officials in charge of the funds were usually the bailiffs, treasurers, wardens, and chamberlains. The chancellors of the two universities assumed financial direction of Elizabeth's visits. In general, the guilds, as the most politically and economically important civic groups, provided the people and hierarchy for raising the money. Taking advantage of their local elites, some towns asked for a fixed amount of money from their councils and liveried companies. In Gloucester, the chamberlain began a "progress war chest" by first collecting all outstanding fines.[17] He then supplemented it through a special tax on the burgesses and the trading companies. The sliding scale rated the tailors at the highest contribution of £4, down to the weavers at 11s. The guilds in Coventry supported the cost of the queen's visit in a similar manner. After her arrival in August 1566, the guild wardens presented £61 10s. to the town treasurer.[18] An orderly scheme in Worcester relied upon financial contributions both from the guilds and from the town officials. The bulk of the moneys came from the civic government of 24 aldermen, 48 common councilors, the treasury, and the constables. The aldermen each paid 40s., for a group assessment of £46; the councilors paid at the lesser rate of 20s. to make up £48 total; funds taken from the town treasury amounted to £53; and the guilds put in close to £32.[19] With the fines collected by the constables, the citizens of Worcester had raised £236 to pay for their entertainment of the queen. The corporation of Leicester followed a similar pattern of financing, but included in its plans was the contingency that Elizabeth might change her mind and bypass the town. In order to be prepared for a visit, the town ordered a collection of ready money to be paid with a fortnight's warning. The 24 aldermen would pay 40s. each, and the 48 councilors would pay 20s. each to the chamberlains.[20] The notice of two weeks would enable the town to buy a gift, organize a reception, and clean up the streets, while it also guarded against wasted efforts should the queen not arrive. The caution of the Leicester officials was justified, in any case, when Elizabeth did not visit the town according to her plans in 1575. By assessing their leaders at higher rates than the citizenry, these four western towns financed a royal visit with a fiscal hierarchy parallel to the social one that governed the corporation.

Ipswich was unusual in levying a general tax upon its inhabitants to underwrite civic expenses during a progress visit. The town records reveal that in June 1561 the council decided all householders of Ipswich should be assessed for the costs of entertaining Elizabeth "at her next comming to the Towns." The council named the assessors to collect the money. Should citizens balk at paying their mandated share, the council threatened them with disfranchisement.[21] The town regularly employed this method of raising funds for civic functions. A similar assessment was made in 1559 to cover debts incurred by legal suits brought to protect the charters and liberties of Ipswich. Assessors met in the moot hall, determined the amounts owed by burgesses and inhabitants, and enforced the tax with the penalty of disfranchisement. Since the whole town theoretically profited from the legal victories, the council reasoned, the general body of citizens should shoulder the costs of those lawsuits. In matters of importance to the whole town, such as civic activities and royal entertainments, Ipswich regularly made such assessments. The town also took action to reimburse people for their personal expenses for the royal visit. The bailiffs would determine the amount of payment of any bills submitted by 15 May, and the reimbursements did indeed occur. In 1571 John Mintor received 20s. in recompense for his share of the royal entertainment, and in 1572 he had "40s. more given to him provided that he give a gen'll release."[22]

This method of fundraising depended for its success upon an initial voluntary compliance, later enforced if necessary by law. Since some inhabitants did not pay on time, the collection of taxes could drag on for years. When the Ipswich council in July 1561 ordered an assessment to provide two boats "decently furnished" for the queen's welcome, however, one person objected. Robert Barker did not pay his share before the queen arrived, and he had not paid it as late as 26 September, a month after she had come and gone. Faced with Barker's refusal to pay his £8 assessment, the council deprived him of his status as freeman. The council ordered him to pay his £8 to the treasurer by 1 November, and it tacked on another £6 as a fine to redeem his freedom. Several aspects of this incident help to explain its seemingly unusual nature. The occasion of Elizabeth's visit was not the first time that Robert Barker had come before the Ipswich council for judgment. In 1560 he violated some town ordinances, for which he was called before the council. After a most unrepentant submission, Barker received a pardon. Two years later in 1562, he was fined £5 for miscalling and misusing the Ipswich bailiffs and councilors. His bellicose behavior, however, did not exile Barker from the inner circles of town power. He had served in Parliament in 1558–59, and he would become a portman and bailiff of Ipswich in 1563, two years after the queen's visit. Barker was, in fact, one of a small group of citizens who did not pay their assessment on time, provoking the council to threaten the shirkers. In March 1563, the council ordered the collectors to levy arrears upon the goods and chattels of those citizens who had not paid; those in violation of the order on 1 May would lose their freedom.[23] By these strategies did civic hosts ensure that members of their community paid for the hospitality extended to the queen.

These financial plans for royal visits reflected the corporate nature of civic hospitality. The entire citizenry played host to the visiting queen, and sharing the costs involved the whole community in the occasion. At the same time, it established necessary limits on the total contributions that the town could expect to collect. Some councils recognized the financial demands attached to civic responsibility, as they required their wealthiest citizens to assume a larger financial burden than the communality. Others adopted the more onerous, if egalitarian, method of taxing inhabitants at the same rate. Either way, the local people paid a share of the costs incurred for the royal welcome, and they thereby had a direct investment in the success of the occasion. Through their money, labor, and attendance, townspeople created the hospitable environment that welcomed Elizabeth. This popular participation—fiscal and physical—in a celebration of civic glory united the citizens in a symbolic recognition of their identity as a town and as subjects of a monarch. The interplay between these two identities formed the ceremonial dialogue that lay at the heart of Elizabethan progresses.

REQUESTS FOR ECONOMIC AID

Many of the towns that entertained Elizabeth used the occasion to petition her for special favors and royal action. These requests focused on local improvements and economic aid ranging from harbors, silting, and fishing rights to markets and relocation of courts. The civic leaders also solicited her intervention in settling local disputes. Because of the opportunity to petition directly, the towns welcomed Elizabeth with a display of civic wealth and talent. Not only did they reap the local benefits of her visit, despite some inconvenience and expense, but the towns also enhanced their reputation by providing entertainments, dinners, and gifts. Civic pride as well as prosperity received a boost from the queen's visit. If the queen denied or ignored the request, however, the town did not consider her visit a failure. The ceremonial component remained intact, with its emphasis on the civic identity. Elizabeth had heard the suit and witnessed the town's ceremonial display of its own civic pride. She might deny the request, but she could not invalidate or easily forget the power and bonds within that civic community. The ceremonies won, in part, for the towns what they might seem to lose financially.

The request for aid came in the middle of the public ceremonies at the town's center or more privately through other representatives at court. Having escorted the queen with a procession into town and presented a gift with yet more speeches, the civic officers used the public forum to bring forward their request. In towns along the southeastern coast, the issues often dealt with the state of the all-important harbors. The Cinque Ports and other coastal towns had sand that silted up the harbors and ruined their trade, and such maritime concerns led citizens to petition Elizabeth for royal aid when she visited their community. During her progress in 1573, Elizabeth stayed three days in Rye, a declining Sussex port experiencing the problems of a silted harbor and a depressed economy. Later that year, the mayor of Rye presented a petition to the Privy Council in which he sought the queen's aid in repairing the "puddle and creek of Rye." Overgrown reeds and bulrushes had clogged the sewers and dikes from Newingden to the sea. For the fishermen and traders to have a useful harbor again, water lines had to be cleaned and scoured. The estimated cost of such a project came to £3,000, money that the people of Rye hoped would come from the royal commissioner of sewers for Kent and Sussex.[24] The town hoped that Elizabeth's earlier inspection of their problems during the summer progress would incline her to grant the request from Rye. By granting the funds to clean the silted harbor, the queen would be returning the favor to a town that had entertained her well. The delayed nature of the request weakened its claim on her royal attention, but the memory of their civic hospitality might also move the queen to support the people of Rye.

The people of Folkestone wanted Elizabeth to visit them in 1573, "in the hope of securing the aid of the crown for their failing haven."[25] Folkestone was suffering from the competition in fishing and trade of nearby Dover and Hythe. The Folkestone trained band of 50 men escorted the queen through Folkestone Down to Dover Castle. Mayor Robert Holiday accompanied them with a civic group of some 300 people and then presented a petition concerning the harbor. The mayor and town clerk later followed the progress retinue to Canterbury to receive the queen's response. Holiday also presented his suit to Lord Cobham as warden of the Cinque Ports, but apparently neither effort brought Folkestone any relief. However poorly their suit fared, the judgment of the citizens was that they could best speak to the queen about important matters through a display of ceremony. A royal denial did not undermine the aura of civic hospitality. Through such ceremonies, the community constructed its own image as a single body formed of its individual citizens. The power of the civic ceremonies was that they expressed the townspeople's unity and hospitality to the queen, a newcomer to their place, while also asking for a favor of her from a stated position of civic strength.

The people of Sandwich struck the same note as their Folkestone neighbors during the queen's southern progress of 1573. Before asking for aid to repair the harbor, the town officials orchestrated a booming welcome that set the visit's motif of martial strength and naval skill. At Sandwich, Elizabeth first received a gift and heard an oration by the minister of St. Clement's parish. Then she watched a spinning demonstration by industrious citizens who relied upon trade to feed the town's energetic economy. After yet another instance of proper civic hospitality with a public banquet, the queen enjoyed a mock battle in which the combatants stormed a fort with guns ablaze.[26] This ceremonial prelude established an image of Sandwich as a town worth maintaining: its people produced goods of value to the commonweal, they were key defenders of the realm against foreign invasion, and the entire community knew how to extend such hospitality to its monarch as would redound to the credit of both guest and host. With the symbolic background set, the message in the foreground appeared.

Mayor John Gilbert capped the occasion with his petition on behalf of all Sandwich's residents for help from the queen in repairing the town harbor. He handed the petition to Elizabeth and received her promise to attend closely to the contents. Showing he understood court politics and patronage, Mayor Gilbert then proceeded to shore up support for his request by approaching nobles in the progress retinue. He solicited the help of Lord Burghley, Lord Admiral Clinton, the earl of Sussex, and the earl of Leicester. When Elizabeth later read his petition, she would then be discussing the request with a group of her close advisors who had already undertaken to champion the citizens of Sandwich. Even though Gilbert deprived the ceremonial presentation of some of its force by not announcing the request before the assembled crowds, he did work behind the scenes to ensure a favorable judgment. To secure relief for their silted harbor, the citizens of Sandwich used both public and private dialogues.

The issue facing Elizabeth during her progress to Norfolk in 1578 concerned the use of the sea. A controversy of long standing over fishing rights had divided the towns of Great Yarmouth and Little Yarmouth. The citizens of Great Yarmouth had traditionally enjoyed a monopoly of fishing privileges in the harbor shared with its neighbor, Little Yarmouth. In 1570, however, the situation changed when the earl of Richmond led his tenants of Little Yarmouth in a legal challenge designed to end that monopoly. Their success won for the inhabitants of Little Yarmouth and nearby Gorleston manor the right to fish in the harbor and sell their catch as they pleased. When Elizabeth visited the area in 1578, therefore, the burgesses of Great Yarmouth sought access to the queen to overturn the ruling and regain their monopoly. While the queen remained in Norwich, her privy councilors visited Great Yarmouth where they learned of the contested fishing rights. After the queen's departure, the burgesses of Great Yarmouth secured an order from the Privy Council that returned control of the harbor to them. The sheriff and justices of the peace for Suffolk received notice that the order prohibited any Gorleston fish markets. The order of the Privy Council mandated that all merchandise, including herring and other fish, brought into the harbor be sold in Great Yarmouth; excepted was the catch in Gorleston and Little Yarmouth boats.[27] The private visit of several privy councilors to Great Yarmouth probably contributed to that town's successful appeal to the council in the following year. By using the opportunity of meeting with courtiers during the queen's progress, Great Yarmouth had prevailed in protecting its civic privileges.

In addition to harbors, towns tried to protect their special industries and traditional civic rights. In the middle of a trade depression that severely hit Bristol merchants in the 1560s and 1570s, the town entertained the queen during her 1574 progress. Trade had influenced many aspects of political life in Bristol. In 1571 the parliamentary election turned on the issue of trade monopolies held by the Merchant Adventurers, an economic advantage that antagonized other city traders. In their first session in London, the newly elected members for Bristol secured an act of Parliament that ended the monopoly of the Merchant Adventurers.[28] Civic expectations were dashed, however, when freer trade did not rejuvenate the town's economy, so civic leaders examined other causes of their distress. The Bristol merchants believed that the declining volume of exports and imports through Bristol's harbor reflected the stormy relations between England and the Iberian powers of Spain and Portugal. Accordingly, the Bristol community equated its economic prosperity with peaceful foreign relations.[29] During the week in which Elizabeth visited the city, the civic ceremonies pursued this message through the combined images of war, peace, military might, and royal mediation. The queen watched as the town staged a mock battle between the allegorical opponents War and Peace. With the background of fireworks, boats, and weapons, a figure personifying the city of Bristol spelled out the civic preference for stability: "Our Traed doth stand on sivill lief, and thear our glory lies; And not on strief, the ruen of staets, a storm that all destroys, A heavy bondage to eatch heart, that Freedom's fruit enjoys."[30] While the guns pounded two forts in the name of concord, the forces of Peace won the three-day battle with the assistance of the queen. The martial ceremony conveyed a request to the queen for the peace that would usher in economic security. The fruit of English freedom on the seas, in the eyes of merchants in Bristol, was the stability of peace. For Elizabeth's purposes, such fruit also included the possession of Spanish gold captured from the duke of Alva, which was the ostensible topic of the aptly named Treaty of Bristol.

Two years later, Bristol counted upon its reputation with Elizabeth in advancing a suit for more economic relief. In 1576 the town sought restitution for shipping losses that reached up to 13 ships and 5 barks, along with their cargos. By sending their chamberlain, Robert Halton, to London with a petition for the earl of Leicester, Bristol officials hoped to use a court favorite to persuade the queen of the suit's merit. They hoped that her previous visit, with its allegorical and personal appeals for aid, would incline the queen to act on their request. Unfortunately, while Elizabeth was "verie sorie" to hear of their losses, she did not translate that sympathy into hard money.[31] Such exchanges between town and sovereign frequently did not satisfy the petitioners, as in the case of Bristol, where the town's several requests brought only partial aid from the queen. The queen's visits to towns, however, enabled the civic groups to try to persuade her of their requests' worth even as they validated their own importance as a corporation through the process of petitioning.

Towns facing an economic decline found that entertaining the itinerant queen offered an arena in which to discuss solutions. The citizens of Stafford seized the opportunity of a progress visit in 1575 to address two major concerns about their local economy. During her visit, Elizabeth enquired about the reasons for the economic decay. City officials pointed to the troubled capping industry and the absence of the assizes from their main county town. They asked for protection of their craft's monopoly against foreign and domestic competition, and they wanted the business of justice for their corporation. In response, the queen promised to renew the statute for capping and agreed that the assizes should return to Stafford. As one of the older towns struggling against the economic troubles experienced by many towns earlier in the century, Stafford appealed directly to Elizabeth to redress their grievances. Whether this royal interest proved effective or whether an economic upsurge strengthened trade, Stafford enjoyed "a mild recovery during Elizabeth's reign."[32]

The once flourishing cloth trade in Worcester had also decayed during the 1570s, as Elizabeth heard in a similar suit from its citizens when she visited Worcester in 1575. The deputy recorder used his welcoming speech to the travelers to describe how the town's cloth trade had declined. The queen, he said, "shall see and fynde the wealth wasted and decayed, the bewty faded, the buylding ruin'd, the three hundred and fowerscore loomes of clothyng comen to the nomeber of one hundred and three score, and thereby above fyve thowsand persons, that were lately well wrought and relieved, now wantyng the same; so that of all that was, ther' is allmost nothyng lefte but a ruynous Citie, or decaied Antiquities." Town officials hoped that increased trade would revitalize their looms and that Elizabeth would protect their foreign ventures by challenging voracious pirates. In addition, Worcester officials wanted more legal protection of its important guilds. Elizabeth heard a petition from the bishop of Hereford for a charter incorporating the weavers, walkers, and clothiers of Worcester. The queen indicated that she understood the necessity of action to preserve a valued town of her realm. She liked "as well of them as I have liked of any people in all my progressive time in all my life," but despite her avowal of support, the town did not receive its charter for the guilds until 1590.[33] Another issue, however, did receive a more timely and favorable resolution. Like Stafford, Worcester wanted the courts relocated in the shire town. During the course of that 1575 progress through Worcestershire, Elizabeth and her ministers decided upon the "restitution to the old Corts to Worcester."[34] Worcester gained some success from its sustained petitions for the guild charter, the return of the courts, and trade concessions. The context of these requests was a series of processions, pageants, speeches, presentation of gifts, and civic entertainments. To judge from the mutual enjoyment of both royal guest and civic host, the ceremonial dialogue of that occasion brought about a satisfactory conclusion to the progress visit.

Towns received economic benefits from a progress visit in two ways: by ceremonially asking for it, and by absorbing it indirectly through local market activity. The arrival of the queen automatically stimulated the demand for goods and services and infused the local markets with scores of new buyers. Although the royal household took care of most supplies for the court on progress, the local civic economies supported the extraneous needs of the court. In addition to these straightforward market exchanges, towns also profited from having access to the queen to seek favors. Towns received direct grants of aid from the queen and subsidiary revenues from the members of the progress retinue who spent money in the locality. Although the presence of the queen could create problems for which communities and individuals sought restitution, in a more positive sense the presence of the court supercharged the local markets, as members of the progress retinue purchased goods and services from the area. Both the corporation and individual members of the community could reap economic benefits from the queen on progress.

Not surprisingly, the area most frequently affected by the infusion of court travelers was in the Thames River valley close to London. Because the queen spent long periods either in London or in a royal palace within 20 miles of the city, inhabitants of the capital felt the impact of repeated royal visits. They seemed to face the purveyors and cart takers on a regular basis, and the needs of the itinerant queen distorted their markets. Years of sporadic inconvenience from the progresses led citizens to appeal for monetary and regulatory relief. The inhabitants of Greenwich found that the queen's repeated trips to her palace there affected their businesses. Easy access by river made Greenwich popular with members of the court, who as temporary residents mingled in the Greenwich markets. While their presence increased the demand for goods and services, they strained the market beyond its capacity. In 1586 the bakers of Greenwich complained that the court was consuming all available grain, forcing them to buy at higher prices from the market three miles away at Gravesend.[35] The queen had been staying in the region for much of the summer and fall, and the court's consumption of foods was drying up local markets. The Greenwich bakers petitioned Lord Cobham for an exemption from the current market regulations governing the sale of corn. As evidence of the economic dislocation, the bakers cited the great numbers of strangers in Greenwich "by reasone nowe of her highnes continuance there." They understood the cause of their troubles and sought relief from the queen whose presence was creating them. In a similar suit in 1603, William Newland petitioned the household officers for compensation. Newland owned farmland near the queen's palace at Richmond. Because of the court's need for freshly killed meat, the barns that held Newland's grain were turned into temporary slaughterhouses for the queen during her lengthy and final stay at Richmond palace. He complained to the sergeant of the acatry that the queen's "contynuall coming" interfered with his farming and prevented him from enjoying the use of his property.[36] In recognition of the justice of his complaint, Newland received an annual fee in addition to his weekly one from the household. The household officers regularly granted dispensations from the orders that regulated the supplies at court. Both the royal household and the merchants recognized that the traveling court strained the markets for local goods, which encouraged them to reorganize the system.

Wherever Elizabeth stayed, her court gave a temporary boost to the local economy. Some of the people most pleased with her presence were the publicans who supplied the court with ale. Although beer remained tasty in storage up to a year, required fewer grains in the finished product, and cost less to produce, the weaker and perishable ale was the drink of choice at court because Elizabeth preferred it. In order to quench the queen's thirst, therefore, extra alehouses sprang up wherever the court traveled. During the progresses, the household officers issued licenses to tavern keepers giving them permission to make and supply ale. The court's demand for ale also brought business to the poorer tapsters who were never far from economic disaster. According to Peter Clark's study, poor people kept alehouses as a way of bringing in "an invaluable secondary income . . . as their principal bulwark against starvation."[37] For these folks living near the edge, the arrival of the court into their locality put money in their pockets and food on their tables. The value of these alehouse licenses lay in their income for the holders, the supply for the consumers, and the patronage controlled by the authorities. Through these licenses, both established and new alehouse keepers gained business from their courtly visitors.

Alehouses specially erected for the progresses received their licenses from the Board of Green Cloth. Outside of that special occasion, the justices of the peace ordinarily controlled the number of alehouses in a county by issuing them licenses. According to the regulatory act of 1552, the justices "within every shire, city, borough, town corporate, franchise or liberty within this realm" had the power "to remove, discharge and put away common selling of ale and beer in the said common ale-houses and tipplinghouses in such town or towns and places where they shall think meet and convenient."[38] This responsibility occupied much judicial time. Selling and brewing ale was a business easily entered into by people without much capital, so the justices had to be vigilant lest illegal houses spring up. The justices also watched that the "tippling-houses" did not harbor vagrants or criminals. Control of the alehouses was a central element in the local effort "to establish higher standards of social discipline" in the community.[39] In 1577 the Privy Council ordered all justices to make a survey of the number of alehouses in their jurisdiction so that the government could tax victuallers to pay for repairs to Dover harbor. But the government also wanted to know how much grain was going into the production of beer instead of the bread that would feed hungry, and possibly rebellious, subjects.[40] Whether people were drinking their nutrition instead of eating it, or plotting sedition within the safe confines of the tavern, the government did not want to let such activities continue freely.

Alehouses licensed for the court on progress, therefore, operated within restrictions of time and space. They existed only in the locality that received the queen, and their licenses expired with the departure of the court. In 1601 William Knollys as comptroller of the household issued a bill of recognizance to establish special alehouses in Greenwich for the duration of the queen's stay there. The bill listed the names of 35 men and one woman who had the authority to operate those alehouses. According to the license, the tavern keepers could not sell beer, ale, or bread in altered or lesser measurers than allowed by law; they also had to obey the price lists set by the clerk of the market. The standard prohibitions against dicing, gaming, and prostitution completed the list of rules.[41] In another recognizance for Greenwich alehouse keepers in May 1602, Knollys and the Board of Green Cloth authorized 21 men under the same conditions to keep alehouses. Because the principals listed had to have two other people sign as their sureties, many of the keepers stood as sureties for other principals; William Tomson's name appeared five times as a surety in addition to his own listing as a principal. Eleven people received licenses from both lists, and two others with the same surname probably had a family connection. Anyone who tried to avoid this legal process and sell ale without authorization faced indictment before the local assize judge.[42] The laws tried to ensure that alehouses did not proliferate beyond the time of the queen's visit and that those taverns sanctioned for her retinue collapsed with her remove.

The power to regulate the alehouses often bred disaffection as opponents contended for the right to issue licenses. This tension remained at its highest in the university towns of Cambridge and Oxford, which traditionally had poor relations between the "town and gown" elements. Before Elizabeth arrived in Cambridge in 1564, she had to settle a dispute between the corporation and the university over the power to license alehouses. The university claimed that the mayor of Cambridge was interfering with the school's ancient privileges of licensing tipplers and victuallers. The mayor defended his right to issue licenses under the statute giving that power to the justices of the peace. In a decision that pleased her scholastic host, Elizabeth recognized the special status of the university entitling it to an exemption from the regular statutory provisions. The university maintained its right to control alehouses within its liberties, as the mayor received a royal order not to "intermeddle" in those affairs again.[43]

Pleased by this royal support, university officials must have blessed their fortune when the queen, during that same visit, seemed ready to expand her economic aid beyond alehouses. During her speech to the University of Cambridge faculty, Elizabeth praised the "sumptuous edifices, erected by several most illustrious princes, my ancestors," that graced the collegiate grounds. Carried away by their stone splendor, the queen spontaneously vowed to build a monument in her name that would match past royal generosity, promising that "from this design, as long as I have any life left, I shall never depart."[44] But this queen who built no palaces founded no colleges either. Her intent was partially realized, at least, by the less publicized actions of a member of her court. As the retinue departed, the duke of Norfolk stepped in to fill the queen's financial shoes. He made a gift of £40 to the fellows of Magdalene College and promised the same sum as an annuity for the college to erect buildings. Through his semiprivate act, the duke of Norfolk recognized the civic and scholastic claims of the host town and subsidized the public ceremony of Elizabeth. Because the queen remained the center of ritual attention during her visit, however, the duke's gesture, coming at the occasion's denouement, did not shift the focus from the queen. In a deft maneuver, the queen claimed the credit through her domination of the public ceremony without having to pay out the moneys to make good on that promise. So through indirect patronage, such as Norfolk's gift, or direct aid from alehouse licenses, the queen financially supported the university community while giving it a victory in its frequent contests with the municipal government. The overall economic impact of the progresses on any community was considerable.

While many town officials forthrightly asked Elizabeth for royal aid, only a few seem to have asked her to arbitrate local grievances. In general, the desire of civic hosts to preserve a corporate image of communal solidarity and status within the region curbed the divisive tongues of local officials. To show her the merits of their town, entertain her well, and ask for favors was one thing; to air the unresolved arguments that fractured the image of civic concord was another. Elizabeth typically faced a delegation of welcoming townspeople whose actions and clothing emphasized the ceremonial inclusion of the visiting monarch within a stable civic community. With all the care taken to hide wandering pigs and madmen from the queen's eyes, town leaders did not eagerly spotlight local controversies that, with their suggestions of civic disunity, might deter the queen from granting aid.

In a few cases, however, civic hosts shed their caution and laid a public problem before Elizabeth for a royal verdict. The town of Coventry regularly used Elizabeth to settle local problems and appealed to her for arbitration. The corporation sought Elizabeth's views on three divisive issues: the operation of a grammar school, the propriety of its Hock Tuesday play, and the fate of a mayor charged with manslaughter. She heard the first two of these suits while staying in Coventry, and the third while on progress through Hampshire. Through their persistence and direct approach, the citizens of Coventry took advantage of their increased access to Elizabeth during the progresses to receive a royal judgment. For Coventry, the risks of displaying civic tensions were less important than having solutions to their problems.

During her visit to Coventry for three days in August 1566, Elizabeth heard about the problems with the town's grammar school.[45] After the mayor's ceremonial welcome, John Throckmorton, the town recorder, broached the topic of the school and outlined the problem in his oration to the queen. "For the better education of the youth of this City in virtue and learning," her father, Henry VIII, had founded a free school. Despite that act, the school was starving for funds because "sinister, underhand, unjust means" had prevented the city from using the income for that purpose. Throckmorton acted on behalf of the city in appealing to Elizabeth for royal justice: "for redress whereof the Mayor and Commonalty of this City most humbly beseech your Majesty to give gracious hearing to their further complaint."[46] The queen approached him afterward with words of praise, and the oratorical skill of Throckmorton moved Elizabeth to consider his request. After the welcoming ceremonies ended, Elizabeth rode to the free school and made a monetary present to the town for its upkeep.

The queen, according to observers, was "extremely incensed" at the destruction of the free school. She ordered Burghley to investigate the charges leveled by Throckmorton and the Coventry officials. The history of the school's foundation explained the confusion. In 1545 Henry VIII had granted the lands of the dissolved St. John's Hospital in Coventry to his clerk of the hanaper, John Hales. In the grant, the king intended to include a provision requiring Hales to establish and maintain a school there with some of the income from the hospital's lands. Hales argued that the designated sum of 4 marks per annum would be too small to support a school, so he made a counterproposal to the king: he offered to give 12 marks annually to support a school provided that the king omit written reference to that condition in the grant. By this clever ruse, which ended up being a gentleman's agreement between king and subject, Hales freed himself to abandon the school entirely without breaking the law. Hales did operate a school for a few years, but soon he began diverting the funds into his own coffers. The city discovered the embezzlement and engaged in an angry but unsuccessful battle to force Hales into compliance with the intent of the grant. Because Throckmorton and the Coventry officials believed that the grant mandated the foundation of a school, they felt justified in complaining to the queen about its abrogation. Any hesitation they might have felt at a public attack on a former court official faded in the context of Hales's rocky relationship with Elizabeth. His support of the secret marriage between Catherine Grey and the earl of Hertford in 1563 had angered the queen. For this offense, Hales spent a year in prison and lived under house arrest almost until his death in 1572.[47] Thus, the citizens of Coventry were blaming an unpopular official for depriving the community of a worthy, needed asset.

Such a complaint, even within the ceremonial moment of public unity, did not seem too risky to the people of Coventry. Because Hales had few local supporters, Coventry's unified commitment to the school enabled civic leaders to air their concerns without fear of harming the town's image. The problem with Hales's school did not reflect poorly on the city because the issue had not divided the community: his offense had hurt the community at large and, therefore, should earn him royal censure. In addition, he was not a favored courtier of the queen, which left him vulnerable to an appeal from the citizens over his head to Elizabeth. Hopeful of the queen's support after her visit, the Coventry officials petitioned the Privy Council but received little satisfaction until Hales's death in 1572. After his will failed to establish funds for the free school, the citizens of Coventry took the issue to Parliament and secured the passage of an act in 1583 that restored the Coventry school.[48] Although the resolution of the school issue came years after the queen visited Coventry, the city took the first step by grabbing the queen's attention as she stood in the town center. Mayor Brownell and Recorder Throckmorton seized the opportunity of her visit to present their petition directly to Elizabeth and to show her the school. The drama of that confrontation eventually paid benefits to the citizens of Coventry.

The second request from Coventry to the queen concerned the entertainment during her 1566 visit, and again in 1575, when she stayed at nearby Kenilworth with the earl of Leicester. As a traditional center of dramatic activity with the medieval Corpus Christi cycle, Coventry also boasted its own Hock Tuesday play, which it wanted to perform before Elizabeth. The play celebrated the victory of Coventry citizens over the Danes in 1002. During that supposed battle, the English women of Coventry had defended their homes against the foreign invaders. A key element in the commemorative play was that the women trussed up their "Danish" captives whom they held for ransom.[49] The play was popular because it extolled the courage of the citizens; it was important because its performance gave the women of Coventry, who had no role in the guilds or any important civic body, a fleeting moment of public involvement in civic society.[50] The pervasive inequalities concerning sex, wealth, and status in Coventry lessened briefly as the carnival atmosphere of the role reversals allowed some tension to escape and temporarily redrew gender relations. The Coventry show, as Lawrence Manley found in London civic pageants, provided an opportunity for citizens to refashion and enhance the history of their community.[51]

Despite the popularity and tradition of the play, in 1561 "was Hox tuesday put down," probably for religious reasons. Although Coventry citizens had performed the play for years without incident, or "without ill exampl of mannerz, papistry, or any superstition," now certain interfering ministers had branded it harmful. The increasingly Protestant outlook of the Elizabethan clergy made some more eager to attack unorthodox dramas and players. Banning the play grieved the townspeople because they could find no good reason for such a drastic action. They "knu no cauz why onless it wear by the zeal of certain theyr Preacherz: men very commendabl for their behaviour and learning, & sweet in their sermons, but sumwhat too sour in preaching awey theyr pastime."[52] The "sour" preachers were depriving the community of a ceremonial display of their civic history and reputation. In petitioning the queen for permission to revive the play for her, the town of Coventry was counting on Elizabeth's love of such entertainments to persuade her to act as their champion. They might also have suspected that the queen would enjoy a show depicting women who took up arms in defense of their country and physically triumphed over men. They judged their monarch well: Elizabeth insisted upon a performance of the Hock Tuesday play in 1566 when she visited Coventry. A popular local festival under attack by a small segment of the town had needed defending by the larger community. By reviving the play after suppression for five years, the town was reaffirming, for the moment, their traditional community standards. The visit of Elizabeth in 1566 offered an ideal opportunity to raise the issue before a sympathetic judge.

Because the queen championed the Hock Tuesday play and enjoyed other pageants during that same visit, her royal support revivified these provincial dramas and helped save them, temporarily, from the suppression that occurred in the York and Chester cycles.[53] Like other communal pageants and feasts, such as May Day and Corpus Christi, the Hock Tuesday shows were losing their meaning and vitality during the later sixteenth century. In part, the erosion of ceremony reflected the economic tensions in

urban and guild life, according to Phythian-Adams, that arose from growing "class loyalties," but the role of religious attitudes should not be dis-
counted.[54] Through a combination of religious and political tensions, such
ceremonies had come under a dual attack from local elites concerned with
order and puritanical reformers determined to purge the new church of
any remnants of the old Catholic ritual calendar.[55] The Coventry controversy suggests how religious differences ultimately altered the local obser-
vance of secular and religious ceremonies. By trying to perform the play in
the years after her last visit, the citizens of Coventry sought to preserve a
form of communal celebration that others, Hutton argues, were abandon-
ing. Elizabeth shared in their efforts, as they put on the Hock Tuesday
play "by the commaundment of the Quenes Counsell" in 1566 and 1575.[56]
Although the rich ceremonial life was declining throughout England by
the end of her reign, Elizabeth was able in Coventry, for a time, to protect
a locally important public festival.

The third time that Coventry traded upon its hospitality in seeking a
favor from Elizabeth followed shortly upon the Hock Tuesday episode.
Two years after her decision on the play, Elizabeth favored the town by
granting to the mayor, bailiffs, and community of Coventry the monopoly
on the manufacture of woolen cloths, "ulterfynes and cromple lysts," usually imported from Flanders.[57] With those favors freshly in mind, the Coventry councilors naturally turned to the queen when a legal tangle developed around the mayor in 1568. Mayor John Harford was walking his dogs
while William Heley, an embroiderer, passed by with his spaniel. When
the dogs began to fight, Heley tried to separate them and save his dog.
Mayor Harford, however, resented Heley's interference in the canine combat and set to beating the unfortunate embroiderer into neutrality. During
the melee, Harford's blows killed Heley. For this crime, the council of Coventry deprived Harford of his mayoralty and arraigned him on charges of
manslaughter. The council then named butcher John Saunders to serve as
mayor until the next regular election. After taking these actions, the aldermen solicited the opinion of town recorder John Throckmorton. When
Throckmorton doubted the legality of Harford's deprivation and Saunders's selection under the corporation charter, Coventry officials turned to
higher authorities. They queried the Privy Council as to the propriety of
their actions against the violent mayor. To deliver their request, the town
sent Edmund Brownell "with all speed" to the traveling government. This
wise choice of messenger indicated the tactful role assumed by the aldermen. Elizabeth and some of the privy councilors had already met Edmund
Brownell during their progress visit to Coventry in 1566, when Brownell
was the mayor who welcomed them.[58] Two years later, the town was hoping that both the message and the messenger would attract royal attention,

and they did. The matter of mayoral manslaughter interested both the council and Elizabeth, who learned of the news from the earl of Leicester. During her progress visit to Southampton in September 1569, Elizabeth sent her decision to Coventry. The queen ordered Harford, then in "ward," to have a fair trial under the "ordinarye course of Justice" without regard to his station. She also concurred in the town's decision to deprive Harford and select Saunders as interim mayor. Thus far the aldermen's actions had met with her approval. Admonishing them not to let her letter prejudice the proceedings against Harford, Elizabeth requested that the council keep her informed as the trial began. She especially was concerned that any sentence of death be delayed until they notified her. If Harford, she wrote, "shall deserve deathe, our meaning is that before any execucion be therefore done, you should certifie us of your proceadinges in the triall." Harford was found guilty of manslaughter but escaped death by striking an agreement with Heley's widow and the council. He promised to pay Mrs. Heley considerable damages; in exchange, he "had his Pardon which cost him very much." By way of further punishment, Harford could never serve as an alderman or magistrate, and he lost his livery.[59]

The importance of this episode lies in the actions taken by the officials of Coventry in approaching the queen. Elizabeth did not allude to these past visits when she was considering the Harford case, as far as we know, but the connection between her entertainments there, the several civic petitions, and the queen's later interest in Coventry suggest that she knew the townspeople well. The people of Coventry had met Elizabeth during her visit in 1566 and had impressed her with their devotion and enthusiasm for their Hock Tuesday play. This relationship paid dividends several years later when the council was questioning its treatment of Mayor Harford: the town had access to the queen, could easily present its petition, and received a favorable hearing at court through the patronage of their lord, the earl of Leicester. Coventry planned its campaign well. It sought advice from a popular and well-connected town recorder and used a mayor known to Elizabeth as its messenger to her court. Both John Throckmorton and Edmund Brownell helped put the town in the best possible light. The care and planning that went into this petition and the other suits about the free school and the play showed the significance civic leaders attached to the queen's visit.

Not every town had such a close and continuous relationship with Elizabeth as did Coventry, whose petitions over 10 years kept the queen apprised of corporate events, but any royal visit encouraged civic hosts to consider what favors they might solicit from the queen. From harbor repairs to aid for local industries, the towns tried to benefit from the queen's decision to stop there on her progress. These requests and petitions indicated that the progresses extended opportunities for subjects and towns alike to communicate their desires directly to the sovereign. Coventry used its petitions not only to secure particular favors but also to maintain its reputation with Elizabeth. Underlying all these issues was the sense of corporate identity that enabled the councilors and citizens to ask for royal assistance while they offered the proper ceremonies of inclusion binding queen and town.

CIVIC IMAGE AND CEREMONIAL DIALOGUE

Beyond these tangible, economic motives of civic hospitality was the role that the royal progresses played in enabling towns to construct and preserve their corporate identity.[60] Through the ceremonies that welcomed the queen—the pageantry, processions, speeches, and gifts—the civic hosts drew together their community to express a unity in the face of their visiting monarch. The presence of the queen encouraged citizens to work together because the entire town, not one person, acted as her host during those progresses. As Elizabeth enhanced her queenly image and the town sought favors from her, they engaged in a "ceremonial dialogue" that included movements, processions, costumes, gifts, entertainments, and speeches. The public exchange of messages between the queen and local officials, merchants, and ordinary people occurred in the ceremony created by these participants to contain such a plurality of voices. Even when the ritual was challenged by a spontaneous interruption or withdrawal, the tensions highlighted the power of the original ceremony and confirmed the value of such communication. The ceremonial dialogue allowed the queen and her hosts to magnify each other's place in society and government while validating their own importance in the larger outside world.

Visibility and a public audience served both queen and town during the progresses. Townspeople extended to the visiting court a public hospitality that set the context for their petitions and their own civic image, while Elizabeth accepted their hospitality, which provided a background for her display of prerogative powers. These interlacing designs of host and guest required a public arena and open display through which the royal icon evoked popular support and the towns remade themselves spatially and visually as a worthy civic body. Through costume, movements, speeches, and presentations, the host and guest fashioned a message of images.[61] Because the ceremony was the message, guest and host each tried to control the ceremonial agenda. Even when the ritual was challenged or warped, the interruption reinforced the power of the original ceremony as the participants headed back to their original script and roles. This script had words, but equally meaningful were the ritual actions and arrangement of costumed officials performing a tableau of civic self-definition that drew a responding message from the participating queen.

The ceremonial communication between ruler and ruled frequently depended on a mobile monarch displayed before a large body of citizenry, as in royal processions and royal progresses. In his studies of Renaissance Florence, Richard Trexler has focused on the ceremonial rules that framed relations between the city and its foreign guests.[62] When a visiting dignitary entered Florence, a delicate and precise maneuvering began. According to the Florentine view of diplomacy, these visits were part of the city's foreign policy: how the city displayed its power before the visitor would determine in what esteem the foreigner would hold Florence. In addition, the image held by Florentines of their own city was crafted through the ceremonies welcoming foreign visitors. The crowds judged how important their visitors were by how many steps the Florentine officials descended before greeting the newcomers. The more illustrious the guest, the farther down the staircase came the welcoming committee; conversely, waiting at the top of the platform while the guest approached up the stairs was a sign from the Florentine rulers to their citizens of their guest's relatively low status. A similar use of space, although not so regularized and canonized, occurred during the entertainments of Elizabeth in her English towns.

This orchestrated ceremony expressed a relationship between ruler and subjects. The most notable ceremonial dialogue in England was the coronation entry of monarchs into London, which developed into a religious courtship between citizens and ruler.[63] Their union occurred during the ruler's ceremonial progression along special streets with stops for instructive pageants. Mediating between the crowds and monarch as a "symbolic buffer," Malcolm Smuts argues, were the liveried companies in their robes, whose central position indicated their civic importance.[64] Another exchange of ritual messages occurred in the ceremony created by the queen's meetings with members of Parliament. The two sides used numbers, location, patterns of speech, and clothing to display their status and constitutional role.[65] In a literary example from 1597, *Jacke of Newberie,* Thomas Deloney depicted a progress of Henry VIII, who finds his way blocked by Jacke and other armed weavers who have taken over an anthill to protest royal taxes. Refusing to come down from the hill to parley with Henry, Jacke in a "violation of ceremonial space" forces the king to come to him and so renegotiates briefly the "traditional patterns of deference between subject and monarch."[66] Moving and standing, approaching and receiving, ascending and descending, all were physical actions that revealed political realities.

Ceremonial rules governed the civic receptions of the visiting monarch.

In some ways, Elizabeth was a "foreign" guest who crossed legal and social borders by entering the liberties of the town. The welcoming entertainments allowed the civic officials to recognize the high status of the monarch even as they stressed their local prestige and loyalty. In 1432 the ceremonies marking the entry of Henry VI into London conjured up displays of the royal authority that the young king lacked in reality.[67] That communal support characterized the receptions given by citizens of York for Henry VI, Richard III, and even Henry VII. The York pageant in 1486 for the conquering Tudor's visit to that Yorkist bastion included the town's mythical founder, Ebrauk, red and white roses, and the six past King Henrys in a civic expression of dynastic support.[68] In Victor Turner's analysis, each party, through such a structure and sense of communitas, "safeguards [its] uniqueness in the very act of realizing their commonness."[69] The public ceremonies began the process of inclusion that brought the queen from the world beyond the town limits into the focal point of civic life, the town center.

The welcoming process that carried the queen across the civic threshold began at the liberties or borders of the town, where town officials greeted her. Forming the images of status and power were the colors, luxurious cloths, approaches and lowerings, groups of people and animals, lights, and tools of office that characterized most of these royal welcomes. In 1566 the city of Coventry sent out sheriffs Julius Hearing and William Wilkes to meet Elizabeth at the edge of town nearest Woolvey. The retinue included 20 "young men" in purple livery, which contrasted boldly with the sheriffs' scarlet robes. The entire group was on horseback. Carrying their white rods of office to give into the queen's hand and receive back from her, the party rode before Elizabeth to Coventry.[70] At Warwick in 1572, the bailiff, town recorder, and burgesses considered it "their bounden duty to attend her Hieghnes at the uttermost confynes of their Libertye." At three in the afternoon, Elizabeth and Lady Warwick drove through the mud "as nere as the coache could be brought nyege to the place" where the Warwick men waited. There the kneeling officials watched as Elizabeth opened wide the carriage doors "that all her subjects present might behold her, which most gladly they desired." The bailiff handed his mace to the queen, which she held during the town recorder's speech and returned afterward to the bailiff. The cavalcade then moved toward the city "with as good speded as they might, and in order rode two and two togither before her Majestie" from the hill to the castle gate.[71] The scene at Worcester in 1575 was similar, except that the queen had a late evening arrival. When her horse reached the liberties, the queen faced a sizable crowd of civic representatives: in addition to the 2 bailiffs, 2 aldermen, the high chamberlain, and a stand-in for the town recorder, there were 12 former bailiffs and at least 50 councilors or aldermen. While the assembled crowd knelt before the queen's horse, each officer of Worcester yielded her "in grateful words and feir speeches" the liberties of the city and followed their words with action by presenting their maces to Elizabeth and receiving them back from her. Bailiff Christopher Dighton extended the ritual by "kyssing his mace" before the queen accepted it, "wch she, bowing her body towards hym, rec'd with a cheerful countenance, and sd, 'It was very well.'"[72] As all knelt, the mounted queen heard an oration of welcome by William Bell before passing into the town center. The initial confrontation between visitor and hosts was colored with hospitality and ritual to emphasize their status, rights, and mutual regard.

The "words" in this ceremonial dialogue were movements, colors, relative sizes and heights, ritual objects, and also the speeches themselves. In his study of political power and ritual, David Kertzer suggests that "ritual can be seen as a form of rhetoric, the propagation of a message through a complex symbolic performance."[73] The rhetoric of the progresses created a conversation between civic pageantry and royal iconography, a dialogue that intertwined the compatible but different messages of queen and townspeople. In an unusual choreography, the queen moved toward her subjects rather than having them approach her. Practical considerations obviously affected the issue of who came and who waited. A progress by definition was the sustained movements of the queen from one host to the next; towns could not uproot their structures and come to her. Embassies of civic officials did carry messages to the court in London but were of necessity pale imitations of the bustling reality of spires, stones, and humanity in their civic home. Nonetheless, the physical openness of the queen as she came into the host community was an important aspect of the political relationship between monarch and subjects that the queen was cultivating, and the hosts sharing, through the institution of progresses. By riding or driving toward the waiting body of town officials, Elizabeth reversed the ceremonial order of stationary monarch and approaching, supplicating subjects. Instead of petitioners moving through the public rooms at court to more private royal quarters where a restricted group had an audience with the queen, Elizabeth traveled to these towns in order to display herself and to participate in an open exchange of messages.

The lavish welcome that built up Elizabeth's image as omnipotent ruler also redounded to the town's credit in a dynamic that magnified the reputation of both town and queen. The vivid colors of the officials' gowns marked that body as special, drawing all eyes to them. Riding out on horseback enlarged the appearance of the group, as it spread out over a wider amount of land and rose above the ground, and suggested a healthy prosperity and energy. Exchanging the mace and rods of office between their holders and the queen evoked the historical claims of English monarchs to rule the entire country through local officers responsible to them. The dominance of the queen appeared also in her elevated and separate position, whether sitting on horseback, in her open coach, or standing before the crowd. She physically was apart from and higher than the dismounted, kneeling committee that bent its civic authority before her. Finally, the body of civic officials would literally surround the queen as they formed a train before and after her. She was in the center of the moving group, which with their bodies had incorporated her into their midst even before the retinue had reached the town center for additional ceremonies of inclusion. The queen had first become a part of the group of civic leaders, who were then presenting her as a member of the community to the townspeople for a popular welcome into the larger corporation.

All the elements of these first contacts between queen and city described their relationship through striking tableaux and movements so that the ordinary observer, as well as the official participants, would understand what was happening. Communicating with the bystanders was often the most important accomplishment that Elizabeth took away from her progress visits, which meant that the pageantry carrying her message could not be only elitist.[74] In private entertainments, such as at Kenilworth, she could elevate her dialogue by adopting a mythical persona and by addressing figures from classical antiquity, but these cultural, linguistic, and literary allusions would not touch everyone in the public, heterogeneous arena of the town. Educated civic leaders would draw greater meaning from classical references than would craftsmen. But the variety of allusions and symbols meant that everyone could appreciate different, if not all, parts of the ceremonial welcome. Her audience gave to the ceremonial dialogue its guidelines and its context, which was why Elizabeth's progresses were so successfully a part of her government. She knew how to converse with her civic audiences through their common language of visual and spatial symbolism.

As the officials led Elizabeth from the outskirts into the town square, the ceremonial dialogue highlighted the queen's natural place in the civic world and the town's generous hospitality. The most direct way for the town to indicate its prosperity and welcome was to give gifts to the queen and key members of her retinue. According to Felicity Heal, "corporations expected to give, rather than to receive, the treat that lubricated relations between themselves and the elite."[75] The gift expressed tangibly the bond between town and monarch, and, unlike a tax, it was freely given. A monetary offering nestled in a beautiful cup was the usual choice, but equally important were the accompanying words that asserted civic loyalty while denigrating the amount of coin. Coventry gave Elizabeth a purse with £100 of angels, a lavish effort which she recognized in her thanks to Mayor Brownell ("I have but few such" gifts). In the choice of coin, also called the angel-noble, the town made a graceful gesture that evoked Elizabeth's religious authority: the queen who defended her kingdom on earth held in her hands golden images of the archangel Michael killing a dragon. The mayor, however, diminished the gold by praising the "harts of all your true loveing subjects" also contained in the purse, which Elizabeth quickly recognized as "Indeed a greate deale more."[76] The human heart displaced the angelic face.

When the bailiff of Warwick presented her with a purse of £20 in sovereigns, Elizabeth swore she was "unwilling to tak any thing of you, because I knowe that a myte of their haunds is as much as a thowsand pounds of some others." She accepted it only because it represented "their good wills." The beleaguered city of Worcester scraped together £50 for a covered silver cup ("the fairest that mought be found in London") full of sovereigns, a "small porc'on" and "simple presents" which they hoped Elizabeth in her "prynceley benygnytie" would accept.[77] She did. In accepting their gifts, Elizabeth was receiving good hearts, good wills, and by extension of imagery, loyalty. Her subjects rendered metallic images of the queen on the sovereign coins to the living sovereign before them as token of their loyalty. This verbal and symbolic dance united the giver and the recipient in a display of loyalty and favor through the ceremony of gift giving.

The monetary gift was but a small part of the more significant negotiations for royal favor that each town expected during a progress visit. The ceremony of inclusion that characterized the queen's arrival at the liberties of the town, bonding visitor and community, was a necessary prelude to the major request. Before the hosts could petition their guest, they had to establish the lines of loyalty and mutual regard that cleared the way for the larger request. Everyone knew how the script should read, and Elizabeth in particular expected such appeals. She thanked the people of Warwick for their gift, "praying God that I may perform, as Mr. Recorder saith, such benefyt as is hopid."[78] Her recognition of the ceremonial agenda underscored the exchange of favors expected during a civic visit.

Both town officials and the entire urban populace created the rituals of inclusion that made Elizabeth part of the civic community. Realizing that a lavish display of civic hospitality spread abroad the good name of their town, residents found visual ways to show their pride in entertaining the queen. Without this nonofficial participation of the larger body of citizenry, the queen would have entered the town in silence and obscurity. For the ceremonial dialogue to exist, an involved observing crowd needed to fill the civic arena. While ordinary citizens did not make speeches to the queen, they did extend a collective welcome to her through their actions.

Looking around her, the queen could read the message from Coventry on the bodies of its citizens: "the popular course of the inhabitants, their greedy taste for your Majesty, the ways and streets filled with company of all ages, desirous of having the fruition of your blessed countenance, the divers shews and stages provided to the utmost of their powers, as not satisfied with one sight of your Royal person; the houses and habitations themselves, lately arisen from their naked barns to a more lively and fresh furnitures, doth sufficiently declare . . . the joyful hearts, the singular affections, the ready and humble good-will of us your true, poor, hearty subjects."[79] It is hard to see how, as Jonathan Goldberg argues, Elizabeth wielded all the ceremonial power and orchestrated the interactions during her entries.[80] The actions of her civic hosts also shaped the ceremony and turned it from a monologue into an exchange of messages.

The same strains came from Warwick, whose "deutifull hartes can shew themselves by externall signes and testymonyes" in the whitewashed houses, clean streets, painted gates, and cheering crowds.[81] Worcester also scrubbed its face to make a good impression upon the queen. The council issued a set of detailed orders that included: painting the gates "in some decent color" with the queen's arms; removing "any donghills or myskyns and timber" from the streets and paving them with gravel; whitelyming all residences "with comeley colours"; and painting the queen's arms in the guildhall and the crosses outside. The commonalty would pay for these and other preparations through a special tax levied by ward. The successful results did impress Elizabeth, who saw Worcester's "heavy hartes . . . now in happy hope" with her arrival late in the evening: "the people, being innumerable, in the streets and Churchyard" cried "God save yr Majestie!" and "every howse in the street having both candles in lanterns, torches and candles burning on every side . . . gave a marvelous light." Exiting the town later, Elizabeth found "the streets beyng replenyshed with people, cryeing to her Majestie, and praying for her, and also she cheerfully and comfortably speaking to the people, and thanks gevyng with a lowd voice."[82] With much energy and effort, the townspeople created a visual, lively message of welcome that was crucial to a successful dialogue between Elizabeth and the town's official leaders: the separate voices of the elite and the populace were united in their civic message.

Such public acclamation, however, did not convey a specific request to the queen. For that, the town relied upon its officials, and the town recorder in particular, who made a public speech of welcome and petition before the assembled crowds in the town center. Despite the different local circumstances and requests, civic speeches to the queen had a common structure, rhetoric, and even occasionally a common author, as in the case of John Throckmorton, who as town recorder greeted Elizabeth in both

Coventry and Worcester. In the typical construction, the speech framed the request within the context of the town's illustrious history, marked by direct royal aid on many occasions, and the recorder saved the specific favor for his conclusion, where that desire mingled with the town's display of continued affection for the queen. Elizabeth heard in Coventry, Warwick, and Worcester how her royal predecessors had long favored these towns by protecting their liberties and fostering trade. The Coventry town recorder's speech opened with the image of England's "politic body" thriving under the healthy and strong leadership of its "head and chief governor."[83] After such long prosperity, however, each town had fallen on hard times and now needed royal assistance. Of these three areas, Worcester claimed to suffer a more serious, sustained economic slump. Having established a worthy civic image and the precedent as well as their need for aid, the town officials then presented a specific request for direct, immediate royal action. Concluding remarks emphasized the towns' confidence in their own future and, of course, Elizabeth's. Every aspect of the ceremonial dialogue from the time the queen entered the town's liberties had pointed toward this public exchange of verbal messages.

Because ceremony gave a structure to the queen's visit and shaped the town's pageantry of welcome and entertainment, the interactions between royal guest and urban host could appear to take on a cloak of staginess or predestination. But while the ceremonies fit into a pattern repeated from town to town, surprises and accidents frequently occurred to strain, interrupt, and alter the planned ceremonial exchange of messages. That both parties of this exchange depended on ceremony was evident in those moments when the system broke down. The spontaneous reactions not coded in the ritual script took the players from that uncertainty back to the structure and guidance of the original story line. From problems with the weather, confusion about the roads, spontaneous repartee, and political tensions, these breaks in the ceremony created risky openings but memorable moments. These moments of minor chaos and disorder yielded to the stronger desire on everyone's part for the familiar ceremony.

Something as mundane as the English weather could destroy the carefully laid plans for the queen's welcome and force the participants to improvise. Both townspeople and queen through mutual efforts kept the ceremonial show going. Because the day was "well spent" when Elizabeth arrived at Kenilworth, the queen could not see the series of nature gods bearing gifts that led up to the castle gate, nor could she make out the new coat of arms and poem painted on it. Lest this effort go to waste, the poet himself appeared and described "everie prezent as he spake . . . and how the posts might agree with the speech" of his poem. Fireworks more appropriately closed this stage of Elizabeth's darkened welcome. Constant rain during that same visit forced the cancellation of George Gascoigne's masque: "being prepared and redy (every Actor in his garment) two or three days together," the show "never came to execution" for "lack of opportunity and seasonable weather."[84] The welcoming committee from Warwick almost missed the queen's arrival entirely a few years earlier. The bailiff and burgesses awaited Elizabeth on the road from Ichington, where she was having lunch. Because "the weather having bene very fowle [a] long tyme before, and the way much staynid with carriage, her Majesty was led an other way."[85] The surprised officials, "having word" of the queen's new route, hurried off to intercept her so that they could perform "their bounden duety to attend her Hieghnes at the uttermost confynes of their Libertye." All were properly arranged, kneeling in the mud, when the queen's coach appeared. Another steady drizzle had turned the road to mud during her visit to Worcester, but this time the queen altered the ceremonial dialogue at her departure. When the elegantly attired bailiffs and aldermen were about to dismount "to have doone their duties on their knees" before Elizabeth as custom dictated, "for that the ways wer fowle, her Majestie said unto them, 'I pray you, keep your horses, and do not alight.'"[86] On this occasion, unlike other mucky times, the queen suspended the ritual to indicate her pleasure with her cordial hosts. Despite inconveniences that dampened these visits, the hosts did not wait for sunlight, return to the town, or try to protect their clothing. On a practical level, the wet and muddy hosts could not simply abandon Elizabeth because of the bad weather; on a theoretical level, their actions worked to advance the ceremony. Both queen and hosts acted together to keep intact the ceremonial structure that gave meaning to the event.

In addition to such acts of God, lesser mortal mishaps jostled the ceremonial agenda. A dispute arose in Warwick over the right to escort the queen from the liberties through the town to the castle. As a baron and high sheriff in the shire, Henry Compton "wold have carried up his rod [mace] into the Towne, which was forbidden him by the Heralds and Gentlemen Ushers," who preferred that honor to go to the town bailiff. Bailiff Philippes "rode into the Castell, still carrieng his mace" according to the herald's orders.[87] The town official took precedence over an important local magnate, as the queen's heralds recognized the legal and ritual rights held by the civic hosts. A more noticeable hitch occurred in 1575, when the people of Coventry went to Elizabeth at Kenilworth for permission to revive their famous Hock Tuesday play, recently banned but which she had once seen and liked. The townspeople considered the play, with its brave women vanquishing foreign invaders, especially appropriate for Elizabeth: "for becauz the matter mencioneth how valiantly our English women for loove of their countree behaved themselvez, expressed in actionz and rymez after their manner, they thought it moought moove sum myrth to her Majestie the rather." When the queen asked to see them perform, the Coventry citizens staged their battle with enthusiasm, firing guns and having the women tie up and conquer the men. Unfortunately, however, Elizabeth's attention had wandered from them to the competing—and boisterously violent—bridale below her window. When everyone realized that she had seen "but a littl of the Coventree Plea," Elizabeth "commaunded thearfore on the Tuesday following to have it full oout: az accordingly it was prezented, whereat her Majestie laught well."[88] And publicly. The queen made amends to the community with a gift of money and deer, both public and tangible offerings, but most important was the public attention she gave to the restaged play. Through her noted expression of interest, the queen was restored to her proper role as engaged participant in the civic festivities in her honor.

Elizabeth had to make amends for a more serious accident that befell the celebrants of her 1572 visit to Warwick. The earl of Warwick sponsored a mock battle (with battering rams and mortars brought from the Tower in London) between local men and the honored earl of Oxford. The sides exchanged shots and fireworks, "terrible to those that have not bene in like experiences, valiant to such as delighted therin, and in dede straunge to them that understood it not; for the wildfyre falling into the ryver Aven, wold for a tyme lye still, and than agayn rise and flye abroade, casting furth many flashes and flambes, whereat the Quene's Majesty took great pleasure" from her perch in Warwick Castle. But disaster loomed. "Whether by negligence or otherwise, it happned that a ball of fyre fell on a house" of Henry Cowper and his wife, who barely escaped the burning timbers. Fireballs "did so flye quiet over the Castell, and into the myds of the Towne, falling downe, some on houses, some in courts and baksides, and some in the streate . . . to the great perill, or else great feare, of the inhabitants." In all, four houses burned to the ground, and a ball shot through a fifth before the "fyre [was] appesid, [and] it was tyme to goo to rest." The ceremonial battle to amuse the queen had unexpectedly turned on the spectators, and the visitors quickly tried to repair the damage to property and emotions. A group of courtiers, including the earl of Oxford and Sir Fulke Greville, fought the fires that night. The next day Elizabeth had "the poore old man and woman that had their house brent brought unto her . . . recomfortid [them] very much, and, by her Grace's bounty, and other courtiers," gave the couple £25 for their pain and loss.[89] Royal sympathy and coin together represented Elizabeth's attempt to return to the time before the blaze, and in order to do so she had to assume responsibility for the damage to the ceremony.

The significance of these episodes lies in the queen's reaction to the accidents. No one expected royal visits to run without mishap, and other serious accidents, in fact, occurred during Elizabeth's progresses without lessening the success of her visits. When the queen was at Oxford in 1566, for example, a stage in Christ Church Hall collapsed and killed three men.[90] After her doctors tried unsuccessfully to save the unfortunate men, the queen then watched the play, which did go on, with obvious enjoyment. The episodes of the Coventry play and errant fireworks reveal the queen's recognition of harm done to the ceremony as well as to the people. While she made amends on a personal level by asking the Coventry folks to return and by reimbursing the Cowpers, the queen played out these apologies within a ceremonial context. In a public audience with the Cowpers, she extended words of comfort and gave them a sizable purse before the witnessing eyes of the town that had earlier presented a similar gift to the arriving queen. She gave money and deer for the same reasons to the Coventry players. The appropriate way to restore the ceremonial dialogue between visiting queen and townspeople was for Elizabeth to see the Hock Tuesday play under the observant gaze of the crowd as the people noted her public laughter. The affront to ceremony needed a proper reconciliation through ritual.

Within the ceremony itself, the internal structure could go awry as challenges and tensions appeared in the speeches and petitions made by town officials. Although most of the speeches adhered to the proven formula (cite the town's past glories and royal favors, indicate a current problem, and ask for a specific remedy), there were uneasy moments when the speakers strayed into turbulent political waters. The resulting tension served as a brief, powerful reminder of the strength of and the control exerted by the ceremonial rules of public speaking.

Each address that Elizabeth heard in Coventry, Warwick, and Worcester transgressed the limits of political discourse from the queen's perspective. Taking advantage of this public access to the queen, town officials shared their opinions on national issues and gave advice to their royal guest. After highlighting key moments from Warwick's history, the town recorder, Edward Aglionby, thanked the queen and her current favorite, Robert Dudley, for their interest in the town. Aglionby catalogued the benefits of royal rule: "the restauracion of God's true religion, the speedie chaunge of warres into peace, of dearth and famine into plentie, of an huge masse of drosse and counterfait monye into fyne golde and silver."[91] But he praised these benefits within the larger context of challenges to Elizabeth's rule, mentioning the most severe threat thus far, the 1569 Revolt of the Northern Earls. He noted that her reign was untouched "with any trowbelous season (the rude blast of one insurrection except) which being soone blowen over and appeased by God's favour and your Majesty's wisdome, hath made your happy Government to shyne more gloriosly." Given the generic content and tone of these speeches, this gratuitous remark about revolt seemed jarring and unnecessary. Perhaps Aglionby's nerves, as he feared, had "put me bothe out of coutenance and remembrance," as he dangerously alluded to the queen's constant worry, rebellion. In a time where thoughts of death or aid to an enemy could constitute treason, subjects addressing their queen needed to mark their words.

Another risky topic of conversation came from William Bell of Worcester. In Bell's address, the queen learned how the once thriving economy of Worcester had collapsed due to "unlooked-for troubles, as the breach of fayth lies in merchants, and restraint of trafyque" which the strong English navy was already policing.[92] By way of thanking Elizabeth and soliciting more help, Bell offered up an extravagant compliment full of unpalatable political theory. "All estates" of Worcester so loved the queen "that if all just laws had not cast upon yor Majestie the inheritance and ryghtful succession in this Kingdom, we myght, my Lords, in merite most justlie have elected her Majestie thereunto." While the expression of loyalty and support fell naturally on the ears of a divinely sanctified ruler, the idea of electing, or even selecting, a monarch according to merit would horrify the recipient of the intended praise. Dropping that thought, Bell reached safer ground by giving Elizabeth an unambiguous purse of money, and "as her looks gave wytness," the queen appeared to like the speech and gift. Elizabeth's response to these two political comments showed her accepting the good and ignoring the questionable. She recognized the loyal intentions of the speakers, who were using the rhetoric of contrast to validate her authority. These two dangerous ideas—questioning royal power in a military and theoretical way—lost their treasonable qualities as they remained with the ceremonial dialogue of the civic speeches.

Less treasonable but equally infringing upon the royal prerogative were the repeated urgings that Elizabeth should marry and provide the country with an heir. John Throckmorton, recorder of Coventry, concluded his request for economic aid and a new school with a bold appeal to the queen: "like as you are a mother to your kingdom, and to the subjects of the same, by justice and mothery care and clemency, so you may, by God's goodness and justice, be a natural mother, and having blest issue of your princely body, may live to see your children's children, unto the third and fourth generation."[93] With her practiced skill, Elizabeth thanked Throckmorton for his fine words and then ignored them. She also finessed the petition of Preacher Griffyn in Warwick, who publicly presented her with a Latin poem urging her to marry. "If it be any matter to be aunswerid," Elizabeth replied, "we will look upon it, and give you aunswer at my Lord of Warwik's house."[94] With that deferment consigning the petition to the ash heap, the queen avoided any more unwelcome public discussion of her marital status, and the ceremonial agenda returned the participants to their typical dialogue.

She was not so fortunate in her visit to Warwick and Kenilworth three years later. In a series of famous entertainments, both the civic hosts and the earl of Leicester created one extended marriage proposal that suffused all the ceremony of that royal visit. The purpose of George Gascoigne's pageant, "The Princely Pleasures at the Courte at Kenelwoorth," was to persuade Elizabeth that marriage to Robert Dudley was in her and the country's best interest, and the sooner the better.[95] Inclement weather forced Dudley to cancel parts of the pageant, but Elizabeth did see Dudley's passion for her staged in the person of Deep Desire, whose "fierie flames" survived the queen's "colde answers." The queen was supposed to appear in the show as the nymph Zabeta (a reference to her name) over whom Juno/Marriage and Diana/Chastity were fighting. Juno despaired of "mak[ing] her once to yeelde unto the wedded life," while Diana left "it to your choice, what kinde of life you best shall like to holde." Perhaps Elizabeth disliked her intended role or preferred to hunt instead, but for whatever reasons this part of the pageant was not performed. However, she could not escape the messages of love. A final show from Sylvanus reminded the queen of her Deep Desire's loyalty: "neither any delay could daunt him, no disgrace could abate his passions, no tyme coulde tyre him, no water quench his flames, nor death itself could amase him with terror." His passion for the queen had turned him into a holly tree, "now furnished on every side with sharpe pricking leaves, to prove the restlesse prickes of his privie thoughts."[96] Three weeks of such public marriage proposals and the growing pressure to stay at Kenilworth for yet more nuptial entertainments required Elizabeth to give Dudley her answer in the same symbolic terms. Queen and courtier had carried on an elaborate, lengthy ceremonial dialogue that pounded on the sole topic of marriage. Elizabeth chose to reply in a properly ceremonial, firm, and succinct way that allowed Dudley no appeal: she packed up and left. Her ceremony answered his. The queen denied the pleas of Deep Desire with a formal departure that kept all unwelcome marital pressure within the confines of ceremony.

Whether the ceremony followed the script or required improvisation, its significance was manifest to the town officials, the crowds of people, and the queen. Each of these participants joined in creating the specific rituals that together formed a conversation of ceremony. Held in an elaborate language of movements, clothing, presents, shows, and speeches, this conversation gave to the attending microcosm of English society—queen and aristocracy, merchants and laborers—an opportunity to speak across the divides of status without challenging the hierarchy. As they remade themselves spatially and symbolically, the participants used the exchange of messages to enhance their reputations and validate their importance to each other and to the outside, watching world. Just how important this communication between monarch and subjects was would become more obvious in the coming years of Stuart silence. A ceremonial distance grew between the participants, according to Goldberg: "whereas Elizabeth played at being part of the pageants, James played at being apart, separate."[97] The ceremonial conversation turned inward, focusing on the smaller groups within the privacy of court and turning dialogues into monologues. The early Stuart kings shifted the emphasis, restricted the audience and participants, and turned the civic processions into royal masques because such Elizabethan public occasions seemed superfluous. In doing so, they lost the crucial public conversation, the dialogue of ceremony that connected civic officials, citizens, court, and queen, and that Elizabeth found so invaluable to her rule.

The larger significance of the civic and royal interaction lay in its reliance upon visual and verbal ceremonies that established a dialogue between the ruler and the citizenry. While both sides could claim equal precedence in the ceremony, Elizabeth through her monarchical powers and towns through their civic identities, the decision to grant favors and aids belonged to the queen. The ceremonial dialogue recognized the status of both parties, but obviously the queen had precedence: the towns might ask, but the queen could order. While the queen did not uniformly grant their requests, the towns did benefit from the process of engaging in that dialogue. Having the opportunity to petition Elizabeth reinforced the sense of civic identity within the town that sometimes was the real legacy of a royal visit. The queen heard many petitions that she chose to ignore, reject, or revoke as soon as they were granted. In the context of civic ritual, royal image making, and ties between sovereign and towns, the ceremonial questions and replies that characterized the royal progresses loom large. Towns enhanced their civic reputation through such ceremonies even as Elizabeth orchestrated the ceremony from a royal perspective. The importance of that ceremonial dialogue lies only partly in whether the royal answer was "yes." Of more significance were the frequency of these exchanges between ruler and townspeople and the mutual satisfaction that characterized them.

SIX

The Royal Agenda:
Personal Monarchy at Work

The public image that Elizabeth presented to civic and private hosts was part of her strategy of rule. In her elaborate dress, public ceremonies, and stately travel, the queen displayed the power and wealth of the crown, even as she rendered herself accessible to the citizens whose support she consistently claimed to need. The queen understood the impact her presence had on a community and, conversely, the leverage she gained from denying access to others. Her movements over 40 years revealed a skillful manipulation of those who formed the audience around her, from local groups to government ministers and foreign ambassadors. But her travels also pointed to the very constraints on that royal authority. The limitations revealed in her travels mirrored the challenges facing her government and her monarchy. Through her granting and denying of access to herself, the queen struck chords of inclusion as well as of ambiguity; she often sought the middle way in policy and in destination. In their scope, direction, and purpose, her progresses enabled the queen to foster religious unity, to control negotiations of marriage, and to construct a military and ceremonial defense of her kingdom. While Elizabeth used the progresses to advance her diplomacy and reiterate the nature of her personal monarchy, her decisions about travel also suggested the political limitations of her power.

RELIGIOUS STABILITY

From the first, Elizabeth used her public appearances to facilitate the process of establishing a national church. The tensions between Catholics and Protestants in the sixteenth century testified to the deeply rooted power of ceremony in people's daily lives.[1] As the queen and her government crafted the religious settlement, Elizabeth maintained her primacy in a church inclusive of the vast majority of her Protestant and Catholic subjects. The progresses gave the queen a natural platform from which to speak on religious matters. Through her own public worship and choice of hosts, Elizabeth used her presence to cultivate religious conformity. But her absence also conveyed a message about the difficulty of religious unification. The queen never risked traveling in the predominantly Catholic northern counties, nor did she conduct any ceremonial dialogue in those areas most challenged by her views. Instead, she moved through the southern half of the island and mingled there with Anglicans, Puritans, and recusants. Thus, in several senses, the queen pursued a middle way. The progresses helped Elizabeth mold religious conformity where it already had the strongest chance of succeeding.

As the English church emerged in the early years of her reign, Elizabeth took part in processions around London that kept her in the public eye. In 1559 Sir William Cecil warned of the dangers from "a lack of good govnmet ecclesiasticall," but Elizabeth was equally sensitive to the dangers from losing her subjects' goodwill. To see and be seen in that delicate time, the queen made two short barge trips on the Thames within a week in late April. Flotillas of boats surrounded the royal barge, while Londoners lined the river banks to share in the music, water games, and fireworks late into the night. The second celebration ended when gunpowder exploded, burning a pinnace and drowning one man.[2] The river became a public stage that gave the queen access to people and a smooth escape should circumstances dictate.

As the Acts of Uniformity and Supremacy led to the deprivation of Marian bishops in late May and June 1559, Elizabeth used brief ceremonial outings to gauge the public response to the change of clergy. On the same day that the mass ended and the new dean of St. Paul's, William Nowell, assumed his duties, Elizabeth "with drumes and trumpetes playhyng" made an evening circuit from Whitehall along the bankside to the palace of the marquis of Winchester and back. All was quiet. Two weeks later she deprived the bishops of Winchester, Lincoln, and London. This alternation of public appearances and religious changes continued through the summer. The day after the muster and tilt at Greenwich on 2 July, the queen rode by barge to Woolwich for dinner on board the *Elizabeth Jonas*. Two days later, she deprived the archbishop of York, Nicholas Heath, and the bishop of Ely, Thomas Thirlby. The queen capped their departure with a joust on 11 July, and by the end of the month she was on progress in Kent and Surrey.[3]

As these excursions confirmed, the queen's support of Protestantism was popular, if to many people incomplete. The "violent and crude" propaganda of early civic pageants argued for a return to true Protestantism as conceived by the Marian exiles.[4] Three years into her reign, a progress into

East Anglia revealed important distinctions between royal and local views of religious propriety. In the name of tradition, ritual, and centrism, Elizabeth had embraced contradictory views that might confuse her subjects. In 1559, for example, she banished tapers from the opening ceremonies of Parliament, and in 1561 she ordered the altars in Westminster Abbey taken down. However, she kept candles and a crucifix for her own private worship in the Chapel Royal.[5] And on the biggest issue of symbolic power, the mass, she fostered a vague interpretation that included many but offended true believers. In the context of such religious uncertainty, progresses opened the queen's eyes to some of her subjects' wayward religious practices and gave her the opportunity to work toward conformity in religion. Through a mixture of royal example and ceremonial dialogue, Elizabeth used her presence to validate the national church that she meant to have.

On her visit to Ipswich in August 1561, the queen had occasion to define her broad religious views for the public. She witnessed apparent laxness in the church services conducted by the puritanically inclined bishop of Norwich, John Parkhurst. The clergy used no surplices, those richly embroidered gowns worn by Catholic priests and mandated by the queen in 1559. More offensive to the queen, "in Cathedrals and Colleges there were so many wives, and widows and children seen." On the issues of vestments and clerical marriage, Elizabeth had strong opinions that separated her from Puritans. By a royal injunction on 9 August, the queen forbade any female presence within the clergy's lodgings on pain of deprivation of any ecclesiastical promotion in the cathedral or college. In Elizabeth's eyes, the women lured the clergy from their divine reflections with worldly enticements, "whereof no small offence groweth to the entente of the founders & to the quiett & orderlye profession of studye & lerninge." While she did not abolish clerical license to marry, which had too many defenders and practitioners, she could mandate a physical separation of clerical husbands and wives that created the impression, at least within cathedral grounds, of an unmarried clergy. She yielded on the reality but sought to preserve the appearance. Such a distinction placed a heavy weight on image, outward sign, and public display in a way that recognized the power such ceremonies wielded. The French ambassador De Maisse summed up the queen's thinking on the matter: "as for the ecclesiastics, they may marry if they wish, as also the canons and the curates, although the Queen takes no pleasure in the sight of a married bishop."[6] Through her visit to Ipswich, the queen advanced her inclusive views of a national church that retained ritual and accepted the inevitability of a married clergy.

All that discussion of marriage must have put the queen in a foul temper in dealing with a nuptial rebellion within her own court. During her progress of 1561, the queen learned of the pregnancy of Lady Catherine Grey, her cousin, a granddaughter of Henry VIII's sister Mary, and the heir presumptive according to the will of Henry VIII. Catherine Grey and Edward Seymour, earl of Hertford, claimed to have been married in a secret ceremony before Christmas, and their union had now proved fertile. Elizabeth was angry that a lady-in-waiting had dared to marry without her sovereign's permission, and Catherine's royal blood made the situation potentially threatening—in fact, her sister Jane had assumed the throne for nine days after the death of Edward VI in 1553. Upon discovery of this pregnancy, the queen committed both Grey and Hertford to the Tower, where Catherine would later die.[7] Years later she forgave the earl of Hertford by visiting him for a magnificent entertainment at Elvetham in 1591.

The discovery of the clandestine marriage, as well as the proliferation of clerical wives, led Elizabeth to have even less patience with the disobedient couple in 1561 than she might have had later. Also, Elizabeth had recently been coping with her own marital difficulties. The previous year had shown Elizabeth that she, unlike Catherine, could not marry the man whom she loved: Amy Robsart's death in 1560 had ended her serious dalliance with Robert Dudley. The secret marriage of her royal cousin troubled the dynastic waters while the public marriages of her clergy embroiled the religious ones. In both cases a practical desire for order motivated the queen's responses.

After her experience in Ipswich, Elizabeth shaped her itinerary to include the two university towns, where her presence would advance religious conformity. She visited Cambridge in 1564 and Oxford in 1566 to assess compliance with the royal injunctions on vestments. The lush decoration and color gave a sense of continuity with the past, which reformers disliked but the queen valued. Given that these schools produced and housed England's finest theologians, Elizabeth needed to have their compliance with the new rules of her church. A royal visit would put the scholars on notice.

The two chancellors of the universities, rival courtiers William Cecil and Robert Dudley, felt pressure to produce such conformity. Cecil groomed Cambridge for a month before the queen's arrival. In a letter to Vice-Chancellor Edward Hawford alerting him of the progress, Cecil gave instructions for housing the queen. But the real reason for the letter was his fear of ceremonial disaster in that hotbed of incipient Puritanism. Two years earlier, Cecil had worried enough about the attitudes at Cambridge that he had considered resigning his chancellorship. He had been "trobled to here how, in that university, a greate parte of the colleges be now of late become full of factions & contentions." Cecil vowed in 1564 that under the direct and public gaze of the queen, Cambridge must be a model of learning, order, and conformity: "I meane both for religion & civill behavior," as well as order and uniformity "in apparel & religion & especially in setting of the communion table." Cecil arrived the day before the queen, on 4 August 1564, and found the Cambridge scholars appropriately attired. He "reioysed to see theym in so comely aparell, theye were in longe gowns, brode slewes, and hoodes, sayinge that the quene shortly after her progresse intendyd to have one uniforme and lyke ordere of aparell for the cler-gie."[8] In response to the queen's visit, they adopted her image of clerical propriety.

The ceremonial occasion gave Elizabeth the perfect venue to display her learning, recognize religious obedience, and bind the community to her monarchy. She spent the days "in Scholasticall exercises of Philosophy, Phisicke, and Divinitie: the nights in Comedies and Tragedies." Speaking to the crowd outside King's College Chapel, Elizabeth "thanked God that had sent her to this university, where she, altogether against her expecta-tion, was so received, that, she thought, she could not be better." Years later Cecil, then Lord Burghley, was still on guard. When a delegation from Cambridge visited the queen at Audley End in 1578, Burghley again made sure they wore the proper black gowns and hoods.[9] The queen found her presence generated an awareness of religious policies that bonds of patron-age enforced.

By visiting despite her "expectation" of religious strife, Elizabeth proved her willingness to venture into a place of limited conflict for the good of her church and crown. With her councilor Cecil managing those loyal Pu-ritans, the risk to royal authority was slight: Elizabeth chose a confronta-tion that she would win for the moment. Cambridge did remain more purely Protestant than the queen preferred, while rapid changes in religious practice led others to cling to past customs. Churches the queen did not visit took advantage, at times, of their anonymity to pursue a more inde-pendent course of religious practice. The churchwardens of Great St. Mary's in Cambridge, for example, did not sell their vestments or plate until 1567 and 1568, when they felt confident that Elizabeth's religious settlement would last longer than her sister's.[10] But the importance of the universities guaranteed a royal visit in the name of religious and political unity.

In terms of court politics, patronage, and religious conformity, her visit to Cambridge set the pattern for Elizabeth's visit to Oxford in 1566. Timing was all that separated them, but the queen's strategy showed in her original plan to visit Oxford on that same Cambridge progress. Only an outbreak of plague delayed her arrival, a deficit felt by the deprived scholars who "had looked for her comming this ther two yeers."[11] In 1566 Elizabeth evened the score with a long visit (31 August–6 September) full of enter-tainments. As chancellor of Oxford, Robert Dudley shouldered the same burden of success as had his fellow councilor Cecil. Dudley too arrived early to bring the Oxford scholars in line with the queen's views on the proper ceremonial. Even the Puritan president of Magdalen College, Laurence Humphreys, conformed by wearing the detested gown for the arrival of the queen. In a caustic reference to his beliefs, Elizabeth supposedly remarked to Humphreys, "that loose gown becomes you mighty well, I wonder your notions should be so narrow."[12] With that bit of acting, the queen commended him for obedience while warning him not to lapse into the old ways when she left. Her public presence exacted a ceremonial change of clothing by the ecclesiastical hosts. In the spring following her visit, the university obeyed orders from the archbishop of Canterbury to destroy "superstitious" plate.[13] On her other visit to Oxford in 1592, the queen again stressed conformity by admonishing the scholars to worship "not according to the opinion of the world, not according to far-fetched, finespun theories, but as the Divine Law commands, and as our law preaches."[14] As at Cambridge, Oxford scholars altered their actions and externals of worship in response to the queen's presence. A royal visit, Elizabeth understood, had a marvelous way of focusing people's attention.

In the next decade, the queen used her ceremonial power to strengthen the church by visiting Canterbury, the seat of her valuable archbishop, Matthew Parker, from 3 to 16 September 1573. Elizabeth regularly attended church during the progresses, creating a dual image of royal and religious authority. Faced with increasingly effective Puritan diatribes against the Anglican prayer book and hierarchy, Parker invited Elizabeth to come to Canterbury in the summer of 1573. He enlisted the help of Burghley to emphasize the importance of the visit: "It would much reioyce and stablishe the people here, in this religion, to see her highnes that Sondaye (being the first sonday of the month, when others also customablie may receive) as a godlie devoute prince, in her cheife and metropoliticall churche, openly to receive the comunyon, which by her favor I would minister unto her."[15] Parker wanted a public ceremony that overwhelmed the audience with a swirl of religious and political pageantry focused on Elizabeth.

He proposed a change from the typical staging of such visits by important personages. The customary schedule began with the guest, bishop, dean, and chapter members gathered in the west end of the cathedral to hear an oration. The guest then walked into the middle of the church nave for prayers. Moving forward toward the communion table, the queen and clerics heard the Eucharist recited. Parker suggested restaging the public worship so that more people could participate. He proposed that Elizabeth hear the service in the common chapter, which could hold a large congregation below while the queen and lords sat above in a gallery. The new blocking would enlarge the audience, but it also removed the queen from the center of the cathedral. In Parker's assessment, the elevated, distant queen gazing down on her subjects would urge spiritual conformity. By coming to Canterbury at Parker's request, Elizabeth lent her ceremonial support to the religious settlement. She reiterated her point by traveling through the eastern part of Sussex, where Protestantism was strong, before returning to Greenwich by the end of September.[16] Through her presence in these areas, Elizabeth validated the essentials of her church before crowds already in agreement.

The queen also called for religious conformity as she crossed the breadth of the island to visit Bristol in 1574. In July, Elizabeth ordered the establishment of a special commission for ecclesiastical causes within the dioceses of Bristol and Gloucester. The religious commission joined her list of reasons for heading to the western port, where she planned to sign a trade agreement and to watch celebrations of English military prowess. The special commission was ready to meet by the time she arrived in August 1574. In an opening ceremony, Elizabeth delivered a prayer to bind her subjects in religious and political unity. She began by thanking God for "preserving me in this long & dangerous journy" and emphasizing her reliance upon that divine strength to protect her from her enemies. She acknowledged receiving her kingdom from God and hoped to render up "a peaceable, quiett, & well ordered State & Kingdome, as also a perfect reformed church to ye furtherance of thy Glory." The implication that the state was not yet peaceable, quiet, and well ordered was one she wished her audience to ponder as the ecclesiastical commission began its duties. Elizabeth closed the prayer by asking her subjects to have "faithfull and obedient hearts willingly to submitt themselves to the obedience of thy word & commandments."[17] Such understanding they should gain from the official agents of the established church, who acted under royal authority. When Elizabeth appealed for right thinking and religious conformity in Bristol, she had already set in motion the means of enforcing this demand.

A progress to Norfolk in 1578, however, revealed the limitations of the queen's ability to reconcile religious differences at the national and local levels. As the queen traveled through Suffolk, Burghley lamented in a letter to Walsingham that at Bury "we fynd ye people very sound, saving in some parts infected with ye bransyk heresy of ye papisticall family of love."[18] Other areas of the two counties had a growing Puritan presence. After the duke of Norfolk's execution in 1572, ecclesiastical patronage in Suffolk assumed a more Protestant tone. Other conservative and secretly Catholic nobles died, and Puritans such as John, Lord Darcy, and Roger, Lord North, were appointed to the commission of the peace. Norwich remained archly Protestant as well. Under the leadership of Bishop John Parkhurst, the worship services began to show signs of Protestant innovation. In 1570 Norwich Cathedral had suffered the attack of iconoclastic Puritans, who entered the choir of the church and "brak down ye organes with other outrages." The angry queen prodded Parkhurst to punish the people responsible for the "lewd disorders" and notified the bishop that she was referring the matter to the archbishop of Canterbury, as she had found Parkhurst "very remiss in observation of ye ordres of ye church."[19] These religious disputes shaped the agenda of Elizabeth's progress to Norwich.

Elizabeth planned a route with hosts whose differing religious beliefs mirrored the conflicts in the counties. Not only did she face a strong Puritan community in Norwich, but the queen also stayed with a set of Catholic sympathizers. Although the idea of a progress had been discussed early in May and the mileage between houses charted in July, her strategy caused last-minute changes to the itinerary, which remained unsettled until the queen's departure. Even Burghley had wrong information, as he predicted Elizabeth would leave Suffolk after visiting Sir William Cordell at Long Melford and return to London via Cambridge. Using her progresses to foster religious unity, Elizabeth stayed with hosts in the Norwich area who were crypto-Catholic supporters of the former duke of Norfolk or even known recusants. They included Sir Edward Clere, Sir Robert Southwell, Sir Roger Woodhouse, and Sir Thomas Kitson, men loyal to her but uncomfortable with the Protestant nature of the Anglican church.[20] During the queen's visit with Edward Rookwood of Euston, a landowner who endured recusancy fines for decades, someone found a figure of the Virgin in his barn. Elizabeth ordered the Catholic icon burned before an approving crowd, and Rookwood was ordered to appear in Norwich on charges of recusancy.[21] While the queen could not ignore public violations of religious law, she chose to stay with Catholic hosts in an apparent effort to assess religious problems within their local context.[22] Her religious signals were intentionally mixed to foster good relations among the traveling court, the government in London, and the people in the county.

As she embraced loyal Catholics in 1578, the queen wrestled with her ministers' demands that she send aid to her fellow Protestants in the Low Countries. On progress in East Anglia, Burghley, Leicester, and Secretary Wilson kept ambassadors Walsingham and Davison informed of Elizabeth's irritation at the thought of sending money abroad. Burghley noted that the queen was "gretly perplexed to thynk that the low contrees may become french." From Norwich, the earl of Leicester commented on the court's geographical propinquity to the Low Countries, "where my thinks I hear every day the voyce of that people but lytle good I imagyn they say." This sourness also infected Wilson's correspondence, as he contrasted the "pryncelie" reception of Elizabeth in Norwich with the impending disaster abroad: "in the middst of al the jolitie it wer good to provide for myschief hereafter, which I do feare is not farre frome us."[23] Surrounded by these calls for Protestant aid on her journey into East Anglia, the queen had an opportunity, should she choose, to show her support for English—and by extension, Dutch—Protestants.

Awaiting the queen in Norwich was the new bishop, Edmund Freke, who had arrived in 1575 "to suppress Puritanism in the diocese." He was a man of conservative religious views who administered an area where strong Catholic sympathies vied with an equally vociferous puritanism. Freke had the reputation of associating with recusants, overlooking errant Catholics, and targeting Puritans. According to his critics, Freke was "attended upon by men most unfitt for his callinge, and to pliable and familiar with suche, as maie be douted no great favorers of this happie peaceable tyme of the gospell."[24] The difficulties began soon after his arrival, when in 1576 the bishop suspended a group of Puritan preachers for publicly debating ecclesiastical policy. The local gentry appealed to sympathetic courtiers such as Sir Nicholas Bacon, Walsingham, and Leicester, who had access to and influence with the queen.

In the civic ceremonies, Elizabeth made a public show of supporting the local Puritan faction. The mayor's welcoming oration brought the religious issue out in the open. After noting the town's prosperity, loyalty, and happiness at her arrival, Mayor Robert Wood described the citizens of Norwich as "most studious of Gods glory & true Religion." Such a comment matched the words inscribed below the royal arms on the town gate: "God and the Queen we serve." The next day, Elizabeth heard a speech from a Dutch minister who thanked her for allowing refugees from the Low Countries to settle in Norwich and for defending the "miserable dispossessed men of Christ's church."[25] Between ceremonies, the queen summoned 23 supposed Catholics, including Rookwood, to appear before the Privy Council there for examination. At the same time, the council ordered Bishop Freke to reinstate the Puritan preachers of Norwich whom he had suspended.

Elizabeth thus dramatized her disapproval of recusancy in the diocese of a prelate accused of leniency in that direction. While Freke attacked Puritans, public opinion held that he tacitly sanctioned the practice of Catholicism. Such a public reprimand of Bishop Freke for his alliance with the Catholic gentry involved the elevation of the Puritan element as well. Elizabeth gratified her courtiers who shared the Puritan views of many East Anglians. According to Sir Thomas Heneage, the queen had returned the troubled county to a religious calm. Writing to Walsingham from court, he said, "My lords, with the rest of the Council, have most considerately straightened divers obstinate and arch Papists that would not come to church; and by some good means, Her Majesty has been brought to believe well of divers zealous and loyal gentlemen of Suffolk and Norfolk, whom the foolish Bishop [Freke] had maliciously complained of to her, as hinderers of her proceedings, and favorers of Presbyterians and Puritans."[26] By publicly disgracing some Catholic hosts and by knighting hosts who practiced religious conformity, Elizabeth hoped to bring Freke in line with both her ecclesiastical hierarchy and his own neighbors. Her approach then was to seek a reconcilation between the bishop and his Puritan charges and bring quiet to Norwich. Elizabeth supported his critics in 1578, without revoking the bishop's ecclesiastical authority. She helped to restrict Catholic activity in Norfolk and Suffolk and to encourage a freer puritanism in those areas. By staying with recusant hosts and supporting local Puritans during the progress of 1578, Elizabeth sought the middle ground of religious inclusion.

On some issues, however, the queen saw no position of compromise, and her travel then became a weapon of exclusion. During the late 1570s, some reformist clergy engaged in prophesyings, a public forum for debating biblical interpretations with the usual intent of adopting a more Puritan outlook. Such free-wheeling discussion of established religious practice offended the queen's sense of her own authority as Supreme Governor of the Church and threatened religious unity. "Whenever she was reminded of their existence," the queen launched an attack on prophesyings.[27] Feeding her anger was the attitude of the new archbishop of Canterbury, Edmund Grindal, who refused to join the royal attack on vocal reformers. As part of an effort to force him to comply, Elizabeth did not allow Grindal to participate in the progresses or act as host. Until his death in 1583, she censured and isolated Grindal, the only one of her three archbishops of Canterbury to experience such royal shunning. But then, he was the only one who never yielded to the queen on an important religious issue. Elizabeth understood how her presence favored a host and her absence could criticize, but with Grindal the limits of her royal diplomacy stood revealed.

The queen's use of travel to foster religious stability changed in the 1580s, when she had failed to craft a religious policy that offered her safety within England and significant alliances abroad. Foreign powers in Spain, France, and Rome were planning the military conquest of the heretical isle. The religious threats became personal ones during the years leading up to the execution of Mary Stuart in 1587. The Armada of 1588 was but the public military representation of a long-standing secret war. In these circumstances, Elizabeth did not make extensive progresses away from the greater London area, nor did she use the ceremonial power of her image in public dialogues. In fact, she did precisely the opposite. To direct the defense of the country, her monarchy, and herself, the queen curtailed her progresses for a decade.

Nonetheless, for the first 20 years of her reign Elizabeth shaped her progresses to advance religious unity. By visiting loyal Catholics, upholding Puritan demands, and publicly participating in her established church's services, Elizabeth used her presence to bring others under the umbrella of conformity. But in her ceremonial exchanges the queen recognized the limits of her personal diplomacy and religious authority. She did not risk the dangers of visiting northern England or Wales even to advance acceptance of her religious settlement. Instead, the progresses revealed a cautious queen who traveled only to places where her popularity and church were secure. When she could not, then she stopped. Elizabeth's movements mirrored her monarchy and the constraints on it.

PERSONAL DIPLOMACY

In governing their kingdoms, sixteenth-century monarchs depended upon direct contact with their subjects as well as foreign visitors. The slow nature of communication and travel, as well as the lack of standing armies or police forces, meant that rulers relied upon their royal displays to reinforce loyalty to their government. Elizabeth made regular public appearances, sponsored official portraits, and engaged in elaborate court rituals that created an interaction between sovereign and subjects. Through her movements and ceremonial moments, the queen created opportunities to deal directly with important people on personal or diplomatic matters. In acting on issues of foreign policy, succession, and marriage, therefore, Elizabeth relied upon the convenience and flexibility of her progresses to bolster her negotiations. As the progresses focused attention on the queen, they also created ways for her to manipulate others through her presence and absence.

Elizabeth's most significant attempts to use travel for diplomatic purposes concerned Mary Stuart. Twice during the 1560s the English and Scottish rulers planned to meet one another, but on both occasions the visits collapsed. In the summer of 1562, Elizabeth proposed to Mary that they meet in York, where together they could enjoy lavish spectacles, entertainments, feasts, and hunting. That historic confrontation would have given them intimate knowledge of the other's goals, methods, and personality hard to translate through the diplomatic dispatches and verbal reports. Elizabeth wanted to assess Mary's motives and take her measure as a monarch, as well as compare her own accomplishments with those of her younger cousin. English parliaments and prelates were hammering out the religious settlement, there were inconclusive negotiations with Scotland about the Treaty of Edinburgh that Elizabeth wanted clarified, and Mary had only recently returned to her native country as its queen. Such were the incentives for Elizabeth to seek to know her rival. On Mary's part, she was coping with the religious blasts from John Knox's trumpet that condemned her, her mother, and her English cousin for reasons that included their heretical Catholicism and damnable gender. Mary Stuart was steering a middle course similar to Elizabeth's by which religious differences would not rend the country. She was curious as well about her elder cousin and eager to travel in such style for promised festivities. Not least on her agenda was being named heir to the English throne.[28]

The English privy councilors did not share their queen's enthusiasm for the meeting. Although Elizabeth could point to numerous precedents for such royal summits, including her father's meetings with his European rivals Emperor Charles V and Francis I of France, the queen's advisors considered the venture too expensive and risky. It would meddle in French politics and cloud the religious picture in England. The English ministers feared that Mary would incite rebellion among her fellow Catholics in Yorkshire. They also pressed Elizabeth to stay in London to conduct delicate negotiations with the French, who were facing a religious civil war. On 7 June 1562, William Cecil wrote to Sir Nicholas Throckmorton in France that the Scottish meeting would unduly strengthen the French Guise party in its dynastic struggles. Cecil confidently predicted that "this resolution being dilatory will come to no effect." Three weeks later Bishop Quadra was reporting to Spain that the proposed rendezvous "seems to be cooling."[29] His analysis did not square with Elizabeth's commitment, however, as the queen rejected her councilors' warnings about the political and financial costs. Under the agreement worked out with Ambassador Maitland, the two queens would meet sometime between 20 August and 20 September 1562 in the conveniently located York. Before they could rendezvous, however, war in France intervened that July. Elizabeth then felt obligated to aid the French Protestants, and she remained in London to take command of the operations. Because of the war, her agreement with Maitland on 6 July meant nothing by 17 July, when Elizabeth reluctantly decided to cancel the northern progress to York.[30] At the same time, she did ask Mary to reschedule their meeting for the summer of 1563, but that meeting, too, never came to pass. In the difficult early years of Elizabeth's reign, religious and international complications deprived her of a most desired progress.

Three years later, Mary asked Elizabeth for a meeting. By 1566, conditions in Scotland had worsened for Mary. With the support of Murray and Maitland, she had only just regained control of Edinburgh after her husband's murder of David Rizzio. In the temporary flush of cordial relations with England, Mary proposed that Elizabeth bring her retinue on a northern progress that summer. The English response was muted in that no lavish preparations occurred as they had in 1562. But the movements of Elizabeth indicated her diplomatic answer: the queen traveled northward during the summer of 1566. Elizabeth journeyed to Stamford in southern Lincolnshire, where she visited William Cecil at his house of Greyfriars on 5 August.[31] Remaining in the county for about a week, Elizabeth was not far from York, a proximity that kept alive the possibility of a meeting with the Scottish queen. Events in Edinburgh, however, took precedence over those in England. Mary had given birth to her son James in June 1566 and found it difficult to conduct any meeting that summer. But Elizabeth indicated by her choice of itinerary that she was keeping open the possibility of the much anticipated rendezvous. Her 1566 progress covered unusual ground for Elizabeth, who did not later repeat this itinerary. Only after Sempringham, some 20 miles north of Stamford and the most northern point in all of Elizabeth's travels, did the queen turn her retinue westward toward Coventry, Warwick, and Oxford. Then Mary Stuart's arrival in England the next year as a fugitive changed all the ground rules for their meeting. New circumstances recast the two queens as fettered guest and reluctant host, and in such conditions Elizabeth continually refused any personal interview with Mary, who spent the summer confined in Sheffield Castle under the care of the earl of Shrewsbury.[32] When Elizabeth visited Warwickshire in August 1572, according to Burghley, the Scottish queen "hath made great means to come to Kennellworth offering to disclose matters of great momet to the Q. majestie but I trust no such grosse error wilbe comytted although I see some towardnes here to admytt it."[33] Even after plots and a revolt, the queen remained intrigued by the chance to meet Mary. In the end, as Burghley hoped, Elizabeth's resolve to isolate her imprisoned cousin remained firm, and in their remaining years the two queens never met. But during that 1562 summer of friendlier relations with Scotland, when France seemed at peace, Elizabeth sought a meeting with her fellow monarch as a sound measure of statecraft. She would have faced her possible successor in Mary Stuart and learned from her nature and mind what to expect in foreign policy. The proposed visit to York in 1562, and the later possibility in 1566, revealed the centrality of progresses in royal diplomacy and an English monarch eager to conduct personal negotiations within her own borders.

Elizabeth used the force of her presence when she faced recurring problems with her highest noble. The misdeeds of the wayward Thomas Howard, fourth duke of Norfolk, gave her ample cause for concern. When the queen visited Norfolk at Charterhouse in London in July 1568, Mary Stuart and Norfolk had yet to cross paths, even though the Scottish queen had begun her exile in England earlier that spring. Elizabeth's visit with Norfolk in 1568 was one of the last times that she did not have to interrogate him about her cousin.[34] In 1569 rumors of Norfolk's involvement with the northern earls' rebellion and his intent to marry Mary Stuart reached Elizabeth. In response to the rumors, the queen devoted part of her progress in September to checking their veracity. During her stay at Tichfield, Hampshire, Elizabeth pressed Norfolk about his intentions, wringing from him the admission that he had discussed marriage with Mary. After that confession, events in the north led Norfolk into further disloyal acts that caused him by the end of September 1569 to lie imprisoned in the Tower.[35] Although Elizabeth had given him an opportunity to absolve himself at Tichfield, the duke had squandered that moment and never fully recovered his position at court. When the highest noble in the kingdom flirted with treason, the queen used a progress to demand answers of him in person.

As knowledge of Norfolk's involvement in the Ridolfi plot spread in 1571, Elizabeth again used a progress to question Norfolk. Worries about the queen's security troubled the Privy Council and created anxiety about her absence from London. The councilors disapproved of her journey because of reports about Ridolfi and other Catholic activity in Flanders: "She was moved by her council that she would remain about London, only upon doubt of some great trouble both inward and beyond the seas. But her Majesty would not forbear her Progress, so as it might be near to London."[36] News of another plot in the name of Mary Stuart had reached the English court in May 1571, but details of it remained incomplete. The pieces formed a coherent picture, at last, during Elizabeth's visit to the duke of Norfolk at Audley End from 29 August to 3 September 1571. There Elizabeth heard Norfolk swear his allegiance to her, an oath supported by other courtiers' testimony to the duke's good character. Based on her understanding that Norfolk had broken with Mary Stuart and her reluctance to condemn such a privileged, consanguineous member of her nobility, Elizabeth "seemed to give favourable ear" to his pleas for forgiveness. Unfortunately for Norfolk, however, his public image was at odds with his secret activities. Walsingham uncovered evidence that Norfolk had sent money to Mary Stuart's supporters. The duke was still tied to the network of papal-French-Scottish agents trying to depose Elizabeth; he had been acting in treasonous complicity with the Scottish queen since 1568.[37] Elizabeth had gone to Audley End both to find out more about Norfolk's rogue foreign policy and to keep him in her good graces, but the duke misplayed his hand by not taking advantage of his meetings with the queen to speak honestly. Elizabeth's diplomatic overtures to Norfolk yielded results during that progress, even though they were not the ones for which she had hoped.

A visit from the queen did not necessarily have the amicable goals of her contact with Norfolk. In 1574 she used the occasion of a progress to

Gloucester to chastise her errant host, Henry, Lord Berkeley. Her displeasure with him had arisen from Berkeley's lineage and his choice of enemies. Berkeley had married Katherine Howard, daughter of Henry Howard, earl of Surrey, and sister to Thomas Howard, fourth duke of Norfolk. He was sanguinely involved, therefore, in the debacle of the Howard family that culminated in the execution of Thomas Howard in 1572. Executing such a senior and powerful noble, Elizabeth knew, would have risky consequences. After the duke's death, Elizabeth remarked to his sister, Lady Berkeley, "wee know you will never love us for the death of your brother."[38] Instead of trying to compensate for his family, Berkeley quarreled at length with the Dudleys during their period of ascendancy in the 1560s and 1570s. While Thomas Howard was in the Tower, Berkeley spurned a marriage alliance with Robert Dudley. In retaliation for the slight, the Dudleys launched a legal attack on the Berkeley title with its leases and lands. In 1574, therefore, the time did not seem propitious for a royal visit to such problematic hosts as Lord and Lady Berkeley.

With these dark rumblings as a background, Elizabeth chose to stay with the Berkeleys on her progress to Bristol in 1574. In a departure from the typical agenda of a progress visit, the queen's time at Berkeley Castle, Gloucestershire, was full of tension, as host and guest picked a quarrel over the etiquette of the hunt. Instead of taking a token number of her host's stock of game, in accordance with the rules of hospitality, Elizabeth enraged Berkeley by hunting most of his deer. He angrily threatened to destroy his herd himself so that the queen could not have the pleasure of doing it.[39] Such unusual hostility between guest and host had larger ramifications beyond the shattered expectations of hospitality. Elizabeth visited Berkeley Castle in order to display her royal power over its politically suspect hosts. Because of his family ties to a renegade courtier and his rejection of an approved marital alliance, the queen had reason to distrust Berkeley. She did not expect to kindle any friendship or support from Berkeley during her visit. Instead, Elizabeth calculated that royal intimidation would serve the same purpose. Her slaughter of his deer graphically captured Berkeley's attention and offered a lesson in the royal wrath and omnipotence that by implication could also strike him down. In addition, the queen continued to champion the Dudley cause against him in the courts. This visit was remarkable for its ugly atmosphere and bloody insults. The exchange of messages in this ceremonial dialogue conveyed a rancor not often seen between queen and host. The Berkeley visit showed Elizabeth in a punishing vein that she did not find necessary to repeat in the rest of her progresses.

While her direct contact with hosts allowed Elizabeth to help or dominate them, her travels also generated public and private meetings with visiting ambassadors attached to her court. Elizabeth enjoyed parading her accomplishments to foreigners who would report their colorful stories home, but more significant were the discussions they shared about current diplomatic problems of treaties, alliances, aid, and matrimony. Her hosts during the progresses became accustomed to the traffic of foreign ambassadors and envoys who sought audiences with the mobile queen. La Mothe Fénélon, the French ambassador, intercepted Elizabeth during her stay with the earl of Bedford at Chenies in July and August of 1570. Fénélon wanted to discuss the details of the recent peace between England and France, urgent business preempting that of ministers Walsingham and Burghley. The queen traveled to Nonsuch in late May 1580 to receive the French ambassador and the prince de Condé, who arrived in England on 19 June. They discussed the possibility of English aid to Henry of Navarre in the newly resumed wars of religion in France. Nonsuch was again the site of foreign receptions when Count Albert of Alasco arrived in the spring and summer of 1583. The commissioners of the Hansa cities met her there in August 1585. Elizabeth arranged to entertain the duc de Bouillon in April 1596 at Greenwich so that they could discuss the continuance of their combined efforts against the Spanish. Convenient transportation along the river and accessible hunting made the royal palaces close to the Thames a popular venue for such diplomatic negotiations. But when her travels led her away from London and she needed to meet with emissaries, private houses served as well. In the summer of 1601, Elizabeth had already gone on her last extended progress when Henry IV of France proposed a meeting with his envoy, the duc de Biron. Elizabeth brought the court back toward London in September to meet the duke at Basing, the Hampshire home of the marquis of Winchester.[40] The presence of ambassadors on her progresses gave Elizabeth a wider, international audience for her displays of state and dynastic power.

Ambassadors followed the traveling court to secure an alliance of marriage with the English queen. During the 1570s in particular, their aims coincided with Elizabeth's approach to foreign policy. She hoped to neutralize potential enemies through the hope of marriage rather than a declaration of war. Conducting foreign policy with a tempting prospect of marriage allowed Elizabeth to keep close control of foreign negotiations and to save the costs of supporting an army and navy in battle.[41] Elizabeth gained a real advantage by taking her suitors on the road with her: her important advisors accompanied her, personal distractions remained at a distance (but close enough to appear if she needed the interruption), and she controlled the itinerary. The foreign visitors had fewer attendants, they experienced delays in sending news home, and they did not know the countryside. She had the initiative in arranging lodgings and orchestrating the nature of the progress. By moving the court Elizabeth created a chaos that isolated her guests while keeping the freedom of maneuver to herself.

During her first years as queen, Elizabeth received a number of marriage proposals that resulted in state visits from foreign suitors. Eric, king of Sweden, made four separate proposals and sent his brother to England as his personal envoy to plead his case. When that approach failed, Eric determined to visit Elizabeth in 1560 and sweep her hesitations away. That September the queen ended her progress from Surrey and Hampshire at Windsor, where she waited for news of her suitor's arrival: "being every hour in a continual expectation of the King of Sweden's coming, [Elizabeth] is looked for to be shortly here at Westminster."[42] While the queen prepared to move to the more central Westminster, the king of Sweden was suffering a voyage of heavy weather that ultimately prevented him from reaching England at all. From a Scandinavian match, the queen turned to consider a Hapsburg one. During her progress in 1566, Spanish ambassador Guzman de Silva traveled with Elizabeth to sound out her views on a marital alliance. "For almost a couple of leagues," de Silva broached the subject of a Hapsburg marriage with either Philip II of Spain or Archduke Charles of the Holy Roman Empire.[43] For hearing marriage proposals, avoiding them, and slipping away without reply, her progresses provided Elizabeth with a helpful flexibility.

With the French suitor, the duc d'Anjou, however, the queen organized a progress to mingle with courtiers who favored the match as well as those set against it. Elizabeth devoted several of her progresses to courtships with Anjou and later his younger brother, the duc d'Alençon. For reasons of the succession, Burghley and Sussex supported Anjou's suit: they wanted an heir of the queen's body, and time for that was rapidly passing. A combination of religious fears, personal jealousy, and xenophobia led Leicester and Hatton to oppose it.[44] The queen heard their conflicting opinions as a way to gauge the wider popular response to her courtship with a Catholic Frenchman. In their defense of the Protestant settlement so dearly and recently won, the warning voices who counseled against the match closely mirrored the overwhelmingly negative reaction of the populace. Elizabeth took a long time to listen to those critics and instead used her progresses to draw out French marital discussions for almost a decade.

When domestic peace in France made an alliance propitious in 1571, Elizabeth and her ministers undertook negotiations with King Charles IX and his mother Catherine de Medici for a marriage with his brother, the duc d'Anjou. During her progress in June 1571, Elizabeth spend two days at Sir Thomas Gresham's house, Osterley, where she worked out some preliminary terms. Elizabeth's dowry was set at 30,000 crowns, and she reluctantly broached the touchy subject of religion in a letter to the French.

While most of her councilors did not know of these plans, Burghley, Leicester, and Walsingham did. A month later at Hampton Court, Elizabeth was denying strenuously that she had promised Anjou freedom to worship as a Catholic. By the time she reached Audley End in September, where she had other concerns to face in regard to the duke of Norfolk, proponents of the marriage were urging her to conclude negotiations. Her ministers in favor of the match had joined with the French envoy, Paul de Foix, to persuade the queen to settle the religious issue quickly and announce the betrothal. At one point, Burghley wrote to Walsingham that if Monsieur "will forbeare his Mass she will assent to the Marriage." Burghley and Lord Buckhurst were entertaining de Foix with elaborate feasts "to increase his honor," and they arranged for the earl of Oxford to pay special attention to the visitor. So concerned were the lords about a threat to the talks that they tried to plan for any eventuality. While entertaining de Foix, Buckhurst learned "how we were like to pas by her h. [Elizabeth] as she did hunte." Buckhurst wrote to Burghley for instructions as to his behavior in various situations: if de Foix saw Elizabeth and asked to join her hunting; if he saw the queen and remarked upon her; if de Foix saw Elizabeth but did not comment; and if he did not see her.[45] Buckhurst did not want a small accidental encounter to derail the talks. It was just the kind of opportunity that the queen might use to end the matter.

A year later, Elizabeth had replaced Anjou as a suitor with his brother Alençon, and the match caused much discussion with Burghley on her progress from Theobalds to Kenilworth. At Theobalds in July 1572 with M. de Foix and the duc de Montmorency, the queen referred both to the Alençon match and the ratification of the Treaty of Blois. Now, however, she appeared more negative about settling the religious issues than previously. A month later at Gorhambury, home of Sir Nicholas Bacon, Elizabeth again raised the religious impediment to the marriage. She told Walsingham to invite Alençon for a visit to discuss his suit, a visit that would remain secret if the king and his mother balked at sending Alençon without any guarantees. As Burghley noted, the queen "is very irresolute to these our countrey matters" and wavered in her opinion of the marriage from day to day. She was not, as Susan Doran argues, "straightforward and direct" in negotiations with her suitors.[46] Instead, through the disturbances of travel, Elizabeth cultivated this irresolution by moving from one host to another. As her lodgings changed, so did her pronouncements about marriage.

By the time the progress reached Kenilworth in August 1572, Burghley nourished some optimism that the betrothal might occur. The queen's instructions to Walsingham revealed how undecided Elizabeth remained: if the French had taken offense at sending Alençon to England, Elizabeth told Walsingham to stress her desire for peace and to downplay the marital alliance.[47] Other events beyond the queen's control, however, ended serious consideration of the marriage. In September London was shocked to hear of the massacre of Huguenots in Paris on St. Bartholomew's Day, 24 August 1572. At Woodstock, Ambassador Fénélon had the impossible task of defending the murders of French Protestants (and Parisians in general) to Elizabeth. In response to the news, Elizabeth put aside consideration of matrimony, with its obvious difficulties, and worked to preserve amity with France. One of her prime concerns in the aftermath of the slaughter was for Walsingham's safety in France. If he could continue negotiating for her with Charles IX, she wanted him to remain there; Burghley, however, thought Walsingham should be recalled. At Reading on 28 September, the queen told the French ambassador that while the king's French subjects were his own business, she thought it "repugnant" that he sued for her hand while killing her coreligionists.[48] The marriage negotiations lay in ruins, because the match was more unpopular in Protestant England than before. Elizabeth dared not risk the French alliance that had occupied so much of her progress in 1572.

By the summer of 1578, support for the match revived at the court. While staying with James Altham at Mark Hall in Essex, Elizabeth pleased Burghley and the earl of Sussex by instructing Walsingham to probe Alençon's thought once again on the old matter. From the court at Bury St. Edmunds in August 1578, Leicester reported to Walsingham the queen's ambivalence about a visit from Monsieur: "she ys afrayd of yt, but wyll allowe no better remedye than to seme to myslyke him for yt." When Alençon finally arrived for a secret visit in August 1579, he enchanted the queen during their private entertainments at Greenwich. Elizabeth fueled the rumors in March 1580 by visiting the French ambassador for a lengthy conversation. To the court observers, "it was considered a great innovation for the Queen to go to his house, and it is looked upon by some as a sure indication that the marriage will take place."[49] The presence of the queen at the ambassador's residence, it was widely believed, revealed her commitment to the match.

Elizabeth calibrated her movements to indicate to the observing public just how she felt about her French suitor at that moment. She knew how her actions fanned the gossip of courtiers and ambassadors, so her decision to escort Alençon out of England in 1582 gave that small act a heightened significance. When Alençon departed in February 1582, concluding a leisurely visit begun the previous November, Elizabeth probably realized that he was going to be the last serious suitor who brought the genuine possibility, if not of children, then at least of marriage. The last chance for the queen to marry had been lost, and even though its failure rested largely with Elizabeth, she still mourned Alençon's departure. She insisted on escorting him from London through Kent to Dover, where he would sail for France, and extended lavish hospitality to him at their stops in Rochester and Canterbury. After he boarded the ship at Dover, the queen vowed to stay "in no place in which she lodged as she went, neither will she come to Whitehall because the places shall not give cause of remembrance to her of him with whom she so unwillingly parted."[50] Her public and ostentatious entertainments, however, came from more than a royal heartache. When Elizabeth closed the marriage negotiations, Alençon had proved inconveniently unwilling to head back to France. His price for leaving England was English aid to the Dutch Protestant rebels in their revolt against Spain, a rebellion that the French prince was championing. With her regal pageantry that the progresses best displayed, Elizabeth was impressing Alençon one last time with the power and wealth of the host who subsidized his campaigns. By taking him on a tour of her ships at Rochester on his final progress through Kent, Elizabeth showed off English sea power to an ally who would have need of it. More important, she wanted Alençon, who was her military arm by proxy, to remember English interests in his continental battles and heed her advice when it came. From a practical aspect, too, escorting the prince from England with a heralded progress ensured that he did leave. Elizabeth used the pageantry of a progress to put ceremonial pressure on Alençon to move toward the Channel and to get on a boat. Since the purpose of the progress was to usher him out of England, the rules of hospitality and ritual obligated him to go. Thus, the queen's final progress with her last suitor displayed to the public her matrimonial judgment as well as her military strength. She orchestrated the ceremony of Alençon's departure to emphasize her willingness to marry, her decision not to, and her regret that the whole business was over. Regardless of how genuine her ceremonial message was, it still had power and meaning.

Elizabeth appreciated the power of her regal presence to signal support or criticism. The correlation between the queen's goals in foreign policy and her movements appeared in the ebbing and flowing that characterized her relationship with Mary Stuart. The power of the queen's absence was never more apparent than in her ultimate refusal to share a room with her Scottish prisoner. As a general principle of government, the fluidity of travel helped Elizabeth manipulate her suitors and play diplomatic games. The progresses created both the personal contact on which her monarchy depended and the chaos and flexibility that typified her approach to decision making.

DEFENSE OF THE REALM

Elizabeth took advantage of progresses to emphasize themes of English military strength and her own divine responsibility for preserving the kingdom. Through her choice of destination and participation in public ceremonies, the queen crafted for herself the military role of protector that her gender deprived her of on the battlefield. On her many visits to fortified towns and harbors, Elizabeth inspected the outposts of national defense. Her peacetime progresses often had martial ceremonies, with ritual displays of force that included cannons, guns, fireworks, ships, and staged battles showing the English ability to defend their country. To the court, the townspeople who participated, and the foreign visitors in the retinue, these combative shows in peacetime affirmed the military power that the queen could summon. But when the military threat was imminent, she retreated to the greater security of the London area to oversee defenses and plot strategy. During the northern uprising of 1569, the expected Spanish invasion in the 1580s, and the trial that led to the execution of Mary Stuart in 1587, Elizabeth stayed in royal palaces around London that offered physical protection and a central location. When the military threat was real, with the exception of her visit to Tilbury, the queen abandoned her progresses and retreated to the security of the London area. She understood that her ceremonial defense, erected through the progresses, worked as diplomacy but crumbled on the battlefield.

Military pageants characterized the queen's travels from the earliest part of her reign. For her coronation in January 1559, an elaborate procession ushered her into the city, where citizens staged pageants that extolled their own corporation's history while suggesting to Elizabeth how she should rule. That spring she celebrated May Day with games, followed two months later by the Greenwich muster and tilt. In July 1559, Elizabeth called out the people of London for a muster at Greenwich. The band of defenders included citizens, soldiers, armorers, and the lord mayor. They crossed London Bridge to spend the night of 1 July 1559 in St. George's Fields before marching to Greenwich the next day. There the crowd offered Elizabeth the entertainment of a staged battle, complete with gunfire, and they closed the day with a tilt before returning to the city.[51] These public ceremonies in the first year of her reign emphasized the community between the new queen and her subjects. Taken as a group, these ceremonies began the dialogue between queen and subjects that characterized Elizabeth's reign and in particular her progresses. They introduced the queen to her people. The symbolism of the event bound the new ruler and her court to the residents of the city of London, on whose loyalty she would most depend. The military overtones had a particular purpose. The tilt, gunfire, and organized bands marching around the field conveyed the image of strength, victory, and unity. For reasons of gender and precedent, Elizabeth wanted the Greenwich muster to highlight her promise and confidence as a military leader. Because as a woman she would not lead troops in battle, her presence at mock ones suggested, nevertheless, her symbolic participation in them. In addition, she wanted to distinguish her successful future from her predecessor, Mary Tudor's, military failures. As a queen and soldier, Elizabeth would do better.

Immediately after the Greenwich muster, Elizabeth made her first visit as queen to a royal ship. The court went to Woolwich and had a banquet aboard the *Elizabeth Jonas* there. She returned for a similar occasion the next April, when the queen went with Lord Russell to Deptford. On board a new galley, they dined sumptuously and afterward watched a naval exercise, with gunfire, hurled stones, and men thrown in the water. A large crowd of spectators on the shore and in boats also enjoyed the event.[52] Elizabeth visited Deptford to check on her ships at least five times during her reign. After her visits in 1559 and 1560, the queen returned in the summers of 1576 and 1577. In April 1581, she went to look at the *Golden Hind* at Deptford with Sir Francis Drake, before launching it in January 1582.[53] These public expressions of interest in her navy used the ceremonial power of the queen's presence to supplement what Elizabeth would not grant: large sums of money to bankroll the fleet. Her visit to Rochester in 1573 showed the queen monitoring the execution of her earlier order to strengthen the naval forces. In his 1823 compendium of documents relating to her progresses, John Nichols observed: "when we consider the peculiar talents of Queen Elizabeth for business, and her close attention to the important affairs of State, we can hardly imagine that amusement was her principal motive for her long continuance in this place."[54] The queen cultivated a soldierly image to encourage unity among her people and to impress foreign rulers as they heard their ambassadors' reports of her movements and festivity. News of her trips to Deptford and the military entertainments there gave the continental rulers an image of the English queen not as a "weaker vessel" but as an armed warrior. Elizabeth used these public martial displays to convey at home and abroad the reputation of English and queenly strength.

She had special need of this martial image during the crisis sparked by the arrival of Mary Stuart in England in 1568. Within a year of the Scottish queen's flight southward, the northern earls had taken up arms on her behalf. Elizabeth faced a rebellion against her government and the influence of William Cecil in particular. At first, Elizabeth was cautious in her travel plans. She limited that summer progress of 1568 to a circuit in the home counties. In July, the Spanish ambassador wrote to Philip II that the queen was "in good health and continued her progress which, as I have said, will only be in the neighborhood, as she is careful to keep near at hand when troubles and disturbances exist in adjacent countries."[55] As rumors circulated in 1569 of a possible marriage between Mary and the duke of Norfolk, Elizabeth became increasingly concerned. She had already determined to visit Southampton, possibly to check on the Spanish ship that had carried the duke of Alva's treasure now in her safe possession, and she stuck to that itinerary. However, at the end of the progress, it was "believed for certain here that she will go direct to Windsor in consequence of the affairs" of Mary Stuart. After spending some time at Hampton Court, Elizabeth did stay at Windsor in September 1569. During the tense fall as the northern earls marched around Yorkshire, the queen lived much of the time at Windsor, "one of her castles to which Elizabeth rarely resorted except when she felt herself to be in grave danger."[56] The queen was at Windsor at the end of October, when she commanded the earls to appear before her court. She spent Christmas at Windsor and continued there during the first weeks of January. Her caution agreed with William Cecil's assessment of the threat to the queen. As a safety measure, he ordered lists of recusants and detained at university the sons of any rebels.[57] This uprising challenged the queen's authority in an especially threatening manner. The rebels were protesting the queen's right to choose her own advisors, the intrusion of royal government into the clannish northern provinces, and the Protestantism of the religious settlement. Of all the plots during her reign, the one in 1569 came closest to succeeding, and at the time Elizabeth viewed it with great seriousness. From her stronghold at Windsor, the queen kept apprised of news by special posts and rallied her forces to resist the rebels. In light of the serious threat to her monarchy, Elizabeth had just cause to seek the protection of Windsor Castle.

After several years of stability, Elizabeth began the series of spectacular progresses that took her far afield from London and the safety of her Thames palaces. She continued, however, to play the martial note in her pageantry and entertainments. Elizabeth used the 1574 visit to Bristol to settle a diplomatic account within an aggressively military setting. At issue was the confiscated treasure belonging to the duke of Alva that English seamen had appropriated in 1569. The queen had claimed the wealth inside the cargo ship but wanted to settle the matter with Spain. The resulting Treaty of Bristol settled all claims to the property, much of which Elizabeth already had in her possession, and temporarily pasted over disagreements between the two countries. The environment from which the treaty came, however, was anything but peaceful. The theme of the entertainments presented by the city was not one of harmony but one of military victory. While the queen and court watched from a timber scaffold in the nearby marshes, 300 harquebusiers and 100 pikemen waged a battle that lasted three days. From land and water they attacked a fort in Trenemill meadow, and a smaller fort behind it had already fallen in the early stages of the battle. This "martiall experiment beinge verie costlie and chargeable (especially in gonnepowder), the Queene and Nobilitie liked verie well of [it] and gave Mr. Maior and his brethren greate thankes for theire doinges." This skirmish involved serious combatants using real equipment: the costumes, sounds, and weapons gave the appearance of an actual battle.[58] The treaty signed in the context of the mock battle indicated the way Elizabeth blended diplomacy with the symbolic entertainments of her progresses. The guns and soldiers in tenacious battle alluded to the strong position of the queen in controlling domestic problems and in dealing with foreign powers. While she wanted to settle the claims on Alva's treasure, the battle made the queen appear not to be bargaining out of weakness or fear of Spanish reprisal. The results of her progress to Bristol in 1574 were an awareness of English military strength, among her own people and foreign visitors alike, and an equitable treaty that gave both countries a peaceful period for regrouping their defenses.

When danger threatened from Spain later in the 1580s, the queen curtailed her progresses and remained near London. With the exception of her 1582 journey with Alençon through nearby Kent, the queen did not have an extended progress between 1580 and 1590. Instead, she stayed in the London area or in the Thames River palaces: Nonsuch, Beddington, Chobham, Windsor, Eltham, Woking, and Syon. In London her residence often was St. James's Palace or Somerset House, in part because the sprawling palace at Whitehall was hard to defend. The expected sailing of the Armada dominated much of English politics in that decade, and Elizabeth wanted to be ready to defend her kingdom.

Exacerbating the threat from Spain was the threat closer to home that Mary Stuart represented. The Spanish and Scottish worry sapped Elizabeth's desire to travel at any great distance from London during the 1580s. As one plot led to another and the Scottish crisis came to a head in 1586, Elizabeth wrapped herself in London's security. In the summer of 1586, the queen did not go on a progress but stayed in her royal residences in the Thames valley. In October Mary went on trial at Fotheringay Castle in Northamptonshire for charges of treason and murder. Although Elizabeth had authorized the trial, she was ambivalent about the precedent it set in trying a monarch and in reaching a possible verdict that she would not want to uphold or execute. During that tense time in the fall of 1586, Elizabeth stayed at Windsor. When Parliament convened in a session dominated by the events at Fotheringay, Elizabeth missed the opening ceremonies and made a "deliberate retreat to Richmond" for the duration of the sitting.[59] She did not want to appear to countenance the parliamentary moves against Mary. Her distance from Parliament caused problems for her ministers, who had to travel between Westminster and Richmond, but such inconvenience was intentional. The queen wanted to slow the proceedings and possibly have them die from attrition so that the life of Mary Stuart would not rest in her hands. She was near enough to London to follow the proceedings, but also at a distance which inconvenienced the members and ministers attacking Mary. The ploy, however, did not save Mary's life: the parliamentary petition for her execution came to Elizabeth at Richmond on 12 November 1586. Still she procrastinated at Richmond by refusing to sign the warrant. Her tired lord treasurer, a committed enemy of Mary, wrote that "these hard accidents happen by her Majesty being so far from hence." At last the council and Parliament won. When Mary Stuart was executed at Fotheringay on 18 February 1587, Elizabeth heard the news from her palace at Greenwich.[60] By choosing an inconvenient residence during the parliamentary maneuvers of 1586–87, Elizabeth showed her desire to protect the life of her cousin as much as she felt able. While Elizabeth at last accepted the legal and political need to execute Mary, she reached that conclusion only after making the process difficult by staying at Richmond.

After the execution of Mary Stuart, rumors spread about the planned invasion of England soon to be launched by Philip II of Spain. What he could not accomplish indirectly by championing the Catholic Stuart claimant to the English throne, Philip had to seek now through direct military action. As the rumors circulated early in 1587 about invading expeditions from Spain, Elizabeth made plans for a defense. She had information from foreign sources that a fleet was gathered "to surpryse" the Isle of Wight in February. In response, she notified the lords lieutenant and their deputies to view their troops "as the necessitie of the tyme & the importaunce of the place requyreth."[61] Later, in the fall of 1587, she requested the formation of a guard to protect her in case of a Spanish invasion. That guard had grown by August 1588 to include 1,200 footmen and 87 horsemen under the charge of Lord Hunsdon. The bishops, as well as the counties, contributed to the queen's defense. Walsingham worked out the arrangements with Archbishop Whitgift in the summer of 1588, whereby each diocese shared the burden of sending men and horses. After many delays, by August the bishops' certificates came to a total of 559 lances and lighthorse and 3,885 footmen for the queen.[62] The summer prior to the August battles saw the Privy Council sitting almost daily at Richmond, and later Westminster, in order to respond quickly to new problems.[63] The queen was never far away.

As lieutenant and captain general, as well as a close friend, the earl of

Leicester felt especially responsible for the queen's safety during July and August of 1588. From the camp at Gravesend on 27 July, he wrote that Elizabeth should now gather her army around her and remain "no dowbts but I think about london." The militia should drill with its weapons and have the carriages and victuallers ready at a moment's notice. Although the queen planned to meet the enemy wherever he landed, Leicester advised against that plan. He suggested that she should visit her troops camped at Tilbury via the safe house at Havering. That arrangement would give her the protection of her army encamped in the outlying villages. After her officers investigated the lodgings, Elizabeth accepted this invitation. Leicester continued to assure her safety while urging her to come rally the troops. "Good swete q[ueen]," he wrote, "alter not your purpose yf god gyve you good health. . . . Your usher also lyketh your lodging, a proper swete clenly house, your camp within a lytle myle of you, & your person to be as sure as at St. James for my lyfe." His men would take great comfort from her presence, and she would cheer thousands in England.[64] From the tone of this letter and his reference to her health, Leicester feared that Elizabeth would change her mind about coming to Tilbury.

During this crisis, Elizabeth wanted to know as much as possible about the risks she assumed. She traveled by land from Greenwich back to Lambeth, where she took a boat from Westminster down the river to Gravesend, and then by carriage to the Tilbury camp two miles inland. Along that small stretch of the Thames were nests of guns in 10 locations that protected the queen on her journey.[65] While the forces of the duke of Parma struggled to reach their ships off the Dutch coast, Elizabeth stayed at Tilbury from 8 to 10 August with her host Thomas Rich at Ardern Hall. The queen's visit to Tilbury, where she reviewed the troops from her white gelding and later spoke rousing words of encouragement to them, remains one of the most colorful episodes of her reign. It also would have inspired her troops had Parma ever landed in Essex. Elizabeth was so consumed with the preparations and dangers that her advisors had to do much talking to convince her to return to St. James's on 11 August.[66]

Elizabeth's actions during the 1580s revealed her cautious and pragmatic approach to the threat from Spain. By staying near London and canceling any long progresses, the queen had more time to react to foreign news and to oversee the execution of her orders. She remained in London, the communications center of the island. Neither did she dissipate her councilors' energies by having them organize any progresses. Her priority of defending the country was a military goal that her travels would not help accomplish. While progresses were excellent settings from which to spread images of military strength and national power, their ceremonial message did not translate into victories on the battlefield or seas. The symbolic dialogue generated by the queen's travels had to yield during the 1580s to literal actions with bloody consequences.

The storms that blew the Armada toward Ireland did not, however, blow away the threats for long. In November 1588, the celebratory service at St. Paul's "to give public thanks to God for the victory" was delayed a week "for fear that a harquebuss might be fired at" the queen.[67] After her most significant victory over Spain, which happened more by luck than military policy, Elizabeth did not resume her progresses with her former enthusiasm of the 1570s. In the 1590s, she made two more extensive progresses that evoked memories of her 1572 and 1575 extravaganzas, but the atmosphere was different. In 1591 she traveled to Hampshire to check on the fortifications there. Earlier in the spring, the queen had received disturbing news of Spanish ships off the Cornish coast on their way to Ireland. Such a threat made her "very melancoly," and her southern itinerary reflected this concern. It was common knowledge at her court and abroad that the reason for this Hampshire progress stemmed from the queen's desire "voir les fortifications de Portesmeue." From 26 to 31 August, Elizabeth stayed in Portsmouth, where she had the customary military entertainments, before traveling near the coast to Southampton on 5 September.[68]

More than the fortifications drew Elizabeth to Portsmouth at that particular time. She also hoped that she might influence the outcome of Henry IV's campaign against the Spanish in Normandy and preserve English interests there. The new Bourbon king had yet to consolidate his hold over a kingdom riven by religion and afflicted by Spanish interference. Elizabeth had sent aid to the Protestant cause in France and wanted to make sure that her "tres cher bon Frere & Cousin Le Roy tres chrestien" was not squandering it.[69] She hoped for a meeting with Henry, so she made herself and her court geographically available should the French king care to cross the Channel. Having never been outside her country, Elizabeth did not contemplate going to visit him. Henry understood from his envoy, De Reau, according to a letter written 5 August (o.s.) from the French camp at Noyon, that Elizabeth would be at Portsmouth "los que nous cerons vers la coste de normandye." De Reau hoped "trouver bon que je vous y alle beser les meyns come Roy de navarre & estre aupres de vous deus heures."[70] Despite the tempting proximity of the English queen, Henry could not leave his country because of the urgency of planning for the siege of Rouen. He sent apologies through Ambassador Beauvoir la Nocle to Elizabeth, who fumed over what she perceived as unnecessary delays in attacking Rouen. In Elizabeth's assessment, Henry had delayed using the English troops during his journey north to meet with his German allies. He had sent Marshal Biron to Normandy in his place, and Elizabeth was not pleased. The French interpretation of the conflict credited the confusion to Elizabeth's vanity. The queen loved "it to be said that great princes have come to see her. During the siege of Rouen, thinking that the King was to come and see her, she went to Portsmouth with a great train, and she appeared to be vexed and to scoff that the king had not come thither."[71] Despite her reputation for vanity, however, Elizabeth was too politically practical to be hurt by Henry's absence. The progress to Portsmouth came primarily from the queen's desire to inspect her defenses and to provoke Henry IV into beginning the siege of Rouen. Undoubtedly Elizabeth looked forward to a meeting with the French king and was disappointed that he chose to remain in France. The main thrust of her travels, however, was the furtherance of English foreign policy and the strengthening of her coastal defenses.

After two satisfying progresses in 1591 and 1592, suspicions of a second attempted invasion in 1593 alarmed the queen and kept her once again close to London. She spent much of the late summer and early fall at Windsor. In August Francis Bacon reported that the queen was much bothered by the dangers in Scotland and France. In September at Windsor the earl of Essex "found the queen so wayward, as I thought it no fit time to deal with her in any suit." Elizabeth deferred her move to Nonsuch upon hearing news of the Spanish landing in Ireland in September 1595. That December she ordered an accounting of recusants by diocese, reflecting the Privy Council's concern "for the present estate of the realm . . . and the diminution of the forces for defence of the realm." The summer of 1596 she spent in palaces near London, including Greenwich, Nonsuch, Eltham, and Richmond, out of a continued apprehension "in this doubtfull tyme." Another scare came in July 1599 with reports of a large Spanish fleet at sea. While Sir Robert Cecil oversaw the mobilization of the fleet and trained bands, Elizabeth traveled between her royal residences around London but had no progress. The court remained at Nonsuch in early August, a situation that pleased the attending John Chamberlain. In a letter written 9 August to Dudley Carleton, Chamberlain noted the comforts of Nonsuch, "where I wish yt [the court] may tarry longe" without the country's going to war. The final Spanish threat to Elizabeth came in August 1601, as English troops landed in Ireland to resist the Spanish invasion of that close neighbor and perennial host to English enemies. Despite the dangers of invasion, the queen had decided to go on a progress through Berkshire, Hampshire, and Surrey. Sir Robert Cecil wrote to Archbishop Whitgift and Chief Justice Popham of his displeasure at the foolhardy risks such travel posed. Warning them to expect the arrival of the queen, Cecil wrote: "Of our Progress, I am sorry I cannot write unto you that it were abridged, you being well able to judge how ill these growing troubles concur with her Majesty being so far removed from her Council: for which purpose, because her Majesty sees you will not come to her, it is like that she will come to you."[72] Although they weighted the risks differently, both queen and her ministers shared the perception that in times of trouble she belonged with her council near London. But for her own reasons, perhaps the desire to make what could be a last progress, Elizabeth overrode her advisors' counsel and made the journey.

During times of peace, Elizabeth created an aura of military prepared-ness by traveling to inspect fortifications, watch mock battles, and con-clude treaties. These ceremonial events conveyed a general message of mil-itary strength. They also conflated her female status with the royal prerogative to defend the kingdom: the public saw her supervise the cere-monial defense of their locality—and by extension the country—and as-sume a martial role that as queen she had to delegate to men. As long as the danger remained hypothetical and distant, her strategy worked. But when Elizabeth faced a challenge to her authority, she sought the security of royal palaces in the Thames River valley and in London. The progresses did not give the queen the protection, the flexibility, or the efficiency that she needed in times of crisis. The chaos and expense of travel undermined her military defense of the kingdom, and the martial ceremonies for royal visits lost their former meaning in the context of real battlefields and casu-alties. Whenever the queen thought the progresses hindered her ability to rule, therefore, she changed strategies and abandoned them.

PARADOX OF ACCESS

While the progresses lay at the heart of Elizabeth's view of monarchy and her personal exercise of royal power, they had unintended consequences that challenged the queen's agenda in traveling. Her desire to interact with her subjects gave hundreds of hosts access to queen and court. Elizabeth's belief that her dynastic security lay in her popularity, however, ran head-long into the reality that her progresses made her more vulnerable. This openness, combined with the chaos of travel, allowed people into the court who ignored her ceremonial messages, who distorted them, and who wanted to harm the queen. In both her government and her travels, there-fore, the queen had to fight to keep control over the ceremonial dialogue and her royal agenda. On progress she included the worthy and excluded the poor to maintain the social and political hierarchies that empowered her monarchy.

When she went on progress, royal officials cleared her roads of undesir-ables. While riding out of Aldersgate in Islington in 1581, Elizabeth "was invironed with a number of begging rogues (as beggars usually haunt such places), which gave the Queen much disturbance." She sent a footman to the lord mayor and recorder of London, who immediately issued warrants. The next day city officers arrested "seventy-four rogues, whereof some were blind, and yet great usurers, and very rich. They were sent to Bridewell, and punished."[73] A common device in warding off vagrants was the far-reaching royal proclamation. "Whereas the Queens moste excellente matie is determined verie shortlie to make her remove from Grenwich unto her castle of Windsore, and soe from there to goe in progresse," began a proclamation of 5 August 1601, all masterless men, boys, vagabonds, rogues, and unauthorized women had to leave and avoid the court within 12 hours of the publication of the order. Other proclamations expanded the list of unauthorized personnel to include unlicensed artificers, launderers, persons "of the inferior sorte," and all their wives and children. Citizens near the court who received expelled people faced three hours in the stocks and the closure of their homes during the length of the royal visit.[74] While the queen sought contact with her subjects in situations where pageantry controlled the interaction, she did not hesitate to clear her court of common loiterers, whose status as outsiders threatened her ceremonial dialogue and potentially her safety.

Only licensed visitors could gain access to the court and queen. To banish idlers hanging about the court, Elizabeth issued proclamations calling justices of the peace to enforce existing vagrancy laws.[75] Porters in the royal household had orders to keep the gates shut against masterless men and women of low degree, and servants in all household departments had similar warnings.[76] Not only would such restrictions provide more security for the queen, but they also would decrease the expense of supplies pilfered by these unauthorized wanderers. To supplement the efforts of local officials, Burghley turned his orderly mind to regulating the household crowds. When the queen needed to guard against a likely Spanish invasion in 1593, Burghley drew up a list of defensive measures directed at the amorphous groups coming and going at court. He advised barring unnecessary persons from court and limiting the numbers of servants. The ushers and clerks of the household should inspect all petitioners seeking a royal audience. No one should use the back doors at court except for the designated servants who would then lock them. Most importantly, the knight harbinger and knight marshal should prevent crowds from lodging near the court on progress by surveying everyone within two miles of the court several times each week. Legitimate followers had to enroll their names in the porter's book or have a special warrant; otherwise, they faced gaol.[77] The negligible impact of these orders underscored the difficulty in policing the court and protecting the queen from her own subjects.

This concern about the crowds at court reflected more than a governmental fear of beggars, vagrants, and masterless people: the queen and her advisors knew that the progresses exposed Elizabeth to attack. Political assassination was so common in western Europe that all rulers had to take precautions against concealed poisons, pistols, and daggers. William of Orange, the French Henrys (Henry III, Henry of Guise, and Henry IV), David Rizzio, Henry Lord Darnley, and George Villiers, duke of Buckingham, all succumbed to assassination plots, and James VI of Scotland survived kidnappings and physical threats. Elizabeth was both bold and calculating in matters of her own safety. In circumstances of hidden dangers, Elizabeth protected herself: at public dinners, for example, she used tasters to guard against poison, and she strengthened her palace guards. But the public nature of the progresses made protecting Elizabeth more difficult. She stayed constantly in unfamiliar surroundings, crowds of people in towns had access to her, and most uncontrollable of all, the personnel in the royal household changed so that strangers could approach the court. Traveling around her realm brought the queen in close proximity to many strange people whose goodwill and respect could only be presumed.

Opportunities to do her harm abounded. In 1559 Elizabeth had an early lesson in the perils of her position as queen. While celebrating her birthday at Hampton Court, Elizabeth learned of a plot to poison Robert Dudley and her when they had dined the month before with the earl of Arundel at Nonsuch.[78] Another apparent attempt on her life was in fact more of an accident. In 1579, while Elizabeth barged down the Thames, Thomas Appletree discharged "a peece raishely and unadvisedly upon the watter" close to the queen's boat. Appletree claimed he accidentally fired his weapon and had no idea of the royal traveler's identity or location. The Privy Council committed Appletree and his companion, Barnaby Actton, to the Marshalsea, but Actton soon gained a pardon through his mother's petition to the council based on the accidental nature of the offense.[79] The risk of these attacks, intentional or accidental, was genuine, and the queen would face them throughout her reign. Nonetheless, in light of the many public meetings and numerous visits in which the queen could have been attacked and was not, Elizabeth enjoyed relative safety during her early progresses.

During the 1570s when she made some of her longest journeys, the queen met with little hostility or direct menace. This interlude, however, gradually ended as the plots sponsored by Philip II and Mary Stuart formed a regular prelude to the invasion of England in 1588. Between 1583 and 1594, Elizabeth survived plots by Francis Throckmorton, Thomas Parry, Anthony Babington, Robert Parsons, and the maligned Dr. Lopez. The holy war launched by Pius V in 1570, with his excommunication of Elizabeth and call for loyal Catholics to kill the English Jezebel, gained a momentum in the 1580s that kept Elizabeth close to London in her well-fortified royal palaces. Even brief trips within the greater London area brought risks. The concerned lord mayor of London, Sir Thomas Pullyson, was worried enough in 1585 about the queen's safety that he offered to guard her as she traveled to Greenwich. In a letter to Walsingham, her minister of security, Pullyson volunteered to bring bowmen from London "to attend the garde of her royall person in this her present shorte progresse."[80] Given the Throckmorton plot and the vigilante signers of the Bonds of Association who pledged to kill anyone ordering or benefiting from the death of Elizabeth, Pullyson did not believe he was overreacting. As he noted, "consideringe the present perilous tymes and contynuall maillice and myschevous purposes of the papistycall factyon," he was logical and prudent in his concern for the queen's safety.

But other, smaller plots troubled the queen no less than the major ones. In a society where the social order rested upon coerced obedience without efficient enforcement of the laws, a minor treason could loom as large as a major rebellion. The government, therefore, did not always distinguish between thoughtless words and serious intent to overthrow the monarchy; it was, in fact, hard to know the difference. After a violent argument with his father-in-law in October 1583, John Somerfield of Warwickshire spoke "lewdly" of the queen, calling her "a serpent and a viper," and conceived a desire to kill her. Despite Somerfield's claim "that he was a man distracted, not know[ing] what he did or intended," he faced indictment. Under questioning from John Doyly of Merton, Somerfield admitted that his "plan" consisted of going to London, finding the queen, and shooting her with his pistol. Doyly also examined Somerfield about his movements, acquaintances, and religious beliefs. He stated that he had not actually gone to London but had remained in "his hovell" all that month; nor did he premeditate his attack on the queen. As for religion, Somerfield denied knowing any Jesuits. When Doyly inquired about his possession of a crucifix, itself a serious offense, Somerfield shifted the guilt to his maid who, he stated, had left the crucifix in his window. Both his angry words and apparent Catholicism convicted Somerfield, who was committed to the Tower on 31 October.[81] Careless words and use of symbols were taken seriously when they touched on the queen's safety. Such cases and the government's response to them occurred more often than the queen would have cared to admit. Although her travels were supposed to elicit feelings of loyalty, her progresses did not persuade all people of either her sanctity or beneficence as queen. The power of the queen's presence could have unsettling, antagonistic consequences.

The laws against encompassing the queen's death by speech, printing unlicensed materials, harboring priests or Jesuits, and possessing crucifixes attacked religious and political nonconformity. Because rumors spread so quickly, harsh punishment struck those who spoke recklessly about the queen's welfare. Accused of spreading rumors of the queen's death during the Lopez scandal in February 1594, William Hancock, a tailor and servant to a musician at court, vigorously denied the charge. By way of defense, Hancock explained that he had heard from John Rogers, a chandler in Whitechapel, that Elizabeth was ill and that her sickness had caused her removal from Hampton Court to Greenwich.[82] He was not discussing her death, he claimed; instead, he was expressing concern for her recovery. Nonetheless, any public discussion of the queen's health was subject to charges of sedition and libel. Parliamentary acts and royal proclamations outlawed seditious and libelous words against the queen in hopes of crushing the pernicious rumors that could fuel a rebellion. People with access to the court had to keep their mouths shut. Idle talkers anywhere could harm the reputation that Elizabeth was cultivating through her progresses.

From angry words to violent action was a small step that court officials feared. Attempts to guard the queen often began with the household, since its organizational problems could place the queen in jeopardy. Every effort to reform the household mentioned restricting the numbers of people at court and requiring them to seek access through a porter. A proclamation of 1594 restrained suspect persons from approaching Elizabeth, but the problem had plagued the household since her accession.[83] The consequences of this uncontrolled access could be severe. In 1585 Edmond Neville, disappointed over a denial of fee farms, joined with Dr. Parry to kill Elizabeth in the name of Catholicism, justice, and the imprisoned Mary Stuart. The conspirators judged that the deed was best "performed especially when hir mat. went abroad to tak the ayre in the fields" of St. James's. As Elizabeth rode in her carriage, Neville and Parry would approach her from two sides and fire their daggers at her, presumably avoiding their own crossfire. Parry commented that when he later tried to kill the queen as she stood alone in the garden at Richmond, she had such a majestic presence reminiscent of her father that he could not harm her.[84] In another progress plot, William Stanley wanted to destroy the queen and crown the duke of Parma king in her place. Stanley and his conspirators thought her 1592 progress into Wiltshire would be "a meane and opportunietie fitt for this practise" and desired "the benefitt therof be not over slipped."[85] A year later, the same thought occurred to Robert Parsons and Gilbert Laton. Parsons advised Laton how he might strangle or stab the queen "and sheweth howe yt might be performed—her matie being in the progresse—and to be executed with a wyer made with jemos or with a poyniard." This opportunity appealed also to Patrick Collen and J. Annias, who thought it easy to shoot or stab the queen as she traveled on progress, "for she taketh no care of her going." In 1598 a disgruntled Edward Squier concocted a poison to kill Elizabeth and the earl of Essex. Because the poison could destroy its target by skin contact alone, Squier rubbed the poison on Essex's dinner chair. He also wandered up to the queen's horse in the stableyard, sprinkled the poison from a pricked bladder onto her saddle, and left unnoticed.[86] The confusion and crowds around the queen on progress made this scenario, and the others, perfectly plausible. The idea of harming Elizabeth while she traveled appears frequently enough to suggest that, for some disgruntled folk, the progresses offered the opportunity for violent, not symbolic, action. Despite efforts to limit access to Elizabeth and restrict the number of licensed people at court, the queen remained vulnerable to attack while on progress. The public meetings with her subjects, which were the essence of the progresses, at the same time provided the opportunity to do Elizabeth harm.

Just as access to the queen was a two-edged sword, so too the symbolic messages of the progresses could slip from the queen's control. Her travels occasionally elicited criticisms of the queen and her court from the very subjects who were supposed to be welcoming them. Such unpredictable responses to Elizabeth's intended political message illustrate again how flexible and shifting were the communications between her subjects and the queen on progress. Through ceremony and symbol Elizabeth might speak of her virtues as queen, but not everyone—especially not those who threatened her life—received and agreed with her message. Potentially treasonous rumors about Elizabeth's private life abounded and checked her ability to protect herself and her image. These challenges to the queen's self-created image resulted in what Susan Frye calls a "slippage of meanings," as the aging Elizabeth worked to protect her royal identity in matters of gender, virginity, and power.[87] The nature of her personal monarchy required Elizabeth to shape her public image, but the limitations of royal authority preordained some of these efforts to failure. Elizabeth could attract public attention, but she could not always control it.

It is not surprising that public criticism of Elizabeth focused on what was most unusual about her: her gender and her sexuality. A young, healthy, energetic woman who wielded power without the controlling hand of either husband or father presented a threat to comfortably held opinions on the roles of men and women. In sixteenth-century society, women were seen as intellectually inferior, sexually voracious, morally weak creatures descended from the temptress Eve, whose lapse led to the expulsion from the Garden of Eden. Women were, according to Aristotle, "imperfect men," and as such, women required the strong guiding hand of fathers or husbands.[88] As a reigning queen, Elizabeth differed from the female norm—she had her throne by the grace of God and her father

Henry VIII—but she still lived in a society where women were to be subordinate.

During the progresses the queen's freedom of movement in the company of admiring courtiers did start tongues wagging. Many rumors focused on the relations between Elizabeth and Robert Dudley, who as master of the horse and close councilor often attended the queen on progress. The rumors gained currency as the genuine attachment between the two became apparent.[89] Because of her admitted feelings for him, his exalted position at court, and Dudley's own intense unpopularity, some critics saw the queen's travels not as a ceremony of statecraft but as an extended tryst. One progress story of 1581 had an attentive Dudley slipping in front of a servant to hand Elizabeth down from her carriage; the slighted servant angrily asserted his right of office by boxing the bold Dudley's ears.[90] Such public signs of affection led to more lurid rumors. A citizen of Ipswich claimed that Elizabeth "looked like one lately come out of childbed." According to the gossipy report of the Spanish ambassador, the reason for her 1564 progress was that "Some say she is pregnant and is going away to lie in." Henry Hawkins publicly stated that "Lord Robert hath had fyve children by the Quene, and she never goethe in progresse but to be delivered."[91] Hawkins's story found its way to a Norfolk preacher, Thomas Scot, who reported it to the slandered Leicester and the justices of the peace, who bound Hawkins over for trial. For Hawkins, the progresses gave Elizabeth and Dudley repeated opportunities to be lovers and to hide (or murder) the purported offspring of their passion well away from the watchful eyes of Londoners. How wrong was his view of court life. Anyone who traveled with the hundreds of people in the queen's retinue would have smiled at the suggestion that Elizabeth found romantic privacy on the road. Had the much-traveled monarch actually gone on progress "to be delivered," Elizabeth truly would have been the mother of her kingdom. The fluidity and chaos of travel, which Elizabeth found helpful in manipulating her court, also inspired those critics uncomfortable with an independent sovereign queen.

Elizabeth addressed the related issues of her gender and her ability to govern by crafting a public image that included both indictment and rebuttal. The queen was careful to recognize (and accept) some of the general concerns about her ability even as she answered them with a defense that played upon social expectations. In her portraits, Elizabeth appeared amidst classical and biblical allusions to virginity that emphasized the wisdom of her own unmarried state and the good governance that she alone provided.[92] She was the pelican that fed its chicks from its bleeding breast and the vestal virgin who carried water in a sieve to prove her virginity; she wore pearls and white ermine to suggest purity, and her hair, like that of young maids, fell freely over her shoulders. Wings of lace, at times gigantic, sprang from her shoulders in homage to Elizabeth as the Fairy Queen, the Queen of Heaven, the Queen of England. Her portraits played on the theme of royal omnipotence by displaying her supervising the defeat of the Spanish Armada; wearing a dress covered with animals of the air, land, and sea over whom she had dominion; wearing another gown decorated with human eyes, ears, and mouths that suggested her omniscience; and hold- ing a rainbow in her hand so that she became the sun without which there would be no light, color, life. Few of them ever chronicled the passage of the years. As Elizabeth aged, her painted image grew younger, distant, asex- ual, and became timeless. In Nanette Salomon's analysis, the flat, distant royal images both displayed the powerful queen and erected a barrier that reminded the viewer of the gulf between queen and subject.[93] Elizabeth referred to herself in terms that recognized the boundaries of gender but twisted them into a testimony to her unique ability to surmount them.

She preserved her authority by reinventing herself through the media of her times—portraits, words, actions, and travels—and by attaching to herself the virtues typically attributed to men. Her clothing in the Armada portrait resembled armor, the shape of her body suggested broad male shoulders, and kingly regalia of crown, orb, scepter, and sword lay in the background.[94] She publicly referred to herself as both male and female, claiming male privileges while appearing to denigrate her unfortunate fem- ininity. In her speeches to Parliament, Elizabeth said that while she might be a weak woman she had the heart and stomach of a king; she could be turned out of the kingdom in her petticoat and still earn her keep; she re- ferred to herself as a king, prince, man; she was married to no man but was mother of all her subjects; she would not wade into deep matrimonial wa- ters with so shallow a wit.[95] Her understanding of the public concern about her gender's liabilities led Elizabeth to mount an oblique defense. Through her rhetoric, Elizabeth used feminine weakness and God's power to sup- port her male independence of action.

And in this effort, the progresses played an important role. On her visits to towns and estates, Elizabeth fashioned a public image that portrayed her as both king and queen, man and woman, divinely favored warrior and judge. But the public comments on her sexuality and the accusations of illegitimacy and infanticide revealed the limitations of the queen's ability to present herself. Loading and unloading wagons as the queen vacillated about leaving Windsor, a carter remarked, "Now I see that the queen is as woman as well as my wife."[96] In the moment of that statement, whether spoken in anger, irritation, amusement, or jest, Elizabeth had lost her regal dignity and distance, the ambiguity of her gender, and her solitary position in English society. Perhaps that was why she kept traveling and engaging in ceremonial dialogue with her subjects about the nature of her personal monarchy. The messages needed repeating.

The progresses allowed Elizabeth to unite the symbolism of her image with the powerful reality of her presence. In fostering religious stability, pursuing diplomatic negotiations, and defending the realm, the queen relied upon her physical presence and the ceremonies attached to it to shape events to her purpose. Sometimes she succeeded, sometimes not. The limitations of her royal authority appeared in the threats against her life and the renegade reactions to her self-constructed, contradictory image. But while these years of access and public interactions did at times reveal the constraints on her authority, her progresses and their ceremonies in many ways contributed to her longevity as queen. Elizabeth's progresses validated the structures of Tudor society that in turn supported her monarchy.

SEVEN

Conclusion

The travels of Elizabeth I revealed a monarchy in flux and a queen in negotiation. The physical motions of the traveling court reflected Elizabeth's dual goals: the consolidation of royal authority to foster national unity, and the manipulation of that power to refigure her own unique embodiment of royalty. To pursue the first, she turned to the progresses as a proven method of engaging the traditional bases of social support. On her travels, she visited the gentry, encouraged religious conformity, championed English causes abroad, and flaunted her country's martial strength. In this way, the progresses allowed her to cultivate popular support of the status quo. Through her choice of hosts and destinations, Elizabeth's actions on the road validated the commonly held views of hierarchy and social order. She remained in the populous, wealthier, Protestant, familiar southern part of the island, never risking her royal authority in areas of serious unrest, and her ceremonial messages emphasized the proper relationship between subjects and sovereign. By embracing her people's hospitality, Elizabeth also drew the gentry to her and, in effect, enlarged her court to include the rotating membership of her progress hosts. Thus she designed her government to draw strength from its sovereign's popularity as one link in a chain of glorious English rulers.

But to pursue the second goal, exerting her authority as a single woman over a society whose political structures excluded women, Elizabeth could not cling to the traditional. She needed to find ways of wielding her unusual power within established social conventions in order to maintain the essential ties between people, court, Parliament, government, and sovereign. In this effort, the progresses served Elizabeth well. Through their turmoil and constant change, they gave her a freedom to maneuver, to delay or avoid decisions, to forge an independent course of action. In insisting on progresses, which her government and household disliked, the queen was repeatedly making the members of her court do something that they preferred to avoid. For the queen, therefore, travel in itself became an expression of her will.

On a wider scale, through her progresses Elizabeth delineated the borders of her royal power. During visits she shaped the moments to highlight the relationship with her loyal subjects, but she did not control every aspect of the visit. Even in the ceremonial dialogue characteristic of her public occasions, the exchanged messages testified to the respective authority of all participants. Her progresses also circumscribed the groups of people whom the queen would meet. By never leaving the country, by avoiding the dangers of the rugged north and west, by concentrating on the south, she chose a safer, more predictable arena for her public visits. Even though Elizabeth embraced the idea of a personal monarchy dependent upon face-to-face exchanges with her subjects, her commitment remained more regional than national.

On her government and court, the impact of travel was significant. To many participants, the progresses siphoned money, effort, and time from the more important business of governing. Over the years, the extra costs of travel strained the purveyance system, forcing a change to composition, while regulation of the queen's household was a distant, even receding goal. But from Elizabeth's perspective, these inconveniences paled next to the benefits of access to her people, flexibility in reaching decisions, and control of her court. In their problematic pageantry, her travels became an extension of the queen's authority and a symbol of her approach to ruling.

Elizabeth's reliance upon her popularity and nurturing of her public image led her to stay with a set of hosts of local and national prominence. These men and woman gained access to the queen to pursue favors and enhance their status, and through these efforts they also acknowledged the power of her personal monarchy. During those days of entertaining Elizabeth, they briefly became part of her court in a relationship that lingered past her departure. As the queen stayed with hundreds of men and women in the countryside, clergy, townspeople, privy councilors, and members of Parliament, she seemed to be collecting the hospitality of the groups essential to maintaining the social order.

The presence of the queen at a host's house or in a town was a potent occasion that Elizabeth knew how to use to great effect. She conducted diplomatic negotiations, in part, through an intentional willingness to be present or to withhold her image. By being present, she indicated support and inclusion; by being absent, she unsettled, critiqued, delayed. Whether in matters of religion, law, or military defense, the queen ruled through her travels.

But this valuable access to Elizabeth had its pitfalls. The queen could not suppress all the slanders and troubling rumors that her progresses seemed to feed, nor could she always trust her safety to the crowds that had access to her. The best she could do was to issue orders banishing vagrants, limiting entrance to the household, and clearing the roads. Although contact with her subjects was the rationale for a progress, in those very moments of a visit the queen put her safety and reputation at risk. The travels intended to enhance her monarchy could slip from her control in ways that might undermine it.

In the end, Elizabeth's progresses mirrored the fortunes of her government, policies, private life, and monarchy. As a new queen negotiating the challenges of shaping a new church, organizing her government, and conducting foreign policy, Elizabeth made a few brief progresses close to London that allowed her to stay with trusted friends. With the blossoming of her relationship with Robert Dudley, her experience in governing, and her confidence in the religious settlement, the queen launched into the longer, relatively adventuresome progresses of the 1570s. But the 1580s brought threats from abroad and plots at home that constricted Elizabeth's movements to the safety of royal palaces along the Thames. She also began to lose the close friends and advisors who had supported her monarchy for decades. Despite their deaths and her own advancing age, the queen strove to keep her progresses alive in the 1590s. The long trips of the early part of that decade, however, had no match at the turn of the century. For both England and Elizabeth, the 1590s contained hardships—economic, political, and symbolic—that remained for her successor to tackle.

The progresses of Elizabeth brought together hundreds of people—hosts, workers, courtiers—in repeated ceremonies focused on the monarch. The face before the crowds, of course, was that of a woman, the daughter of Henry VIII, the monarch whose language proclaimed her to be both king and queen. With her horses, tents, and court at the ready, Elizabeth could add her progresses to the formidable bag of strategies that enabled her to confound adversaries, govern her kingdom, and shape her princely image. And ultimately the paradoxes within the progresses of Elizabeth mirrored the strengths and weaknesses of her government.

The last Tudor has received criticism for failing to address significant problems that continued to plague her Stuart successors. On the one hand, Elizabeth had built a national church whose inclusiveness alienated both Protestants and Catholics in the seventeenth century. She presided over a financial system that could not respond well in the long run to the increased royal demands placed upon it. Many in her government yearned for the day when "God Save the Queen" required a new ending and they would receive the offices and grants from the new king that the old queen had withheld. Her parsimony heightened expectations of liberality from the Stuarts, whose maleness seemed in many eyes to rectify a cosmic gaffe of queenly rule. On the other hand, her very success in defending the country against its Catholic enemies and surviving for four decades as monarch conditioned people to expect much from her successor. In her failures she hampered James I and Charles I, and in her triumphs she embodied a royal image that, to critics, the Stuarts did not match. All in all, she bequeathed a mixed legacy.

So, too, did her progresses contain the ambiguities that characterized the reign and accomplishments of Elizabeth I. She intended that her travels reinforce the popularity that she required as queen, so her court made regular journeys into the towns and counties of southern England. Yet that royal imperative evaporated when the context of her image making shifted to the north. By all accounts, the queen kept a close eye on her funds and made many decisions of policy on the basis of financial gains or losses. But when given evidence of her progresses' drain on the treasury, the queen turned away and planned the next journey. She worked hard at the business of monarchy, including the mundane tasks associated with the court, bureaucracy, and Parliament. Despite the pleas of respected ministers who bemoaned the deleterious effects her travels had on the government and on the smooth operation of royal affairs, Elizabeth insisted both on progresses and on responsible rule. And when her movements caused a flurry of rumors about her sexuality, gender, and competence, the queen continued to seek opportunities to meet her subjects and to interact spontaneously with them on occasions that she could not fully control.

These mixed messages illuminated the essence of the Elizabethan monarchy and the queen's multiple agendas. What all these contradictions shared was the queen's goal of dynastic and self preservation. The progresses made access to the queen a central issue of her reign, and by choosing whom to visit and whom to avoid, the queen exerted her authority on a daily basis. Such access was regulated and temporary, determined by the queen's will. So too did she shape the life and context of her court through her decision to travel. The unsettled operations of the itinerant government underscored the unchanging dominance of the queen at its center. As a master of double meanings, paradox, and misdirection, Elizabeth found in her progresses the quintessential way to enact her sovereignty.

APPENDIX I

Lists

Number of Household Servants, Elizabeth I and James I, after 1613
(PRO L. S. 13/168, ff. 368–71)

Dept.	Eliz	After 1613	1613 Book	New Book
Countinghouse	4	5	2	4
Bakehouse	18	18	12	16
Pantry	12	12	10	11
Buttery	10	12	10	10
Cellar	11	15	10	11
Pitcherhouse	4	4	2	3
Spicery	5	5	3	4
Chandlery	5	6	5	5
Ewery	7	7	6	7
Laundry	6	8	5	6
Confectionary	4	6	4	4
Wafery	2	2	1	2
Kitchens	70	82	76	78
Boilinghouse	3	3	2	2
Larder	10	11	8	9
Acatry	16	16	13	13
Poultry	10	11	7	8
Scaldinghouse	6	6	5	6
Pastry	14	13	9	11
Scullery	16	17	12	13
Woodyard	9	10	8	9
Herbingers	5	9	6	6
Almnery	5	5	3	4
Porters at Gate	6	7	6	6
Cartakers	4	6	4	4
Officers of the Hall	26	32	20	20
Messengers	1	1	1	1
Bellringers	1	1	1	1
Woodbearers	2	2	2	2
Wineporters	8	8	8	8
Longcarts	4	4	4	4
Guilder	1	1	1	1
Totals	305	345	266	289

Gifts given by the city of Norwich to the officers and servants of the queen's retinue in this her progress Ano [1578] according to usual custom (Bod. Rawl. MS, B 146, f. 116)

Clerk of the market		40 s.
Gentleman ushers		40 s.
Sword bearer from cities limits		20 s.
Grooms of the chamber		20 s.
Yeoman waiters		20 s.
Porters		20 s.
Officers of the spicery		20 s.
Serjeant at arms		40 s.
5 Ordinary messengers		40 s.
Yeomen of the mall [mail]		20 s.
Yeomen of the flagons		26 s. 8 d.
Marshall		26 s. 8 d.
Footmen	£ 3	6 s. 8 d.
Trumpeters		53 s. 4 d.
4 Harbingers		26 s. 8 d.
Surveyor of the ways		20 s.
Officers of the buttery		20 s.
Cooks and boilers		20 s.
Musicians of the viols		20 s.
Black guard		20 s.
Officers of the cellary		20 s.
8 Musicians who follow the tent		20 s.
Musicians		20 s.
Heralds at arms	£ 5	
Total	£37	

APPENDIX 2

Tables

In compiling the tables, I used the following sources: Chambers, "Court Calendar," in *Elizabethan Stage,* vol. 4; Colvin, *History of the King's Works;* Pevsner and Nairn, *Buildings of England;* Arlott, *John Speed's England;* the *DNB;* Williams, *Tudor Regime;* Kinney, *Titled Elizabethans;* Bindoff, *History of Parliament: House of Commons;* and Hasler, *History of Parliament: Commons;* and county and city histories listed in the Bibliography.

These charts do not attempt to locate the queen every day of her reign. Instead, I have focused on her lengthy trips away from London as "progresses," while her day trips around the greater London area appear as "London visits." Her movements among palaces in London, Windsor, Richmond, Oatlands, Hampton Court, Syon, Nonsuch, Greenwich, and Eltham are included only if they began a progress away from the city. The brackets and question marks in the tables indicate, for the most part, Chambers's clarifications and uncertainties, of which many unfortunately remain. Royal palaces in the queen's possession or leased out are marked with "r." I have adopted notation placing first the year and then the month and day. Letters help to keep the order when uncertainty exists. For example, in late August 1560, Elizabeth visited Odiham, Hartley Wintney, and Bagshot in that order, according to Chambers, but the exact dates are unknown. The "a, b, c" attached to the "28?–30?" days maintain that arrangement.

1. Chronology of Royal Visits and Progresses

Place	Co	R	Host	Date
Hadley	Midd		Stamford?, Lady Alice	58-11-22-23
Charterhouse	Lon		North, Lord	58-11-23-28
Baynard's Castle	Lon	r	Pembroke, Earl of	59-04-25
Woolwich	Midd		ship banquet, Elizabeth Jonas	59-07-03
Dartford	Kent	r	royal	59-07-17-18
Cobham Hall	Kent		Cobham, Lord	59-07-18-21
Gillingham	Kent			59-07-22?
Otford	Kent	r		59-07-23-28
Eltham	Kent	r		59-08-04
Croydon	Surrey		A of Canterbury	59-08-05-6?
Nonsuch	Surrey		Arundel, Earl of	59-08-06-10
West Horsley	Surrey		Clinton, Lord [Admiral]	59-08-17-23
Deptford	Kent			60-04-24-27
Lambeth	Surrey		A of Canterbury	60-07-29
Sutton Place	Surrey		Weston, Sir Henry	60-08-05
Woking?	Surrey	r	Weston, Sir Henry	60-08-05
Farnham	Surrey		B of Winchester	60-08-07-08
Rotherfield	Hants		Norton, John?	60-08-08?-12?a
Southwick	Hants		White, John	60-08-08?-12?b
Portsmouth, Netley Castle	Hants			60-08-12-13
Southampton	Hants			60-08-13-16
Winchester	Hants			60-08-16-23
Micheldever	Hants		Clerk, Edmund	60-08-23
Basing	Hants		Winchester, Marquis of	60-08-23-28
Odiham	Hants		Paulet?, Chidiock	60-08-28?-30?a
Hartley Wintney	Hants		Mason?, Sir John	60-08-28?-30?b
Bagshot	Surrey	r	Weston, Sir Henry?	60-08-28?-30?c
Horsley	Surrey		Clinton?, Lord [Admiral]	60-10
dinner	Lon		Dudley, Robert	61-06-24
Charterhouse	Lon		North, Lord	61-07-10-14
Strand	Lon		Cecil, William	61-07-13
Wanstead	Essex		Rich, Lord	61-07-14
Havering	Essex	r		61-07-14-19
Pyrgo	Essex		Grey, Lord John [d. 1569]	61-07-16
Loughton Hall	Essex		Darcy?, Lord	61-07-17
Ingatestone	Essex		Petre, Sir William	61-07-19-21
New Hall in Boreham	Essex	r	Sussex, Earl of	61-07-21-26
Felix Hall	Essex		Long?, Henry	61-07-26
Colchester	Essex		Lucas, Sir Thomas	61-07-26-30
Layer Marney	Essex		Tuke, George	61-07-26?-30?a
St. Osyth	Essex		Darcy, Lord	61-07-30/08-02
Harwich	Essex			61-08-02-05
Ipswich	Suffolk			61-08-05-11
Shelley Hall	Suffolk		Tilney, Philip	61-08-11
Smallbridge	Suffolk		Waldegrave, William	61-08-11-14
Hedingham	Essex		Oxford, Earl of	61-08-14-19
Gosfield	Essex		Wentworth, Sir John	61-08-19-21

1. Chronology of Royal Visits and Progresses (*continued*)

Place	Co	R	Host	Date
Lees	Essex		Rich, Lord	61-08-21-25
Great Hallingbury [Hastingbury]	Essex		Morley, Lord	61-08-25-27
Standon	Hert		Sadler, Sir Ralph	61-08-27-30
Hertford [Castle]	Hert	r		61-08-30/09-16
Hatfield?	Hert	r		61-09-16a?
Enfield	Midd	r		61-09-16b-22
Baynard's Castle	Lon	r	Pembroke, Earl of	62-01-15-16
Nonsuch	Surrey		Arundel, Earl of	62-63
Lambeth	Surrey		A of Canterbury	63-07-20/08-01?
Stanwell	Midd			63-08-02
Baynard's Castle	Lon	r	Pembroke, Earl of	64-06-28
Sackville House	Lon		Sackville, Sir Richard	64-07-05
Cecil House	Lon		Cecil, Sir William	64-07-06
Whitehall	Lon		Northampton, Marchioness of	64-07-15
Theobalds	Hert		Cecil, Sir William	64-07-27?
Enfield	Midd	r		64-07-31/08-01
Hertford Castle	Hert	r		64-08-01?-04?a
Aldbury	Hert		Hyde, Thomas	64-08-01?-04?b
Haslingfield	Cams		Worthington, Mr.	64-08-04-05
Grantchester	Cams			64-08-05
Cambridge	Cams		King's College	64-08-05-10
Long Stanton	Cams		B of Ely	64-08-10a
Hinchinbrook	Hunt		Cromwell, Sir Henry	64-08-10b
Kimbolton	Hunt		Wingfield, Thomas?	64-08-11-17a
Boughton	Nhants		Montague, Edward	64-08-11-17b
Launde	Leic		Cromwell, Henry Lord	64-08-18?
Braybrooke Castle	Nhants		Griffin, Sir Thomas	64-08-19/9-11a
Dallington?	Nhants		Corbett, Sir Andrew	64-08-19/9-11b
Northampton	Nhants		Crispe, Mr.	64-08-19/9-11c
Easton Neston	Nhants		Fermor, Sir John	64-08-19/9-11d
Grafton	Nhants	r		64-08-19/9-11e
Thornton	Bucks		Tyrrell, George	64-08-19/9-11f
Toddington	Bed		Cheyne, Sir Henry	64-08-19/9-11g
St. Albans	Hert	r	Lee, Sir Richard	64-08-19/9-11h
Great Hampden?	Bucks		Hampden, Griffith	64-08-19/9-11j
Princes Risborough?	Bucks		Penton, Mr.	64-08-19/9-11k
Shardeloes in Amersham?	Bucks		Totehill, William	64-08-19/9-11m
Harrow	Midd			64-09-12
Osterley	Midd		Gresham, Sir Thomas	64-09-12?b
Gray's Inn	Lon		Dudley, Robert	65-03-06
	Lon		Dudley, Robert	65-05-12
Durham Place	Lon	r	Knollys, Henry/Cave, Margaret	65-07-16
Ankerwyke	Berks		Smith, Sir Thomas	65-08-08
Sunninghill	Berks	r		65-08/9a
Farnham	Surrey			65-08/9b

1. Chronology of Royal Visits and Progresses (*continued*)

Place	Co	R	Host	Date
Bagshot	Surrey	r		65-08/9c
Osterley	Midd		Gresham, Sir Thomas	65-09
Nonsuch	Surrey		Arundel, Earl of	65-10-29?/11-02?
tilt at wedding	Lon		Warwick, Earl of/Russell	65-11-11
Baynard's Castle	Lon	r	Pembroke, Earl of	66-02-14
wedding	Lon		Southampton, Earl of/Browne	66-02-24-26
Bermondsey				
(E of Sussex)	Surrey		Mildmay, Thomas/Radcliffe	66-07-01
Hendon	Midd		Herbert, Edward?	66-07-08
Shenley	Hert		Pulteney, Michael	66-07-09-20a
Hatfield	Hert	r		66-07-09-20b
Knebworth	Hert		Lytton, Rowland	66-07-09-20c
Bygrave	Hert		Warren?, William	66-07-09-20d
Wrest	Bed		Suffolk, Duchess of	66-07-09-20e
Houghton				
Conquest	Bed		Ellensbury, Dame	66-07-09-20f
Willington	Bed		Gostwick, John	66-07-09-20g
Bletsoe	Bed		St. John, Lord	66-07-09-20h
Bushmead	Bed		Gery, William	66-07-09-20j
Kimbolton	Hunt		Wingfield, Thomas?	66-07-21
Leighton				
Bromswold	Hunt			66-07-22-28a
Fotheringay Castle	Nhants	r		66-07-22-28b
Apethorpe	Nhants		Mildmay, Sir Walter	66-07-22-28c
Colly Weston	Nhants	r		66-07-29,08-03
Stamford	Lincs		Cecil, Sir William, Greyfriars	66-08-05
Grimsthorpe				
[castle]	Lincs		Suffolk, Duchess of	66-08-06-16a
Sempringham	Lincs		Clinton, Lord [Admiral]	66-08-06-16b
Irnham	Lincs		Thimelby, Richard	66-08-06-16c
Exton	Rut		Harington, Sir James	66-08-06-16d
Kingscliffe	Nhants		Thorpe?, John? d. 1596	66-08-06-16e
Deene	Nhants		Brudenell, Edmund	66-08-06-16f
Dingley	Nhants		Griffin, Edward	66-08-06-16g
Coventry	War		Whitefriars	66-08-17-19
Kenilworth	War		Dudley, Robert (Leicester)	66-08-19-22
Warwick [Castle]	War		Warwick, Earl of	66-08-22?-23?
Charlecote	War		Lucy, Sir Thomas	66-08-24?
Broughton	Oxon		Fiennes, Richard	66-08-24?-25?
Woodstock	Oxon	r		66-08-26-31
Oxford	Oxon			66-08-31/09-06
Rycote	Oxon		Norris, Sir Henry	66-09-06-07
Bradenham	Bucks		Windsor, Lord	66-09-07-09
Bagshot	Surrey	r		66-09
Croydon	Surrey		A of Canterbury?	67-01-17?/02-01?a
Nonsuch	Surrey		Arundel, Earl of	67-01-21-27
Osterley	Midd		Gresham, Sir Thomas	67-01-27/02-01
Arundel House	Lon		Arundel, Earl of	67-02-10
Kingston	Surrey			67-08-01a

1. Chronology of Royal Visits and Progresses (*continued*)

Place	Co	R	Host	Date
Beddington?	Surrey		Carew, Francis	67-08-01b
Woking	Surrey	r		67-08-18?
Guildford Manor	Surrey	r		67-08-20-21
Loseley?	Surrey		More, William	67-08-22-23?
Farnham	Surrey		B of Winchester	67-08-24-25,29
Odiham	Hants			67-08-30a?
Bagshot	Surrey	r		67-08-30b?
Charterhouse	Lon			68-01-02
Hackney	Midd			68-02
Charterhouse	Lon		Norfolk, Duke of	68-07-06?-12?
Havering	Essex	r		68-07-13-15
Giddy Hall in Romford	Essex		Cooke, Sir Anthony	68-07-16-18a
Pyrgo	Essex		Grey, Lord John [d. 1569]	68-07-16-18b
Copt Hall	Essex		Heneage, Thomas [Sir]	68-07-19
Enfield	Midd	r		68-07-22, 25
Hatfield	Hert	r		68-07-30/ 08-03,04,07
Knebworth	Hert		Lytton, Rowland	68-08-01a
St. Albans	Hert	r	Rowlett, Sir Ralph	68-08-08
Dunstable	Bed		Wingate, Edward	68-08-09-13a
Brickhill	Bucks		Duncombe?, Thomas	68-08-09-13b
Whaddon	Bucks		Grey, Lord [Arthur Grey]	68-08-09-13c
Buckingham, parsonage	Bucks		Davers?, William	68-08-09-13d
Easton Neston	Nhants		Fermor, Sir John	68-08-14,21
Grafton Regis	Nhants	r		68-08-22-26a
Charlton	Nhants		Lane, Sir Robert	68-08-22-26b
Bicester	Oxon		More, Mr.	68-08-27
Rycote	Oxon		Norris, Sir Henry	68-08-27/09-12a
Ewelme	Oxon	r		68-08-27/09-12b
Wallingford, at college	Berks	r	Parry, Thomas	68-08-27/09-12c
Yattendon	Berks		Norris?, Sir Henry	68-08-27/09-12d
Donnington Castle	Berks			68-08-27/09-12e
Newbury	Berks			68-09-12-13
Aldermaston	Berks		Forster, William?	68-09-14-17
Reading	Berks	r	Stafford, Mr.; Gare, Mr.	68-09-18?
Lambeth	Surrey		A of Canterbury	69-07-21
Chertsey	Surrey		FitzWilliam?, Sir William	69-08-05?-08?
Woking	Surrey	r		69-08-09
Guildford	Surrey	r		69-08-10,12
Farnham	Surrey		B of Winchester	69-08-14,17,20,22
Kingsley	Hants		Backhouse, Nicholas	69-08-23-26a
Odiham	Hants			69-08-23-26b
Basing	Hants		Winchester, Marquis of	69-08-27,29/ 09-01
Abbotstone	Hants		St. John, Lord	69-09-01?-04?a

1. Chronology of Royal Visits and Progresses (*continued*)

Place	Co	R	Host	Date
Soberton	Hants		Lawrence, Lady Anne	69-09-01?-04b
Tichfield	Hants		Southampton, Lady	69-09-04,06
Southampton	Hants			69-09-06?,
Tower				08,09,14
Melchet	Hants		Audley, Richard?	69-09-15-21a
Mottisfont	Hants		Sandys, Lord	69-09-15-21b
Wherwell	Hants		Poynings, Sir Adrian	69-09-15-21c
Hurstbourne?	Hants		Oxenbridge, Sir Robert	69-09-15-21d
Steventon	Hants		Pexall, Sir Richard	69-09-15-21e
Vine in Sherborne				
St. John	Hants		Sandys, Lady	69-09-22
Hartley Wintney	Hants		Mason, Lady	69-09-22?-23?a
Bagshot	Surrey	r	Sutton, Sir Henry	69-09-22?-23?b
Bisham	Berks		Hoby, Lady	69-12
Ham House	Surrey		Châtillon, Madame de	70-03-19
Osterley	Midd		Gresham, Sir Thomas	70-07-16-18
Denham	Bucks		Peckham, Sir George	70-07-18-19
Chenies	Bucks		Bedford, Earl of	70-07-19/08-13
Pendley	Hert		Verney, Edmund	70-08-15-17
Toddington	Bed		Cheyne, Sir Henry	70-08-19-20
Houghton				
Conquest	Bed		Ellensbury, Dame	70-08-21-23a
Segenhoe in				
Ridgmont	Bed		Grey, Peter	70-08-21-23b
Wing	Bucks		Dormer, Sir William	70-08-24?
Eythorpe [Eydrop]	Bucks		Dormer, Sir William	70-08-25?-29?
Rycote	Oxon		Norris, Sir Henry	70-08-30/
				09-02,06,07
Ewelme	Oxon	r		70-09-08?-16?
Reading	Berks	r		70-09-17,24-26
Philberds in Bray	Berks	r	Neville, Sir Thomas	70-09-26?-29?
Bishopsgate	Lon		Gresham, Sir Thomas	71-01-23
St. George's Fields	Surrey			71-04-20
wedding	Lon		Northampton, Marquis/	71-04-29
			Helena von Snavenberg	
Bermondsey	Surrey		Sussex, Earl of	71-04/07? twice
Osterley	Midd		Gresham, Sir Thomas	71-06-07-08
Horsley	Surrey		Lincoln, Earl of	71-07/08a
Byfleet	Surrey	r		71-07/08b
Gunnersbury	Midd			71-08-08?a
Hendon	Midd		Herbert, Edward	71-08-08?b
Hatfield	Hert	r		71-08-15-21
Knebworth	Hert		Lytton, Rowland	71-08-22?a
Brent Pelham				
[Burnt]	Hert		Morley, Lord	71-08-26
Saffron Walden	Essex			71-08-27?a
Audley End	Essex		Norfolk, Duke of	71-08-29/09-03
Horham Hall in				
Thaxted	Essex		Cutts, Sir John	71-09-05

1. Chronology of Royal Visits and Progresses (*continued*)

Place	Co	R	Host	Date
Lees (Henham Park)	Essex		Rich, Lord	71-09-07-08
Rookwood Hall in Roding Abbess	Essex		Browne, Wiston	71-09-09?
Mark Hall in Latton	Essex		Altham, James	71-09-13,14,17
Stanstead Abbots	Hert		Bashe, Edward	71-09-20
Theobalds	Hert		Cecil, William, Lord Burghley	71-09-22
Hadley	Midd		Stamford, Lady	71-09-22?a
Harrow	Midd		Wightman, William	71-09-22?b
wedding	Lon		Oxford, Earl of/Cecil, Anne	71-12-16?-23?
wedding	Lon		Somerset, Edward/Elizabeth Hastings	71-12-23
Bishopsgate	Lon		Fisher, Jasper	72-07-15?a
Bethnal Green	Midd		White, Lady Joan	72-07-15?b
Havering	Essex	r		72-07-19-20
Birch Hall in Theydon Bois	Essex		Elderton, Edward?	72-07-21?
Theobalds	Hert		Cecil, William	72-07-22-25
Enfield	Midd	r		72-07-25?a
Hatfield	Hert	r		72-07-25?b
Gorhambury	Hert		Bacon, Sir Nicholas	72-07-25-28
Dunstable	Bed		Wingate?, Edward	72-07-28-29
Woburn	Bed		Bedford, Earl of	72-07-29-31
Chicheley	Bucks		Weston, Elizabeth	72-07-30?
Salden	Bucks		Fortescue, John [Sir]	72-08-01-04
Easton Neston	Nhants		Fermor, Sir John	72-08-04-08
Beachampton	Bucks		Pigott, Thomas?	72-08-04?
Edgecott	Nhants		Chauncy, William	72-08-10
Bishop's Itchington	War		Fisher, Edward	72-08-11
Warwick Castle	War		Warwick, Earl of	72-08-11-13
Kenilworth	War		Dudley, Robert	72-08-13-16
Warwick Castle	War		Warwick, Earl of	72-08-16-18
Warwick Priory	War		Fisher, Thomas	72-08-16a
Kenilworth	War		Dudley, Robert	72-08-18-23
Charlecote	War		Lucy, Sir Thomas	72-08-23a
Compton Wyniates	War		Compton, Lord	72-08-23b
Great Tew	Oxon		Rainsford, Henry	72-08-24?
Woodstock	Oxon	r		72-08-27, 09-07-19
Langley	Oxon		Unton, Sir Edward	72-09a
Holton	Oxon		Browne, Sir Christopher	72-09b
Ewelme	Oxon	r		72-09c
Reading	Berks	r		72-09-21-28
Philberds in Bray	Berks		Neville, Sir Thomas	72-09-28
Fold in South Mimms	Midd		Waller, Mr.	73-02-24/03-10a

1. Chronology of Royal Visits and Progresses (*continued*)

Place	Co	R	Host	Date
Islehampstead				
Latimer	Bucks		Sandys, Miles	73-02-24/03-10b
Gorhambury	Hert		Bacon, Sir Nicholas	73-02-24/03-10c
Brockett Hall in				
Hatfield	Hert		Brockett, John	73-02-24/03-10d
Northiaw	Hert		Warwick, Earl of	73-02-24/03-10e
Theobalds	Hert		Cecil, William	73-02-24/03-10f
Bishopsgate	Lon		Fisher, Jasper	73-03-07
Croydon	Surrey		A of Canterbury	73-07-14-21
Orpington	Kent		Hart, Sir Percival	73-07-21-24
Otford	Kent	r		73-07-24
Knole in				
Sevenoaks	Kent			73-07-24-29
Bastead	Kent			73-07-29
Comfort in Birling	Kent		Abergavenny, Lord	73-07-29/08-01
Oxenheath in				
West Peckham?	Kent		Cotton, Sir Thomas	73-08-01
Eridge	Sussex		Abergavenny, Lord	73-08-01-07
Mayfield?	Sussex		Gresham, Sir Thomas?	73-08-01?-07?
Kilndown	Kent			73-08-07a?
Bedgebury in				
Goudhurst	Kent		Culpepper, Alexander	73-08-07b-08
Hemstead in				
Benenden	Kent		Guildford, Thomas	73-08-08-11
Northiam	Sussex		Bishop, George	73-08-11
Rye	Sussex			73-08-11-14
Winchelsea	Sussex		Savage?, Mr.	73-08-11?-14?
Northiam	Sussex			73-08-14
Sissinghurst in				
Cranbrook	Kent		Baker, Richard	73-08-14-17
Boughton				
Malherbe	Kent		Wotton, Thomas	73-08-17-19
Smarden	Kent			73-08-17?-19?
Hothfield	Kent		Tufton, John	73-08-19-21
Olantigh in Wye	Kent		Kempe, Sir Thomas	73-08-21-22
Brabourne	Kent		Scott, Sir Thomas	73-08-22
Westenhanger	Kent	r		73-08-22-25
Sandgate Castle	Kent			73-08-25
Dover	Kent	r	Cobham, Lord [as constable]	73-08-25-31
Folkestone	Kent		Fisher, Thomas?	73-08-26
Sandwich	Kent		Manwood, Roger?	73-08-31/09-03
Wingham	Kent			73-09-03
Canterbury	Kent		St. Augustine's	73-09-03-16
Canterbury	Kent		A of Canterbury	73-09-07
Faversham	Kent			73-09-16-18
Tunstall	Kent		Cromer, William	73-09-18-19
Gillingham	Kent			73-09-19
Rochester	Kent		The Crown	73-09-19-23

1. Chronology of Royal Visits and Progresses (*continued*)

Place	Co	R	Host	Date
Bulley Hill, ship at				
Rochester	Kent		Watts, Richard	73-09-23-24
Cobham	Kent		Cobham, Lord	73-09-24a
Sutton	Surrey			73-09-24b
Dartford	Kent	r		73-09-24c-26
Deptford	Kent			73-11 (twice)
	Lon		Lincoln, Earl of	74-02-18-20a
Osterley	Midd		Gresham, Sir Thomas	74-02-18-20b
Lambeth	Surrey		A of Canterbury	74-03-02-03
Merton Abbey	Surrey		Lovell, Gregory?	74-05-30
Stanwell	Midd			74-07-07a
Colnbrook	Bucks			74-07-07b
Binfield	Berks			74-07-15a?
Reading	Berks	r		74-07-15b-23
Caversham or				
Rotherfield				
Greys	Oxon		Knollys, Sir Francis	74-07-23
Ewelme	Oxon	r		74-07-23-24
Holton	Oxon		Browne, Christopher	74-07-24
Woodstock	Oxon	r		74-07-24/08-02
Langley	Oxon		Unton, Sir Edward	74-08-02-03
Burford	Oxon			74-08-03
Sherborne	Glos		Dutton, Thomas	74-08-03-04
Sudeley Castle	Glos		Chandos, Lady	74-08-04-05
Boddington	Glos		Denne, Mr.	74-08-06-09?
Gloucester	Glos			74-08-10a
Churcham?	Glos			74-08-10b?
Frocester	Glos		Huntley, George	74-08-10c-11
Iron Acton	Glos		Pointz, Sir Nicholas	74-08-11a?
Berkeley Castle	Glos		Berkeley, Lord	74-08-11b-12
Berkeley Hearne?	Glos			74-08-13a
Bristol St.				
Lawrence	Glos		[St. Lawrence church in Bristol]	74-08-13b
Bristol	Glos		Young, Sir John	74-08-14-21
Keynsham	Som		Brydges, Henry?	74-08-21a
Morecroft	Wilts		Croft?, Stokes	74-08-21b
Bath	Som			74-08-21c-23
Hazelbury	Wilts		Bonham, John	74-08-23
Lacock	Wilts		Sherington, Sir Henry	74-08-23-28
Erlestoke [Stoke				
earle]	Wilts		Brouncker, William	74-08-28-31
Heytesbury	Wilts		Hawker, Mr.	74-08-31/09-03
Longleat	Wilts		Thynne, Sir John	74-09-02
Wylye?	Wilts		Mervyn, Lady	74-09-03
Wilton	Wilts		Pembroke, Earl of	74-09-03-06
Clarendon Park	Wilts	r	from Wilton; ruins	74-09-06a?
Salisbury	Wilts		B of Salisbury	74-09-06b-09
Amesbury	Wilts			74-09-07?

1. Chronology of Royal Visits and Progresses (*continued*)

Place	Co	R	Host	Date
Winterslow	Wilts		Thistlethwaite?, Giles	74-09-09
Mottisfont	Hants		Sandys, Lord	74-09-09-10
Somborne	Hants		Gifford, Henry?	74-09-10
Winchester	Hants			74-09-10-13
Abbotstone	Hants		Winchester, Marquis of	74-09-13
Alresford	Hants			74-09-14a
Herriard	Hants		Puttenham, George	74-09-14b
Odiham	Hants			74-09-14-16
Farnham	Surrey		B of Winchester	74-09-15,19
Bagshot	Surrey	r		74-09-24-25
Nonsuch	Surrey		Arundel, Earl of	74-10-19-22
Mortlake	Surrey		Dee, Dr.	75-03-16
Chiswick	Midd			75-04a
Osterley	Midd		Gresham, Sir Thomas	75-04b
Baynard's Castle	Lon	r	Pembroke, Lady	75-05-05-08
Stoke Newington	Midd		Dudley, John	75-05-23
Theobalds	Hert		Cecil, William	75-05-24/06-06
Broxbourne	Hert		Penruddock, Sir George	75-06-06-07a
Woodhall	Hert		Butler, Sir John	75-06-06-07b
Hatfield	Hert	r		75-06-07-14
Luton	Bed		Rotherham, George	75-06-15-18a
Toddington	Bed		Cheyne, Lord [Henry]	75-06-15-18b
Segenhoe in Ridgmont	Bed		Grey, Peter	75-06-15-18c
Holcutt	Bed		Charnock, Richard	75-06-15-18d
Chicheley	Bucks		Weston, Elizabeth	75-06-15-18e
Grafton	Nhant	r		75-06-19/07-06
Fawsley	War		Knightley, Sir Richard	75-07-07?
Long Itchington	War		Dudley, Robert	75-07-09
Kenilworth	War		Dudley, Robert	75-07-09-27
Meriden	War		Foster, William	75-07-28-29a
Middleton	War		Willoughby, Sir Francis	75-07-28-29b
Swinfen	Staff		Dyott?, John	75-07-28-29c
Lichfield	Staff			75-07-30a/08-03
Beaudesert	Staff		Paget, Lord	75-07-30b
Alrewas	Staff		Griffith, Walter	75-07-30c
Colton	Staff		Gresley, Lady Katharine	75-08-01-06a
Chartley	Staff		Essex, Lady	75-08-01-06b
Stafford Castle	Staff		Stafford, Lord	75-08-07-08
Ellenhall	Staff		Harcourt, Walter?	75-08-09-11a
Chillington	Staff		Giffard, John	75-08-09-11b
Dudley Castle	Wor		Dudley, Lord	75-08-12
Hartlebury Castle	Wor		B of Worcester	75-08-12-13
Worcester	Wor		B of Worcester	75-08-13-20
Hindlip	Wor		Habington, John	75-08-16
Hallow Park	Wor		Habington, John	75-08-18
Batenhall Park	Wor		Bromley, Thomas [Sir]	75-08-19
Elmley Bredon	Glos		Daston, Anne	75-08-20-22
Evesham?	Wor			75-08-21?

1. Chronology of Royal Visits and Progresses (*continued*)

Place	Co	R	Host	Date
Campden	Glos		Smythe, Thomas	75-08-22-26a
Sudeley Castle	Glos		Chandos, Lord	75-08-22-26b
Sherborne	Glos		Dutton, Thomas	75-08-22-26c
Langley	Oxon		Unton, Sir Edward	75-08-27
Cornbury	Oxon		Stafford?, Thomas	75-08-29
Woodstock	Oxon	r		75-08-29/10-03
Holton	Oxon		Browne, Christopher	75-10-04-05?
Rycote	Oxon		Norris, Lord	75-10-06-08
Bradenham [Bradnam]	Bucks		Windsor, Lord Frederick	75-10-09a
Wooburn [Uburne]	Bucks		Goodwin, Sir John	75-10-09b
Philberds in Bray	Berks		Neville, Sir Thomas	75-10-09c
Colnbrook	Bucks			75-12-20
Leicester House	Lon		Dudley, Robert	76-05-09-10
Osterley	Midd		Gresham, Sir Thomas	76-05-10-12
Pyrford	Surrey		Lincoln, Earl of	76-05-12-15
Nonsuch	Surrey		Arundel, Earl of	76-05-15-17
Beddington	Surrey		Carew, Sir Francis	76-05-17-19
Hatfield	Hert	r		76-06-07?
Deptford	Kent			76-06-18
Eltham	Kent	r		76-06
Highgate	Midd		Lichfield, Thomas?	76-07a
Fold? at Barnet	Midd		Waller, Mr.	76-07b
Hendon	Midd		Herbert, Edward	76-07c
Stratford at Bow	Midd		Young, Richard?	76-07-30
Havering	Essex	r		76-07-30/08-07
Pyrgo	Essex		Grey, Henry	76-08-05a?
Harolds Park	Essex		hunting	76-08-05b?
Chigwell Hall	Essex		Petre, Sir John	76-08-07a
Loughborough	Essex		Stonard, John	76-08-07b
Upshire?	Essex			76-08-10
Mark Hall in Latton	Essex		Altham, James	76-08-10-11
Hatfield Broadoak	Essex		Barrington, Sir Thomas	76-08-11
Great Hallingbury [Hastingbury]	Essex		Morley, Lord	76-08-11-14
Stanstead Abbots	Hert		Bashe, Edward	76-08-14-19
Hertford Castle	Hert	r		76-08-19-22
Hatfield	Hert	r		76-08-24
Hertford [Castle]	Hert	r		76-08-26-28
Northiaw	Hert		Warwick, Earl of	76-08-30
St. Albans	Hert	r		76-08-30/09-01
Gorhambury	Hert		Bacon, Sir Nicholas	76-09-01
Latimer	Bucks		Sandys, Miles	76-09-01-03
Chalfont St. Giles	Bucks		Gardiner, John?	76-09-03?
Hedgerley	Bucks		Drury, Sir Robert	76-09-03
Windsor	Berks	r		76-09-03-10
Folly John Park	Berks			76-09-03-10?

1. Chronology of Royal Visits and Progresses (*continued*)

Place	Co	R	Host	Date
Thorpe	Surrey		Polsted, Richard	76-09-10
Byfleet	Surrey	r		76-09-10-11
Pyrford	Surrey		Lincoln, Earl of	76-09-11-12
Guildford	Surrey	r		76-09-12
Loseley in				
Artington	Surrey		More, Sir William	76-09-12-13
Farnham	Surrey		B of Winchester	76-09-13?-20
Odiham	Hants			76-09-20-22
Mr. Hall's	Berks			76-09-22
Reading	Berks	r		76-09-22/10-08
Rotherfield Greys	Oxon		Knollys, Sir Francis	76-10-08
Hurst	Berks		Ward, Richard	76-10-08-09
Windsor	Berks	r		76-10-09-12
Wanstead?	Essex		Dudley, Robert	77-02-26/03-03
Leicester House	Lon		Dudley, Robert	77-05-09-10
Stoke Newington	Midd		Dudley, John	77-05-14?
Theobalds	Hert		Cecil, William	77-05-15-17?
Northiaw	Hert		Warwick, Earl of	77-05-18?
Gorhambury	Hert		Bacon, Sir Nicholas	77-05-18-22
Fold? at Barnet	Midd		Waller, Mr.	77-05-23-25?a
Highgate	Midd		Lichfield, Thomas?	77-05-23-25?b
Southwark	Surrey		George Earl of Cumberland	77-06-24
Deptford	Kent			77-07
Isleworth				
[Thistleworth]	Midd		Derby, Countess of, [Margaret]	77-07-24
Barn Elms	Surrey		Walsingham?, Sir Francis	77-07-26a
Mortlake Park				
Lodge	Surrey		Dudley, Robert	77-07-26b
Pyrford	Surrey		Lincoln, Earl of	77-09-04-07?
Hanworth	Midd	r	Somerset, Duchess of	77-09-12
Sir John Zouch			Zouch, Sir John	77-09
Thorpe	Surrey		Polsted?, Richard	77-09-23
Sunninghill	Berks	r		77-09
Osterley	Midd		Gresham, Sir Thomas	78-02
Putney	Surrey		Lacy?, John	78-02-25-27
Leicester House	Lon		Dudley, Robert	78-02-27/03-03?
Leicester House	Lon		Dudley, Robert	78-04-05,28
Tottenham	Midd		Compton, Lord	78-05-06-07
Theobalds	Hert		Cecil, William	78-05-07-10
Stanstead Abbots	Hert		Bashe, Edward	78-05-10-12
Copt Hall	Essex		Heneage, Sir Thomas	78-05-12-13
Wanstead	Essex		Dudley, Robert	78-05-13-16
West Ham	Essex		Meautys, Henry?	78-07-11?
Havering	Essex	r		78-07-12-20
Theydon Garnon	Essex		Branch, John	78-07-21-22
Mark Hall in				
Latton	Essex		Altham, James	78-07-23
Standon	Hert		Sadler, Sir Ralph	78-07-24
Berden Priory	Essex		Averie, Margery	78-07-25?

I. Chronology of Royal Visits and Progresses (*continued*)

Place	Co	R	Host	Date
Audley End	Essex		Howard, Thomas	78-07-26-30
Barham Hall in				
Linton	Suffolk		Milsent, Robert	78-07-31a
Keddington	Suffolk		Barnardiston, Thomas	78-07-31b
De Greys in				
Cavendish	Suffolk		Colt, Sir George	78-08-01
Long Melford	Suffolk		Cordell, Sir William	78-08-03-05
Lawshall	Suffolk		Drury, Sir William	78-08-05
Bury St. Edmunds	Suffolk			78-08-05-06
Onehouse?	Suffolk		Drury, Sir William	78-08-07-09a
Stowmarket?	Suffolk			78-08-07-09b
Euston	Suffolk		Rookwood, Edward	78-08-10
Kenninghall	Norf		Surrey, Earl of	78-08-11-12
Bracon Ash	Norf		Townsend, Thomas	78-08-16
Norwich	Norf		B of Norwich	78-08-16-22
Costessey	Norf		Jerningham, Lady Mary	78-08-19
Mount Surrey on				
Mousehold Hill	Norf		Surrey, Earl of	78-08-20
Kimberley	Norf		Woodhouse, Sir Roger	78-08-22 or 23
Wood Rising	Norf		Southwell, Sir Robert	78-08-24
Breckles	Norf		Woodhouse, Francis	78-08-25-26?
Thetford	Norf		Clere, Sir Edward	78-08-27
Hengrave	Suffolk		Kitson, Sir Thomas	78-08-28-30
Chippenham	Cams		Revett, Thomas	78-09-01
Kirtling	Cams		North, Lord	78-09-01-03
Horseheath	Cams		Alington, Sir Giles	78-09-04
Waltons in				
Ashdon [now				
Bartlow]	Essex		Tyrell, Edward	78-09-05-06?
Horham Hall in				
Thaxted	Essex		Cutts, Sir John	78-09-07,11
Manuden	Essex		Crawley, Thomas	78-09-12-13?
Hadham Hall	Hert		Capel, Henry	78-09-14
Hyde Hall in				
Sawbridgeworth	Hert		Heigham, Henry?	78-09-14?
Hatfield				
Broadoak?	Essex		Barrington, Sir Thomas	78-09-15
Rookwood Hall in				
Roding Abbess	Essex		Browne, Wiston	78-09-18
Theydon Bois	Essex		Elderton, Mrs.	78-09-18?
Gaynes Park	Essex		Fitzwilliam, Sir William	78-09-19
Loughborough	Essex		Stonard, John	78-09-21-22
Wanstead	Essex		Dudley, Robert	78-09-23?
Putney	Surrey		Lacy, John	79-01-31?
Leicester House	Lon		Dudley, Robert	79-01/02
Wanstead	Essex		Dudley, Robert	79-04-28?/05-02
Wanstead	Essex		Dudley, Robert	79-06-24-26
Gravesend	Kent			79-07-15-17a
Deptford	Kent			79-07-15-17b

1. Chronology of Royal Visits and Progresses (*continued*)

Place	Co	R	Host	Date
Wanstead	Essex		Dudley, Robert	79-08-30-31
Stratford at Bow	Midd		Young, Richard?	79-09-09
Havering	Essex	r		79-09-11-14
Ingatestone	Essex		Petre, Lady	79-09-15-16?
New Hall in				
Boreham	Essex		Sussex, Earl of	79-09-17-18
Moulsham	Essex		Mildmay, Sir Thomas	79-09-19-24a
Thoby	Essex		Berners, Anthony?	79-09-19-24b
Brentwood				
[Burntwood]	Essex		Searle, John?	79-09-19-24c
Giddy Hall in				
Romford	Essex		Cooke, Richard	79-09-25-27
Ilford, at				
St. Mary's				
Hospital?	Essex		Fanshawe, Thomas	79-09-27?
Charterhouse	Lon			80-02
Nonsuch	Surrey			80-05-26-29
Putney	Surrey		Lacy, John	80-05-26?
Beddington	Surrey		Carew, Sir Francis	80-06
Molesey	Surrey			80-07-11 or 12
Chobham	Surrey			80-07/08a
Chobham	Surrey		Bray, Edward?	80-07/08b
Chobham	Surrey		Wolley, John	80-07/08c
Pyrford	Surrey		Lincoln, Earl of	80-07/08d
Sunninghill	Berks	r		80-08-16-20
Woking	Surrey	r		80-08-25?-27?
Molesey	Surrey		Brand, Thomas	80-09-13
Mortlake	Surrey		Dee, Dr. John	80-09-17
Mortlake	Surrey		Dee, Dr.	80-10-10
Harmondsworth	Midd		Drury, Mr.	80-11a
Colnbrook	Bucks		Draper, Henry?	80-11b
Windsor	Berks	r		80-11c
Eton College	Bucks			80-11d
Ditton Park	Surrey			80-11e
Nonsuch	Surrey			80-11f
Deptford, Golden				
Hind	Kent		Drake, Sir Francis	81-04-04
Eltham	Kent	r		81-06-26-30
Aldersbrook in				
Little Illford?	Essex		Fuller, Nicholas?	81-07-05-08a
Loughborough	Essex		Stonard, Francis	81-07-05-08b
Leyton	Essex		Paulett, Lady Mary	81-07-05-08c
Wanstead	Essex		Dudley, Robert	81-07-27-29
Eltham	Kent	r		81-09
Sundridge	Kent		Isley, William	81-09
Nonsuch	Surrey			81-09-22-23
Streatham	Surrey		Forth, Dr. Robert	81-09-22?
Beddington	Surrey		Carew, Sir Francis	81-10-03
Putney	Surrey		Lacy, John	81-11-16 or 17

I. Chronology of Royal Visits and Progresses (*continued*)

Place	Co	R	Host	Date
Deptford	Kent		launch of Golden Lion	82-01
Southfleet	Kent		Sedley, William?	82-02-01
Rochester	Kent		The Crown	82-02-01-03
Sittingbourne	Kent		The George	82-02-03-05
Canterbury	Kent		Manwood, Sir Roger	82-02-05-06
Sandwich	Kent		Manwood, Mr.	82-02-08
Dover	Kent		St. James [sign of Queen's Arms]	82-02-09-11?
Canterbury	Kent	r		82-02-12
Faversham	Kent			82-02-13
Newington	Kent			82-02-14
Rochester	Kent			82-02-14-16
Bulley Hill	Kent		Watts, Anne?	82-02-15?
Swanscombe	Kent		Weldon, Ralph	82-02-16
Horseman Place in Dartford	Kent		Beer, Nicholas?	82-02-16-17
Highgate	Midd		Sheffield, Lady	82-03
Wanstead	Essex		Dudley, Robert	82-04
Somerset House	Lon	r	Hunsdon, Lord (wedding, Sir Edw)	82-05-20-22
Nonsuch	Surrey			82-07-10-12
Putney	Surrey		Lacy, John	82-07-10?
Beddington	Surrey		Carew, Sir Francis	82-07/08?
Molesey	Surrey		Brand, Thomas	82-08-17
Woking	Surrey	r		82-08/09?
Chobham	Surrey		Wolley, John	82-08/09?
Pyrford	Surrey		Lincoln, Earl of	82-09-01-02
Byfleet	Surrey	r	Askewe, Lady Anne	82-09-01?
Egham	Surrey		Kellefet, Richard	82-09-20
Folly John	Berks			82-09a
Mote Park				82-09b
Sunninghill	Berks	r		82-09c
Colnbrook	Bucks			83-01-12?
Barn Elms	Surrey		Walsingham, Sir Francis	83-02-11
Somerset House	Lon	r	Hunsdon, Lord	08-03
wedding	Lon		Southwell, Robert/Howard, Elizabeth	83-04-13
Clapham	Surrey		Worsopp, John	83-04-18
Theobalds	Hert		Cecil, William	83-05-27-31/ 06-01a
Ponsbourne	Hert		Cock, Sir Henry	83-05-27-31/ 06-01b
Edmonton	Midd		Nicholas, Lady	83-05-27-31/ 06-01c
Hackney	Midd		Hayward, Sir Rowland	83-05-27-31/ 06-01d
Chelsea	Midd	r		83-07-30a
Mortlake	Surrey			83-07-30b
Sion	Midd			83-07-30c

1. Chronology of Royal Visits and Progresses (*continued*)

Place	Co	R	Host	Date
Nonsuch	Surrey			83-07
Streatham	Surrey			83-07
Woking	Surrey	r		83-08-27?a
Loseley	Surrey		More, Sir William	83-08-27?b
Guildford	Surrey	r		83-08-27?c
Petworth?	Sussex		Northumberland, Earl of	83-08-27?d
Pyrford	Surrey		Lincoln, Earl of	83-08
Sunninghill	Berks	r		83-08
Chobham	Surrey		Wolley, John	83-09a
Egham	Surrey			83-09b
Arundel House	Lon		Arundel, Earl of	83-10?/12?
Brentford	Midd		Wilkes, Thomas	83-11-25?
Heneage House			Heneage, Sir Thomas	84-01/02
Tower Hill	Lon		Lumley, Lord	84-01/02
Stockwell	Surrey			84-06-09
Nonsuch	Surrey			84-07-17-21
Kingston	Surrey		Evelyn, George	84-08-07
Cobham	Surrey		Gavell?, Robert	84-08
Egham	Surrey			84-09-02a
Sunninghill	Berks	r		84-09-02b
Burley Bushes				84-09-02c
Bagshot	Surrey	r	Weston, Sir Henry	84-09-02d
Blackwater	Hants			84-09-02e
Nonsuch	Surrey			84-11-05
Putney	Surrey		Lacy, John	84-11-12
Arundel House	Lon			84-12
Lambeth	Surrey		A of Canterbury	85-03-26-30
Croydon	Surrey		A of Canterbury	85-03-30?a
Beddington	Surrey		Carew, Sir Francis	85-03-30?b
Lambeth	Surrey		A of Canterbury	85-04-03
Lewisham	Kent			85-04
Croydon	Surrey			85-05-02?
Theobalds	Hert			85-05-18
Edmonton	Midd		Brassey, Mr.	85-05-18a
Tottenham High Cross	Midd		Martin, Richard	85-05-18b
Barn Elms	Surrey			85-07-11
Nonsuch	Surrey			85-07-20-24
Putney	Surrey		Lacy, John	85-07-27-29
Wimbledon	Surrey			85-08-25?
Beddington	Surrey		Carew, Sir Francis	85-08
Westminster	Lon	r	Lord Admiral	85-11-17-19
Lambeth	Surrey		Burgh, Lord	85-12-20-21
Croydon	Surrey			86-04-26/05-01
Putney	Surrey		Lacy, John	86-07-12
Colnbrook	Bucks			86-10-24
Nonsuch	Surrey			87-05-01 or 02
Streatham	Surrey		Forth, Dr. Robert	87-05-25?
Beddington	Surrey		Carew, Sir Francis	87-05

1. Chronology of Royal Visits and Progresses (*continued*)

Place	Co	R	Host	Date
Theobalds	Hert		Cecil, William	87-07-09a
Hackney	Midd		Hayward, Sir Rowland	87-07-09b
Enfield	Midd	r	Middlemore, Henry	87-07-09c
Waltham Forest	Essex			87-07-09d
Cheshunt	Hert		Talbot, Lord	87-07-09e
Northiaw	Hert		Warwick, Earl of	87-07-20-21
Barnet	Hert		Waller, Mr.	87-08-13a
Harrow	Midd		Wightman, William	87-08-13b
Sion	Midd			87-08-13c
West Molesey	Surrey		Brand, Thomas	87-08-13d
Westminster	Lon	r	Lord Admiral dinner	87-10-24
Westminster	Lon	r	Lord Admiral	87-11-17-21
Barn Elms	Surrey		Walsingham, Sir Francis	87-11-20
Ely House	Lon		Hatton, Sir Christopher	87-11-21/12-06
Fulham	Midd		B of London	88-01-16-20a
Hounslow	Midd		Crompton, Thomas	88-01-16-20b
Kensington	Midd		Malinge, Mr.	88-01-16-20c
Lambeth	Surrey		A of Canterbury	88-01-16-20d
Hackney	Midd		Hayward, Sir Rowland	88-04-13-16a
Tottenham High				
Cross	Midd		Martin, Richard	88-04-13-16b
Stoke Newington?	Midd		Townsend, Roger?	88-04-13-16c
Erith	Kent		Compton, Thomas?	88-04/05a
Croydon	Surrey		A of Canterbury	88-04/05b
Lewisham	Kent			88-04/05c
Wanstead	Essex		Dudley, Robert	88-05-07
Putney	Surrey		Lacy, John	88-07-29
Tilbury	Essex		camp	88-08-08-10a
Ardern Hall in				
Horndon	Essex		Rich, Thomas	88-08-08-10b
Belhus in Aveley?	Essex		Barrett, Edward	88-08-08-10c
Ely House	Lon		Hatton, Sir Christopher	88-08-19
Barn Elms	Surrey		Walsingham, Sir Francis	89-05-26-28
Highgate	Midd			89-06-11?
Nonsuch	Surrey			89-06-18-19
Merton Abbey	Surrey		Lovell, Gregory	89-06-18?
West Molesey	Surrey		Brand, Thomas	89-08-10?
Putney	Surrey		Lacy, John	89-12-02
Bedford House?	Lon		Warwick, Earl of	90-01-27
Hackney	Midd		Hayward, Sir Rowland	90-05-31
Waltham Forest	Essex		Bartlett, Sir Richard	90-06
Ely House	Lon		Hatton, Sir Christopher	90-06-04-06
Sydenham House	Kent		Aubrey?, William	90-07-28/08-06a
Beddington	Surrey		Carew, Sir Francis	90-07-28/08-06b
Chessington	Surrey		Harvey, William	90-07-28/08-06c
Stoke d'Abernon	Surrey		Leyfield, Thomas	90-07-28/08-06d
Woking	Surrey	r		90-08-30-31
Chobham	Surrey		Bray, Edward?	90-08-31/09-06a
Sunninghill	Berks	r		90-08-31/09-06b

1. Chronology of Royal Visits and Progresses (*continued*)

Place	Co	R	Host	Date
Ditton Park	Surrey			90-09a
Folly St. John Park	Berks?		Norris, Mr.	90-09b
Putney	Surrey		Lacy, John	90-11-08?
Sydenham Park	Kent			90-11
Ely House	Lon		Hatton, Sir Christopher	90-11
Mortlake	Surrey			90-12-04
East Sheen	Surrey			90-12-14
Lambeth	Surrey		A of Canterbury	91-02-11-13
Hackney	Midd		Hayward, Sir Rowland	91-05-09-10
Tottenham High Cross	Midd		Martin, Sir Richard	91-05-10?
Theobalds	Hert		Cecil, William	91-05-10-20
Enfield	Midd	r	Wroth, Robert	91-05-21-23a
Havering	Essex	r		91-05-21-23b
Croydon?	Surrey			91-07-01?
Burghley House	Lon		Cecil, William	91-07-19
Mitcham	Surrey		Blank, Margaret Lady	91-07-29?
Nonsuch	Surrey			91-08-01-02
Beddington	Surrey		Carew, Sir Francis	91-08-02a
Leatherhead	Surrey		Tilney, Edmund	91-08-02b
East Horsley	Surrey		Cornwallis, Thomas	91-08-03
Clandon Park	Surrey		Weston, Sir Henry	91-08-03?
Guildford	Surrey	r		91-08-04
Loseley	Surrey		More, Sir William	91-08-05-09
Katherine Hall	Surrey			91-08-09?
Farnham	Surrey		B of Winchester	91-08-10-14
Bramshott	Hants		Mervyn, Edmund	91-08-14
Cowdray	Sussex		Montague, Lord	91-08-14-20
Holt, The	Sussex		Delawarr, Lord	91-08-14b
Oseburn Priory	Sussex		Montague, Lord	91-08-17
West Dean	Sussex		Lewknor, Sir Richard	91-08-20
Chichester	Sussex		Lumley, Lord	91-08-20-22
Stanstead	Sussex		Lumley, Lord	91-08-26
Portsmouth	Hants		Sussex, Earl of	91-08-26-31
Southwick	Hants		White, John	91-08-31/09-01
Tichfield	Hants		Southampton, Earl of	91-09-02-03
South Stoneham?	Hants		Caplen, John	91-09-04?
Southampton	Hants			91-09-05-06
Fairthorne	Hants		Serle, Francis?	91-09-07?
Bishop's Waltham	Hants		B of Winchester	91-09-08-09
Warnford	Hants		Neale, William	91-09-10-11a
Tichborne	Hants		Tichborne, Sir Benjamin	91-09-10-11b
Winchester	Hants		B of Winchester	91-09-10-11c
Abbotstone	Hants		Winchester, Marquis of	91-09-10-11d
Wield	Hants		Wallop, William	91-09-10-11e
Farleigh	Hants		Wallop, Sir Henry	91-09-12-13
Basing	Hants		Winchester, Maruis of	91-09-13-16
Vine in Sherborne St. John?	Hants		Sandys, Lord	91-09-18

1. Chronology of Royal Visits and Progresses (*continued*)

Place	Co	R	Host	Date
Odiham	Hants		More, Edward	91-09-19-20
Elvetham	Hants		Hertford, Earl of	91-09-20-23
Farnham	Surrey		B of Winchester	91-09-23-24
Bagshot?	Surrey	r		91-09-24
Sutton in Woking	Surrey		Weston, Sir Henry	91-09-26-27
Ely House	Lon		Hatton, Sir Christopher	91-11-11
Hammersmith	Midd		Payne, William	92-04-07
Osterley	Midd		Gresham, Lady	92-04-07-09
Wimbledon	Surrey		Cecil, Sir Thomas	92-04-14-17
Croydon	Surrey		A of Canterbury	92-04-17-21?
Beddington	Surrey		Carew, Sir Francis	92-04-18
Sydenham	Kent		Aubrey, William	92-04-21
Nonsuch	Surrey	r		92-07-29-31
Mitcham	Surrey		Dent, John	92-07-29?
West Molesey	Surrey		Brand, Thomas	92-08-09-10a
Hanworth	Midd	r		92-08-09-10b
Eastridge in Colnbrook	Bucks		The Ostrich Inn?	92-08-09-10c
Eton College	Bucks			92-08-09-10d
Maidenhead	Berks		The Lion	92-08-09-10e
Bisham	Berks		Russell, Lady	92-08-11-13
John Haynes	Berks			92-08-14a
Hurst	Berks		Ward, Edward?	92-08-14b
Reading	Berks	r	Davies, Mr.	92-08-15-19
Burghfield	Berks		Plowden, Francis?	92-08-19
Aldermaston	Berks		Forster, Sir Humphrey	92-08-19-22
Chamberhouse in Thatcham	Berks		Fuller, Nicholas	92-08-23?
Shaw near Newbury	Berks		Dolman, Thomas	92-08-24-26
Donnington Park	Berks		hunting	92-08-25?
Hampstead Marshall	Berks		Parry, Thomas	92-08-26-27?
Avington	Berks		Choke, Richard?	92-08-27a?
Ramsbury	Wilts		Pembroke, Earl of	92-08-27b-29?
Burderhope [Burdrope]	Wilts		Stevens, Thomas	92-08-29
Lydiard Tregoze	Wilts		St. John, Sir John	92-09-01
Down Ampney	Glos		Hungerford, Anthony	92-09-01-02
Cirencester	Glos		Danvers, Sir John	92-09-02-07
Rendcombe	Glos		Berkeley, Sir Richard	92-09-08?
Whittington	Glos		Cotton, John	92-09-09
Sudeley Castle	Glos		Chandos, Lord	92-09-09-12
Alderton	Glos		Hickford, Sir John	92-09-11?
Northleach	Glos		Dutton?, William	92-09-13?
Sherborne	Glos		Dutton, William	92-09-14-15
Taynton?	Oxon		Bray?, Mr.	92-09-15?
Burford	Oxon		Tanfield, Laurence [Sir]	92-09-15-16
Witney	Oxon		Yate, James	92-09-16-18

1. Chronology of Royal Visits and Progresses (*continued*)

Place	Co	R	Host	Date
Woodstock	Oxon	r		92-09-18-23
Ditchley	Oxon		Lee, Sir Henry	92-09-22?
Yarnton	Oxon		Spencer, Sir William	92-09-23
Oxford	Oxon			92-09-23-28
Holton	Oxon		Browne, George	92-09-28
Rycote	Oxon		Norris, Lord	92-09-28/10-01
Princes Risborough	Bucks		Reve, John (at parsonage)	92-10-01?
Hampden	Bucks		Hampden, Mrs.	92-10-02-03
Chequers in Elsborough?	Bucks		Hawtrey, William	92-10-03-04a
Amersham?	Bucks			92-10-03-04b
Chenies	Bucks		Bedford, Lady	92-10-04-05
Latimer?	Bucks		Sandys, Edwin	92-10-06?
Denham	Bucks		Norris, John	92-10-07
Uxbridge	Midd		Clifford, Francis?	92-10-08?
Bedfont	Midd		Draper, John	92-10-09
Chelsea	Midd	r	Lord Admiral	93-01
Strand	Lon		Cecil, Sir Robert	93-01-30/02-01
Putney?	Surrey		Lacy, John	93-01-30/02-01b
Burghley House	Lon		Cecil, William	93-02-05-14
Croydon	Surrey		A of Canterbury	93-05-02-14
Streatham	Surrey		Forth, Dr. Robert	93-05-02?
Nonsuch	Surrey	r		93-05-14-22
Egham	Surrey		Kellefet, Richard	93-08-01?
Sunninghill	Berks	r		93-08
Laleham	Midd		Tomson, Lawrence?	93-12-01
Somerset House	Lon	r	Hunsdon, Lord	94-03-19
Lambeth	Surrey		A of Canterbury	94-05-29?
Syon	Midd	r		94-06-03
Wimbledon	Surrey		Cecil, Sir Thomas	94-06-03
Richmond	Surrey	r		94-06-04?
Osterley	Midd		Gresham, Anne Lady	94-06-05?
Highgate	Midd		Cornwallis, Sir William	94-06-07
Willesden	Midd		Payne, Mr.	94-06-07
Hendon	Midd		Fortescue, Sir John	94-06-08-12a
Friern Barnet	Midd		Popham, Sir John	94-06-08-12b
Theobalds	Hert		Cecil, William	94-06-13-23?
Pyneste near Waltham				94-06-24?a
Enfield	Midd	r	Wroth, Robert	94-06-24?b
Loughborough	Essex		Stonard, Francis	94-06-24?c
Hackney	Midd		Hayward, Katharine Lady	94-07-05?
Strand	Lon		Cecil, Sir Robert	94-07-12
Kew	Surrey		Puckering, Sir John	94-08-14
Nonsuch	Surrey	r		94-10-01-2
Camberwell	Surrey		Scott, Bartholomew	94-10-01a
Mitcham	Surrey		Blank, Lady	94-10-01b
Combe	Surrey		Vincent, Thomas	94-10-25?

1. Chronology of Royal Visits and Progresses (*continued*)

Place	Co	R	Host	Date
Battersea	Surrey			94-11-14
Savoy	Lon		Heneage, Sir Thomas	94-12-07
wedding	Lon		Earl of Derby/Lady Elizabeth Vere	95-01-26
Burghley House	Lon		Cecil, William	95-01-30/02-01
Lambeth	Surrey		A of Canterbury	95-02-18
Nonsuch	Surrey	r		95-08-18-22
Mitcham	Surrey		Dent, John?	95-08-18?
Beddington	Surrey		Carew, Sir Francis	95-08/10
Combe	Surrey		Vincent, Thomas	95-10-19?
Barn Elms	Surrey		Essex, Earl of	95-11-04
Putney	Surrey		Lacy, John	95-11-14
Kew	Surrey		Puckering, Sir John	95-12-11
Huntingdon House			Huntingdon, Lady	95-12-20
Putney	Surrey		Lacy, John	95-12-23
Putney	Surrey		Lacy, John	96-04-02-03
Burghley House	Lon		Cecil, William	96-04-08
Lambeth	Surrey		Burgh, Lord	96-10-01-02
Mitcham	Surrey			96-10-01-02b
Kingston	Surrey		Cox, John?	96-10-12
Putney	Surrey		Lacy, John	96-11-17
Strand	Lon		Cecil, Sir Robert	96-12-23
Chelsea	Midd	r	Nottingham, Earl of	96-02-19
Putney	Surrey		Lacy, John	97-03
Scadbury	Kent		Walsingham, Sir Thomas	97-07-20-22
Eltham	Kent	r		97-07-20a
Chislehurst	Kent		Carmarden, Richard	97-07-20b
Hackney	Midd		Hayward, Lady	97-08-17a?
Ruckhold in Leyton	Essex		Hicks, Michael	97-08-17b-19
Claybury	Essex		Knyvett, Thomas	97-08-19
Havering	Essex	r		97-08-19-30
Pyrgo	Essex		Grey, Sir Henry	97-08-31a
Loughborough	Essex		Stonard, Francis	97-08-31b
Loughton	Essex		Wroth, Robert (hunt)	97-08-31c
Bracy, Mrs.	Essex		Bracy, Mrs.	97-09-05
Theobalds	Hert		Cecil, William	97-09-05, 07, 09
Enfield Chase	Midd	r	Cecil, Sir Robert	97-09-10-12a
Waltham forest	Essex		Colston, Ralph (his walk)	97-09-10-12b
Edmonton	Midd		Woodward, Mr.	97-09-10-12c
Highgate	Midd		Cornwallis, Sir William	97-09-13, 18, 19
Kensington	Midd		Cope, Walter	97-09-19
Putney	Surrey		Lacy, John	97-09-19-20
Putney	Surrey		Lacy, John	97-10-20a
Chelsea	Midd	r	Delawarr, Lord	97-10-20b
Burghley House	Lon		Cecil, William	98-07-05
Eltham	Kent	r	Miller, Hugh; Lee, John	98-07
Newington	Kent		Saunderson, Mr.	98-09

1. Chronology of Royal Visits and Progresses (*continued*)

Place	Co	R	Host	Date
Nonsuch	Surrey	r		98-09-12-13
Mitcham	Surrey		Caesar, Julius	98-09-12?
Beddington	Surrey		Carew, Sir Francis	98-09
Kingston	Surrey		Evelyn, George?	98-10-10?
Chelsea	Midd	r	Shrewsbury, Lord	98-11-13 or 14
Chelsea	Midd	r	Shrewsbury, Lord	99-02-10
Holborn?	Lon		Derby, Alice, Countess of	99-06-25
Wimbledon	Surrey		Burghley, Thomas Lord	99-07-27-30
Vauxhall	Surrey		Caron, Sir Noel	99-07-27?
Beddington	Surrey		Carew, Sir Francis	99-08-16-17
Kingston	Surrey		Evelyn, George	99-10-03?
Putney	Surrey		Lacy, John	99-11-13a
Chelsea	Midd	r	Nottingham, Earl of; Gorges, Sir Arthur	99-11-13b
York House	Lon		Essex, Earl of	99-11-28
Putney	Surrey		Lacy, John	99-12-07
Chelsea	Midd	r	Nottingham, Earl of	1600-01-19-21
Lumley House	Lon		Lumley, Lord	1600-06-10
Blackfriars	Lon		Russell, Lady, and Cobham, Lord	1600-06-16-17
Newington	Surrey		Carey, Mr.	1600-07-29
Tooting	Surrey		Lacy, John	1600-08-05-06
Beddington	Surrey		Carew, Sir Francis	1600-08-13-16
Croydon	Surrey			1600-08-14
Kingston	Surrey		Evelyn, George	1600-08
Molesey	Surrey		Edmondes, Dorothy Lady	1600-08-24?
Hanworth	Midd	r	Killigrew, William	1600-09-04
Esher	Surrey		Drake, Richard	1600-09-09
Thorpe	Surrey		Bereblock, Mr.	1600-09
Sunbury	Midd		Boteler, Sir Philip	1600-10-09
Chelsea	Midd	r	Shrewsbury, Earl of	1600-11-13
Sackville House	Lon		Glemham, Lady	1600-12-04?
Strand	Lon		Cecil, Sir Robert	1600-12-22
Highgate	Midd		Cornwallis, Sir William	1601-05-01
Chelsea	Midd	r	Lincoln, Earl of?	1601-05-02
Lambeth	Surrey			1601-05-23
Eltham	Kent	r	Miller, Hugh	1601-07
Blackwall				1601-07
Fulham	Midd		B of London	1601-08-06-08a
Brentford	Midd			1601-08-06-08b
Hanworth	Midd	r	Killigrew, William	1601-08-06-08c
Staines	Midd		The Bush Inn	1601-08-08
Stoke Poges	Bucks		Coke, Sir Edward	1601-08-13
Old Windsor	Berks		Meredith, William?	1601-08a
Little Park				1601-08b
Mote Park				1601-08c
Folly John Park	Berks		Duck, Anthony?	1601-08d
Philberds in Bray	Berks		Goddard, William?	1601-08e
Hurst	Berks		Ward, Sir Richard	1601-08-28

1. Chronology of Royal Visits and Progresses (*continued*)

Place	Co	R	Host	Date
Reading	Berks	r	Davies, Mr.	1601-08-28/09-01
Caversham	Oxon		Knollys, Sir William	1601-02-04a
Englefield	Berks		Norris, Sir Edward	1601-02-04b
Basing	Hants		Winchester, Marquis of	1601-09-05-19
Aldermaston	Berks		Forster, Sir Humphrey	1601-09-05a
Silchester Heath	Hants			1601-09-05b
Beaurepaire [Baropey]	Hants		Remington, Sir Robert	1601-09-05c?
South Warnborough	Hants		White, Richard	1601-09-20
Crondall	Hants		Paulet, Mr.	1601-09-21?
Farnham	Surrey		B of Winchester	1601-09-22-23
Seale	Surrey		Woodruff, Lady	1601-09-23a?
Loseley	Surrey		More, Sir George	1601-09-23b
Clandon	Surrey		Weston, Sir Richard	1601-09-24-27a
Stoke d'Abernon	Surrey		Vincent, Thomas?	1601-09-24-27b
Absey Court [Ebbesham Court]	Surrey		Blanden, Mr.	1601-09-24-27c
Putney	Surrey		Lacy, John	1602-02-19
Wimbledon	Surrey		Burghley, Lord	1602-04-09or10
Lambeth	Surrey		A of Canterbury	1602-04-19a
Blackfriars	Lon		Hunsdon, Lord	1602-04-19b
Sydmonscourt	Kent			1602-05-01a
Lewisham	Kent		Buckley, Sir Richard	1602-05-01b
St. James Park	Lon		Chandos, Lady/Knollys, Sir William	1602-05-05
Eltham	Kent	r	Stanhope, Sir John; Miller, Hugh; Walsingham, Sir Thomas	1602-07-15?
Chiswick	Midd		Russell, Sir William	1602-07-28
Lambeth	Surrey		A of Canterbury	1602-07-28
Hounslow	Midd		Whitby, Mr.	1602-07-29-30a
Harlington	Midd		Copinger, Ambrose	1602-07-29-30b
Harefield	Midd		Egerton, Sir Thomas	1602-07-31/08-03
Hitcham	Bucks		Clarke, Sir William	1602-08-03-09
Taplow	Bucks		Guilford, Sir Henry	1602-08-07
Riddings in Datchet	Bucks		Hanbury, Richard?	1602-08-10a
Thorpe	Surrey		Oglethorpe, Mr.	1602-08-10b
Woking	Surrey	r		1602-09/10a
Chertsey	Surrey		Hammond, John	1602-09/10b
"in the forest"			Brooke, Mr.	1602-09/10c
			Bromley, Mr.	1602-09/10d
			Woodward, Mr.	1602-09/10d
Bedfont	Midd		Draper, John	1602-10-02a
West Drayton	Midd		Hunsdon, Lord	1602-10-02b
Putney	Surrey		Lacy, John	1602-11-15
Savoy	Lon		Cecil, Sir Robert	1602-12-06
Arundel House	Lon		Nottingham, Earl of	1602-12-06-23?

1. Chronology of Royal Visits and Progresses (*continued*)

Place	Co	R	Host	Date
Blackfriars	Lon		Hunsdon, Lord	1602-12-06-23b?
Charterhouse	Lon		Walden, Lord Howard de	1603-01-17
Putney	Surrey		Lacy, John	1603-01-21

2. Visits by County, Alphabetical

County	Progress Visits	London Visits	Total Visits
Bedfordshire	16	0	16
Berkshire	35	15	50
Buckinghamshire	33	6	39
Cambridgeshire	7	0	7
Essex	67	19	86
Gloucestershire	23	0	23
Hampshire	55	1	56
Hertfordshire	38	20	58
Huntingdonshire	4	0	4
Kent	58	21	79
Leicestershire	1	0	1
Lincolnshire	4	0	4
London	4	67	71
Middlesex	29	75	104
Norfolk	9	0	9
Northamptonshire	18	0	18
Oxfordshire	36	0	36
Rutland	1	0	1
Somerset	2	0	2
Staffordshire	9	0	9
Suffolk	13	0	13
Surrey	49	178	227
Sussex	12	1	13
Warwickshire	17	0	17
Wiltshire	15	0	15
Worcestershire	7	0	7

3. Visits by County, Ranked

County	Progress Visits	London Visits	Total Visits
Essex	67	19	86
Kent	58	21	79
Hampshire	55	1	56
Surrey	49	178	227
Hertfordshire	38	20	58
Oxfordshire	36	0	36
Berkshire	35	15	50
Buckinghamshire	33	6	39
Middlesex	29	75	104
Gloucestershire	23	0	23
Northamptonshire	18	0	18
Warwickshire	17	0	17
Bedfordshire	16	0	16
Wiltshire	15	0	15
Suffolk	13	0	13
Sussex	12	1	13
Norfolk	9	0	9
Staffordshire	9	0	9
Cambridgeshire	7	0	7
Worcestershire	7	0	7
Huntingdonshire	4	0	4
Lincolnshire	4	0	4
London	4	67	71
Somerset	2	0	2
Leicestershire	1	0	1
Rutland	1	0	1

4. Visits to Towns

Place	Co	R	Host	Date
Alresford	Hants			74-09-14a
Amersham?	Bucks			92-10-03-04b
Bath	Som			74-08-21c-23
Brentwood				79-09-19-24c
[Burntwood]	Essex		Searle, John?	
Bristol	Glos		Young, Sir John	74-08-14-21
Bristol St.				74-08-13b
Lawrence	Glos		[St. Lawrence church in Bristol]	
Buckingham,				68-08-06-16d
parsonage	Bucks		Davers?, William	
Bulley Hill	Kent		Watts, Anne?	82-02-15?
Burford	Oxon			74-08-03
Burford	Oxon		Tanfield, Laurence [Sir]	92-09-15-16
Bury St. Edmunds	Suffolk			78-08-05-06
Cambridge	Cams		King's College	64-08-05-10
Campden	Glos		Smythe, Thomas	75-08-22-26a
Canterbury	Kent		St. Augustine's	73-09-03-16
Canterbury	Kent		Manwood, Sir Roger	82-02-05-06
Canterbury	Kent	r		82-02-12
Canterbury,				73-09-07
A of C	Kent		A of Canterbury	
Chichester	Sussex		Lumley, Lord	91-08-20-22
Cirencester	Gloss		Danvers, Sir John	92-09-02-07
Colchester	Essex		Lucas, Sir Thomas	61-07-26-30
Coventry	War		Whitefriars	66-08-17-19
Dover	Kent	r	Cobham, Lord [as constable]	73-08-25-31
Dover	Kent		St. James [sign of Queen's Arms]	82-02-09-11?
Eastridge in				92-08-09-10c
Colnbrook	Bucks		The Ostrich Inn?	
Faversham	Kent			73-09-16-18
Faversham	Kent			82-02-13
Folkestone	Kent		Fisher, Thomas?	73-08-26?
Giddy Hall in				68-07-16-18a
Romford	Essex		Cooke, Sir Anthony	
Giddy Hall in				79-09-25-27
Romford	Essex		Cooke, Richard	
Gloucester	Glos			74-08-10a
Harwich [on				
Channel]	Essex			61-08-02-05
Hertford Castle	Hert	r		64-08-01?-04?a
Hertford Castle	Hert	r		76-08-19-22
Hertford Castle	Hert	r		61-08-30/09-16
Hertford Castle	Hert	r		76-08-26-28
Ipswich	Suffolk			61-08-05-11
Lichfield	Staff			75-07-30a/08-03
Maidenhead	Berks		The Lion	92-08-09-10e
Newbury	Berks			68-09-12-13
Northampton	Nhants		Crispe, Mr.	64-08-19/9-11c

4. Visits to Towns (*continued*)

Place	Co	R	Host	Date
Northleach	Glos		Dutton?, William	92-09-13?
Norwich	Norf		B of Norwich	78-08-16-22
Oxford	Oxon			66-08-31/09-06
Oxford	Oxon			92-09-23-28
Philberds in Bray	Berks		Neville, Sir Thomas	70-09-26?-29?
Philberds in Bray	Berks		Neville, Sir Thomas	72-09-28
Philberds in Bray	Berks		Neville, Sir Thomas	75-10-09c
Portsmouth	Hants		Sussex, Earl of	91-08-26-31
Portsmouth, Netley Castle	Hants			60-08-12-13
Reading	Berks	r	Stafford, Mr.; Gare, Mr.	68-09-18?
Reading	Berks	r		70-09-17, 24-26
Reading	Berks	r		72-09-21-28
Reading	Berks	r		74-07-15b-23
Reading	Berks	r		76-09-22/10-08
Reading	Berks	r	Davies, Mr.	92-08-15-19
Reading	Berks	r	Davies, Mr.	1601-08-28/09-01
Rochester	Kent		The Crown	73-09-19-23
Rochester	Kent		The Crown	82-02-01-03
Rochester	Kent			82-02-14-16
Rye	Sussex			73-08-11-14
Saffron Walden	Essex			71-08-27?a
Salisbury	Wilts		B of Salisbury	74-09-06b-09
Sandwich	Kent		Manwood, Roger?	73-08-31/09-03
Sandwich	Kent		Manwood, Mr.	82-02-08
Sittingbourne	Kent		The George	82-02-03-05
Southampton	Hants			60-08-13-16
Southampton	Hants			91-09-05-06
Southampton Tower	Hants			69-09-06?, 08, 09, 14
St. Albans	Hert	r	Lee, Sir Richard	64-08-19/9-11h
St. Albans	Hert	r	Rowlett, Sir Ralph	68-08-08
St. Albans	Hert	r		76-08-30/09-01
Stamford	Lincs		Cecil, Sir William, Greyfriars	66-08-05
Stowmarket?	Suffolk			78-08-07-09b
Thetford	Norf		Clere, Sir Edward	78-08-27
Warwick Castle	War		Warwick, Earl of	72-08-11-13
Warwick Castle	War		Warwick, Earl of	72-08-16-18
Warwick Castle	War		Warwick, Earl of	66-08-22?-23?
Winchelsea	Sussex		Savage?, Mr.	73-08-11?-14?
Winchester	Hants			60-08-16-23
Winchester	Hants			74-09-10-13
Winchester	Hants		B of Winchester	91-09-10-11c
Witney	Oxon		Yate, James	92-09-16-18
Woolwich	Midd		ship banquet, Elizabeth Jonas	59-07-03
Worcester	Wor		B of Worcester	75-08-13-20

5. Lengths of Progresses

Year	Start	End	Days	Stops	Days per Stay
1559	July 7	Aug 10	24	7	3.43
1560	Aug 5	Aug 30?	25	13	1.92
1561	July 10	Sept 16?	68	24	2.83
1564	July 27?	Sept 12?	47	25	1.88
1566	July 8	Sept 7	61	32	1.91
1567	Aug 20?	Aug 31?	11	6	1.83
1568	July 13	Sept 18?	67	24	2.79
1569	Aug 5?	Sept 23?	49	19	2.58
1570	July 16	Sept 29?	75	13	5.77
1571	Aug 8?	Sept 22?	45	15	3.00
1572	July 15?	Sept 28	75	30	2.50
1573	July 14	Sept 24	72	38	1.89
1574	July 15?	Sept 25	72	42	1.71
1575	May 23	Oct 9	139	44	3.16
1576	July 30	Oct 12	75	34	2.21
1578	July 11?	Sept 23?	74	40	1.85
1579	Sept 9	Sept 27?	18	9	2.00
1582	Feb 1	Feb 17	17	13	1.31
1591	July 29?	Sept 27	61	37	1.65
1592	Aug 9?	Oct 9	61	44	1.39
1597	Aug 17?	Sept 20	34	15	2.27
1601	Aug 28	Sept 26?	29	16	1.81
1602	July 28	Aug 10?	13	9	1.44

6. Hosts on Progress and London Visits

Host	Place	Co	Date
A of Canterbury	Croydon	Surrey	59-08-05-6?
A of Canterbury	Lambeth	Surrey	60-07-29
A of Canterbury	Lambeth	Surrey	63-07-20/08-01?
A of Canterbury	Lambeth	Surrey	69-07-21
A of Canterbury	Croydon	Surrey	73-07-14-21
A of Canterbury	Canterbury	Kent	73-09-07
A of Canterbury	Lambeth	Surrey	74-03-02-03
A of Canterbury	Lambeth	Surrey	85-03-26-30
A of Canterbury	Croydon	Surrey	85-03-30?a
A of Canterbury	Lambeth	Surrey	85-04-03
A of Canterbury	Lambeth	Surrey	88-01-16-20d
A of Canterbury	Croydon	Surrey	88-04-04/05b
A of Canterbury	Lambeth	Surrey	91-02-11-13
A of Canterbury	Croydon	Surrey	92-04-17-21?
A of Canterbury	Croydon	Surrey	93-05-02-14
A of Canterbury	Lambeth	Surrey	94-05-29?
A of Canterbury	Lambeth	Surrey	95-02-18
A of Canterbury	Lambeth	Surrey	1602-04-19a
A of Canterbury	Lambeth	Surrey	1602-07-28

6. Hosts on Progress and London Visits (*continued*)

Host	Place	Co	Date
A of Canterbury?	Croydon	Surrey	67-01-17?/02-01?a
Abergavenny, Lord	Comfort in Birling	Kent	73-07-29/08-01
Abergavenny, Lord	Eridge	Sussex	73-08-01-07
Alington, Sir Giles	Horseheath	Cams	78-09-04
Altham, James	Mark Hall in Latton	Essex	71-09-13, 14, 17
Altham, James	Mark Hall in Latton	Essex	76-08-10-11
Altham, James	Mark Hall in Latton	Essex	78-07-23
Arundel, Earl of	Nonsuch	Surrey	59-08-06-10
Arundel, Earl of	Nonsuch	Surrey	62-63
Arundel, Earl of	Nonsuch	Surrey	65-10-29?/11-02?
Arundel, Earl of	Nonsuch	Surrey	67-01-21-27
Arundel, Earl of	Arundel House	Lon	67-02-10
Arundel, Earl of	Nonsuch	Surrey	74-10-19-22
Arundel, Earl of	Nonsuch	Surrey	76-05-15-17
Arundel, Earl of	Arundel House	Lon	83-10?/12?
Askewe, Lady Anne	Byfleet	Surrey	82-09-01?
Aubrey, William	Sydenham	Kent	92-04-21
Aubrey?, William	Sydenham House	Kent	90-07-28/08-06a
Audley, Richard?	Melchet	Hants	69-09-15-21a
Averie, Margery	Berden Priory	Essex	78-07-25?
B of Ely	Long Stanton	Cams	64-08-10a
B of London	Fulham	Midd	88-01-16-20a
B of London	Fulham	Midd	1601-08-06-08a
B of Norwich	Norwich	Norf	78-08-16-22
B of Salisbury	Salisbury	Wilts	74-09-06b-09
B of Winchester	Farnham	Surrey	60-08-07-08
B of Winchester	Farnham	Surrey	67-08-24-25, 29
B of Winchester	Farnham	Surrey	69-08-14, 17, 20, 22
B of Winchester	Farnham	Surrey	74-09-15, 19
B of Winchester	Farnham	Surrey	76-09-13?-20
B of Winchester	Farnham	Surrey	91-08-10-14
B of Winchester	Bishop's Waltham	Hants	91-09-08-09
B of Winchester	Winchester	Hants	91-09-10-11c
B of Winchester	Farnham	Surrey	91-09-23-24
B of Winchester	Farnham	Surrey	1601-09-22-23
B of Worcester	Hartlebury Castle	Wor	75-08-12-13
B of Worcester	Worcester	Wor	75-08-13-20
Backhouse, Nicholas	Kingsley	Hants	69-08-23-26a
Bacon, Sir Nicholas	Gorhambury	Hert	72-07-25-28
Bacon, Sir Nicholas	Gorhambury	Hert	73-02-24/03-10c
Bacon, Sir Nicholas	Gorhambury	Hert	76-09-01
Bacon, Sir Nicholas	Gorhambury	Hert	77-05-18-22
Baker, Richard	Sissinghurst in Cranbrook	Kent	73-08-14-17
Barnardiston, Thomas	Keddington	Suffolk	78-07-31b
Barrett, Edward	Belhus in Aveley?	Essex	88-08-08-10c
Barrington, Sir Thomas	Hatfield Broadoak	Essex	76-08-11

6. Hosts on Progress and London Visits (*continued*)

Host	Place	Co	Date
Barrington, Sir Thomas	Hatfield Broadoak?	Essex	78-09-15
Bartlett, Sir Richard	Waltham Forest	Essex	90-06
Bashe, Edward	Stanstead Abbots	Hert	71-09-20
Bashe, Edward	Stanstead Abbots	Hert	76-08-14-19
Bashe, Edward	Stanstead Abbots	Hert	78-05-10-12
Bedford, Earl of	Chenies	Bucks	70-07-19/08-13
Bedford, Earl of	Woburn	Bed	72-07-29-31
Bedford, Lady	Chenies	Bucks	92-10-04-05
Beer, Nicholas?	Horseman Place in Dartford	Kent	82-02-16-17
Bereblock, Mr.	Thorpe	Surrey	1600-09
Berkeley, Lord	Berkeley Castle	Glos	74-08-11b-12
Berkeley, Sir Richard	Rendcombe	Glos	92-09-08?
Berners, Anthony?	Thoby	Essex	79-09-19-24b
Bishop, George	Northiam	Sussex	73-08-11
Blanden, Mr.	Absey Court [Ebbesham Court]	Surrey	1601-09-24-27c
Blank, Lady	Mitcham	Surrey	94-10-01b
Blank, Margaret Lady	Mitcham	Surrey	91-07-29?
Bonham, John	Hazelbury	Wilts	74-08-23
Boteler, Sir Philip	Sunbury	Midd	1600-10-09
Bracy, Mrs.	Bracy, Mrs.	Essex	97-09-05
Branch, John	Theydon Garnon	Essex	78-07-21-22?
Brand, Thomas	Molesey	Surrey	80-09-13
Brand, Thomas	Molesey	Surrey	82-08-17
Brand, Thomas	West Molesey	Surrey	87-08-13d
Brand, Thomas	West Molesey	Surrey	89-08-10?
Brand, Thomas	West Molesey	Surrey	92-08-09-10a
Brassey, Mr.	Edmonton	Midd	85-05-18a
Bray, Edward?	Chobham	Surrey	80-07/08b
Bray, Edward?	Chobham	Surrey	90-08-31/09-06a
Bray?, Mr.	Taynton?	Oxon	92-09-15?
Brockett, John	Brockett Hall in Hatfield	Hert	73-02-24/03-10d
Bromley, Mr.			1602-09/10d
Bromley, Thomas [Sir]	Batenhall Park	Wor	75-08-19
Brooke, Mr.	"in the forest"		1602-09/10c
Brouncker, William	Erlestoke [Stoke earle]	Wilts	74-08-28-31
Browne, Christopher	Holton	Oxon	74-07-24
Browne, Christopher	Holton	Oxon	75-10-04-05?
Browne, George	Holton	Oxon	92-09-28
Browne, Sir Christopher	Holton	Oxon	72-09b

6. Hosts on Progress and London Visits (*continued*)

Host	Place	Co	Date
Browne, Wiston	Rookwood Hall in Roding Abbess	Essex	71-09-09?
Browne, Wiston	Rookwood Hall in Roding Abbess	Essex	78-09-18
Brudenell, Edmund	Deene	Nhants	66-08-06-16f
Brydges, Henry?	Keynsham	Som	74-08-21a
Buckley, Sir Richard	Lewisham	Kent	1602-05-01b
Burgh, Lord	Lambeth	Surrey	85-12-20-21
Burgh, Lord	Lambeth	Surrey	96-10-01-02
Burghley, Lord	Wimbledon	Surrey	1602-04-09 or 10
Burghley, Thomas Lord	Wimbledon	Surrey	99-07-27-30
Butler, Sir John	Woodhall	Hert	75-06-06-07b
Caesar, Julius	Mitcham	Surrey	98-09-12?
camp	Tilbury	Essex	88-08-08-10a
Capel, Henry	Hadham Hall	Hert	78-09-14
Caplen, John	South Stoneham?	Hants	91-09-04?
Carew, Sir Francis	Beddington?	Surrey	67-08-09-13b
Carew, Sir Francis	Beddington	Surrey	76-05-17-19
Carew, Sir Francis	Beddington	Surrey	80-06
Carew, Sir Francis	Beddington	Surrey	81-10-03
Carew, Sir Francis	Beddington	Surrey	82-07/08?
Carew, Sir Francis	Beddington	Surrey	85-03-30?b
Carew, Sir Francis	Beddington	Surrey	85-08
Carew, Sir Francis	Beddington	Surrey	87-05
Carew, Sir Francis	Beddington	Surrey	90-07-28/08-06b
Carew, Sir Francis	Beddington	Surrey	91-08-02a
Carew, Sir Francis	Beddington	Surrey	92-04-18
Carew, Sir Francis	Beddington	Surrey	95-08/10
Carew, Sir Francis	Beddington	Surrey	98-09
Carew, Sir Francis	Beddington	Surrey	99-08-16-17
Carew, Sir Francis	Beddington	Surrey	1600-08-13-16
Mr. Carey	Newington	Surrey	1600-07-29
Carmarden, Richard	Chislehurst	Kent	97-07-20b
Caron, Sir Noel	Vauxhall	Surrey	99-07-27?
Cecil, Sir Robert	Strand	Lon	93-01-30/02-01
Cecil, Sir Robert	Strand	Lon	94-07-12
Cecil, Sir Robert	Strand	Lon	96-12-23
Cecil, Sir Robert	Enfield Chase	Midd	97-09-10-12a
Cecil, Sir Robert	Strand	Lon	1600-12-22
Cecil, Sir Robert	Savoy	Lon	1602-12-06
Cecil, Sir Thomas	Wimbledon	Surrey	92-04-14-17
Cecil, Sir Thomas	Wimbledon	Surrey	94-06-03
Cecil, Sir William	Cecil House	Lon	64-07-06
Cecil, Sir William	Theobalds	Hert	64-07-27?
Cecil, Sir William, Greyfriars	Stamford	Lincs	66-08-05
Cecil, William	Strand	Lon	61-07-13
Cecil, William	Theobalds	Hert	72-07-22-25
Cecil, William	Theobalds	Hert	73-02-24/03-10f

6. Hosts on Progress and London Visits (*continued*)

Host	Place	Co	Date
Cecil, William	Theobalds	Hert	75-05-24/06-06
Cecil, William	Theobalds	Hert	77-05-15-17?
Cecil, William	Theobalds	Hert	78-05-07-10
Cecil, William	Theobalds	Hert	83-05-27-31/06-01a
Cecil, William	Theobalds	Hert	87-07-09a
Cecil, William	Theobalds	Hert	91-05-10-20
Cecil, William	Burghley House	Lon	91-07-19
Cecil, William	Burghley House	Lon	93-02-05-14
Cecil, William	Theobalds	Hert	94-06-13-23?
Cecil, William	Burghley House	Lon	95-01-30/02-01
Cecil, William	Burghley House	Lon	96-04-08
Cecil, William	Theobalds	Hert	97-09-05, 07, 09
Cecil, William	Burghley House	Lon	98-07-05
Cecil, William, Lord Burghley	Theobalds	Hert	71-09-22
Chandos, Lady/ Knollys, Sir William	St. James Park	Lon	1602-05-05
Chandos, Lady	Sudeley Castle	Glos	74-08-04-05
Chandos, Lord	Sudeley Castle	Glos	75-08-22-26b
Chandos, Lord	Sudeley Castle	Glos	92-09-09-12
Charnock, Richard	Holcutt	Bed	75-06-15-18d
Chauncy, William	Edgecott	Nhants	72-08-10
Châtillon, Madame de	Ham House	Surrey	70-03-19
Cheyne, Lord [Henry]	Toddington	Bed	75-06-15-18b
Cheyne, Sir Henry	Toddington	Bed	64-08-19/09-11g
Cheyne, Sir Henry	Toddington	Bed	70-08-19-20
Choke, Richard?	Avington	Berks	92-08-27a?
Clarke, Sir William	Hitcham	Bucks	1602-08-03-09
Clere, Sir Edward	Thetford	Norf	78-08-27
Clerk, Edmund	Micheldever	Hants	60-08-23
Clifford, Francis?	Uxbridge	Midd	92-10-08?
Clinton, Lord [Admiral]	West Horsley	Surrey	59-08-17-23
Clinton, Lord [Admiral]	Sempringham	Lincs	66-08-06-16a
Clinton?, Lord [Admiral]	Horsley	Surrey	60-10
Cobham, Lord	Cobham Hall	Kent	59-07-18-21
Cobham, Lord	Cobham	Kent	73-09-24a
Cobham, Lord, as constable]	Dover	Kent	73-08-25-31
Cock, Sir Henry	Ponsbourne	Hert	83-05-27-31/06-01b
Coke, Sir Edward	Stoke Poges	Bucks	1601-08-13
Colston, Ralph (his walk)	Waltham forest	Essex	97-09-10-12b
Colt, Sir George	De Greys in Cavendish	Suffolk	78-08-01

6. Hosts on Progress and London Visits (*continued*)

Host	Place	Co	Date
Compton, Lord	Compton Wyniates	War	72-08-23b
Compton, Lord	Tottenham	Midd	78-05-06-07
Compton, Thomas?	Erith	Kent	88-04/05a
Cooke, Richard	Giddy Hall in Romford	Essex	79-09-25-27
Cooke, Sir Anthony	Giddy Hall in Romford	Essex	68-07-16-18a
Cope, Walter	Kensington	Midd	97-09-19
Copinger, Ambrose	Harlington	Midd	1602-07-29-30a
Corbett, Sir Andrew	Dallington?	Nhants	64-08-19/9-11b
Cordell, Sir William	Long Melford	Suffolk	78-08-03-05
Cornwallis, Sir William	Highgate	Midd	94-06-07
Cornwallis, Sir William	Highgate	Midd	97-09-13, 18, 19
Cornwallis, Sir William	Highgate	Midd	1601-05-01
Cornwallis, Thomas	East Horsley	Surrey	91-08-03
Cotton, John	Whittington	Glos	92-09-09
Cotton, Sir Thomas	Oxenheath in West Peckham?	Kent	73-08-01
Cox, John?	Kingston	Surrey	96-10-12
Crawley, Thomas	Manuden	Essex	78-09-12-13?
Crispe, Mr.	Northampton	Nhants	64-08-19/09-11c
Croft?, Stokes	Morecroft	Wilts	74-08-21b
Cromer, William	Tunstall	Kent	73-09-18-19
Crompton, Thomas	Hounslow	Midd	88-01-16-20b
Cromwell, Henry Lord	Launde	Leic	64-08-18?
Cromwell, Sir Henry	Hinchinbrook	Hunt	64-08-10b
Culpepper, Alexander	Bedgebury in Goudhurst	Kent	73-08-07b-08
Cutts, Sir John	Horham Hall in Thaxted	Essex	71-09-05
Cutts, Sir John	Horham Hall in Thaxted	Essex	78-09-07, 11
Danvers, Sir John	Cirencester	Glos	92-09-02-07
Darcy, Lord	St. Osyth	Essex	61-07-30/08-02
Darcy?, Lord	Loughton Hall	Essex	61-07-17
Daston, Anne	Elmley Bredon [Elmley]	Glos	75-08-20-22
Davers?, William	Buckingham, parsonage	Bucks	68-08-09-13d
Davies, Mr.	Reading	Berks	92-08-15-19
Davies, Mr.	Reading	Berks	1601-08-28/09-01
Dee, Dr.	Mortlake	Surrey	75-03-16
Dee, Dr.	Mortlake	Surrey	80-10-10
Dee, Dr. John	Mortlake	Surrey	80-09-17
Delawarr, Lord	Holt, The	Sussex	91-08-14b

6. Hosts on Progress and London Visits (*continued*)

Host	Place	Co	Date
Delawarr, Lord	Chelsea	Midd	97-10-20b
Denne, Mr.	Boddington	Glos	74-08-06-09?
Dent, John	Mitcham	Surrey	92-07-29?
Dent, John?	Mitcham	Surrey	95-08-18?
Derby, Alice Countess of	Holborn?	Lon	99-06-25
Derby, Countess of	Isleworth [Thistleworth]	Midd	77-07-24
Dolman, Thomas	Shaw near Newbury	Berks	92-08-24-26
Dormer, Sir William	Wing	Bucks	70-08-24?
Dormer, Sir William	Eythorpe [Eydrop]	Bucks	70-08-25?-29?
Drake, Richard	Esher	Surrey	1600-09-09
Drake, Sir Francis	Deptford, Golden Hind	Kent	81-04-04
Draper, Henry?	Colnbrook	Bucks	80-11b
Draper, John	Bedfont	Midd	92-10-09
Draper, John	Bedfont	Midd	1602-09/10a
Drury, Mr.	Harmondsworth	Midd	80-11a
Drury, Sir Robert	Hedgerley	Bucks	76-09-03
Drury, Sir William	Lawshall	Suffolk	78-08-05
Drury, Sir William	Onehouse?	Suffolk	78-08-07-09a
Duck, Anthony?	Folly John Park	Berks	1601-08d
Dudley, John	Stoke Newington	Midd	75-05-23
Dudley, John	Stoke Newington	Midd	77-05-14?
Dudley, Lord	Dudley Castle	Wor	75-08-12
Dudley, Robert	dinner	Lon	61-06-24
Dudley, Robert	Gray's Inn	Lon	65-03-06
Dudley, Robert		Lon	65-05-12
Dudley, Robert	Kenilworth	War	72-08-13-16
Dudley, Robert	Kenilworth	War	72-08-18-23
Dudley, Robert	Mortlake Park Lodge	Surrey	77-07-26b
Dudley, Robert	Leicester House	Lon	78-02-27/03-03?
Dudley, Robert	Kenilworth	War	75-07-09-27
Dudley, Robert	Leicester House	Lon	76-05-09-10
Dudley, Robert	Wanstead?	Essex	77-02-26/03-03
Dudley, Robert	Leicester House	Lon	77-05-09-10
Dudley, Robert	Leicester House	Lon	78-04-05, 28
Dudley, Robert	Wanstead	Essex	78-05-13-16
Dudley, Robert	Wanstead	Essex	78-09-23?
Dudley, Robert	Leicester House	Lon	79-01/02
Dudley, Robert	Wanstead	Essex	79-04-28?/05-02
Dudley, Robert	Wanstead	Essex	79-06-24-26
Dudley, Robert	Wanstead	Essex	79-08-30-31
Dudley, Robert	Wanstead	Essex	81-07-27-29
Dudley, Robert	Wanstead	Essex	82-04
Dudley, Robert	Wanstead	Essex	88-05-07
Dudley, Robert	Long Itchington	War	75-07-09
Dudley, Robert	Kenilworth	War	66-08-19-22

6. Hosts on Progress and London Visits (*continued*)

Host	Place	Co	Date
Duncombe?, Thomas	Brickhill	Bucks	68-08-06-16b
Dutton, Thomas	Sherborne	Glos	74-08-03-04
Dutton, Thomas	Sherborne	Glos	75-08-22-26c
Dutton, William	Sherborne	Glos	92-09-14-15
Dutton?, William	Northleach	Glos	92-09-13?
Dyott?, John	Swinfen	Staff	75-07-28-29c
Earl of Derby/Lady Elizabeth Vere	wedding	Lon?	95-01-26
Edmondes, Dorothy Lady	Molesey	Surrey	1600-08-24?
Egerton, Sir Thomas	Harefield	Midd	1602-07-31/08-03
Elderton, Edward?	Birch Hall in Theydon Bois	Essex	72-07-21?
Elderton, Mrs.	Theydon Bois	Essex	78-09-18?
Ellensbury, Dame	Houghton Conquest	Bed	66-07-9-20f
Ellensbury, Dame	Houghton Conquest	Bed	70-08-21-23a
Essex, Earl of	Barn Elms	Surrey	95-11-04
Essex, Earl of	York House	Lon	99-11-28
Essex, Lady	Chartley	Staff	75-08-01-06b
Evelyn, George	Kingston	Surrey	84-08-07
Evelyn, George	Kingston	Surrey	99-10-03?
Evelyn, George	Kingston	Surrey	1600-08
Evelyn, George?	Kingston	Surrey	98-10-10?
Fanshawe, Thomas	Ilford, at St. Mary's Hospital?	Essex	79-09-27?
Fermor, Sir John	Easton Neston	Nhants	64-08-19/09-11d
Fermor, Sir John	Easton Neston	Nhants	68-08-14, 21
Fermor, Sir John	Easton Neston	Nhants	72-08-04-08
Fiennes, Richard	Broughton	Oxon	66-08-24?-25?
Fisher, Edward	Bishop's Itchington	War	72-08-11
Fisher, Jasper	Bishopsgate	Lon	72-07-15?a
Fisher, Jasper	Bishopsgate	Lon	73-03-07
Fisher, Thomas	Warwick Priory	War	72-08-16a
Fisher, Thomas?	Folkestone	Kent	73-08-26?
Fitzwilliam, Sir William	Gaynes Park	Essex	78-09-19
Fitzwilliam?, Sir William	Chertsey	Surrey	69-08-05?-08?
Forster, Sir Humphrey	Aldermaston	Berks	92-08-19-22
Forster, Sir Humphrey	Aldermaston	Berks	1601-09-05a
Forster, William?	Aldermaston	Berks	68-09-14-17?
Fortescue, John [Sir]	Salden	Bucks	72-08-01-04
Fortescue, Sir John	Hendon	Midd	94-06-08-12a
Forth, Dr. Robert	Streatham	Surrey	81-09-22?
Forth, Dr. Robert	Streatham	Surrey	87-05-25?
Forth, Dr. Robert	Streatham	Surrey	93-05-02?

6. Hosts on Progress and London Visits (*continued*)

Host	Place	Co	Date
Foster, William	Meriden	War	75-07-28-29a
from Wilton; ruins	Clarendon Park	Wilts	74-09-06a?
Fuller, Nicholas	Chamberhouse in Thatcham	Berks	92-08-23?
Fuller, Nicholas?	Aldersbrook in Little Ilford?	Essex	81-07-05-08a
Gardiner, John?	Chalfont St. Giles	Bucks	76-09-03?
Gavell?, Robert	Cobham	Surrey	84-08
George Earl of Cumberland	Southwark	Surrey	77-06-24
Gery, William	Bushmead	Bed	66-07-9-20j
Giffard, John	Chillington	Staff	75-08-09-11b
Gifford, Henry?	Somborne	Hants	74-09-10
Glemham, Lady	Sackville House	Lon	1600-12-04?
Goddard, William?	Philberds in Bray	Berks	1601-08e
Goodwin, Sir John	Wooburn [Uburne]	Bucks	75-10-09b
Gostwick, John	Willington	Bed	66-07-9-20g
Gresham, Anne Lady	Osterley	Midd	94-06-05?
Gresham, Lady	Osterley	Midd	92-04-07-09
Gresham, Sir Thomas	Osterley	Midd	64-09-12?b
Gresham, Sir Thomas	Osterley	Midd	65-09
Gresham, Sir Thomas	Osterley	Midd	67-01-27/02-01
Gresham, Sir Thomas	Osterley	Midd	70-07-16-18
Gresham, Sir Thomas	Bishopsgate	Lon	71-01-23
Gresham, Sir Thomas	Osterley	Midd	71-06-07-08
Gresham, Sir Thomas	Osterley	Midd	74-02-18-20b
Gresham, Sir Thomas	Osterley	Midd	75-04b
Gresham, Sir Thomas	Osterley	Midd	76-05-10-12
Gresham, Sir Thomas	Osterley	Midd	78-02
Gresham, Sir Thomas?	Mayfield?	Sussex	73-08-01?-07?
Gresley, Lady Katharine	Colton	Staff	75-08-01-06a
Grey, Henry	Pyrgo	Essex	76-08-05b
Grey, Lord John [d. 1569]	Pyrgo	Essex	61-07-16
Grey, Lord John [d. 1569]	Pyrgo	Essex	68-07-16-18a

6. Hosts on Progress and London Visits (*continued*)

Host	Place	Co	Date
Grey, Lord [Arthur Grey, 14th Baron]	Whaddon	Bucks	68-08-09-13c
Grey, Peter	Segenhoe in Ridgmont	Bed	70-08-21-23a
Grey, Peter	Segenhoe in Ridgmont	Bed	75-06-15-18c
Grey, Sir Henry	Pyrgo	Essex	97-08-31a
Griffin, Edward	Dingley	Nhants	66-08-06-16g
Griffin, Sir Thomas	Braybrooke Castle	Nhants	64-08-19/09-11a
Griffith, Walter	Alrewas	Staff	75-07-30c
Guildford, Thomas	Hemstead in Benenden	Kent	73-08-08-11
Guilford, Sir Henry	Taplow	Bucks	1602-08-07
Habington, John	Hindlip	Wor	75-08-16
Habington, John	Hallow Park	Wor	75-08-18
Hammond, John	Chertsey	Surrey	1602-09/10b
Hampden, Griffith	Great Hampden?	Bucks	64-08-19/09-11j
Hampden, Mrs.	Hampden	Bucks	92-10-02-03
Hanbury, Richard?	Riddings in Datchet	Bucks	1602-08-10a
Harcourt, Walter?	Ellenhall	Staff	75-08-09-11a
Harington, Sir James	Exton	Rut	66-08-06-16d
Hart, Sir Percival	Orpington	Kent	73-07-21-24
Harvey, William	Chessington	Surrey	90-07-28/08-06c
Hatton, Sir Christopher	Ely House	Lon	87-11-21/12-06
Hatton, Sir Christopher	Ely House	Lon	88-08-19
Hatton, Sir Christopher	Ely House	Lon	90-06-04-06
Hatton, Sir Christopher	Ely House	Lon	90-11
Hatton, Sir Christopher	Ely House	Lon	91-11-11
Hawker, Mr.	Heytesbury	Wilts	74-08-31/09-03
Hawtrey, William	Chequers in Elsborough?	Bucks	92-10-03-04a
Hayward, Katharine, Lady	Hackney	Midd	94-07-05?
Hayward, Lady	Hackney	Midd	97-08-17a?
Hayward, Sir Rowland	Hackney	Midd	83-05-27-31/06-01d
Hayward, Sir Rowland	Hackney	Midd	87-07-09b
Hayward, Sir Rowland	Hackney	Midd	88-04-13-16a
Hayward, Sir Rowland	Hackney	Midd	90-05-31
Hayward, Sir Rowland	Hackney	Midd	91-05-09-10

6. Hosts on Progress and London Visits (*continued*)

Host	Place	Co	Date
Heigham, Henry?	Hyde Hall in Sawbridgeworth	Hert	78-09-14?
Heneage, Sir Thomas	Copt Hall	Essex	78-05-12-13
Heneage, Sir Thomas	Heneage House		84-01/02
Heneage, Sir Thomas	Savoy	Lon	94-12-07
Heneage, Thomas [Sir]	Copt Hall	Essex	68-07-19
Herbert, Edward	Hendon	Midd	71-08-08?b
Herbert, Edward	Hendon	Midd	76-07c
Herbert, Edward?	Hendon	Midd	66-07-08
Hertford, Earl of	Elvetham	Hants	91-09-20-23
Hickford, Sir John	Alderton	Glos	92-09-11?
Hicks, Michael	Ruckhold in Leyton	Essex	97-08-17b-19
Hoby, Lady	Bisham	Berks	69-12
Howard, Thomas	Audley End	Essex	78-07-26-30
Hungerford, Anthony	Down Ampney	Glos	92-09-01-02
Hunsdon, Lord	Somerset House	Lon	83-03
Hunsdon, Lord	Somerset House	Lon	94-03-19
Hunsdon, Lord	Blackfriars	Lon	1602-04-19b
Hunsdon, Lord	West Drayton	Midd	1602-10-02b
Hunsdon, Lord	Blackfriars	Lon	1602-12-06-23b?
Hunsdon, Lord (wedding, Sir Edward)	Somerset House	Lon	82-05-20-22
hunting	Harolds Park	Essex	76-08-05b?
hunting	Donnington Park	Berks	92-08-25?
Huntingdon, Lady	Huntingdon House		95-12-20
Huntley, George	Frocester	Glos	74-08-10c-11
Hyde, Thomas	Aldbury	Hert	64-08-01?-04?b
Isley, William	Sundridge	Kent	81-09
Jerningham, Lady Mary	Costessey	Norf	78-08-19
Kellefet, Richard	Egham	Surrey	82-09-20
Kellefet, Richard	Egham	Surrey	93-08-01?
Kempe, Sir Thomas	Olantigh in Wye	Kent	73-08-21-22
Killigrew, William	Hanworth	Midd	1600-09-04
Killigrew, William	Hanworth	Midd	1601-08-06-08c
King's College	Cambridge	Cams	64-08-05-10
Kitson, Sir Thomas	Hengrave	Suffolk	78-08-28-30
Knightley, Sir Richard	Fawsley	War	75-07-07?
Knollys, Henry/ Cave, Margaret	Durham Place	Lon	65-07-16
Knollys, Sir Francis	Caversham or Rotherfield Greys	Oxon	74-07-23

6. Hosts on Progress and London Visits (*continued*)

Host	Place	Co	Date
Knollys, Sir Francis	Rotherfield Greys	Oxon	76-10-08
Knollys, Sir William	Caversham	Oxon	1601-09-02-04a
Knyvett, Thomas	Claybury	Essex	97-08-19
Lacy, John	Putney	Surrey	79-01-31?
Lacy, John	Putney	Surrey	80-05-26?
Lacy, John	Putney	Surrey	81-11-16 or 17
Lacy, John	Putney	Surrey	82-07-10?
Lacy, John	Putney	Surrey	84-11-12
Lacy, John	Putney	Surrey	85-07-27-29
Lacy, John	Putney	Surrey	86-07-12
Lacy, John	Putney	Surrey	88-07-29
Lacy, John	Putney	Surrey	89-12-02
Lacy, John	Putney	Surrey	90-11-08?
Lacy, John	Putney?	Surrey	93-01-30/02-01b
Lacy, John	Putney	Surrey	95-11-14
Lacy, John	Putney	Surrey	95-12-23
Lacy, John	Putney	Surrey	96-04-02-03
Lacy, John	Putney	Surrey	96-11-17
Lacy, John	Putney	Surrey	97-03
Lacy, John	Putney	Surrey	97-09-19-20
Lacy, John	Putney	Surrey	97-10-20a
Lacy, John	Putney	Surrey	99-11-13a
Lacy, John	Putney	Surrey	99-12-07
Lacy, John	Tooting	Surrey	1600-08-05-06
Lacy, John	Putney	Surrey	1602-02-19
Lacy, John	Putney	Surrey	1602-11-15
Lacy, John	Putney	Surrey	1603-01-21
Lacy?, John	Putney	Surrey	78-02-25-27
Lane, Sir Robert	Charlton	Nhants	68-08-22-26b
launch of Golden Lion	Deptford	Kent	82-01
Lawrence, Lady Anne	Soberton	Hants	69-09-01?-04?b
Lee, Sir Henry	Ditchley	Oxon	92-09-22?
Lee, Sir Richard	St. Albans	Hert	64-08-19/09-11h
Lewknor, Sir Richard	West Dean	Sussex	91-08-20
Leyfield, Thomas	Stoke d'Abernon	Surrey	90-07-28/08-06d
Lichfield, Thomas?	Highgate	Midd	76-07a
Lichfield, Thomas?	Highgate	Midd	77-05-23-25?b
Lincoln, Earl of	Horsley	Surrey	71-07/08a
Lincoln, Earl of		Lon	74-02-18-20a
Lincoln, Earl of	Pyrford	Surrey	76-05-12-15
Lincoln, Earl of	Pyrford	Surrey	76-09-11-12
Lincoln, Earl of	Pyrford	Surrey	77-09-04-07?
Lincoln, Earl of	Pyrford	Surrey	80-07/08d
Lincoln, Earl of	Pyrford	Surrey	82-09-01-02
Lincoln, Earl of	Pyrford	Surrey	83-08
Lincoln, Earl of?	Chelsea	Midd	1601-05-02

6. Hosts on Progress and London Visits (*continued*)

Host	Place	Co	Date
Long?, Henry	Felix Hall	Essex	61-07-26
Lord Admiral	Westminster	Lon	85-11-17-19
Lord Admiral	Westminster	Lon	87-11-17-21
Lord Admiral	Chelsea	Midd	93-01
Lord Admiral dinner	Westminster	Lon	87-10-24
Lovell, Gregory	Merton Abbey	Surrey	89-06-18?
Lovell, Gregory?	Merton Abbey	Surrey	74-05-30
Lucas, Sir Thomas	Colchester	Essex	61-07-26-30
Lucy, Sir Thomas	Charlecote	War	66-08-24?
Lucy, Sir Thomas	Charlecote	War	72-08-23a
Lumley, Lord	Tower Hill	Lon	84-01/02
Lumley, Lord	Chichester	Sussex	91-08-20-22
Lumley, Lord	Stanstead	Sussex	91-08-26
Lumley, Lord	Lumley House	Lon	1600-06-10
Lytton, Rowland	Knebworth	Hert	66-07-9-20c
Lytton, Rowland	Knebworth	Hert	68-08-01a
Lytton, Rowland	Knebworth	Hert	71-08-22?a
Malinge, Mr.	Kensington	Midd	88-01-16-20c
Manwood, Mr.	Sandwich	Kent	82-02-08
Manwood, Roger?	Sandwich	Kent	73-08-31/09-03
Manwood, Sir Roger	Canterbury	Kent	82-02-05-06
Martin, Richard	Tottenham High Cross	Midd	85-05-18b
Martin, Richard	Tottenham High Cross	Midd	88-04-13-16b
Martin, Richard	Tottenham High Cross	Midd	91-05-10?
Mason, Lady	Hartley Wintney	Hants	69-09-22?-23?a
Mason?, Sir John	Hartley Wintney	Hants	60-08-28?-30?b
Meautys, Henry?	West Ham	Essex	78-07-11?
Meredith, William?	Old Windsor	Berks	1601-08a
Mervyn, Edmund	Bramshott	Hants	91-08-14
Mervyn, Lady	Wylye?	Wilts	74-09-03
Middlemore, Henry	Enfield	Midd	87-07-09c
Mildmay, Sir Thomas	Moulsham	Essex	79-09-19-24a
Mildmay, Sir Walter	Apethorpe	Nhants	66-07-22-28c
Mildmay, Thomas/ Radcliffe, Frances	Bermondsey	Surrey	66-07-01
Miller, Hugh	Eltham	Kent	1601-07
Miller, Hugh; Lee, John	Eltham	Kent	98-07
Milsent, Robert	Barham Hall in Linton	Suffolk	78-07-31a
Montague, Edward	Boughton	Nhants	64-08-11-17b
Montague, Lord	Cowdray	Sussex	91-08-14-20
Montague, Lord	Oseburn Priory	Sussex	91-08-17
More, Edward	Odiham	Hants	91-09-19-20
More, Mr.	Bicester	Oxon	68-08-27
More, Sir George	Loseley	Surrey	1601-09-23b

6. Hosts on Progress and London Visits (*continued*)

Host	Place	Co	Date
More, Sir William	Loseley in Artington	Surrey	76-09-12-13
More, Sir William	Loseley	Surrey	83-08-27?b
More, Sir William	Loseley	Surrey	91-08-05-09
More, William	Loseley?	Surrey	67-08-22-23?
Morley, Lord	Great Hallingbury [Hastingbury]	Essex	61-08-25-27
Morley, Lord	Brent Pelham [Burnt]	Hert	71-08-26
Morley, Lord	Great Hallingbury [Hastingbury]	Essex	76-08-11-14
Neale, William	Warnford	Hants	91-09-10-11a
Neville, Sir Thomas	Philberds in Bray	Berks	70-09-26?-29?
Neville, Sir Thomas	Philberds in Bray	Berks	72-09-28
Neville, Sir Thomas	Philberds in Bray	Berks	75-10-09c
Nicholas, Lady	Edmonton	Midd	83-05-27-31/06-01c
Norfolk, Duke of	Charterhouse	Lon	68-07-06?-12?
Norfolk, Duke of	Audley End	Essex	71-08-29/09-03
Norris, John	Denham	Bucks	92-10-07
Norris, Lord	Rycote	Oxon	75-10-06-08
Norris, Lord	Rycote	Oxon	92-09-28/10-01
Norris, Mr.	Folly St. John Park	Berks	90-09b
Norris, Sir Edward	Englefield	Berks	1601-09-02-04b
Norris, Sir Henry	Rycote	Oxon	66-09-06-07
Norris, Sir Henry	Rycote	Oxon	68-08-27/09-12?a
Norris, Sir Henry	Rycote	Oxon	70-08-30/09-02, 06, 07
Norris?, Sir Henry	Yattendon	Berks	68-08-27/09-12?d
North, Lord	Charterhouse	Lon	58-11-23-28
North, Lord	Charterhouse	Lon	61-07-10-14
North, Lord	Kirtling	Cams	78-09-01-03
Northampton, Marchioness of	Whitehall	Lon	64-07-15
Northampton, Marquis/Helena von Snavenberg	wedding	Lon	71-04-29
Northumberland, Earl of	Petworth?	Sussex	83-08-27?d
Norton, John?	Rotherfield	Hants	60-08-08?-12?a
Nottingham, Earl of	Chelsea	Midd	97-02-19
Nottingham, Earl of	Chelsea	Midd	1600-01-19-21
Nottingham, Earl of	Arundel House	Lon	1602-12-06-23?
Nottingham, Earl of; Gorges, Sir Arthur	Chelsea	Midd	99-11-13b
Oglethorpe, Mr.	Thorpe	Surrey	1602-08-10b
Oxenbridge, Sir Robert	Hurstbourne?	Hants	69-09-15-21d
Oxford, Earl of	Hedingham	Essex	61-08-14-19

6. Hosts on Progress and London Visits (*continued*)

Host	Place	Co	Date
Oxford, Earl of/			
Cecil, Anne	wedding	Lon	71-12-16?-23?
Paget, Lord	Beaudesert	Staff	75-07-30b?
Parry, Thomas	Wallingford, at college	Berks	68-08-27/09-12?c
Parry, Thomas	Hampstead Marshall	Berks	92-08-26-27?
Paulet, Mr.	Crondall	Hants	1601-09-21
Paulet?, Chidiock	Odiham	Hants	60-08-28?-30?a
Paulett, Lady Mary	Leyton	Essex	81-07-05-08c
Payne, Mr.	Willesden	Midd	94-06-07
Payne, William	Hammersmith	Midd	92-04-07
Peckham, Sir George	Denham	Bucks	70-07-18-19
Pembroke, Earl of	Baynard's Castle	Lon	59-04-25
Pembroke, Earl of	Baynard's Castle	Lon	62-01-15-16
Pembroke, Earl of	Baynard's Castle	Lon	64-06-28
Pembroke, Earl of	Baynard's Castle	Lon	66-02-14
Pembroke, Earl of	Wilton	Wilts	74-09-03-06
Pembroke, Earl of	Ramsbury	Wilts	92-08-27b-29?
Pembroke, Lady	Baynard's Castle	Lon	75-05-05-08
Penruddock, Sir George	Broxbourne	Hert	75-06-06-07a
Penton, Mr.	Princes Risborough?	Bucks	64-08-19/09-11k
Petre, Lady	Ingatestone	Essex	79-09-15-16?
Petre, Sir John	Chigwell Hall	Essex	76-08-07a
Petre, Sir William	Ingatestone	Essex	61-07-19-21
Pexall, Sir Richard	Steventon	Hants	69-09-15-21e
Pigott, Thomas?	Beachampton	Bucks	72-08-04?
Plowden, Francis?	Burghfield	Berks	92-08-19
Pointz, Sir Nicholas	Iron Acton	Glos	74-08-11a?
Polsted, Richard	Thorpe	Surrey	76-09-10
Polsted?, Richard	Thorpe	Surrey	77-09-23
Popham, Sir John	Friern Barnet	Midd	94-06-08-12b
Poynings, Sir Adrian	Wherwell	Hants	69-09-15-21c
Puckering, Sir John	Kew	Surrey	95-12-11
Pulteney, Michael	Shenley	Hert	66-07-09-20a
Puttenham, George	Herriard	Hants	74-09-14b
Rainsford, Henry	Great Tew	Oxon	72-08-24?
Remington, Sir Robert	Beaurepaire [Baropey]	Hants	1601-09-05c?
Reve, John (at parsonage)	Princes Risborough	Bucks	92-10-01?
Revett, Thomas	Chippenham	Cams	78-09-01
Rich, Lord	Wanstead	Essex	61-07-14
Rich, Lord	Lees	Essex	61-08-21-25
Rich, Lord	Lees (Henham Park)	Essex	71-09-07-08
Rich, Thomas	Ardern Hall in Horndon	Essex	88-08-08-10b
Rookwood, Edward	Euston	Suffolk	78-08-10
Rotherham, George	Luton	Bed	75-06-15-18a

6. Hosts on Progress and London Visits (*continued*)

Host	Place	Co	Date
Rowlett, Sir Ralph	St. Albans	Hert	68-08-08
Russell, Lady	Bisham	Berks	92-08-11-13
Russell, Lady and Cobham, Lord	Blackfriars	Lon	1600-06-16-17
Russell, Sir William	Chiswick	Midd	1602-07-28
Sackville, Sir Richard	Sackville House	Lon	64-07-05
Sadler, Sir Ralph	Standon	Hert	61-08-27-30
Sadler, Sir Ralph	Standon	Hert	78-07-24
Sandys, Edwin	Latimer?	Bucks	92-10-06?
Sandys, Lady	Vine in Sherborne St. John	Hants	69-09-22
Sandys, Lord	Mottisfont	Hants	69-09-15-21b
Sandys, Lord	Mottisfont	Hants	74-09-09-10
Sandys, Lord	Vine in Sherborne St. John?	Hants	91-09-18
Sandys, Miles	Islehampstead Latimer	Bucks	73-02-24/03-10b
Sandys, Miles	Latimer	Bucks	76-09-01-03
Saunderson, Mr.	Newington	Kent	98-09
Savage?, Mr.	Winchelsea	Sussex	73-08-11?-14?
Scott, Bartholomew	Camberwell	Surrey	94-10-01a
Scott, Sir Thomas	Brabourne	Kent	73-08-22
Searle, John?	Brentwood [Burntwood]	Essex	79-09-19-24c
Sedley, William?	Southfleet	Kent	82-02-01
Serle, Francis?	Fairthorne	Hants	91-09-07?
Sheffield, Lady	Highgate	Midd	82-03
Sherington, Sir Henry	Lacock	Wilts	74-08-23-28
ship banquet, Elizabeth Jonas	Woolwich	Midd	59-07-03
Shrewsbury, Earl of	Chelsea	Midd	1600-11-13
Shrewsbury, Lord	Chelsea	Midd	98-11-13 or 14
Shrewsbury, Lord	Chelsea	Midd	99-02-10
Smith, Sir Thomas	Ankerwyke	Berks	65-08-08
Smythe, Thomas	Campden	Glos	75-08-22-26a
Somerset, Duchess of	Hanworth	Midd	77-09-12
Somerset, Edward/ Elizabeth Hastings	wedding	Lon	71-12-23
Southampton, Earl of	Tichfield	Hants	91-09-02-03
Southampton, Earl of/Browne, Mary	wedding	Lon	66-02-24-26
Southampton, Lady	Tichfield	Hants	69-09-04, 06

6. Hosts on Progress and London Visits (*continued*)

Host	Place	Co	Date
Southwell, Robert/ Howard, Elizabeth	wedding	Lon	83-04-13
Southwell, Sir Robert	Wood Rising	Norf	78-08-24
Spencer, Sir William	Yarnton	Oxon	92-09-23
St. Augustine's	Canterbury	Kent	73-09-03-16
St. James [sign of Queen's Arms]	Dover	Kent	82-02-09-11?
St. John, Lord	Bletsoe	Bed	66-07-09-20j
St. John, Lord	Abbotstone	Hants	69-09-01?-04?a
St. John, Sir John	Lydiard Tregoze	Wilts	92-09-01
Stafford, Lord	Stafford Castle	Staff	75-08-07-08
Stafford, Mr.; Gare, Mr.	Reading	Berks	68-09-18?
Stafford?, Thomas	Cornbury	Oxon	75-08-29
Stamford, Lady	Hadley	Midd	71-09-22?a
Stamford?, Lady Alice	Hadley	Midd	58-11-22-23
Stanhope, Sir John; Miller, Hugh; Walsingham, Sir Thomas	Eltham	Kent	1602-07-15?
Stevens, Thomas	Burderhope [Burdrope]	Wilts	92-08-29
Stonard, Francis	Loughborough	Essex	81-07-05-08b
Stonard, Francis	Loughborough	Essex	94-06-24?c
Stonard, Francis	Loughborough	Essex	97-08-31b
Stonard, John	Loughborough	Essex	76-08-07b
Stonard, John	Loughborough	Essex	78-09-21-22
Suffolk, Duchess of	Wrest	Bed	66-07-09-20e
Suffolk, Duchess of	Grimsthorpe [castle]	Lincs	66-08-06-16a
Surrey, Earl of	Kenninghall	Norf	78-08-11-12
Surrey, Earl of	Mount Surrey on Mousehold Hill	Norf	78-08-20
Sussex, Earl of	New Hall in Boreham	Essex	61-07-21-26
Sussex, Earl of	Bermondsey	Surrey	71-04/07? twice
Sussex, Earl of	New Hall in Boreham	Essex	79-09-17-18
Sussex, Earl of	Portsmouth	Hants	91-08-26-31
Sutton, Sir Henry	Bagshot	Surrey	69-09-22?-23?b
Talbot, Lord	Cheshunt	Hert	87-07-09e
Tanfield, Laurence [Sir]	Burford	Oxon	92-09-15-16
The Bush Inn	Staines	Midd	1601-08-08
The Crown	Rochester	Kent	73-09-19-23
The Crown	Rochester	Kent	82-02-01-03

6. Hosts on Progress and London Visits (*continued*)

Host	Place	Co	Date
The George	Sittingbourne	Kent	82-02-03-05
The Lion	Maidenhead	Berks	92-08-09-10e
The Ostrich Inn?	Eastridge in Colnbrook	Bucks	92-08-09-10d
Thimelby, Richard	Irnham	Lincs	66-08-06-16c
Thistlethwaite?, Giles	Winterslow	Wilts	74-09-09
Thorpe?, John? d. 1596	Kingscliffe	Nhants	66-08-06-16e
Thynne, Sir John	Longleat	Wilts	74-09-02
Tichborne, Sir Benjamin	Tichborne	Hants	91-09-10-11b
Tilney, Edmund	Leatherhead	Surrey	91-08-02b
Tilney, Philip	Shelley Hall	Suffolk	61-08-11
Tomson, Lawrence?	Laleham	Midd	93-12-01
Totehill, William	Shardeloes in Amersham?	Bucks	64-08-19/09-11m
Townsend, Roger?	Stoke Newington?	Midd	88-04-13-16c
Townsend, Thomas	Bracon Ash	Norf	78-08-16
Tufton, John	Hothfield	Kent	73-08-19-21
Tuke, George	Layer Marney	Essex	61-07-26?-30?a
Tyrell, Edward	Waltons in Ashdon [now Bartlow]	Essex	78-09-05-06?
Tyrrell, George	Thornton	Bucks	64-08-19/09-11f
Unton, Sir Edward	Langley	Oxon	72-09a
Unton, Sir Edward	Langley	Oxon	74-08-02-03
Unton, Sir Edward	Langley	Oxon	75-08-27
Verney, Edmund	Pendley	Hert	70-08-15-17
Vincent, Thomas	Combe	Surrey	94-10-25?
Vincent, Thomas	Combe	Surrey	95-10-19?
Vincent, Thomas?	Stoke d'Abernon	Surrey	1601-09-24-27b
Waldegrave, William	Smallbridge	Suffolk	61-08-11-14
Walden, Lord Howard de	Charterhouse	Lon	1603-01-17
Waller, Mr.	Fold in South Mimms	Midd	73-02-24/03-10a
Waller, Mr.	Fold? at Barnet	Midd	76-07b
Waller, Mr.	Fold? at Barnet	Midd	77-05-23-25?a
Waller, Mr.	Barnet	Hert	87-08-13a
Wallop, Sir Henry	Farleigh	Hants	91-09-12-13
Wallop, William	Wield	Hants	91-09-10-11e
Walsingham, Sir Francis	Barn Elms	Surrey	83-02-11
Walsingham, Sir Francis	Barn Elms	Surrey	87-11-20
Walsingham, Sir Francis	Barn Elms	Surrey	89-05-26-28
Walsingham, Sir Thomas	Scadbury	Kent	97-07-20-22

6. Hosts on Progress and London Visits (*continued*)

Host	Place	Co	Date
Walsingham?, Sir Francis	Barn Elms	Surrey	77-07-26a
Ward, Edward?	Hurst	Berks	92-08-14a
Ward, Richard	Hurst	Berks	76-10-08-09
Ward, Sir Richard	Hurst	Berks	1601-08-28
Warren?, William	Bygrave	Hert	66-07-09-20d
Warwick, Earl of	Northiaw	Hert	73-02-24/03-10e
Warwick, Earl of	Warwick Castle	War	66-08-22?-23?
Warwick, Earl of	Warwick Castle	War	72-08-11-13
Warwick, Earl of	Warwick Castle	War	72-08-16-18
Warwick, Earl of	Northiaw	Hert	76-08-30
Warwick, Earl of	Northiaw	Hert	77-05-18?
Warwick, Earl of	Northiaw	Hert	87-07-20-21
Warwick, Earl of	Bedford House?	Lon	90-01-27
Warwick, Earl of/ Russell, Lady Anne	tilt at wedding	Lon	65-11-11
Watts, Anne?	Bulley Hill	Kent	82-02-15?
Watts, Richard	Bulley Hill, ship at Rochester	Kent	73-09-23-24
Weldon, Ralph	Swanscombe	Kent	82-02-16
Wentworth, Sir John	Gosfield	Essex	61-08-19-21
Weston, Elizabeth	Chicheley	Bucks	72-07-30?
Weston, Elizabeth	Chicheley	Bucks	75-06-15-18e
Weston, Sir Henry	Sutton Place	Surrey	60-08-05
Weston, Sir Henry	Woking?	Surrey	60-08-05
Weston, Sir Henry	Bagshot	Surrey	84-09-02d
Weston, Sir Henry	Clandon Park	Surrey	91-08-03?
Weston, Sir Henry	Sutton in Woking	Surrey	91-09-26-27
Weston, Sir Henry?	Bagshot	Surrey	60-08-28?-30?c
Weston, Sir Richard	Clandon	Surrey	1601-09-24-27a
Whitby, Mr.	Hounslow	Midd	1602-07-29-30a
White, John	Southwick	Hants	60-08-08?-12?b
White, John	Southwick	Hants	91-08-31/09-01
White, Lady Joan	Bethnal Green	Midd	72-07-15?b
White, Richard	South Warnborough	Hants	1601-09-20
Whitefriars	Coventry	War	66-08-17-19
Wightman, William	Harrow	Midd	71-09-22?b
Wightman, William	Harrow	Midd	87-08-13b
Wilkes, Thomas	Brentford	Midd	83-11-25?
Willoughby, Sir Francis	Middleton	War	75-07-28-29b
Winchester, Marquis of	Basing	Hants	60-08-23-28
Winchester, Marquis of	Basing	Hants	69-08-27, 29/09-01
Winchester, Marquis of	Abbotstone	Hants	74-09-13

6. Hosts on Progress and London Visits (*continued*)

Host	Place	Co	Date
Winchester, Marquis of	Abbotstone	Hants	91-09-10-11d
Winchester, Marquis of	Basing	Hants	91-09-13-16
Winchester, Marquis of	Basing	Hants	1601-09-05-19
Windsor, Lord	Bradenham [Bradnam]	Bucks	66-09-07-09
Windsor, Lord Frederick	Bradenham [Bradnam]	Bucks	75-10-09a
Wingate, Edward	Dunstable	Bed	68-08-09-13a
Wingate?, Edward	Dunstable	Bed	72-07-28-29
Wingfield, Thomas?	Kimbolton	Hunt	64-08-11-17a
Wingfield, Thomas?	Kimbolton	Hunt	66-07-21
Wolley, John	Chobham	Surrey	80-07/08c
Wolley, John	Chobham	Surrey	82-08/09?
Wolley, John	Chobham	Surrey	83-09a
Woodhouse, Francis	Breckles	Norf	78-08-25-26?
Woodhouse, Sir Roger	Kimberley	Norf	78-08-22 or 23
Woodruff, Lady	Seale	Surrey	1601-09-23a?
Woodward, Mr.	Edmonton	Midd	97-09-10-12c
Woodward, Mr.			1602-09/10e
Worsopp, John	Clapham	Surrey	83-04-18
Worthington, Mr.	Haslingfield	Cams	64-08-04-05
Wotton, Thomas	Boughton Malherbe	Kent	73-08-17-19
Wroth, Robert	Enfield	Midd	91-05-21-23a
Wroth, Robert	Enfield	Midd	94-06-24?b
Wroth, Robert (hunt)	Loughton	Essex	97-08-31c
Yate, James	Witney	Oxon	92-09-16-18
Young, Richard?	Stratford at Bow	Midd	76-07-30
Young, Richard?	Stratford at Bow	Midd	79-09-09
Young, Sir John	Bristol	Glos	74-08-14-21
Zouch, Sir John			77-09

7. Privy Councilors as Hosts

Name	Dates on Council
Arundel, Earl of	1558–80
Bacon, Sir Nicholas	1558–79
Bedford, Earl of	1558–85
Bromley, Sir Thomas	1579–87
Buckhurst, Lord	1586–1608
Cave, Sir Ambrose	1558–68
Cecil, Sir Robert	1591–1612
Cecil, Sir William	1558–98
Cheyney, Sir Thomas	1558–58
Clinton, Lord	1558–85
Cobham, Lord, 10th	1586–96
Croft, Sir James	1566–90
Davison, William	1586–87
Derby, Earl of	1558–72
Derby, Earl of, 4th	1586–93
Dudley, Lord Robert	1563?–88
Egerton, Sir Thomas	1596–1617
Essex, Earl of, 2nd	1593–1601
Fortescue, Sir John	1587–95
Hatton, Sir Christopher	1577–91
Heath, Archbishop of York	1558–59
Heneage, Sir Thomas	1587–95
Herbert, Dr. John	1600–1619
Howard of Effingham, Charles, 2nd	1586–1624
Howard of Effingham, William	1558–73
Hunsdon, Lord Henry, 1st	1577–96
Hunsdon, Lord George, 2nd	1597–1603
Knollys, Sir Francis	1559–96
Knollys, Sir William	1596–1632
Mason, Sir John	1558–66
Mildmay, Sir Walter	1566–89
Norfolk, Duke of, 4th	1563?–72
North, Lord Roger	1596–1600
Northampton, Marquis of	1558–71
Parry, Sir Thomas	1558–60
Paulet, Sir Amyas	1585–88
Pembroke, Earl of	1558–70
Perrot, Sir John	1589–92
Petre, Sir William	1558–72
Popham, Sir John	1599–1607
Puckering, Sir John	1592–96
Rogers, Sir Edward	1558–67
Sackville, Sir Richard	1558–66
Sadler, Sir Ralph	1566–87
Shrewsbury, Earl of	1558–60
Shrewsbury, Earl of, 6th	1571–90
Shrewsbury, Earl of, 7th	1601–1616
Sidney, Sir Henry	1575–86
Smith, Sir Thomas	1571–77

7. Privy Councilors as Hosts (*continued*)

Name	Dates on Council
Stanhope, Sir John	1601–1621
Sussex, Earl of, 3rd	1570–83
Walsingham, Sir Francis	1573–90
Warwick, Earl of	1573–90
Whitgift, John	1583–1604
Wilson, Dr. Thomas	1577–81
Winchester, Marquis of	1558–72
Wolley, John	1586–96
Worcester, Earl, 4th	1601–1628
Wotton, Dr. Nicholas	1562–67
Wotton, Sir Edward	1602–1626

8. Women as Primary Hosts

Host	Place	Co	R	Date
Askewe, Lady Anne	Byfleet	Surrey	r	82-09-01?
Averie, Margery	Berden Priory	Essex		78-07-25?
Bedford, Lady	Chenies	Bucks		92-10-04-05
Blank, Lady	Mitcham	Surrey		94-10-01b
Blank, Margaret, Lady	Mitcham	Surrey		91-07-29?
Bracy, Mrs.	Bracy, Mrs.	Essex		97-09-05
Chandos, Dorothy, Lady, and Knollys, Sir William	St. James Park	Lon		1602-05-05
Chandos, Lady	Sudeley Castle	Glos		74-08-04-05
Châtillon, Madame de	Ham House	Surrey		70-03-19
Daston, Anne	Elmley Bredon [Elmley]	Glos		75-08-20-22
Derby, Alice Countess of	Holborn?	Lon		99-06-25
Derby, Countess of [Margaret, d. 1596]	Isleworth [Thistleworth]	Midd		77-07-24
Edmondes, Dorothy, Lady	Molesey	Surrey		1600-08-24?
Elderton, Mrs.	Theydon Bois	Essex		78-09-18
Ellensbury, Dame	Houghton Conquest	Bed		66-07-09-20f
Ellensbury, Dame	Houghton Conquest	Bed		70-08-21-23a
Essex, Lady	Chartley	Staff		75-08-01-06b
Glemham, Lady	Sackville House	Lon		1600-12-04?
Gresham, Anne, Lady	Osterley	Midd		94-06-05?
Gresham, Lady	Osterley	Midd		92-04-07-09
Gresley, Lady Katharine	Colton	Staff		75-08-01-06a
Hampden, Mrs.	Hampden	Bucks		92-10-02-03
Hayward, Katharine, Lady	Hackney	Midd		94-07-05?
Hayward, Lady	Hackney	Midd		97-08-17a?
Hoby, Lady	Bisham	Berks		69-12

8. Women as Primary Hosts (*continued*)

Host	Place	Co	R	Date
Huntingdon, Lady	Huntingdon House			95-12-20
Jerningham, Lady Mary	Costessey	Norf		78-08-19
Lawrence, Lady Anne	Soberton	Hants		69-09-01?-04?b
Mason, Lady	Hartley Wintney	Hants		69-09-22?-23?a
Mervyn, Lady	Wylye?	Wilts		74-09-03
Nicholas, Lady	Edmonton	Midd		83-05-27-31/ 06-01c
Northampton, Marchioness of	Whitehall	Lon		64-07-15
Paulett, Lady Mary	Leyton	Essex		81-07-05-08c
Petre, Lady	Ingatestone	Essex		79-09-15-16?
Russell, Lady	Bisham	Berks		92-08-11-13
Russell, Lady, and Cobham, Lord (hosts)	Blackfriars	Lon		1600-06-16-17
Sandys, Lady	Vine in Sherborne St. John	Hants		69-09-22
Sheffield, Lady	Highgate	Midd		82-03
Somerset, Duchess of	Hanworth	Midd	r	77-09-12
Southampton, Lady	Tichfield	Hants		69-09-04, 06
Stamford, Lady	Hadley	Midd		71-09-22?a
Stamford?, Lady Alice	Hadley	Midd		58-11-22-23
Suffolk, Duchess of	Grimsthorpe [castle]	Lincs		66-08-06-16a
Suffolk, Duchess of	Wrest	Bed		66-07-09-20e
Watts, Anne?	Bulley Hill	Kent		82-02-15?
Weston, Elizabeth	Chicheley	Bucks		72-07-30?
Weston, Elizabeth	Chicheley	Bucks		75-06-15-18e
White, Lady Joan	Bethnal Green	Midd		72-07-15?b
Woodruff, Lady	Seale	Surrey		1601-09-23a?

9. Clergy as Hosts

Host	Place	Co	Date	Name
A of Canterbury	Canterbury	Kent	73-09-07	Parker
A of Canterbury	Croydon	Surrey	59-08-05-06?	Parker, Matthew, 1559–75
A of Canterbury	Croydon	Surrey	73-07-14-21	Parker
A of Canterbury	Croydon	Surrey	85-03-30?a	Whitgift
A of Canterbury	Croydon	Surrey	88-04-04/05b	Whitgift
A of Canterbury	Croydon	Surrey	92-04-17-21?	Whitgift
A of Canterbury	Croydon	Surrey	93-05-02-14	Whitgift
A of Canterbury	Lambeth	Surrey	60-07-29	Parker
A of Canterbury	Lambeth	Surrey	63-07-20/08-01?	Parker
A of Canterbury	Lambeth	Surrey	69-07-21	Parker
A of Canterbury	Lambeth	Surrey	74-03-02-03	Parker
A of Canterbury	Lambeth	Surrey	85-03-26-30	Whitgift, John, 1583–1604
A of Canterbury	Lambeth	Surrey	85-04-03	Whitgift
A of Canterbury	Lambeth	Surrey	88-01-16-20d	Whitgift
A of Canterbury	Lambeth	Surrey	91-02-11-13	Whitgift
A of Canterbury	Lambeth	Surrey	94-05-29?	Whitgift
A of Canterbury	Lambeth	Surrey	95-02-18	Whitgift
A of Canterbury	Lambeth	Surrey	1602-04-19a	Whitgift
A of Canterbury	Lambeth	Surrey	1602-07-28	Whitgift
A of Canterbury?	Croydon	Surrey	67-01-17?/02-01?a	Parker
B of Ely	Long Stanton	Cams	64-08-10a	Cox, Richard, 1559–81
B of London	Fulham	Midd	88-01-16-20a	Aylmer, John, 1577–94
B of London	Fulham	Midd	1601-08-06-08a	Bancroft, Richard, 1597–1604
B of Norwich	Norwich	Norf	78-08-16-22	Freke, Edmund, 1575–84
B of Salisbury	Salisbury	Wilts	74-09-06b-09	Gheast [Guest], Edmund, 1571–77
B of Winchester	Bishop's Waltham	Hants	91-09-08-09	Cooper
B of Winchester	Farnham	Surrey	60-08-07-08	Horne
B of Winchester	Farnham	Surrey	67-08-24-25, 29	Horne, Robert, 1561–80
B of Winchester	Farnham	Surrey	69-08-14, 17, 20, 22	Horne
B of Winchester	Farnham	Surrey	74-09-15, 19	Horne
B of Winchester	Farnham	Surrey	76-09-13?-20	Horne
B of Winchester	Farnham	Surrey	91-08-10-14	Cooper, Thomas, 1584–97
B of Winchester	Farnham	Surrey	91-09-23-24	Cooper
B of Winchester	Farnham	Surrey	1601-09-22-23	Bilson, Thomas, 1597–1616
B of Winchester	Winchester	Hants	91-09-10-11c	Cooper
B of Worcester	Hartlebury Castle	Wor	75-08-12-13	Bullingham, Nicholas, 1571–76
B of Worcester	Worcester	Wor	75-08-13-20	Bullingham
	Chobham	Surrey	80-07/08a	

10. Members of Parliament, Justices of the Peace, Sheriffs as Hosts

Host	Co	MP or County	Court or Gov Office
Abergavenny, Lord	Kent	son MP	
Alington, Sir Giles	Cams	MP, JP, S	
Altham, James	Essex	son MP	
Aubrey, William	Kent	MP	Master of Requests, Ct of High Commission
Averie, Margery	Essex	husband MP, JP	
Bacon, Sir Nicholas	Hert	MP, JP	Lord Keeper of Great Seal, PC
Baker, Richard	Kent	MP, S	
Barrington, Sir Thomas	Essex	MP, JP, S	
Bashe, Edward	Hert	MP, JP, S	Gen Surveyor
Bedford, Earl of	Bucks	Marian MP, JP, S	ambassador
Berners, Anthony?	Essex	family MP	
Bonham, John	Wilts	father MP	
Brockett, John	Hert	MP, JP, S	
Bromley, Thomas [Sir]	Wor	MP	Chancellor, Solicitor General
Brouncker, William	Wilts	MP, JP, S	
Burghley, Thomas, Lord	Surrey	MP, JP, S	Pres, Council of the North
Butler, Sir John	Hert	MP, JP, S	
Caesar, Julius	Surrey	MP	Master of Requests
Capel, Henry	Hert	MP, JP, S	
Caplen, John	Hants	MP	
Carew, Francis	Surrey	MP, JP, S	courtier
Cecil, Sir Robert	Lon	MP, JP	Principal Secretary, Master Ct of Wards
Cecil, Sir William	Lon	MP, JP	Lord Treasurer, Keeper of Privy Seal, Master Ct of Wards
Chandos, Lady	Glos	husband MP	husband Council of Marches
Cheyne, Sir Henry	Bed	MP, JP, S	
Clere, Sir Edward	Norf	MP, JP, S	
Clifford, Francis?	Midd	MP, JP, S	Council of North
Cobham, Lord	Kent	MP, JP	PC, Lord Chamberlain
Cock, Sir Henry	Hert	MP, JP, S	Cofferer of Household
Coke, Sir Edward	Bucks	MP, JP, Recorder	Attorney General, Speaker of House
Compton, Lord	War	MP, S	courtier
Cooke, Richard	Essex	MP, JP	Groom Privy Chamber
Cooke, Sir Anthony	Essex	MP, JP	Gent Pensioner
Cope, Walter	Midd	MP, JP	feodary Ct of Wards
Copinger, Ambrose	Midd	MP	
Corbett, Sir Andrew	Nhants	MP, JP	Council of Marches
Cordell, Sir William	Suffolk	MP, JP	Master of Rolls, Speaker of House
Cornwallis, Sir William	Midd	MP, JP	
Cox, John?	Surrey	MP	feodary Ct of Wards
Cromer, William	Kent	MP, JP, S	
Cromwell, Henry, Lord	Leic	MP, JP, S	
Cutts, Sir John	Essex	MP, JP, S	
Danvers, Sir John	Glos	MP, JP, S	Council of Marches
Darcy, Lord	Essex	father MP	
Delawarr, Lord	Sussex	father MP	
Delawarr, Lord	Midd	MP, JP	Chamberlain of Exchequer

10. Members of Parliament, Justices of the Peace, Sheriffs as Hosts (*continued*)

Host	Co	MP or County	Court or Gov Office
Dormer, Sir William	Bucks	MP, JP, S	
Drake, Richard	Surrey	MP, JP	Equerry of Stable, Groom Privy Chamber
Drake, Sir Francis	Kent	MP, JP	Vice Admiral
Drury, Sir Robert	Bucks	MP, JP, S	
Drury, Sir William	Suffolk	MP, JP, S	Exchequer
Dudley, John	Midd	MP	
Dudley, Robert	Lon	MP, JP	Master of Horse, Lord Steward Household, Constable
Edmondes, Dorothy, Lady	Surrey	husband MP, JP	
Egerton, Sir Thomas	Midd	MP	Lord Keeper, Master of Rolls, PC
Fanshawe, Thomas	Essex	MP, JP	Clerk Exchequer
Fermor, Sir John	Nhants	MP, JP, S	
Fiennes, Richard	Oxon	MP, S	
Fisher, Jasper	Lon	MP, JP	Clerk Chancery
Fisher, Thomas	War	MP, JP	
Fitzwilliam, Sir William	Essex	MP, JP	Lord Deputy Ireland, Lord Justice
Forster, Sir Humphrey	Berks	MP, JP, S	
Forster, William?	Berks	MP, S	
Fortescue, John [Sir]	Bucks	MP	Chancellor Exchequer, Keeper Wardrobe, PC
Fuller, Nicholas	Berks	MP	
Giffard, John	Staff	MP, S	
Gifford, Henry?	Hants	MP, JP, S	
Glemham, Lady	Lon?	husband MP	
Gostwick, John	Bed	family MP	
Gresham, Lady	Midd	husband MP, JP, S	
Grey, Lord John [d. 1569]	Essex	son MP	
Grey, Sir Henry	Essex	MP, JP	Master of Hounds, Gent Pensioner
Guildford, Thomas	Kent	MP, JP	
Hampden, Griffith	Bucks	MP, JP, S	
Hanbury, Richard?	Bucks	MP	
Harcourt, Walter?	Staff	MP, JP	
Harington, Sir James	Rut	MP, JP, S	
Hatton, Sir Christopher	Lon	MP, JP	Vice Chamberlain, Gent Privy Chamber, Gent Pensioner
Hawker, Mr.	Wilts	MP	
Hawtrey, William	Bucks	MP, S	
Hayward, Katharine, Lady	Midd	husband MP, JP, S	
Heneage, Sir Thomas	Essex	MP, JP	Treasurer of Chamber, PC, Gent Privy Chamber
Hertford, Earl of	Hants	MP	
Hicks, Michael	Essex	MP, JP	
Hungerford, Anthony	Glos	MP	
Hunsdon, Lord	Lon	MP	Lord Chamberlain Household, PC, Captain Gent Pensioners

10. Members of Parliament, Justices of the Peace, Sheriffs as Hosts (*continued*)

Host	Co	MP or County	Court or Gov Office
Hunsdon, Lord	Lon	MP	Lord Chamberlain, Knight Marshall Household
Huntley, George	Glos	MP, JP, S	
Jerningham, Lady Mary	Norf	family MP	
Kempe, Sir Thomas	Kent	MP, JP, S	
Killigrew, William	Midd	MP	Treasurer Chamber, Groom Privy Chamber
Knightley, Sir Richard	War	MP, JP, S	
Knollys, Henry/Cave, Margaret	Lon	MP	
Knollys, Sir Francis	Oxon	MP, JP	Vice-Chamberlain, PC, Treasurer Chamber and Household
Knollys, Sir William	Oxon	MP, JP	Comptroller and Treasurer Household, PC, Gent Pensioner
Knyvett, Thomas	Essex	MP	Privy Chamber, Warden Tower Mint
Lane, Sir Robert	Nhants	MP, JP	
Lawrence, Lady Anne	Hants	husband MP	
Lee, Sir Henry	Oxon	MP, JP	Royal Champion
Lee, Sir Richard	Hert	MP	military posts
Lewknor, Sir Richard	Sussex	MP, JP	
Lichfield, Thomas?	Midd	MP	Gent Privy Chamber
Long?, Henry	Essex	MP, S	
Lord Admiral	Lon	MP	Lord Admiral, PC, Chamberlain of Household
Lucas, Sir Thomas	Essex	MP, S	
Lucy, Sir Thomas	War	MP, JP, S	Council of Marches
Manwood, Sir Roger	Kent	MP	Chief Baron Exchequer
Mason, Lady	Hants	husband MP, JP	husband Treasurer Chamber, PC, Master of Requests
Mildmay, Sir Thomas	Essex	MP, JP, S	
Mildmay, Sir Walter	Nhants	MP, JP	Undertreasurer, PC, Chancellor Exchequer
Montague, Edward	Nhants	MP, JP, S	
Montague, Lord	Sussex		ambassador
More, Edward	Hants	MP, JP	Gent Pensioner
More, Sir George	Surrey	MP, JP	Chamberlain of Receipt, Exchequer
More, Sir William	Surrey	MP, JP, S	Chamberlain Exchequer
Morley, Lord	Essex	family MP	
Neale, William	Hants	son MP	Auditor Exchequer
Norris, Sir Edward	Berks	MP, JP	Sewer of Household, Clerk Petty Bag
Norris, Sir Henry	Oxon	MP, JP, S	ambassador, Capt of Light Horse
North, Lord	Lon	MP, JP	Treasurer Household, PC, Ambassador
Northumberland, Earl of	Sussex	MP, JP, S	Council of North
Norton, John?	Hants	MP	
Oxenbridge, Sir Robert	Hants	MP, JP, S	Princess' Household
Parry, Thomas	Berks	MP, JP, S	ambassador
Paulet, Mr.	Hants	MP, JP	
Paulet?, Chidiock	Hants	MP	

10. Members of Parliament, Justices of the Peace, Sheriffs as Hosts (*continued*)

Host	Co	MP or County	Court or Gov Office
Peckham, Sir George	Bucks	family MP	
Pembroke, Earl of	Lon	MP	Steward Household
Penruddock, Sir George	Hert	MP, JP, S	Provost Marshall, Esquire of Body
Petre, Sir John	Essex	MP, JP, S	
Petre, Sir William	Essex	MP, JP	
Plowden, Francis?	Berks	family MP	
Pointz, Sir Nicholas	Glos	MP, JP, S	Esquire of Body
Polsted, Richard	Surrey	MP, JP, S	
Popham, Sir John	Midd	MP	Queen's Bench, PC, Speaker of House
Poynings, Sir Adrian	Hants	MP, JP	
Puckering, Sir John	Surrey	MP, JP	Lord Keeper, PC, Council of Marches
Pulteney, Michael	Hert	MP	
Rich, Lord	Essex	MP, JP	
Rich, Lord	Essex	father MP	
Rookwood, Edward	Suffolk	father MP	
Rotherham, George	Bed	MP, JP, S	
Rowlett, Sir Ralph	Hert	MP, JP, S	
Russell, Lady	Berks	husband MP, JP	
Russell, Sir William	Midd	MP, JP	Gent Pensioner
Sackville, Sir Richard	Lon	MP, JP	Under Treasurer Exchequer, PC
Sadler, Sir Ralph	Hert	MP, JP	PC
Sandys, Miles	Bucks	MP	Queen's Bench, Clerk of Crown
Scott, Sir Thomas	Kent	MP, JP, S	
Shrewsbury, Earl of	Midd	MP, JP	PC
Smith, Sir Thomas	Berks	MP, JP	Principal Secretary, Keeper Privy Seal, PC
Southwell, Sir Robert	Norf	MP, JP, S	
Spencer, Sir William	Oxon	MP, S	Auditor of Exchequer
St. John, Lord	Bed	MP, JP, S	
St. John, Sir John	Wilts	father MP	
Stafford, Lord	Staff	MP, JP	Council of Marches
Stamford?, Lady Alice	Midd	husband MP, JP	
Stanhope, Sir John	Kent	MP, JP	Vice Chamberlain, PC, Gent Privy Chamber
Sussex, Earl of	Essex	MP, JP	Lord Chamberlain, Capt Gent Pensioners, PC, Council of North
Sussex, Earl of	Hants	MP	military offices
Tanfield, Laurence [Sir]		MP, JP	
Thynne, Sir John	Wilts	MP, JP, S	
Tichborne, Sir Benjamin	Hants	MP, JP, S	
Tilney, Edmund	Surrey	MP	Master of Revels
Tomson, Lawrence?	Midd	MP	
Townsend, Roger?	Midd	MP	
Townsend, Thomas	Norf	father MP	
Tufton, John	Kent	son MP	
Unton, Sir Edward	Oxon	MP, JP, S	
Verney, Edmund	Hert	brother MP	

10. Members of Parliament, Justices of the Peace, Sheriffs as Hosts (*continued*)

Host	Co	MP or County	Court or Gov Office
Vincent, Thomas	Surrey	MP, JP	
Waldegrave, William	Suffolk	MP, S	
Wallop, Sir Henry	Hants	MP, JP	Lord Justice
Wallop, William	Hants	MP, JP, S, Mayor	
Walsingham, Sir Francis	Surrey	MP, JP	Principal Secretary, PC
Walsingham, Sir Thomas	Kent	MP, JP	Chief Keeper Wardrobe
Ward, Richard	Berks	MP, JP	Cofferer Household, Clerk of Greencloth
Watts, Richard	Kent	MP	
Wentworth, Sir John	Essex	son MP	
Weston, Elizabeth	Bucks	husband MP, JP	Queen's serjeant
Weston, Sir Henry	Surrey	MP, JP, S	
Weston, Sir Richard	Surrey	MP, JP	
Wightman, William	Midd	MP	Mint, Exchequer
Winchester, Marquis of	Hants	MP, S	Lord Treasurer
Windsor, Lord	Bucks	father MP	
Wingfield, Thomas?	Hunt	son MP	
Wolley, John	Surrey	MP, JP	Latin Secretary, Ct of High Commission
Woodhouse, Sir Roger	Norf	MP, JP	
Woodruff, Lady	Surrey	husband MP, S, Mayor	
Wotton, Thomas	Kent	MP, S	
Wroth, Robert	Midd	MP, JP, S	
Young, Sir John	Glos	MP, JP, S	
Zouch, Sir John		MP, S	

11. Hosts with Catholic Ties

Host	Co	Date	RC Ties
Arundel, Earl of	Lon	83-10?/12?	RC
Baker, Richard	Kent	73-08-14-17	father, daughter RC
Clere, Sir Edward	Norf	78-08-27	son RC
Compton, Lord	War	72-08-23b	RC
Cornwallis, Sir William	Midd	94-06-07	father RC
Danvers, Sir John	Glos	92-09-02-07	son RC
Delawarr, Lord	Sussex	91-08-14b	daughter RC
Delawarr, Lord	Midd	07-10-20b	sister RC
Dormer, Sir William	Bucks	70-08-24?	RC
Drury, Sir Robert	Bucks	76-09-03	son RC
Egerton, Sir Thomas	Midd	1602-07-31/08-03	RC, conformed
Fermor, Sir John	Nhants	64-08-19/09-11d	RC, conformed
Gardiner, John?	Bucks	76-09-03?	nephew RC
Giffard, John	Staff	75-08-09-11b	RC
Glemham, Lady	Lon?	1600-12-04?	husband's family RC
Hungerford, Anthony	Glos	92-09-01-02	RC, converted
Kempe, Sir Thomas	Kent	73-08-21-22	RC, wife RC
Lawrence, Lady Anne	Hants	69-09-01?-04?b	family RC
Lewknor, Sir Richard	Sussex	91-08-20	brother RC
Mason, Lady	Hants	69-09-22?-23?a	husband RC
Montague, Lord	Sussex	91-08-14-20	RC
More, Edward	Hants	91-09-19-20	RC
Northumberland, Earl of	Sussex	83-08-27?d	RC
Oxenbridge, Sir Robert	Hants	69-09-15-21d	RC
Paulet?, Chidiock	Hants	60-08-28?-30?a	RC
Petre, Lady	Essex	79-09-15-16?	RC
Petre, Sir John	Essex	76-08-07a	mother, wife RC
Petre, Sir William	Essex	61-07-19-21	wife RC
Plowden, Francis?	Berks	92-08-19	father RC
Pointz, Sir Nicholas	Glos	74-08-11a?	RC
Rookwood, Edward	Suffolk	78-08-10	RC
Sackville, Sir Richard	Lon	64-07-05	wife RC
Southampton, Earl of/			
Browne, Mary	Lon	66-02-24-26	RC
Stafford, Lord	Staff	75-08-07-08	RC
Tichborne, Sir Benjamin	Hants	91-09-10-11b	family RC
Waldegrave, William	Suffolk	61-08-11-14	wife RC
Weston, Elizabeth	Bucks	72-07-30?	husband RC
Weston, Sir Henry	Surrey	60-08-05	RC

ABBREVIATIONS

APC	*Acts of the Privy Council*
BL	British Library, London
BL Add.	British Library, Additional MSS
BL Harl.	British Library, Harleian MSS
BL Lans.	British Library, Landsdowne MSS
Bod.	Bodleian Library, Oxford
Bod. Rawl.	Bodleian Rawlinson MSS
CSPD	*Calendar of State Papers, Domestic Series*
CSPD Add.	*Calendar of State Papers, Domestic Series, Addenda*
CSP Spanish	*Calendar of Letters and State Papers relating to English Affairs, Preserved principally in the Archives of Simancas*
DNB	*Dictionary of National Biography*
HMSO	Her Majesty's Stationery Office
H.M.C.	*Historical Manuscripts Commission*
IHR	Institute of Historical Research, London
PRO	Public Record Office, London
PRO S.P.	Public Record Office, State Papers
PRO L.S.	Public Record Office, Lord Steward's
PRO E.	Public Record Office, Exchequer
TBGAS	*Transactions of the Bristol and Gloucestershire Archaeological Society*
VCH	*Victoria County History*

NOTES

I. INTRODUCTION

1. Neale, *Queen Elizabeth I.*
2. Strong, *Cult of Elizabeth; Art and Power;* and *Gloriana.*
3. Bergeron, *English Civic Pageantry.*
4. Christy, "Progresses of Queen Elizabeth."
5. Breight, "Realpolitik and Elizabethan Ceremony."
6. Woodworth, "Purveyance."
7. Turner, *Ritual Process,* and *From Ritual to Theatre;* Geertz, "Centers, Kings, and Charisma," and *Interpretation of Cultures;* Weissman, *Ritual Brotherhood;* Trexler, *Public Life in Renaissance Florence;* Muir, *Civic Ritual in Renaissance Venice;* Giesey, "Models of Rulership"; Bryant, "Configurations of the Community."
8. Manley, *Literature and Culture.*
9. Smuts, "Public Ceremony and Royal Charisma," 66, 68.
10. Wilson, *Entertainments for Elizabeth I,* 42, 56–57.
11. Montrose, "'Shaping Fantasies.'"
12. Cerasano and Wynne-Davies, *Gloriana's Face,* 1–24.
13. Levin, *Heart and Stomach of a King.*
14. Doran, *Monarchy and Matrimony;* Haigh, *Elizabeth I;* MacCaffrey, *Elizabeth I.*
15. Guy, *Reign of Elizabeth I.*
16. Beckingsale, *Elizabeth I,* 21.

2. PATTERNS OF THE PROGRESSES

1. Alexander, *First of the Tudors,* 49–52.
2. Chrimes, *Henry VII,* 306. In *Early English Stages, 1300–1660,* 3:54, Wickham locates the origin of the royal progress in this 1486 journey: "Initiated by Henry VII to bolster his still contested claim to the throne, it [the royal progress] developed sluggishly and did not really come into its own until late in the sixteenth century" in connection with displays and shows. In political and symbolic terms, however, progresses were a medieval phenomenon as well.
3. Samman, "Progresses of Henry VIII," 69.
4. *Calendar of State Papers Domestic Series of the Reign of Edward VI, 1547–1553,* nos. 627, 688, 704, 711.
5. Loades, *Mary Tudor,* 45, 224–27, 332–37; Dutton, *English Court Life,* 54–63.
6. Willson, *King James VI & I,* 88–92, 389–93; Gregg, *King Charles I,* 257.
7. See Mattingly, *Renaissance Diplomacy.*
8. Frye, "Elizabeth I at Tilbury."
9. These ceremonies are described in Strong, *Art and Power,* and Dickens, *Courts of Europe.*
10. *Cest la Deduction du sumptueux ordre plaisantz spectacles et magnifiques theatres dresses, et exhibes par les citoiens de Rouen . . . a la sacree Maieste du Tres christian Roy de France, Henry*

secod . . . et . . . Katharine de Medicis, 1551, Folger Shakespeare Library, DC 114.3 C4 1551. See also McFarlane, *Entry of Henry II into Paris,* 15–75.

11. Kipling, "Richard II's 'Sumptuous Pageants,'" 88–94. The numerous royal entries and their symbolic shows are detailed in Withington, *English Pageantry,* 1:124–92.

12. Bryant, "Configurations of the Community," 20–25.

13. Withington, *English Pageantry,* 1:148–53.

14. Alexander, *First of the Tudors,* 11; Attreed, "Politics of Welcome," 216–18.

15. Attreed, "Politics of Welcome," 220–23; Anglo, *Spectacle, Pageantry, and Early Tudor Policy,* 22–28; Alexander, *First of the Tudors,* 49–52.

16. Anglo, *Spectacle, Pageantry, and Early Tudor Policy,* 117–23.

17. Withington, *English Pageantry,* 1:170; Dutton, *English Court Life,* 45.

18. Anglo, *Spectacle, Pageantry, and Early Tudor Policy,* 293–94, 301; Withington, *English Pageantry,* 1:185–86.

19. Withington, *English Pageantry,* 1:188–92; Dutton, *English Court Life,* 54.

20. Anglo, *Spectacle, Pageantry, and Early Tudor Policy,* 347–58; Bergeron, *English Civic Pageantry,* 11.

21. Chambers, *Elizabethan Stage,* 4:86.

22. PRO S.P. 12/159/39.

23. *CSPSpanish, 1558–67,* 679.

24. Stow, *Annales,* 656–57; Nichols, ed., "Diary of Machyn," 309. This outbreak killed one out of five Londoners, according to Palliser, *Age of Elizabeth,* 36.

25. PRO S.P. 12/29/122; BL Harl. MS 6990, no. 18, ff. 38–39. The earl of Bedford remained in Bristol to avoid the plague in Exeter in 1570 (PRO S.P. 12/73/12, 76). For similar reasons, Sir Nicholas Bacon fled Gorhambury in 1578 (H.M.C. *Salisbury,* 13, Folger microfilm 164.53, 202.111). For other exchanges about the plague, see PRO S.P. 46/49/115, S.P. 46/57/99, S.P. 12/155/82.

26. *CSPSpanish, 1558–67,* 373.

27. BL Harl. MS 6992, no. 8, f. 15.

28. H.M.C. *Bath,* 5:35; IHR Talbot film, 1/50, Burghley to the earl of Shrewsbury.

29. PRO S.P. 12/152/69.

30. Strype, *Annals of the Reformation,* 1:pt. 2, 90; Birch, *Memoirs of the Reign of Queen Elizabeth,* 1:31.

31. Birch, *Memoirs of the Reign of Queen Elizabeth,* 1:133–37; Chambers, *Elizabethan Stage,* 4:100.

32. PRO S.P. 12/245/80, Thomas Phelippes to W. Sterell.

33. MacNalty, *Elizabeth Tudor,* 238; Chambers, *Elizabethan Stage,* 4:86.

34. Peck, *Desiderata Curiosa,* 1:bk. 5, 13.

35. PRO S.P. 12/271/171–73; Chambers, *Elizabethan Stage,* 4:112.

36. Nichols, *Progresses,* 3:595; Neale, *Queen Elizabeth I,* 405; Chambers, *Elizabethan Stage,* 4:115.

37. McClure, ed., *Letters of Chamberlain,* 1:166; *CSPD Add.,* 285/52/260.

38. See Appendix.

39. See Colvin, *History of the King's Works,* 3:79, 231.

40. From a comparison of progress hosts to the charts about the Privy Council created by Williams in *Tudor Regime,* 453–56.

41. Some who died after brief terms, such as Sir Thomas Cheyney (d. 1558) and Sir Thomas Parry (d. 1560), obviously had little opportunity as privy councilors to receive a royal visit.

42. In compiling these lists, I relied upon biographical information in Bindoff, *History of Parliament: House of Commons;* Hasler, *History of Parliament: Commons;* and the *DNB,* a method with obvious limitations.

43. Simon Adams, "The Patronage of the Crown in Elizabethan Politics: The 1590s," in Guy, *Reign of Elizabeth I*, 31, 45.

44. Religious views as described in Bindoff, *History of Parliament: House of Commons;* Hasler, *History of Parliament: Commons;* and the *DNB.*

45. Anne Browne (dau. of Sir William Browne, lord mayor of London), his second wife, died in March 1582. Christy, "Progresses of Queen Elizabeth"; Emmison, *Tudor Secretary;* Chambers, *Elizabethan Stage,* 4:79.

46. Progresses without independent female hosts were in 1559, 1560, 1561, 1568, 1573, 1576.

47. Royal visits to Theobalds are recorded in Nichols, *Progresses,* vols. 1–3, passim; Read, *Secretary Cecil and Queen Elizabeth* and *Lord Burghley and Queen Elizabeth,* passim; Chambers, *Elizabethan Stage,* 4:77–115.

48. Groos, ed., *Diary of Baron Waldstein,* 83–85; Read, *Lord Burghley and Queen Elizabeth,* 122.

49. BL Harl. MS 6992, no. 52, f. 104.

50. Read, *Lord Burghley and Queen Elizabeth,* 371–79.

51. Birch, *Memoirs of the Reign of Queen Elizabeth,* 1:448.

52. Wells, "Kenilworth Castle and Priory," 68; Chambers, *Elizabethan Stage,* 4:83–99.

53. Nichols, *Progresses,* 2:4–6.

54. *CSPSpanish, 1568–79,* 682; H.M.C. *Bath,* 5: 90; IHR Talbot film, 2/31.

55. *VCH Warwickshire,* 2:137–38.

56. Bod. Western MS, Malone 5.

57. BL Harl. MS 6992, no. 6, f. 11.

58. Wernham, *After the Armada,* 324; Chambers, *Elizabethan Stage,* 4:106; Nichols, *Progresses,* 3:80.

59. PRO S.P. 12/239/123, S.P. 12/239/244.

60. Wernham, *After the Armada,* 324–28, 372; Chambers, *Elizabethan Stage,* 4:106.

61. McClure, ed., *Letters of Chamberlain,* 1:98–99, 101. For other instances, see Chambers, *Elizabethan Stage,* 4:77–116.

62. Lodge, *Illustrations of British History,* 2:18; Nicolas, ed., *Memoirs of Hatton,* 25–27.

63. McClure, ed., *Letters of Chamberlain,* 1:139.

64. *CSPSpanish, 1587–1603,* 504; Neale, *Queen Elizabeth I,* 317.

3. THE CHALLENGE OF ROYAL TRAVEL

1. H.M.C. *Bath,* 5:158; IHR Dudley film, 1/151.

2. Christy, "Progresses of Queen Elizabeth," 116. See Hughes and Larkin, *Tudor Royal Proclamations,* and Dasent, *Acts of the Privy Council,* for the location of the queen and Privy Council meetings.

3. BL Harl. MS 4186: Journal of the Privy Council, 1579.

4. Pulman, *Elizabethan Privy Council,* 164–65.

5. Ibid., 150–53; Elton, *Tudor Constitution,* 90.

6. Birch, *Memoirs of the Reign of Queen Elizabeth,* 1:164.

7. PRO S.P. 12/96/108.

8. PRO S.P. 12/109/10, S.P. 12/45/80; BL Harl. MS 6992, no. 8, f. 15; PRO S.P. 12/105/30.

9. PRO S.P. 12/243/7.

10. PRO S.P. 15/32/141; Hasler, *History of Parliament: Commons,* 2:296.

11. BL Harl. MS 6991, no. 7, f. 15.

12. *CSPSpanish, 1580–86,* 175–76.

13. PRO S.P. 84/43/47: "parce que personne de mes gens ne scavoient le chemin ou esoit la court."

14. PRO S.P. 12/282/94; Williams, *Tudor Regime*, 456; Hasler, *History of Parliament: Commons*, 2:296.

15. PRO S.P. 12/6/51.

16. Nichols, *Progresses*, 3:27–28.

17. Harington, *Nugae Antiquae*, 1: 169.

18. Hurstfield, *The Queen's Wards*, 54. For a study of her gentlemen pensioners, see W. J. Tighe, "The Gentlemen Pensioners in Elizabethan Politics and Government" (Ph.D. diss., Cambridge University, 1984).

19. PRO S.P. 46/49/97.

20. Lodge, *Illustrations of British History*, 1:435–40.

21. Nichols, *Progresses*, 1:385, 544, 2:400–403.

22. BL Lans. MS 5, no. 36, f. 122, no. 37, f. 124, no. 36, f. 122.

23. Woodworth, "Purveyance," 8–11; Newton, "Tudor Reforms," 249.

24. PRO L.S.. 13/168/368–71: List of the number of servants in the royal household under Elizabeth and James, compiled after 1613.

25. Woodworth, "Purveyance," 7–8.

26. Nichols, *Progresses*, 1:385; Bod. Rawl. MS, B 146, f. 116.

27. Mullett, *Bubonic Plague and England*, 99.

28. BL Harl. MS 1641, ff. 12–13; Harl. MS 1642, ff. 12–14; Harl. MS 1644, ff. 66–72; PRO L.S.. 13/279/9.

29. PRO L.S.. 13/279/9; BL Harl. MS 1644, ff. 66–72; Chambers, *Elizabethan Stage*, 1:34–35, 108–9; Cheyney, *History of England*, 1:54–55; Dunlop, *Palaces & Progresses*, 122.

30. Newton, "Tudor Reforms," 251–52; Nichols, *Progresses*, 1:269.

31. BL Lans. MS 59, no. 27, Harl. MS 589, no. 23, f. 159.

32. Woodworth, "Purveyance," 12–13.

33. BL Add. MS 34320, f. 118: From the Household Book, 1570–1603, of William Cholmley.

34. Woodworth, "Purveyance," 55–66.

35. BL Add. MS 34320, f. 118.

36. BL Add. MS 34320, f. 122; Woodworth, "Purveyance," 63.

37. PRO S.P. 46/60/29.

38. Slicher Van Bath, *Agrarian History of Western Europe*, 84–85.

39. PRO L.S. 13/279/12; Clark, *English Alehouse*, 177.

40. PRO L.S. 13/168/31–34, L.S. 13/168/53–55; see Clark, *English Alehouse*.

41. BL Harl. MS 1641, f. 4; Harl. MS 1642, f. 4; Harl. MS 1644, f. 25.

42. PRO S.P. 12/127/71, S.P. 12/205/49, S.P. 12/240/123. Harrison, *Description of England*, 307.

43. BL Lans. MS 59, no. 25.

44. Woodworth, "Purveyance," 4, 18–19, 28–32.

45. PRO L.S. 13/179/11.

46. Clapham, *Elizabeth of England*, 87; Woodworth, "Purveyance," 34–38.

47. Woodworth, "Purveyance," 71–73.

48. Ibid., 32–34; Nichols, *Progresses*, 1:411.

49. Nichols, ed., "Diary of Machyn," 189.

50. Cockburn, *Assize Records: Essex Indictments*, nos. 389, 892, 1402, 1403.

51. Cockburn, *Assize Records: Kent Indictments*, no. 1483, and *Assize Records: Hertfordshire Indictments*, no. 400.

52. Cockburn, *Assize Records: Surrey Indictments*, no. 1770. For other cases of conversion against purveyors, see Cockburn, *Assize Records: Essex Indictments*, no. 2253, and *Assize Records: Kent Indictments*, no. 2235; also Nichols, ed., "Diary of Machyn," 223.

53. Cockburn, *Assize Records: Essex Indictments*, no. 2154.

54. Woodworth, "Purveyance," 34–36.

55. PRO S.P. 12/256/22; PRO L.S. 13/168/60–64.

56. PRO S.P. 12/212/21, S.P. 12/209/137; Ellis, *Original Letters,* 4:11–13.

57. Elton, *Tudor Constitution,* 41; Woodworth, "Purveyance," 18–22; Elton, *Parliament of England,* 102–4, 191–92.

58. Neale, *Elizabeth and Her Parliaments,* 1:122, 2:187–88.

59. Ibid., 2:208–15; Woodworth, "Purveyance," 22–24.

60. PRO S.P. 12/127/84; PRO L.S. 13/168/58; Woodworth, "Purveyance," 4–6, 39; BL Harl. MS 589, no. 22, f. 158.

61. Woodworth, "Purveyance," 39, 41, 45.

62. Scott, *Joint-Stock Companies,* 1:93.

63. PRO S.P. 12/239/137; Woodworth, "Purveyance," 4, 15, 25–26, 41; BL Lans. MS 83, no. 53, ff. 142–44.

64. Hume, *History of England,* 4:229; MacCaffrey, *Elizabeth I,* 376. See also MacCaffrey, *Shaping of the Elizabethan Regime,* 180; and Bergeron, *English Civic Pageantry,* 9; Howarth, *Images of Rule,* 6; Russell, *Crisis of Parliaments,* 205–6; Stone, *Crisis of the Aristocracy,* 453. Hosts' large expenses are addressed by Haigh, *Elizabeth I,* 152; Wilson, *Entertainments for Elizabeth I,* 52–57; Bindoff, *Tudor England,* 197–98; Froude, *History of England,* 12:583; Rowse, *England of Elizabeth,* 338. In *King Charles I,* Gregg states that the progresses "saved the King money, for he was entertained at his subjects' charge" (257).

65. Johnson, *Elizabeth I,* 228.

66. Newton, "Tudor Reforms," 251; Heal, *Hospitality.*

67. Harrison, *De Maisse,* 11.

68. Dietz, *English Public Finance,* 412; Woodworth, "Purveyance," 7; Williams, *Tudor Regime,* 49–52; Newton, "Tudor Reforms," 251–52.

69. BL Lans. MS 16, no. 54, f. 114.

70. Nichols, *Progresses,* 1:43–44.

71. BL Harl. MS 589, no. 31, f. 185; BL Add. MS 34320, f. 115.

72. PRO E. 101/432/5, nos. 1–7.

73. BL Harl. MS 589, no. 30, ff. 176–84.

74. *CSPD Add.,* 23/29. *Collection of Ordinances and Regulations,* 293; Woodworth, "Purveyance," 71; BL Harl. MS 589, no. 35, f. 199.

75. PRO S.P. 12/288/75; Chambers, *Elizabethan Stage,* 4:104.

76. PRO S.P. 12/96/107; Groos, ed., *Diary of Baron Waldstein,* 29–32; Darby, *Historical Geography,* 289.

77. PRO S.P. 12/125/132; PRO E. 101/430/nos. 1–4.

78. Dietz, *English Public Finance,* 412.

79. BL Harl. MS 1641, ff. 12–13; Harl. MS 1642, ff. 12–14; Harl. MS 1644, ff. 66–72.

80. Dietz, *English Public Finance,* 410.

81. Nichols, *Progresses,* 2:343–45.

82. See Platt, *Great Rebuildings;* Thurley, *Royal Palaces;* Dunlop, *Palaces & Progresses;* Colvin, *History of the King's Works,* 3:79, 231, 4:30.

83. PRO S.P. 12/56/187, S.P. 12/57/189.

84. Bod. Rawl. MS, A 195C, ff. 237–334.

85. PRO S.P. 12/250/65.

86. Dietz, *English Public Finance,* 104.

87. PRO S.P. 12/259/171.

88. Bod. Ashmole MS, 840, 567.

89. Hasler, *History of Parliament: Commons,* 3:593; BL Cotton MS, Vespasian C, 14, vol. 2, no. 205, ff. 188–96.

90. *CSP Spanish, 1558–67,* 249; BL Add. MS 35831, no. 22, f. 37.

91. BL Lans. MS 21, nos. 63 and 65; Woodworth, "Purveyance," 13.
92. BL Lans. MS 16, no. 51, ff. 106–9; Woodworth, "Purveyance," 58–59; Chambers, *Elizabethan Stage,* 4:89.
93. BL Lans. MS 21, nos. 63 and 65.
94. BL Lans. MS 34, no. 32, f. 91.
95. BL Lans. MS 21, no. 67.
96. BL Harl. MS 589, nos. 31 and 32, ff. 185–86.

4. PRIVATE HOSTS

1. Stone, *Family and Fortune,* 213, 246.
2. BL Cotton MS, Titus B, 13, f. 173.
3. Heal, *Hospitality,* 26–28, 47–48, 188, 389–92.
4. Macfarlane, *Family Life of Josselin,* 154, 171.
5. Wrightson, *English Society,* 51–54.
6. Harrison, *Description of England,* 227.
7. Frye, *Elizabeth I,* 69.
8. Burgon, *Life of Gresham,* 2:447; Dunlop, *Palaces & Progresses,* 120.
9. Groos, ed., *Diary of Baron Waldstein,* 164–65.
10. Nicolas, ed., *Memoirs of Hatton,* 325; BL Harl MS 6993, no. 21, f. 39; Chambers, *Elizabethan Stage,* 4:100.
11. Nicolas, ed., *Memoirs of Hatton,* 124–25, 334.
12. Ibid., 125–26, 155.
13. Read, *Lord Burghley and Queen Elizabeth,* 216.
14. H.M.C. *Salisbury,* 11:314.
15. Ibid., 361.
16. Oliver Lawson Dick, ed., *Aubrey's Brief Lives* (Harmondsworth: Penguin Books, 1982), 310.
17. Chambers, *Elizabethan Stage,* 4:114; McClure, ed., *Letters of Chamberlain,* 1:127–32.
18. Ellis, *Original Letters,* 2:275–76.
19. Smith, *Servant of the Cecils,* 108; Chambers, *Elizabethan Stage,* 4:111.
20. Ellis, *Original Letters,* 2:264; O'Day, "Ecclesiastical Patronage of the Lord Keeper," 92, 109; Nichols, *Progresses,* 1:308–9.
21. Ellis, *Original Letters,* 2:271.
22. Nichols, *Progresses,* 2:60–62; Chambers, *Elizabethan Stage,* 4:93–94.
23. Nicolas, ed. *Memoirs of Hatton,* 68.
24. Ibid., 269; Johnson, *Elizabeth I,* 229; Chambers, *Elizabethan Stage,* 4:107.
25. Batho, "Finances of an Elizabethan Nobleman," 448; Hasler, *History of Parliament: Commons,* 3:203; Chambers, *Elizabethan Stage,* 4:106; *DNB,* 44:409–11.
26. Heal, *Hospitality,* 26–27, 389–92.
27. Nichols, *Progresses,* 1:192; 426, 485; 2:94; 3:101–21, 195, 90, 131, 586.
28. Ibid., 3:252.
29. Ibid., 2:132; 3:68, 83, 429, 441–42, 499, 568.
30. Ibid., 2:236; Johnson, *Elizabeth I,* 229.
31. Emmison, *Tudor Food and Pastimes,* 93–97; Collier, *Egerton Papers,* 341.
32. Chambers, *Elizabethan Stage,* 4:79; Emmison, *Tudor Secretary,* 245.
33. Emmison, *Tudor Secretary,* 237–43.
34. Ibid., 273–74.
35. Emmison, *Tudor Food and Pastimes,* 96.
36. Birch, *Memoirs of the Reign of Queen Elizabeth,* 1:12; Chambers, *Elizabethan Stage,* 4:91; Nichols, *Progresses,* 2:236.

37. Collier, *Egerton Papers*, 340–57; Johnson, *Elizabeth I*, 229; Chambers, *Elizabethan Stage*, 4:115.

38. See Heal, *Hospitality*, passim.

39. Peck, *Desiderata Curiosa*, 1:33; Stone, *Crisis of the Aristocracy*, 452; Emmison, *Tudor Food and Pastimes*, 97 (uses figure of £1,000).

40. Folger microfilm, Hatfield Accounts, Box G/16, ff. 29–30; Chambers, *Elizabethan Stage*, 4:91.

41. Read, *Lord Burghley and Queen Elizabeth*, 556; Read, "Lord Burghley's Household Accounts," 345.

42. PRO S.P. 12/238/237. For dates of her visits, see Appendix, Table 1: Chronology of Royal Visits and Progresses, and Chambers, *Elizabethan Stage*, vol. 4, passim.

43. Bod. Western MS, Smith 28.

44. PRO S.P. 46/22/145.

45. Macfarlane, *Family Life of Josselin*, 52–54.

46. Stone, *Crisis of the Aristocracy*, 450, 549–73.

47. Bevington, *Tudor Drama and Politics*, 179.

48. Read, *Lord Burghley and Queen Elizabeth*, 272–77; Chambers, *Elizabethan Stage*, 4:100.

49. Nichols, *Progresses*, 3:241–45; Read, *Lord Burghley and Queen Elizabeth*, 100.

50. PRO S.P. 15/17/39; Chambers, *Elizabethan Stage*, 4:85.

51. PRO S.P. 12/263/79; Williams, *Tudor Regime*, 398–99; *DNB*, 53:66.

52. PRO S.P. 12/259/54; Chambers, *Elizabethan Stage*, 4:77, 89.

53. PRO S.P. 12/265/196; Hasler, *History of Parliament: Commons*, 2:148.

54. H.M.C. *Pepys*, 1:443.

55. Dewar, *Sir Thomas Smith*, 88–117; Strype, *Life of Thomas Smith*, 88; Hasler, *History of Parliament: Commons*, 3:400.

56. PRO S.P. 12/80/117; MacCaffrey, *Elizabeth I*, 135–39.

57. Lodge, *Illustrations of British History*, 2:368.

58. Nicolas, ed., *Memoirs of Hatton*, 346.

59. H.M.C. *Salisbury*, 10:301; *DNB*, 32:380.

60. MacCaffrey, *Elizabeth I*, 377, emphasizes the "staggering" costs to royal hosts; according to Rowse, *England of Elizabeth*, 253, "some gentlemen begged off in a panic" when faced with a royal visit; to Willson, *King James VI and I*, 320, visits were "an expensive honor"; Hume, *History of England*, 4:229, called Elizabeth's visits "a great oppression on the nobility."

61. H.M.C. *Pepys*, 2:315; Chambers, *Elizabethan Stage*, 4:85.

62. Ellis, *Original Letters*, 2:266; Chambers, *Elizabethan Stage*, 4:88.

63. Nichols, *Progresses*, 2:7.

64. Hasler, *History of Parliament: Commons*, 3:86–88; Chambers, *Elizabethan Stage*, 4:84–106.

65. Collinson, *Elizabethan Puritan Movement*, 146–49.

66. BL Lans. MS 17, no. 44, f. 98; Nichols, *Progresses*, 1:340.

67. BL Lans. MS 17, no. 44, f. 98.

68. Chambers, *Elizabethan Stage*, 4:89.

69. H.M.C. *Salisbury*, 10:283.

70. Ibid., 180.

71. Dick, ed., *Aubrey's Brief Lives*, 262; Chambers, *Sir Henry Lee*, 169–72; Yates, *Astraea*, 94; Chambers, *Elizabethan Stage*, 4:107.

72. PRO S.P. 12/284/97 (1602 August 6).

73. McClure, ed., *Letters of Chamberlain*, 1:160.

74. Stone, *Crisis of the Aristocracy,* 454.
75. H.M.C. *Salisbury,* 11:184–85.
76. Ibid., 10:305, 11:189.
77. Ibid., 10:332. This letter to Robert Cecil was written by Gorges in September 1600.
78. N. M. Fuidge in Hasler, *History of Parliament: Commons,* 1:618.
79. Heal, *Hospitality,* 338.
80. McClure, ed., *Letters of Chamberlain,* 1:174–79; Chambers, *Elizabethan Stage,* 1:6.

5. CIVIC HOSTS

1. Nichols, *Progresses,* 1:529.
2. Essex Record Office transcript no.122 (D/P 94/5/1, Chelmsford Churchwarden's Accounts, 1561); Rev. Francis Haslewood, "Notes from the Records of Smarden Church," *Archaelogia cantiana: Transactions of the Kent Archeological Society* 9 (1874): 235; Nichols, *Progresses,* 3:489.
3. H.M.C. *Southampton and King's Lynn,* 18; L. E. W. O. Fullbrook-Leggatt, "Medieval Gloucester," *TBGAS,* 67 (1946–48): 260–61.
4. Warwick County Record Office, CR 1618, WA/1/1, f. 83; Nichols, *Progresses,* 1:337–39, 417, 533–55; H.M.C. *Southampton and King's Lynn,* 18; Robert Hall Warren, "Mediaeval Chapels of Bristol," *TBGAS* 30 (1907): 184.
5. Cambridge University Library, Ff. 5.14, ff. 88–94; Nichols, *Progresses,* 1:280, 337, 352, 378, 536–42; 2:276. Haslewood, "Notes from Records of Smarden Church," ci–cii; Fullbrook-Leggatt, "Medieval Gloucester," 260–61.
6. Nichols, *Progresses,* 2:275.
7. H.M.C. *Southampton and King's Lynn,* 18, 175; Nichols, *Progresses,* 1:417, 529, 548; Ricart, *Maire of Bristowe,* 58–59. Coventry Record Office, MS D, 68; Ingram, *Early English Drama: Coventry,* 232; Dugdale, *Antiquities of Warwickshire,* 1:149.
8. Essex Record Office film, T/A 401/2; Nichols, *Progresses,* 1:536–42; Fullbrook-Leggatt, "Medieval Gloucester," 260–61.
9. H.M.C. *Southampton and King's Lynn,* 18; Nichols, *Progresses,* 1:548–51. Bod. Rawl. MS, B 146, f. 116.
10. Tittler, "Political Culture," 155.
11. Thomas Dorman, "Visits of Two Queens to Sandwich," *Archaelogia cantiana: Transactions of the Kent Archeological Society* 16 (1886): 58–61.
12. Poole, *Coventry,* 23; "Transactions at Bristol," *TBGAS,* 15 (1980):37; Suffolk Record Office, Ipswich, HD36/2781/118.
13. Nichols, *Progresses,* 1:352, 417, 529, 548–51; H.M.C. *Southampton and King's Lynn,* 18; Fullbrook-Leggatt, "Medieval Gloucester," 260–61; Essex Record Office film, T/A 401/2.
14. Warwick County Record Office, CR1618, WA/1/1, f. 83.
15. Essex Record Office film, T/A 401/2.
16. Heal, *Hospitality,* 300–310.
17. C. H. Dancey, "Silver Plate and Insignia of the City of Gloucester," *TBGAS,* 30 (1907):107.
18. Ingram, *Early English Drama: Coventry,* 231–32.
19. Nichols, *Progresses,* 1:550–51. The Weavers gave £13 6s.; the Walkers £6 13s. 4d.; the Shoemakers and Drapers each £3; the Mercers, Brewers, and Chawlers each £2; and the constables collected £57 5s. 1d.
20. Nichols, *Progresses,* 1:417.
21. BL Add. MS 25334, vol. 1, f. 65; *East Anglian Miscellany* 7 (1913):18–19; Chambers, *Elizabethan Stage,* 4:79; Bacon, *Annalls of Ipswiche,* 254–55, 259–60.
22. Bacon, *Annalls of Ipswiche,* 264, 294, 297.

23. Ibid., 252–60, 262–63; Hasler, *History of Parliament: Commons*, 1:248, 394–95.

24. Manning, *Religion and Society*, 3, 7, 273; Nichols, *Progresses*, 1:334; PRO S.P. 12/93/108.

25. Canon Jenkins, "On the Municipal Records of Folkestone," *Archaelogia cantiana: Transactions of the Kent Archeological Society* 10 (1876):lxxvi, cxiii; Nichols, *Progresses*, 1:336; Chambers, *Elizabethan Stage*, 4:89.

26. Nichols, *Progresses*, 1:337–39.

27. PRO S.P. 12/129/108; Suckling, *History and Antiquities of Suffolk*, 1:365.

28. Hasler, *History of Parliament: Commons*, 1:162–63; Vanes, "Overseas Trade of Bristol"; Sacks, *Trade, Society, and Politics*, and *Widening Gate*.

29. Bergeron, *English Civic Pageantry*, 28–30, 46; Chambers, *Elizabethan Stage*, 4:90.

30. From Thomas Churchyard's entertainment, as cited in Nichols, *Progresses*, 1:395–405.

31. Vanes, "Overseas Trade of Bristol," 13.

32. Nichols, *Progresses*, 1:532; Clark and Slack, *English Towns in Transition*, 31.

33. Nichols, *Progresses*, 1:545–48; *VCH Worcestershire*, 2:289–90.

34. PRO S.P. 12/105/56.

35. PRO S.P. 12/189/129.

36. PRO L.S. 13/168/69.

37. Clark, *English Alehouse*, 95–98, 41, 72–80, 172.

38. Elton, *Tudor Constitution*, 477; Williams, *Tudor Regime*, 210–11.

39. Wrightson, *English Society*, 167.

40. Sharpe, *In Contempt of All Authority*, 41–42; Clark, *English Alehouse*, 41, 72–80, 172.

41. PRO L.S. 13/168/31–34.

42. PRO L.S. 13/168/53–55; Cockburn, *Assize Records: Surrey Indictments*, nos. 3052, 3053.

43. PRO S.P. 12/34/57.

44. Peck, *Desiderata Curiosa*, 2:bk. 7, 43–46.

45. The year of this visit often is given erroneously as 1565, as in Nichols, *Progresses*, 1:192. The confusion arises from the dating of the mayoral terms, which makes the Coventry Annals a "chronological tangle": before 1556, the mayor of Coventry was elected at Candlemas, 2 February, for a year's term; from 1556 until 1834, the mayoral term began on 1 November (*City of Coventry Municipal Handbook;* Burbidge, *Old Coventry and Lady Godiva*, 209–10). All accounts agree that Edmund Brownell was mayor of Coventry during this August visit, and Brownell's term ran from November 1565 until the end of October 1566, placing Elizabeth in Coventry in 1566 (Coventry Record Office, 535/1, f. 14; Ingram, *Early English Drama: Coventry*, 486, 572). The City Annals mention an "unlooked for" visit of Elizabeth in 1568, perhaps made as a side trip from her progress in Northamptonshire to Kenilworth, but other sources do not refer to such a visit (Ingram, *Early English Drama: Coventry*, 243, 575; Coventry Record Office, MS F, f. 27; Chambers, *Elizabethan Stage*, 4:83.

46. Nichols, *Progresses*, 1:195; *VCH Warwickshire*, 2:324; Poole, *Coventry*, 89.

47. Hasler, *History of Parliament: Commons*, 2:238–39; Levine, *Elizabethan Succession Question*, 63–76.

48. Poole, *Coventry*, 245–51.

49. Ingram, *Early English Drama: Coventry*, 583–84; Bergeron, *English Civic Pageantry*, 33; Nichols, *Progresses*, 1:446–56; Duffy, *Stripping of the Altars*, 12–13.

50. Phythian-Adams, "Ceremony and the Citizen," 59, 63, 67. See also his *Desolation of a City*.

51. Manley, *Literature and Culture*, 125–35, 184–85.

52. Ingram, *Early English Drama: Coventry*, 215, 272–74; Bergeron, *English Civic Pageantry*, 33; Greaves, *Society and Religion*, 453; Duffy, *Stripping of the Altars*, 579.

53. *VCH Warwickshire,* 8:218.

54. Phythian-Adams, "Ceremony and the Citizen," 80; Weimann, *Shakespeare and Popular Tradition,* 165.

55. Hutton, *Rise and Fall,* chap. 4, esp. 119–38; James, *Society, Politics, and Culture,* 42–47.

56. Ingram, *Early English Drama: Coventry,* xx, 276.

57. H.M.C. *Shrewsbury and Coventry,* 15: App. 10, 125.

58. Coventry Record Office, MS D, 68.

59. Two paragraphs taken from BL Harl. MS 6388, f. 36; Coventry Record Office, MS D, 69, and 535/1, f. 14; Harris, *Coventry Leet Book,* 819–21.

60. Processions and civic identity are explored in Duffy, *Stripping of the Altars,* 44, 136; Hanawalt and Reyerson, *City and Spectacle;* Muir, *Civic Ritual in Renaissance Venice;* Strong, *Art and Power;* Weissman, *Ritual Brotherhood.*

61. For a discussion of royal display in a "visible expression of power," see Smuts, "Art and Material Culture," 86–112.

62. Trexler, *Public Life in Renaissance Florence,* and *Libro Cerimoniale of the Florentine Republic.*

63. Manley, *Literature and Culture,* chap. 5.

64. Smuts, "Public ceremony and royal charisma," 73.

65. David Harris Sacks, "The Countervailing of Benefits: Monopoly, Liberty, and Benevolence in Elizabethan England," in Hoak, *Tudor Political Culture,* 289.

66. I am indebted to Evelyn Tribble for her helpful discussions of these concepts. See her article, "We Will Do No Harm with Our Swords," 148–52.

67. Bryant, "Configuration of the Community," 23–24.

68. Attreed, "Politics of Welcome," 220–22.

69. Victor Turner, *Dramas, Fields, and Metaphors,* 274.

70. Nichols, *Progresses,* 1:192; Dugdale, *Antiquities of Warwickshire,* 1:149.

71. Warwick Record Office, Black Book of Warwick (microfilm), PG 3381, f. 65; Nichols, *Progresses,* 1:310.

72. Nichols, *Progresses,* 1:533–42.

73. Kertzer, *Ritual, Politics, and Power,* 101.

74. Anglo, *Images of Tudor Kingship,* 109: "Esoteric and complex ideas [in civic pageantry] were likely to lose the audience." Gordon Kipling, "Richard II's 'Sumptuous Pageants' and the Idea of the Civic Triumph," in Bergeron, *Pageantry in Shakespearean Theatre,* 83–103: civic pageants celebrated "the communal political bond which united the sovereign and his people" (98).

75. Heal, *Hospitality,* 314; see also Tittler, "Political Culture," 155.

76. Coventry Record Office, Annals of the City of Coventry, 1348–1684, MS D, 68; Nichols, *Progresses,* 1:192.

77. Nichols, *Progresses,* 1:315, 547–48.

78. Ibid., 1:315.

79. Ibid., 1:196.

80. Goldberg, *James I,* 28–32.

81. For an itemized account of the town's preparations for Elizabeth, see Warwick Record Office, Corporation Accounts, 1546–69, CR1618, WA/1/1, ff. 79, 83; Nichols, *Progresses,* 1:314.

82. Nichols, *Progresses,* 1:533–35, 540–42.

83. Ibid., 1:193.

84. Ibid., 1:433–34, 485–86, 515.

85. Ibid., 1:310.

86. Ibid., 1:540.

87. Ibid., 1:317–18.
88. Ingram, *Early English Drama: Coventry*, 271–75; Harl. MS 6388, f. 37; Nichols, *Progresses*, 1:446–56. For an analysis of the Hock Tuesday play's importance, see Phythian-Adams, "Ceremony and the Citizen," 57–85.
89. Nichols, *Progresses*, 1:319–20.
90. Ibid., 1:210.
91. Ibid., 1:312.
92. Ibid., 1:547.
93. Ingram, *Early English Drama: Coventry*, 232; Nichols, *Progresses*, 1:197.
94. Nichols, *Progresses*, 1:316.
95. McCoy, *Rites of Knighthood*, 42–45; Bergeron, *English Civic Pageantry*, 30–32; Doran, "Juno versus Diana"; Frye, *Elizabeth I*, 56–96. Regarding Dudley's activities in the region, see Adams, "'Because I am of that country.'"
96. Nichols, *Progresses*, 1:496, 502–13, 520; Chambers, *Elizabethan Stage*, 1:123.
97. Goldberg, *James I*, 31.

6. THE ROYAL AGENDA

1. See Duffy, *Stripping of the Altars;* Hutton, *Rise and Fall;* Scarisbrick, *The Reformation;* Collinson, *Religion of Protestants.*
2. PRO S.P. 12/4/135; Nichols, ed., "Diary of Machyn," 196; Nichols, *Progresses*, 1:67.
3. Collinson, *Elizabethan Puritan Movement*, 31; Strype, *Annals of the Reformation*, 1:pt. 1, 206–11; Nichols, ed., "Diary of Machyn," 200; Nichols, *Progresses*, 1:68–69; Chambers, *Elizabethan Stage*, 4:77; "Diary of Machyn," 202–3; Strype, *Annals of the Reformation*, 1:pt. 1, 210–11.
4. Strong, "Elizabethan Pageantry," 38; Yates, *Astraea*, 109; King, "Royal Image," 104–32; McCoy, "'The Wonderfull Spectacle,'" 217–27.
5. Neale, *Elizabeth and Her Parliaments*, 1:42; Nichols, ed., "Diary of Machyn," 256; MacCaffrey, *Shaping of the Elizabethan Regime*, 113; Levin, *Heart and Stomach of a King*, 17–18; Duffy, *Stripping of the Altars*, 565–70; Hutton, *Rise and Fall*, 118–25.
6. Nichols, *Progresses*, 1:96; Chambers, *Elizabethan Stage*, 4:79; Collinson, *Elizabethan Puritan Movement*, 61; Peck, *Desiderata Curiosa*, 2: bk. 7, 22; Strype, *Annals of the Reformation*, 1: pt. 1, 405; Harrison, *De Maisse*, 21.
7. Neale, *Queen Elizabeth I*, 110; Levine, *Elizabethan Succession Question*, 15.
8. Peck, *Desiderata Curiosa*, 2: bk. 7, 23–24, 28–29; Cambridge University Library, Ff. 5.14, ff. 88–94.
9. Stow, *Annales*, 657; Strype, *Annals of the Reformation*, 1: pt. 2, 106–8; Peck, *Desiderata Curiosa*, 2: bk. 7, 34; Cambridge University Library, Baker MS 24, 252–58 and MS 29, 367; BL Add. MS 5845, f. 226. Fuller accounts of the 1564 visit can also be found in BL Add. MS 5845, ff. 191–93.
10. Spufford, *Contrasting Communities*, 243.
11. Stow, *Annales*, 660; Plummer, *Elizabethan Oxford*, 200; Collinson, *Elizabethan Puritan Movement*, 73; Boas, *University Drama*, 89–108.
12. Nichols, *Progresses*, 1:206–47; Chambers, *Elizabethan Stage*, 4:83; Peck, *Desiderata Curiosa*, 2: bk. 7, 47.
13. Nichols, *Progresses*, 1:247–49.
14. Rice, *Public Speaking*, 99; Plummer, *Elizabethan Oxford;* Cambridge University Library, Patrick Papers, no. 34, ff. 5–9, and Baker MS 36, 446–48.
15. Nichols, *Progresses*, 1:340, 353; BL Lans. MS 17, no. 44, f. 98; Collinson, *Elizabethan Puritan Movement*, 135; Strype, *Annals of the Reformation*, 2: bk. 1, 466.
16. Manning, *Religion and Society*, 243; Chambers, *Elizabethan Stage*, 4:89.

NOTES TO PAGES 141–51

17. F. Douglas Price, "Commission for Ecclesiastical Causes for the Dioceses of Bristol and Gloucester, 1574," *TBGAS*, 59 (1937): 62–63; Chambers, *Elizabethan Stage*, 4:90; PRO S.P. 12/98/41; BL Lans. MS 115, no. 45, f. 108.

18. PRO S.P. 83/8/18.

19. MacCulloch, "Power, Privilege, and the County Community," 137, 144; Collinson, *Elizabethan Puritan Movement*, 203; Smith, *County and Court*, 218; PRO S.P. 12/73/171.

20. PRO S.P. 12/125/98–102; Nichols, *Progresses*, 2:92; Cambridge University Library, Baker MS 29, 377; Nichols, *Progresses*, 2:108; MacCulloch, "Power, Privilege, and the County Community," 75–77; Smith, *County and Court*, 222, 214, 185, 65, 32.

21. MacCullough, "Power, Privilege, and the County Community," 145–46; *VCH Essex*, 4:193; Chambers, *Elizabethan Stage*, 4:95; Nichols, *Progresses*, 2:216–17; Smith, *County and Court*, 218. For Rookwood's later recusancy fines, see PRO S.P. 12/188/38; Lambeth Palace MS 2004, f. 40.

22. MacCullough, "Power, Privilege, and the County Community," 145.

23. PRO S.P. 83/8/25, 36, 34.

24. Smith, *County and Court*, 201–3, 208–15; PRO S.P. 12/126/41.

25. Norfolk Record Office, Colman MS 634, unpaginated. For preparations for her visit, see Norfolk Record Office, St. George's Guild Book, 295.

26. PRO S.P. 45/25/197.

27. Collinson, *Elizabethan Puritan Movement*, 173, 191; Strype, *Annals of the Reformation*, 2: pt. 1, 477–500.

28. Wormald, *Mary Queen of Scots*, 130–33.

29. BL Add. MS 35831, no. 22, f. 37; *CSPSpanish, 1558–67*, 249.

30. *CSPSpanish, 1558–67*, 254; Neale, *Queen Elizabeth I*, 115–16.

31. Read, *Secretary Cecil and Queen Elizabeth*, 349, 376; Chambers, *Elizabethan Stage*, 4:83.

32. Durant, *Bess of Hardwick*, 79.

33. PRO S.P. 12/89/25.

34. Chambers, *Elizabethan Stage*, 4:84; MacCaffrey, *Shaping of the Elizabethan Regime*, 243.

35. MacCaffrey, *Shaping of the Elizabethan Regime*, 323–27; Chambers, *Elizabethan Stage*, 4:84–85.

36. Read, *Lord Burghley and Queen Elizabeth*, 40.

37. PRO S.P. 12/80/117; Read, *Lord Burghley and Queen Elizabeth*, 38–41; MacCaffrey, *Shaping of the Elizabethan Regime*, 412–14.

38. Stone, *Family and Fortune*, 246–49. Stone incorrectly dates the queen's visit to Berkeley Castle as occurring in 1573 instead of 1574. The progress of 1573 took Elizabeth through Kent, the opposite direction of Gloucestershire.

39. Stone, *Family and Fortune*, 248; Manning, "Poaching as Symbolic Substitute."

40. Dr. Williams's Library, Morrice 31/D, 65; Read, *Lord Burghley and Queen Elizabeth*, 224–25; MacCaffrey, *Elizabeth I*, 201–4; Birch, *Memoirs of the Reign of Queen Elizabeth*, 1:30–31; Chambers, *Elizabethan Stage*, 4:100–101; Dent, *Quest for Nonsuch*, 168–69; Birch, *Memoirs*, 1:467; Harrison, *De Maisse*, iii–x; H.M.C. *Salisbury*, 11:381.

41. Christopher Haigh, in *Elizabeth I*, chap. 7, emphasizes how Elizabeth tried, but often failed, to control her military commanders when they were in the field or at sea.

42. Nichols, *Progresses*, 1:87; Neale, *Queen Elizabeth I*, 76; Chambers, *Elizabethan Stage*, 4:78; Lodge, *Illustrations of British History*, 1:423.

43. *CSPSpanish, 1558–67*, 564.

44. Nicolas, ed., *Memoirs of Hatton*, 81; Hasler, *History of Parliament: Commons*, 2:276; Doran, *Monarchy and Matrimony;* Adler, "Imaginary Toads in Real Gardens."

45. Williams's Library, Morrice 31/D, 288–93; Chambers, *Elizabethan Stage,* 4:86; Williams's Library, Morrice 31/D, 298–300, 338, 347–51; Black, *Reign of Elizabeth,* 121; PRO S.P. 12/80/21.

46. Williams's Library, Morrice 31/D, 547–57; Read, *Lord Burghley and Queen Elizabeth,* 85–86; Doran, *Monarchy and Matrimony,* 217.

47. Williams's Library, Morrice 31/D, 569–72, 574–75.

48. Ibid., 611–29; Read, *Lord Burghley and Queen Elizabeth,* 87–92; Black, *Reign of Elizabeth,* 127–29; Kingdon, *St. Bartholomew's Day Massacres.*

49. PRO S.P. 83/7/53, 76, 92, 93; Read, *Lord Burghley and Queen Elizabeth,* 35; Chambers, *Elizabethan Stage,* 4:95; PRO S.P. 83/8/14; *CSPSpanish, 1580–86,* 16; Black, *Reign of Elizabeth,* 302.

50. Nichols, *Progresses,* 2:345–47, 386.

51. Chambers, *Elizabethan Stage,* 4:77; Frye, *Elizabeth I,* 22–55; Nichols, *Progresses,* 1:69–72.

52. Chambers, *Elizabethan Stage,* 4:77; Nichols, ed., "Diary of Machyn," 232; Hasted, *History of Kent,* 17.

53. Chambers, *Elizabethan Stage,* 4:92–99.

54. Nichols, *Progresses,* 1:354; Folger MS V. b. 296, p. 356.

55. *CSPSpanish, 1568–79,* 50, 189, 192–93; Chambers, *Elizabethan Stage,* 4:85; Read, *Lord Burghley and Queen Elizabeth,* 346–47.

57. Chambers, *Elizabethan Stage,* 4:85; *CSPD Add.,* 14/100; 17/16, 29; Fletcher, *Tudor Rebellions,* 94, 101–6; PRO S.P. 12/60/15.

58. Ricart, *Maire of Bristowe,* 59; Boynton, *Elizabethan Militia,* 115–16.

59. IHR Talbot film, 1/250; Neale, *Elizabeth and Her Parliaments,* 2:105; Read, *Lord Burghley and Queen Elizabeth,* 352–61, 364.

60. IHR Talbot film, 1/258, 1/260; Read, *Lord Burghley and Queen Elizabeth,* 364; Mattingly, *The Armada,* 16.

61. PRO S.P. 12/198/137.

62. Lambeth Palace MS 2009, ff. 15, 21, 36.

63. Read, *Lord Burghley and Queen Elizabeth,* 416–17, 429.

64. PRO S.P. 12/213/80, S.P. 12/214/86.

65. BL Add. MS 44839.

66. Mattingly, *The Armada,* 347–51; Chambers, *Elizabethan Stage,* 4:103; IHR Dudley film, 2/246; Ellis, *Original Letters,* 2nd ser., 3:141; Johnson, *Elizabeth I,* 319–21; Frye, "Elizabeth I at Tilbury."

67. *CSPSpanish, 1587–1603,* 480, 493–94.

68. PRO S.P. 12/238/240, S.P. 84/43/70; Chambers, *Elizabethan Stage,* 4:106.

69. Folger MS V. b. 131.

70. PRO S.P. 78/25/161.

71. PRO S.P. 78/25/384; Harrison, *De Maisse,* 39.

72. Birch, *Memoirs of the Reign of Queen Elizabeth,* 1:117, 123; Chambers, *Elizabethan Stage,* 4:106–8; Wernham, *After the Armada,* 458; Lambeth Palace MS 2004, no. 4, f. 4; PRO S.P. 12/259/12; Birch, *Memoirs of the Reign of Queen Elizabeth,* 1:294; Chambers, *Elizabethan Stage,* 4:110, 111–12; Boynton, *Elizabethan Militia,* 198; Sawyer, *Memorials of Affairs of State,* 1:90; McClure, ed., *Letters of Chamberlain,* 1:80–82; H.M.C. *Salisbury,* 11:353–54; Chambers, *Elizabethan Stage,* 4:114.

73. Nichols, *Progresses,* 2:303.

74. PRO L.S. 13/168/40, 14.

75. PRO S.P. 12/268/87; Aydelotte, *Rogues and Vagabonds,* 68; Youngs, *Proclamations of the Tudor Queens,* 37, 73–77.

76. PRO L.S. 13/168/5–10, 15–22.

77. PRO S.P. 12/247/98.

78. *CSPSpanish, 1558–67,* 95; Chambers, *Elizabethan Stage,* 4:77.

79. PRO S.P. 12/131/159, 162.

80. PRO S.P. 12/179/26.

81. PRO S.P. 12/163/54–67; Peck, *Desiderata Curiosa,* 1: bk. 4, 20.

82. PRO S.P. 12/247/79.

83. Birch, *Memoirs of the Reign of Elizabeth,* 1:149–51, 59.

84. PRO S.P. 12/176/154–60; Clapham, *Elizabeth of England,* 88.

85. PRO S.P. 12/113/173.

86. PRO S.P. 12/244/112, S.P. 12/247/61, S.P. 12/268/144–45.

87. Frye, *Elizabeth I,* 11.

88. Fletcher, *Gender, Sex, and Subordination,* 60–80; Margaret R. Sommerville, *Sex & Subjection: Attitudes to Women in Early-Modern Society* (New York: St. Martin's Press, 1995), 8–39, 51–61; Merry E. Wiesner, *Women and Gender in Early Modern Europe* (Cambridge: Cambridge University Press, 1992), 9–38.

89. For a discussion of the queen's marital history, see Doran, *Monarchy and Matrimony.*

90. PRO S.P. 15/28/113.

91. Levin, *Heart and Stomach of a King,* 81; *CSPSpanish,* 1:362; 2:491, quoted in Levin, 81; PRO S.P. 12/148/157.

92. Roy Strong analyzes the iconography of her portraits in *Gloriana.*

93. Salomon, "Positioning Women in Visual Convention."

94. Andrew Belsey and Catherine Belsey, "Icons of Divinity: Portraits of Elizabeth I," in Lucy Gent and Nigel Llewellyn, eds., *Renaissance Bodies: The Human Figure in English Culture, c. 1540–1660* (London: Reaktion Books, 1990), 11–18.

95. See an analysis of these important issues in Levin, *Heart and Stomach of a King,* esp. chap. 4; Montrose, "'Shaping Fantasies,'" 47–50.

96. Birch, *Memoirs of the Reign of Queen Elizabeth* 1:154–55. Elizabeth's ability to create and shape her public images is extensively analyzed in Frye, *Elizabeth I.*

BIBLIOGRAPHY

MANUSCRIPT SOURCES

Bodleian Library
  Ashmole MSS: Nos. 384, 802, 824, 837, 840, 855, 858, 1134, 1729
  Rawlinson MSS: A 195C, B 146, Poet 187
  Tanner MSS: Nos. 76, 115, 306
  Western MSS: Auct. F.5.13; E. Mus. 18; Latin Misc. E. 23; Malone 5; Smith 28; Willis 70
British Library
  Additional MSS: Nos. 2623, 4105, 4106, 4131, 4160, 5845, 6342, 12497, 12506, 12507,
    25334, 32092, 32350, 34320, 34324, 35831, 36970, 38170, 44746, 44839, 46375, 62540
  Cotton MSS: Titus B, 12; Vespasian C, 14
  Harleian MSS: 293; 589, nos. 22–26, 29–32, 35, 40; 894, no. 3; 1196, no. 142; 1641; 1642;
    1644; 1877, no. 59; 1988, no. 42; 4186; 6388; 6990, no. 18; 6991, nos. 7, 13; 6992, nos.
    6, 8, 52; 6993, no. 21
  Lansdowne MSS: 4, nos. 6, 7; 5, nos. 1, 36–38; 16, nos. 21, 40, 51, 52, 54, 76; 17, no. 44;
    21, nos. 7, 41, 42, 63–67; 34, nos. 23–25, 32, 33; 59, nos. 25–28; 83, nos. 49, 51, 53, 60,
    62, 64; 115, no. 45; 116, no. 26; 638, no. 18
  Royal MSS: 18A, no. 46
Cambridge University Library
  Baker MSS: Nos. 24, 29, 31, 36
  Dd.3.85(14). Accounts
  Ff. 5.14, no. 9 (1304). Elizabeth at Cambridge
  Oo. 6.115. List of Norwich mayors
  Patrick Papers, no. 34
Coventry City Record Office
  Chamberlain's Accounts
  535/1. The History of Coventry
  Minutes, Acts of the Town Council, 1556–1642
  MSS A 14(a) and C
  MSS D, E, and F. Annals of the City of Coventry
Essex Record Office, Chelmsford
  D/Dp A9–10. Petre Accounts
  D/P 94/5. Chelmsford Churchwarden's Accounts
  D/Y 2/2–8. Mordant MSS
  T/A 465. Colchester Assembly Book
  T/A 401/2. Microfilm of Saffron Walden Accounts
Folger Shakespeare Library
  DC 114.3 C4 1551. *C'est la Deduction* . . .
  Microfilm of Hatfield Accounts, Box G/16
  Microfilm of Hatfield Manuscripts, H. M. C. *Salisbury*
  V. b. 131. Letter, Elizabeth to Henry IV

V.b. 296. Dering family remembrance book
Z.d. rolls 12–17. Lists of New Year's gifts
Institute of Historical Research
    Microfilm of the Devereux, Dudley, and Talbot family papers
Lambeth Palace Library
    Papers of Anthony Bacon
    Lambeth Palace MSS: Nos. 1727, 2003, 2004, 2008, 2009, 2014, 7242
Norfolk Record Office
    Colman MS 634
    Norfolk Record Society, nos. 10968, 15300, 17044, 19404
    Press B, case 10, shelf D (Rep. 149)
    St. George's Guild Book
    Y/C4/272. Yarmouth Corporation Records
Public Record Office
    Exchequer
        E. 101. King's Remembrancer, Accounts Various
        E. 351. Enrolled Household Accounts
    Lord Chamberlain's Department
        L.C. 2. Special Events
        L.C. 5. Miscellanea
        L.C. 9. Accounts
    Lord Steward's Department (Board of Green Cloth)
        L.S. 13/168, 179. Records, 1589–1815
        L.S. 13/279. Treatises of the Household
    State Paper Office
        S.P. 12. State Papers Domestic, Elizabeth I
        S.P. 15. State Papers Domestic, Addenda, Elizabeth I
        S.P. 46. Supplementary Collections
        S.P. 46/49. Papers of Nicholas Williamson of Sawley, Derbys., 1586–94
        S.P. 46/57. Papers of John Astwick of Flamstead, Herts., 1565–1613
        S.P. 46/60. Papers of John Gamage of Kinsey, Bucks., 1573–80
        S.P. 46/76. Bayning Papers, 1614–40
        S.P. 70. State Papers Foreign, Elizabeth I
        S.P. 78. State Papers, France, Elizabeth I
        S.P. 83. State Papers, Holland and Flanders, Elizabeth I
        S.P. 84. State Papers, Holland, Elizabeth I
Suffolk Record Office, Ipswich
    C6/1. Assembly Books
    C5/12. General Court Records
    C9/2. Treasurer's Accounts, 1560–71
    HD36. Borough Muniments
Warwick County Record Office
    CR/136/B 2454. Account of Elizabeth at Harefield
    CR1618. WA/1/1. Corporation Accounts, 1546–69
    CR1618. W14/4. Miscellaneous Papers
    CR1618. W19/4. Notes on tipplers and alehouse keepers
    CR1908. 227/1. Bailiffs' Accounts, 1559–1716
    PG 3381. Microfilm of the Black Book of Warwick
Dr. Williams's Library, London
    Morrice 31/D. Letterbook

PRINTED PRIMARY SOURCES

Akrigg, G. P. V., ed. *Letters of King James VI & I.* Berkeley: University of California Press, 1984.

Arlott, John, ed. *John Speed's England: A Coloured Facsimile of the Maps and Text from the Theatre of the Empire of Great Britaine, First Edition, 1611.* 4 vols. London: Phoenix House, 1953.

Bacon, Nathaniel. *The Annalls of Ipswiche.* Ed. William H. Richardson. Ipswich: S. H. Cowell, 1884.

Birch, Thomas. *Memoirs of the Reign of Queen Elizabeth, from the year 1581 till her death.* 2 vols. London: A. Millar, 1754.

Bradner, Leicester, ed. *The Poems of Queen Elizabeth I.* Providence: Brown University Press, 1964.

Calendar of Letters and State Papers relating to English Affairs, Preserved principally in the Archives of Simancas. Liechtenstein: Kraus Reprint, 1971.

Calendar of State Papers, Domestic Series, of the Reign of Edward VI, 1547–1553. Ed. C. S. Knighton. Rev. ed. London: HMSO, 1992.

Calendar of State Papers, Domestic Series, of the Reigns of Edward VI, Mary, Elizabeth, 1547–1625. Liechtenstein: Kraus Reprint, 1967.

Calendar of State Papers, Domestic Series, of the Reign of Elizabeth, with Addenda. Liechtenstein: Kraus Reprint, 1967.

Clapham, John. *Elizabeth of England: Certain Observations Concerning the Life and Reign of Queen Elizabeth.* Ed. Evelyn Plummer Read and Conyers Read. Philadelphia: University of Pennsylvania Press, 1951.

Clifford, Arthur, ed. *The State Papers and Letters of Sir Ralph Sadler.* 2 vols. Edinburgh: James Ballantyne, 1809.

Cockburn, J. S., ed. *Calendar of Assize Records: Essex Indictments Elizabeth I.* London: HMSO, 1978.

———. *Calendar of Assize Records: Hertfordshire Indictments Elizabeth I.* London: HMSO, 1975.

———. *Calendar of Assize Records: Kent Indictments Elizabeth I.* London: HMSO, 1979.

———. *Calendar of Assize Records: Surrey Indictments Elizabeth I.* London: HMSO, 1980.

———. *Calendar of Assize Records: Sussex Indictments Elizabeth I.* London: HMSO, 1975.

A Collection of Ordinances and Regulations for the Government of the Royal Household . . . from King Edward III to King William and Queen Mary. London: John Nichols, 1790.

Collier, J. Payne, ed. *The Egerton Papers.* London: John Bowyer Nichols and Son, 1840.

Dasent, J. R., ed. *Acts of the Privy Council of England.* 32 vols. London: HMSO, 1890–1907.

Eland, G., ed. *Thomas Wotton's Letter-Book, 1574–1586.* London: Oxford University Press, 1960.

Ellis, Henry, ed. *Original Letters Illustrative of English History.* Vol. 2. 1st ser. London: Harding, Triphook, & Lepard, 1824.

———. *Original Letters Illustrative of English History.* Vol. 3, 2nd series. London: Harding & Lepard, 1827.

———. *Original Letters Illustrative of English History.* Vol. 4. 3rd ser. London: Richard Bentley, 1846.

Elton, G. R. *The Tudor Constitution: Documents and Commentary.* Cambridge: Cambridge University Press, 1982.

Groos, G. W., ed. *The Diary of Baron Waldstein: A Traveller in Elizabethan England.* London: Thames & Hudson, 1981.

Halliwell, James Orchard, ed. *The Private Diary of Dr. John Dee.* Camden Society, O. S., vol. 19. London, 1842.

Harington, Sir John. *Nugae Antiquae.* Ed. Thomas Park. 2 vols. London: J. Wright, 1804.

Harris, Mary Dormer, ed. *The Coventry Leet Book; or, Mayor's Register . . . 1420–1555.* 2 vols. London: Kegan Paul, 1907–13.

Harrison, G. B., ed. *De Maisse: A Journal of all that was accomplished by Monsieur De Maisse Ambassador in England from King Henri IV to Queen Elizabeth Anno Domini 1597.* London: Nonesuch Press, 1931.

———. *The Letters of Queen Elizabeth.* London: Cassell, 1935.

Harrison, William. *The Description of England.* Ed. Georges Edelen. Ithaca: Cornell University Press, 1968.

Hayward, Sir John. *Annals of the First Four Years of the Reign of Queen Elizabeth.* Ed. John Bruce. Camden Society, O. S., vol. 7. London: John Bowyer Nichols and Son, 1840.

H. M. C. Calendar of the Manuscripts of the Most Honourable the Marquess of Bath. Vol. 5, *Talbot, Dudley, and Devereux Papers, 1533–1659.* London: HMSO, 1980.

H. M. C. Calendar of the Manuscripts of the Most. Hon. the Marquis of Salisbury, K. G. London: HMSO, 1883.

H. M. C. The Manuscripts of the Shrewsbury and Coventry Corporations. 15th Report, Appendix 10. London: HMSO, 1899.

H. M. C. The Manuscripts of the Corporations of Southampton and King's Lynn. 11th Report, Appendix, Part 3. London: HMSO, 1887.

H. M. C. Report on the Pepys Manuscripts. London: HMSO, 1911.

Hughes, Paul F., and James F. Larkin, eds. *Tudor Royal Proclamations.* 3 vols. New Haven: Yale University Press, 1964–69.

Ingram, R. W., ed. *Records of Early English Drama: Coventry.* Toronto: University of Toronto Press, 1981.

Kemp, Thomas, ed. *The Book of John Fisher, Town Clerk and Deputy Recorder of Warwick, 1580–1588.* Warwick: Henry T. Cooke and Son, n.d.

Laneham, Robert. *Entertainment of Queen Elizabeth at Killingworth.* N.p., 1575.

Lodge, Edmund. *Illustrations of British History, Biography, and Manners in the Reigns of Henry VIII, Edward VI, Mary, Elizabeth, & James I.* 2nd ed. 3 vols. London: John Chidley, 1838.

McClure, Norman Egbert, ed. *The Letters of John Chamberlain.* 2 vols. Philadelphia: American Philosophical Society, 1939.

MacCulloch, Diarmaid, ed. *The Chorography of Suffolk.* Suffolk Records Society, vol. 19. London: Dramrite Printers, 1976.

Mares, F. H., ed. *The Memoirs of Robert Carey.* Oxford: Clarendon Press, 1972.

Murdin, William. *A Collection of State Papers relating to affairs in the reign of Queen Elizabeth, from the year 1571 to 1596.* London: William Bowyer, 1759. Rpt., 1978.

Nichols, John. *The Progresses and Public Processions of Queen Elizabeth.* 3 vols. London: John Nichols and Son, 1823.

Nichols, John Gough, ed. "The Diary of Henry Machyn." Camden Society, O. S., no. 42, 1848.

Nicolas, Sir Harris, ed. *Memoirs of the Life and Times of Sir Christopher Hatton.* London: Richard Bentley, 1847.

Ogle, Octavius, ed. *Royal letters addressed to Oxford, and now existing in the City Archives.* Oxford: James Parker, 1892.

Peck, Francis. *Desiderata Curiosa.* 2 vols. London, 1732.

Plummer, Charles, ed. *Elizabethan Oxford: Reprints of Rare Tracts.* Oxford Historical Society, vol. 8. Oxford: Clarendon Press, 1887.

The Princelye Pleasures at the courte at Kenelworth. London: Richard Johns, 1576. Rpt., 1821.

Ricart, Robert. *The Maire of Bristowe is Kalendar.* Ed. Lucy Toulmin Smith. Camden Society, n. s., vol. 5. Westminster: J. B. Nichols and Sons, 1872.

Sawyer, Edmund. *Memorials of Affairs of State in the Reigns of Queen Elizabeth and King James I, collected from the original papers of the Right Honourable Sir Ralph Winwood.* 3 vols. London: W. B. for T. Ward in the Inner Temple Lane, 1725.

Smith, A. Hassell, and Gillian M. Baker, eds. *The Papers of Nathaniel Bacon of Stiffkey.* Vol. 2, *1578–1585.* Norfolk Record Society, vol. 49, 1983.

Stow, John. *Annales; or, A general chronicle of England.* London: Richard Meighen, 1631.

Suffolk in 1568, Being the Return for a Subsidy granted in 1566. Suffolk Green Books, no. 12. Bury St. Edmunds: Paul & Mathew, 1909.

Wall, Alison D., ed. *Two Elizabethan Women: Correspondence of Joan and Maria Thynne, 1575–1611.* Wiltshire Record Society, vol. 38. Stoke-on-Trent: J. G. Fenn, 1983.

Youngs, Frederic A. *The Proclamations of the Tudor Queens.* Cambridge: Cambridge University Press, 1976.

SECONDARY SOURCES

Adams, Simon. "'Because I am of that countrye & mynde to plant myself there': Robert Dudley, Earl of Leicester and the West Midlands." *Midland History* 20 (1995): 21–71.

Adler, Doris. "Imaginary Toads in Real Gardens." *English Literary Renaissance* 11, no. 3 (1981): 235–60.

Alexander, Michael Van Cleave. *The First of the Tudors: A Study of Henry VII and His Reign.* Totowa, N.J.: Rowman & Littlefield, 1980.

Altman, Joel B. *The Tudor Play of Mind: Rhetorical Inquiry and the Development of Elizabethan Drama.* Berkeley: University of California Press, 1978.

Anglo, Sydney. *Images of Tudor Kingship.* London: Seaby, 1992.

———. *Spectacle, Pageantry, and Early Tudor Policy.* Oxford: Clarendon Press, 1969.

Appleby, Andrew B. *Famine in Tudor and Stuart England.* Liverpool: Liverpool University Press, 1978.

Archer, Ian. *The Pursuit of Stability: Social Relations in Elizabethan London.* Cambridge: Cambridge University Press, 1991.

Ashton, Robert. *The Crown and the Money Market, 1603–40.* Oxford: Clarendon Press, 1960.

Atkinson, Tom. *Elizabethan Winchester.* London: Faber & Faber, 1963.

Attreed, Lorraine. "The Politics of Welcome: Ceremonies and Constitutional Development in Later Medieval English Towns." In Barbara A. Hanawalt and Kathryn Reyerson, eds., *City and Spectacle in Medieval Europe,* 208–31. Minneapolis: University of Minnesota Press, 1994.

Axton, Marie. *The Queen's Two Bodies: Drama and the Elizabethan Succession.* London: Royal Historical Society, 1977.

Aydelotte, Frank. *Elizabethan Rogues and Vagabonds.* London: Frank Cass, 1967.

Bak, Janos M., ed. *Coronations: Medieval and Early Modern Monarchic Ritual.* Berkeley: University of California Press, 1990.

Bassnett, Susan. *Elizabeth I: A Feminist Perspective.* New York: Berg Press, 1988.

Batho, Gordon R. "The Finances of an Elizabethan Nobleman: Henry Percy, Ninth Earl of Northumberland (1564–1632)." *Economic History Review,* 2nd ser. 9 IX (1957): 433–50.

Beckingsale, B. W. *Elizabeth I.* London: B. T. Batsford, 1963.

Beier, A. L. "The Social Problems of an Elizabethan Country Town: Warwick, 1580–90." In Peter Clark, ed., *Country Towns in Pre-industrial England,* 45–86. Leicester: Leicester University Press, 1981.

Beier, A. L., David Cannadine, and James M. Rosenheim, eds. *The First Modern Society: Essays in Honour of Lawrence Stone.* Cambridge: Cambridge University Press, 1989.

Belsey, Andrew and Catherine Belsey. "Icons of Divinity: Portraits of Elizabeth I," in Lucy Gent and Nigel Llewellyn, eds., *Renaissance Bodies: The Human Figure in English Culture, c. 1540–1660,* 11–35. London: Reaktion Books, 1990.

Bentley, Gerald Eades. *The Jacobean and Caroline Stage.* 7 vols. Oxford: Oxford University Press, 1941–68.

Bergeron, David M. *English Civic Pageantry, 1558–1642.* London: Edward Arnold, 1971.

———, ed. *Pageantry in the Shakespearean Theatre.* Athens: University of Georgia Press, 1985.

Berry, Philippa. *Of Chastity and Power: Elizabethan Literature and the Unmarried Queen.* London: Routledge, 1989.

Berry, William. *County Genealogies: Pedigrees of the Families in the County of Kent.* London: Sherwood, Gilbert, & Piper, 1830.

Bevington, David. *Tudor Drama and Politics.* Cambridge: Harvard University Press, 1968.

Bigland, Ralph. *Observations on Marriages, Baptisms, and Burials, as Preserved in Parochial Registers.* London: W. Richardson & S. Clark, 1764.

Bindoff, S. T., ed. *The History of Parliament: The House of Commons, 1509–1558.* 3 vols. London: Secker & Warburg, 1982.

———. *Tudor England.* Harmondsworth: Penguin Books, 1950.

Bindoff, S. T., J. Hurstfield and C. H. Williams, eds. *Elizabethan Government and Society: Essays Presented to Sir John Neale.* London: Athlone Press, 1961.

Black, J. B. *The Reign of Elizabeth, 1558–1603.* Oxford: Clarendon Press, 1949.

Boas, Frederick S. *University Drama in the Tudor Age.* New York: Benjamin Blom, 1914. Rpt., 1966.

Bowler, Gerald. "English Protestants and Resistance Writings, 1553–1603." Ph.D. diss., University of London, 1981.

Boynton, Lindsay. *The Elizabethan Militia, 1558–1638.* London: Routledge & Kegan Paul, 1967.

Breight, Curt. "Realpolitik and Elizabethan Ceremony: The Earl of Hertford's Entertainment of Elizabeth at Elvetham, 1591." *Renaissance Quarterly,* 45 (1992): 20–48.

Bryant, Arthur C. *The Elizabethan Deliverance.* London: Collins, 1980.

Bryant, James C. *Tudor Drama and Religious Controversy.* Macon, Ga.: Mercer University Press, 1984.

Bryant, Lawrence M. "Configurations of the Community in Late Medieval Spectacles: Paris and London during the Dual Monarchy." In Barbara A. Hanawalt and Kathryn Reyerson, eds., *City and Spectacle in Medieval Europe,* 3–33. Minneapolis: University of Minnesota Press, 1994.

Burbidge, F. Bliss. *Old Coventry and Lady Godiva.* Birmingham: Cornish Brothers, n.d.

Burgon, John William. *The Life and Times of Sir Thomas Gresham.* 2 vols. New York: Burt Franklin, 1964.

Buxton, John. *Elizabethan Taste.* London: Macmillan, 1963.

Byrne, Muriel St. Clare. *Elizabethan Life in Town and Country.* London: Methuen, 1925.

Calderwood, William. "The Elizabethan Protestant Press: A Study of the Printing and Publishing of Protestant Religious Literature in English, Excluding Bibles and Liturgies, 1558–1603." Ph.D. diss., University of London, 1977.

Campbell, Mildred. *The English Yeoman under Elizabeth and the Early Stuarts.* London: Merlin Press, 1960. Rpt., 1967.

Cerasano, S.P., and Marion Wynne-Davies, eds. *Gloriana's Face: Women, Public and Private, in the English Renaissance.* Detroit: Wayne State University Press, 1992.

Chambers, E. K. *The Elizabethan Stage.* 4 vols. Oxford: Clarendon Press, 1923.

———. *Sir Henry Lee: An Elizabethan Portrait.* Oxford: Clarendon Press, 1936.

Cheyney, Edward P. *A History of England from the Defeat of the Armada to the Death of Elizabeth.* 2 vols. New York: Longmans, Green, 1926.

Chrimes, S. B. *Henry VII.* Berkeley: University of California Press, 1972.

Christophers, Richard Albert. "Social and Educational Background of the Surrey Clergy, 1520–1620." Ph.D. diss., University of London, 1975.

Christy, Miller. "The Progresses of Queen Elizabeth through Essex and the Houses in Which she Stayed." *Essex Review* 26 (1917): 115–29, 181–97.

Clark, Peter, ed. *Country Towns in Pre-industrial England.* Leicester: Leicester University Press, 1981.

———, ed. *The Early Modern Town.* London: Longman Press, 1976.

———. *The English Alehouse: A Social History, 1200–1830.* London: Longman Group, 1983.

Clark, Peter, and Paul Slack, eds. *Crisis and Order in English Towns, 1500–1700.* London: Routledge & Kegan Paul, 1972.

———, eds. *English Towns in Transition, 1500–1700.* London: Oxford University Press, 1976.

Collinson, Patrick. *Archbishop Grindal, 1519–1583: The Struggle for a Reformed Church.* London: Jonathan Cape, 1979.

———. *The Elizabethan Puritan Movement.* Berkeley: University of California Press, 1967.

———. *Godly People: Essays on English Protestantism and Puritanism.* London: Hambledon Press, 1983.

———. *The Religion of Protestants: The Church in English Society, 1559–1625.* Oxford: Clarendon Press, 1982.

Colvin, H. M. *The History of the King's Works.* 6 vols. London: HMSO, 1963–82.

Cooper, Charles. *The English Table in History and Literature.* London: Sampson Low, Marston, 1929. Rpt., 1968.

Creighton, Mandell. *The Age of Elizabeth.* New York: Charles Scribner's Sons, 1890.

Cromwell, Thomas. *History and Description of the Ancient Town and Borough of Colchester in Essex.* Vol. 1. London: Robert Jennings, 1825.

Dancey, C. H. "Silver Plate and Insignia of the City of Gloucester." *Transactions of the Bristol and Gloucestershire Archaeological Society* 30 (1907), 91–122.

Darby, H. C. *An Historical Geography of England before A.D. 1800.* Cambridge: Cambridge University Press, 1936.

Dent, John. *The Quest for Nonsuch.* London: Hutchinson, 1962.

Dewar, Mary. *Sir Thomas Smith: A Tudor Intellectual in Office.* London: Athlone Press, 1964.

Dickens, A. G., ed. *The Courts of Europe: Politics, Patronage, and Royalty, 1400–1800.* New York: McGraw-Hill, 1978.

Dietz, Frederick C. *English Public Finance, 1558–1641.* New York: Century, 1932.

———. *The Exchequer in Elizabeth's Reign.* Smith College Studies in History 8, no. 2 (1923): 65–118.

Doran, Susan. "Juno versus Diana: The Treatment of Elizabeth I's Marriage in Plays and Entertainments, 1561–1581." *Historical Journal* 38, no. 2 (1995): 257–74.

———. *Monarchy and Matrimony: The Courtships of Elizabeth I.* London: Routledge, 1995.

———. "The Political Career of Thomas Radcliffe, 3rd Earl of Sussex (1526?-1583)." Ph.D. diss., University of London, 1977.

Dorman, Thomas. "Visits of Two Queens to Sandwich." *Archaelogia cantiana: Transactions of the Kent Archeological Society* 16 (1886): 58–61.

Dowling, Maria. "Scholarship, Politics, and the Court of Henry VIII." Ph.D. diss., London School of Economics and Political Science, 1981.

Duffy, Eamon. *The Stripping of the Altars: Traditional Religion in England, c. 1400–c. 1580.* New Haven: Yale University Press, 1992.

Dugdale, Sir William. *The Antiquities of Warwickshire.* 2nd ed. 2 vols. London, 1730.

Dunlop, Ian. *Palaces & Progresses of Elizabeth I.* London: Jonathan Cape, 1962.

Durant, David N. *Bess of Hardwick: Portrait of an Elizabethan Dynast.* London: Weidenfeld & Nicolson, 1977.

Dutton, Ralph. *English Court Life from Henry VII to George II.* London: B. T. Batsford, 1963.

Elton, G. R. *England under the Tudors.* London: Methuen, 1962.

———. *The Parliament of England, 1559–1581.* Cambridge: Cambridge University Press, 1989.

———. *Studies in Tudor and Stuart Politics and Government: Tudor Politics, Tudor Government.* Cambridge: Cambridge University Press, 1974.

Emmison, F. G. *Elizabethan Life: Home, Work, & Land.* Chelmsford: Essex County Council, 1976.

———. *Tudor Food and Pastimes.* London: Ernest Benn, 1964.

———. *Tudor Secretary: Sir William Petre at Court and Home.* London: Longmans, Green, 1961.

Erickson, Carolly. *The First Elizabeth.* New York: Summit Books, 1983.

Feiling, Sir Keith. *England under the Tudors and Stuarts, 1485–1688.* London: Oxford University Press, 1927. Rpt., 1963.

Fisher, F. J. "The Development of London as a Centre of Conspicuous Consumption in the Sixteenth and Seventeenth Centuries," *Transactions of the Royal Historical Society,* 4th ser. 30 (1948): 37–50.

Fletcher, Anthony. *Gender, Sex, and Subordination in England, 1500–1800.* New Haven: Yale University Press, 1995.

———. *Tudor Rebellions.* London: Longman Group, 1977.

Froude, James Anthony. *History of England from the Fall of Wolsey to the Death of Elizabeth.* 12 vols. New York: Charles Scribner, 1870.

Frye, Susan. *Elizabeth I: The Competition for Representation.* Oxford: Oxford University Press, 1993.

———. "The Myth of Elizabeth I at Tilbury." *Sixteenth Century Journal* 23 (1992): 95–114.

Fullbrook-Leggatt, L. E. W. O. "Medieval Gloucester." *Transactions of the Bristol and Gloucestershire Archaeological Society* 67 (1946–48): 217–306.

Geertz, Clifford. "Centers, Kings, and Charisma." In Sean Wilentz, ed., *Rites of Power,* 13–38. Philadelphia: University of Pennsylvania Press, 1985.

———. *The Interpretation of Cultures.* New York: Basic Books, 1973.

Giesey, Ralph E. "Models of Rulership in French Royal Ceremonial." In Sean Wilentz, ed., *Rites of Power,* 41–64. Philadelphia: University of Pennsylvania Press, 1985.

Glanville, Gordon Harris. "Aspects of the History of the County of Surrey, 1580–1620." Ph.D. diss., University of London, 1972.

Gleason, J. H. *The Justices of the Peace in England, 1558 to 1640.* Oxford: Clarendon Press, 1969.

Glyde, John, comp. *The New Suffolk Garland.* Ipswich, 1866.

Goldberg, Jonathan. *James I and the Politics of Literature: Jonson, Shakespeare, Donne, and Their Contemporaries.* Baltimore: Johns Hopkins University Press, 1983.

Greaves, Richard L. *Society and Religion in Elizabethan England.* Minneapolis: University of Minnesota Press, 1981.

Green, John Richard. *History of the English People.* 4 vols. New York: Harper & Brothers, 1878.

Greenblatt, Stephen. *Renaissance Self-Fashioning.* Chicago: University of Chicago Press, 1980.

————, ed. *Representing the English Renaissance*. Berkeley: University of California Press, 1988.

Gregg, Pauline. *King Charles I*. London: J. M. Dent & Sons, 1981.

Guizot, M. *History of England*. 4 vols. Boston: Dana Estes, 1800.

Guth, Delloyd J. and John W. McKenna, eds. *Tudor Rule and Revolution: Essays for G. R. Elton from His American friends*. Cambridge: Cambridge University Press, 1982.

Guy, John, ed. *The Reign of Elizabeth I: Court and Culture in the Last Decade*. Cambridge: Cambridge University Press, 1995.

————. *Tudor England*. New York: Oxford University Press, 1988.

Haigh, Christopher. *Elizabeth I: Profile in Power*. London: Longman, 1988.

Haller, William. *The Rise of Puritanism*. New York: Harper & Brothers, 1938. Rpt., 1957.

Hanawalt, Barbara A., and Kathryn Reyerson, eds. *City and Spectacle in Medieval Europe*. Minneapolis: University of Minnesota Press, 1994.

Hasler, P. W. *The History of Parliament: The House of Commons, 1558–1603*. 3 vols. London: HMSO, 1981.

Haselwood, Rev. Francis. "Notes from the Records of Smarden Church." *Archaelogia cantiana: Transactions of the Kent Archeological Society* 9 (1874): 224–35.

Hasted, Edward. *Hasted's History of Kent. Part 1, The Hundred of Blackheath*. Ed. Henry H. Drake. London: Mitchell & Hughes, 1886.

Havran, Martin J. "The Character and Principles of an English King: The Case of Charles I." *Catholic Historical Review* 69, no. 2 (1983): 169–208.

Heal, Felicity. *Hospitality in Early Modern England*. Oxford: Clarendon Press, 1990.

Heisch, Allison. "Queen Elizabeth I and the Persistence of Patriarchy." *Feminist Review*, Feb. 1980, 45–56.

Hirst, L. Fabian. *The Conquest of Plague*. Oxford: Clarendon Press, 1953.

Hoak, Dale, ed. *Tudor Political Culture*. Cambridge: Cambridge University Press, 1995.

Hogrefe, Pearl. *Women of Action in Tudor England*. Ames: Iowa State University Press, 1977.

Hopkins, Lisa. *Elizabeth I and Her Court*. London: Vision Press, 1990.

Hoskins, W. G. "An Elizabethan Provincial Town: Leicester." In J. H. Plumb, ed., *Studies in Social History*, 33–67. London: Longmans, Green, 1955. Rpt., 1969.

Howarth, David. *Images of Rule: Art and Politics in the English Renaissance, 1485–1649*. Berkeley: University of California Press, 1997.

Hudson, Winthrop S. *The Cambridge Connection and the Elizabethan Settlement of 1559*. Durham: Duke University Press, 1980.

Hume, David. *The History of England*. 6 vols. New York: Harper & Brothers, 1879.

Hunt, William. *The Puritan Moment: The Coming of Revolution in an English County*. Cambridge: Harvard University Press, 1983.

Hurstfield, Joel. *Freedom, Government, and Corruption in Elizabethan England*. London: Jonathan Cape, 1973.

————. *The Queen's Wards*. London: Longmans, Green, 1958.

Hutton, Ronald. *The Rise and Fall of Merry England: The Ritual Year, 1400–1700*. Oxford: Oxford University Press, 1994.

Innes, Arthur D. *England under the Tudors*. London: Methuen, 1924.

Ives, E. W. *Faction in Tudor England*. London: The Historical Association, 1979.

James, Mervyn. *Society, Politics, and Culture: Studies in Early Modern England*. Cambridge: Cambridge University Press, 1986.

Jenkins, Canon. "On the Municipal Records of Folkestone." *Archaelogia cantiana: Transactions of the Kent Archeological Society*, 10 (1876): lxix–lxxxv.

Jenkins, Elizabeth. *Elizabeth the Great*. New York: Coward-McCann, 1959.

Johnson, Paul. *Elizabeth I*. New York: Holt, Rinehart, & Winston, 1974.

Jordan, W. K. *Philanthropy in England, 1480–1660*. London: George Allen & Unwin, 1959.

Kertzer, David I. *Ritual, Politics, and Power.* New Haven: Yale University Press, 1988.

King, John N. "The Royal Image, 1535–1603." In Dale Hoak, ed., *Tudor Political Culture,* 104–32. Cambridge: Cambridge University Press, 1995.

———. *Tudor Royal Iconography.* Princeton: Princeton University Press, 1989.

Kingdon, Robert M. *Myths about the St. Bartholomew's Day Massacres, 1572–1576.* Cambridge: Harvard University Press, 1988.

Kinney, Arthur. *Titled Elizabethans.* Hamden, Conn.: Archon Books, 1973.

Kipling, Gordon. "Richard II's 'Sumptuous Pageants' and the Idea of the Civic Triumph." In David M. Bergeron, ed., *Pageantry in the Shakespearean Theatre,* 88–94. Athens: University of Georgia Press, 1985.

La Mar, Virginia A. *Travel and Roads in England.* Washington, D.C.: Folger Shakespeare Library, 1960. Rpt., 1966.

Levin, Carole. *"The Heart and Stomach of a King": Elizabeth I and the Politics of Sex and Power.* Philadelphia: University of Pennsylvania Press, 1994.

Levine, Mortimer. *The Early Elizabethan Succession Question, 1558–1568.* Stanford: Stanford University Press, 1966.

———. "The Place of Women in Tudor Government." In D. J. Guth and J. W. McKenna, eds., *Tudor Rule and Revolution,* 109–123. Cambridge: Cambridge University Press, 1982.

Linnell, Rev. C. L. S. "Suffolk Church Monuments." *Proceedings of the Suffolk Institute of Archaeology* 27, p. 1 (1955).

Loades, David. *Mary Tudor: A Life.* Oxford: Basil Blackwell, 1990.

Lockyer, Roger. *Tudor and Stuart Britain, 1471–1714.* New York: St. Martin's Press, 1964.

Lovejoy, A. O. *The Great Chain of Being: A Study of the History of an Idea.* Cambridge: Harvard University Press, 1936.

Luke, Mary M. *Gloriana: The Years of Elizabeth I.* New York: Coward, McCann, & Geoghegan, 1973.

Lyon, Bryce. *A Constitutional and Legal History of Medieval England.* 2nd ed. New York: W. W. Norton, 1980.

MacCaffrey, Wallace T. *Queen Elizabeth I.* London: Edward Arnold, 1993.

———. *Queen Elizabeth and the Making of Policy, 1572–1588.* Princeton: Princeton University Press, 1981.

———. *The Shaping of the Elizabethan Regime.* Princeton: Princeton University Press, 1968.

McCoy, Richard C. *The Rites of Knighthood: The Literature and Politics of Elizabethan Chivalry.* Berkeley: University of California Press, 1989.

———. "'The Wonderfull Spectacle': The Civic Progress of Elizabeth I and the Troublesome Coronation." In Janos M. Bak, ed., *Coronations,* 212–27. Berkeley: University of California Press, 1990.

MacCulloch, Diarmaid Ninian John. "Power, Privilege, and the County Community: County Politics in Elizabethan Suffolk." Ph. D. diss., Cambridge University, 1977.

Macfarlane, Alan. *The Family Life of Ralph Josselin.* New York: W. W. Norton, 1970. Rpt., 1977.

McFarlane, I. D. *The Entry of Henry II into Paris, 16 June 1549.* Binghamton: Medieval & Renaissance Texts & Studies, 1982.

MacNalty, Sir Arthur Salusbury. *Elizabeth Tudor: The Lonely Queen.* New York: Frederick Ungar, 1961.

Manley, Lawrence. *Literature and Culture in Early Modern London.* Cambridge: Cambridge University Press, 1995.

Manning, Roger B. "Poaching as a Symbolic Substitute for War in Tudor and Early Stuart England." *Journal of Medieval and Renaissance Studies* 22, no. 2 (1992): 185–210.

———. *Religion and Society in Elizabethan Sussex: A Study of the Enforcement of the Religious Settlement, 1558–1603.* Leicester: Leicester University Press, 1969.

Mattingly, Garrett. *The Armada*. Boston: Houghton Mifflin, 1959.
———. *Renaissance Diplomacy*. Baltimore: Penguin Books, 1964.
Mepham, W. A. "Visits of Professional Touring Companies to Essex, 1537–1642." *Essex Review* 57 (1948): 205–16.
Montrose, Louis. "'Shaping Fantasies': Figurations of Gender and Power in Elizabethan Culture." In Stephen Greenblatt, ed., *Representing the English Renaissance*, 31–40. Berkeley: University of California Press, 1988.
Morant, Philip. *The History and Antiquities of the County of Essex*. 2 vols. London, 1763–68.
Morris, Christopher. *The Tudors*. London: Fontana Press, 1974.
Muir, Edward. *Civic Ritual in Renaissance Venice*. Princeton: Princeton University Press, 1981.
Mullett, Charles F. *The Bubonic Plague and England*. Lexington: University Press of Kentucky, 1956.
Neale, J. E. *Elizabeth I and Her Parliaments. Vol. 1, 1559–1581*. London: Jonathan Cape, 1953.
———. *Elizabeth I and Her Parliaments. Vol. 2, 1584–1601*. London: Jonathan Cape, 1957.
———. *The Elizabethan House of Commons*. London: Jonathan Cape, 1949. Rpt., 1976.
———. *Queen Elizabeth I: A Biography*. London: Jonathan Cape, 1934. Rpt., 1957.
———. "The Sayings of Queen Elizabeth." *History* 10 (1925): 212–33.
Newton, A. P. "Tudor Reforms in the Royal Household." In R. W. Seton-Watson, ed., *Tudor Studies Presented by the Board of Studies in History in the University of London to Albert Frederick Pollard*, 231–56. New York: Russell & Russell, 1924. Rpt., 1970.
Notestein, Wallace. "The English Woman, 1580–1650." In J. H. Plumb, ed., *Studies in Social History*, 71–107. London: Longmans, Green, 1955. Rpt., 1969.
O'Day, Margaret Rosemary. "Clerical Patronage and Recruitment in England in the Elizabethan and Early Stuart Periods, with Special Reference to the Diocese of Coventry and Lichfield." Ph.D. diss., University of London, 1972.
———. "The Ecclesiastical Patronage of the Lord Keeper, 1558–1642," *Transactions of the Royal Historical Society*, 5th ser. 23 (1973): 89–109.
Orgel, Stephen. *The Illusion of Power: Political Theatre in the English Renaissance*. Berkeley: University of California Press, 1975.
Palliser, D. M. *The Age of Elizabeth: England under the Later Tudors, 1547–1603*. London: Longman Group, 1983.
Patten, John. *English Towns, 1500–1700*. Folkestone: William Dawson & Sons, 1978.
Pevsner, Nicholas, and Judy Nairn, eds. *The Buildings of England*. 46 vols. Harmondsworth: Penguin Books, 1951–79.
Philipott, Thomas. *Villare cantianum; or, Kent Surveyed and Illustrated*. 2nd ed. Lynn: W. Whittingham, 1776.
Phythian-Adams, Charles. "Ceremony and the Citizen: The Communal Year at Coventry, 1450–1550." In Peter Clark and Paul Slack, eds., *Crisis and Order in English Towns, 1500–1700*, 57–85. London: Routledge & Kegan Paul, 1972.
———. *Desolation of a City: Coventry and the Urban Crisis of the Late Middle Ages*. Cambridge: Cambridge University Press, 1979.
———, ed. *Societies, Cultures, and Kinship, 1580–1850*. Leicester: Leicester University Press, 1993.
Platt, Colin. *The Great Rebuildings of Tudor and Stuart England*. London: University College, 1994.
Plowden, Alison. *The Young Elizabeth*. New York: Stein & Day, 1971.
Plumb, J. H., ed. *Studies in Social History: A Tribute to G. M. Trevelyan*. London: Longmans, Green, 1955. Rpt., 1969.
Poole, Benjamin, comp. *Coventry: Its History & Antiquities*. London: John Russell Smith, 1870.

Pound, John F. *The Norwich Census of the Poor, 1570*. Norfolk Record Society Publications, vol. 40, 1971.

———. *Poverty and Vagrancy in Tudor England*. London: Longman Group, 1971.

Powell, W. R., ed. *The Victoria History of the Counties of England: A History of the County of Essex*. Vols. 4–8. London: Oxford University Press, 1956–83.

Price, F. Douglas. "Commission for Ecclesiastical Causes for the Dioceses of Bristol and Gloucester, 1574." *Transactions of the Bristol and Gloucestershire Archaeological Society* 59 (1937): 61–184.

Priestley, Edgar John. "The Manor and Palace of Eltham, Kent, 1086–1663." M. Ph. thesis, University of London, 1973.

Pulman, Michael Barraclough. *The Elizabethan Privy Council in the Fifteen-Seventies*. Berkeley: University of California Press, 1971.

Read, Conyers. *Lord Burghley and Queen Elizabeth*. London: Jonathan Cape, 1960.

———. "Lord Burghley's Household Accounts." *Economic History Review,* 2nd ser., 9 (1956): 343–48.

———. *Mr. Secretary Cecil and Queen Elizabeth*. Rpt. New York: Alfred A. Knopf, 1961.

———. *The Tudors*. New York: W. W. Norton, 1969.

Rice, George P., Jr. *The Public Speaking of Queen Elizabeth*. New York: Columbia University Press, 1951.

Ridley, Jasper. *Elizabeth I*. New York: Viking, 1987.

Roberts, R. S. "Epidemics and Social History." *Medical History* 12 (1968): 305–16.

Rowse, A. L. *The Elizabethan Renaissance: The Life of the Society*. New York: Charles Scribner's Sons, 1971.

———. *Eminent Elizabethans*. Athens: University of Georgia Press, 1983.

———. *The England of Elizabeth: The Structure of Society*. New York: Macmillan, 1950.

———. *Ralegh and the Throckmortons*. London: Macmillan, 1962.

Rubin, Miri. "Religious Culture in Town and Country: Reflections on a Great Divide." In David Abulafia, Michael Franklin, and Miri Rubin, eds., *Church and City, 1000–1500: Essays in Honour of Christopher Brooke,* 3–22. Cambridge: Cambridge University Press, 1992.

Russell, Conrad. *The Crisis of Parliaments: English History, 1509–1660*. Oxford: Oxford University Press, 1978.

Rutledge, Douglas F., ed. *Ceremony and Text in the Renaissance*. Newark: University of Delaware Press, 1996.

Rutton, William Loftie. "Wentworth, of Gosfield, Co. Essex." *Essex Archaeological Society Transactions,* n.s. 3 (1889): 209–21.

Sacks, David Harris. *Trade, Society, and Politics in Bristol, 1500–1640*. New York: Garland 1985.

———. *The Widening Gate: Bristol and the Atlantic Economy, 1450–1700*. Berkeley: University of California Press, 1991.

Salomon, Nanette. "Positioning Women in Visual Convention: The Case of Elizabeth I." In Betty S. Travitsky and Adele F. Seef, eds., *Attending to Women in Early Modern England,* 64–95. Newark: University of Delaware Press, 1994.

Salzman, L. F. *England in Tudor Times: An Account of Its Social Life and Industries*. New York: Russell & Russell, 1926. Rpt., 1969.

Samaha, Joel. *Law and Order in Historical Perspective: The Case of Elizabethan Essex*. New York: Academic Press, 1974.

Samman, Neil. "The Progresses of Henry VIII, 1509–1529." In Diarmaid MacCulloch, ed., *The Reign of Henry VIII: Politics, Policy, and Piety,* 59–73. London: Macmillan, 1995.

Scalingi, Paula Louise. "The Scepter or the Distaff: The Question of Female Sovereignty, 1516–1607." *Historian* 41 (1978): 59–75.

Scarisbrick, J. J. *The Reformation and the English People.* Oxford: Basil Blackwell, 1984.

Schelling, Felix E. *The Queen's Progress and Other Elizabethan Sketches.* London: T. Werner Laurie, 1904.

Schofield, R. S. "The Geographical Distribution of Wealth in England, 1334–1649." *Economic History Review* 2nd ser. 18, no. 3 (1965): 483–510.

Scott, William Robert. *The Constitution and Finance of English, Scottish, and Irish Joint-Stock Companies to 1720.* 3 vols. Cambridge: Cambridge University Press, 1912. Rpt., 1951.

Sharpe, Buchanan. *In Contempt of All Authority: Rural Artisans and Riot in the West of England, 1586–1660.* Berkeley: University of California Press, 1980.

Sharpe, Kevin, and Peter Lake, eds. *Culture and Politics in Early Stuart England.* London: Macmillan, 1994.

Sheils, William. "The Puritans in Church and Politics in the Diocese of Peterborough, 1570–1610." Ph.D. diss., University of London, 1974.

Shrewsbury, J. F. D. *A History of Bubonic Plague in the British Isles.* Cambridge: Cambridge University Press, 1970.

Silcock, R. H. "County Government in Worcestershire, 1603–1660." Ph. D. diss., University of London, 1974.

Slicher Van Bath, B. H. *The Agrarian History of Western Europe, A.D. 500–1850.* Trans. Olive Ordish. London: Edward Arnold, 1963.

Smith, A. Hassell. *County and Court: Government and Politics in Norfolk, 1558–1603.* Oxford: Clarendon Press, 1974.

Smith, Alan G. R. *Servant of the Cecils: The Life of Sir Michael Hickes, 1543–1612.* London: Jonathan Cape, 1977.

Smith, Lacey Baldwin. *Elizabeth Tudor: Portrait of a Queen.* Boston: Little, Brown, 1975.

Smuts, R. Malcolm. "Art and the Material Culture of Majesty in Early Stuart England." In Smuts, ed., *The Stuart Court and Europe.* Cambridge: Cambridge University Press, 1996.

———. *Court Culture and the Origins of a Royalist Tradition in Early Stuart England.* Philadelphia: University of Pennsylvania Press, 1987.

———. "Public Ceremony and Royal Charisma: The English Royal Entry in London, 1485–1642." In A. L. Beier, David Cannadine, and James M. Rosenheim, eds., *The First Modern Society,* 65–94. Cambridge: Cambridge University Press, 1989.

Somerset, Anne. *Elizabeth I.* London: Weidenfeld & Nicolson, 1991.

Sommerville, Margaret R. *Sex & Subjection: Attitudes to Women in Early-Modern Society.* New York: St. Martin's Press, 1995.

Spufford, Margaret. *Contrasting Communities: English Villagers in the Sixteenth and Seventeenth Centuries.* Cambridge: Cambridge University Press, 1974.

Stephens, W. B., ed. *The Victoria History of the Counties of England: A History of the County of Warwick.* Vols. 2–8. London: Oxford University Press, 1964–69.

Stone, Lawrence. *The Causes of the English Revolution.* New York: Harper Torchbooks, 1972.

———. *Crisis of the Aristocracy, 1558–1641.* Oxford: Clarendon Press, 1965.

———. *Family and Fortune: Studies in Aristocratic Finance in the Sixteenth and Seventeenth Centuries.* Oxford: Clarendon Press, 1973.

Strangford, Viscount, ed. "Household Expenses of the Princess Elizabeth during Her Residence at Hatfield." *Camden Miscellany,* vol. 2, 1853.

Strong, Roy. *Art and Power: Renaissance Festivals, 1450–1650.* Berkeley: University of California Press, 1984.

———. *The Cult of Elizabeth.* Berkeley: University of California Press, 1977.

———. "Elizabethan Pageantry as Propaganda." Ph.D. diss., University of London, 1962.

———. *Gloriana: The Portraits of Queen Elizabeth I.* New York: Thames & Hudson, 1987.

Strype, John. *Annals of the Reformation.* Oxford, 1824. Rpt., New York: Burt Franklin, 1968.

———. *The Life of the Learned Sir Thomas Smith.* New York: Burt Franklin Reprints, 1974.

Suckling, Rev. Alfred. *The History and Antiquities of the County of Suffolk.* 2 vols. London: John Weale, 1846.

Taylor-Smither, Larissa J. "Elizabeth I: A Psychological Profile." *Sixteenth Century Journal* 15, no. 1 (Spring 1984): 47–72.

Thomas, J. H. *Town Government in the Sixteenth Century.* London: George Allen & Unwin, 1933.

Thurley, Simon. *The Royal Palaces of Tudor England.* New Haven: Yale University Press, 1993.

Tillyard, E. M. W. *The Elizabethan World Picture.* New York: Vintage Books, 1943.

Tittler, Robert. "Political Culture and the Built Environment of the English Country Town, c. 1540–1620." In Dale Hoak, ed., *Tudor Political Culture.* Cambridge: Cambridge University Press, 1995.

———. "Seats of Honor, Seats of Power: The Symbolism of Public Seating in the English Urban Community, c. 1560–1620." *Albion* 24 (1992): 205–23.

Travitsky, Betty S., and Adele F. Seef, eds. *Attending to Women in Early Modern England.* Newark: University of Delaware Press, 1994.

Trexler, Richard C. *The Libro Cerimoniale of the Florentine Republic.* Geneva: Librairie Droz, 1978.

———. *Public Life in Renaissance Florence.* Ithaca: Cornell University Press, 1991.

Tribble, Evelyn B. "'We Will Do No Harm with Our Swords': Royal Representation, Civic Pageantry, and the Displacement of Popular Protest in Thomas Deloney's *Jacke of Newberie.*" In Alvin Vos, ed., *Place and Displacement in the Renaissance,* 147–57. New York: Medieval & Renaissance Texts & Studies, 1995.

Trousdale, Marion. *Shakespeare and the Rhetoricians.* Chapel Hill: University of North Carolina Press, 1982.

Turner, Victor. *Dramas, Fields, and Metaphors: Symbolic Action in Human Society.* Ithaca: Cornell University Press, 1975.

———. *From Ritual to Theatre: The Human Seriousness of Play.* New York: PAJ Publications, 1982.

———. *The Ritual Process: Structure and Anti-structure.* Ithaca: Cornell University Press, 1969.

Vanes, Jean Mary. "The Overseas Trade of Bristol in the Sixteenth Century." Ph.D. diss., University of London, 1975.

Vos, Alvin, ed. *Place and Displacement in the Renaissance.* New York: Medieval & Renaissance Texts & Studies, 1995.

Waldman, Milton. *Elizabeth and Leicester.* Boston: Houghton Mifflin, 1945.

———. *England's Elizabeth.* Boston: Houghton Mifflin, 1933.

Warren, Robert Hall. "Mediaeval Chapels of Bristol." *Transactions of the Bristol and Gloucestershire Archaeological Society* 30 (1907): 181–211.

Webb, John. *Great Tooley of Ipswich: Portrait of an Early Tudor Merchant.* Suffolk Records Society Publication, 1962.

Weimann, Robert. *Shakespeare and the Popular Tradition in the Theater.* Ed. Robert Schwartz. Baltimore: Johns Hopkins University Press, 1978.

Weissman, Ronald R. E. *Ritual Brotherhood in Renaissance Florence.* New York: Academic Press, 1982.

Wells, Edith Nellie. "Kenilworth Castle and Priory." M.A. thesis, University of Birmingham, 1923.

Wernham, R. B. *After the Armada: Elizabethan England and the Struggle for Western Europe, 1588–1595.* Oxford: Clarendon Press, 1984.

Wickham, Glynne. *Early English Stages, 1300–1660.* 3 vols. London: Routledge & Kegan Paul, 1981.

Wiesner, Merry E. *Women and Gender in Early Modern Europe.* Cambridge: Cambridge University Press, 1992.

Wilentz, Sean, ed. *Rites of Power: Symbolism, Ritual, and Politics since the Middle Ages.* Philadelphia: University of Pennsylvania Press, 1985.

Williams, Penry. "Court and Polity under Elizabeth I." *Bulletin of the John Rylands University Library* 65, no. 2 (Spring 1983): 259–86.

———. *The Tudor Regime.* Oxford: Clarendon Press, 1979. Rpt., 1983.

Williamson, James A. *The Tudor Age.* New York: David McKay, 1961.

Willis-Bund, J. W., et al. *The Victoria History of the County of Worcester,* 4 vols. Westminster: A. Constable and Co., 1910–24.

Willson, David Harris. *King James VI & I.* New York: Oxford University Press, 1967.

Wilson, Jean. *Entertainments for Elizabeth I.* Totowa, N. J.: Rowman & Littlefield, 1980.

Wilson, Violet A. *Queen Elizabeth's Maids of Honour and Ladies of the Privy Chamber.* London: Bodley Head, 1922.

Withington, Robert. *English Pageantry.* 2 vols. Cambridge: Harvard University Press, 1918–20.

Wood, Anthony. *Survey of the Antiquities of the City of Oxford composed in 1661–6.* Ed. Andrew Clark. 3 vols. Oxford: Clarendon Press, 1889.

Woodworth, Allegra. "Purveyance for the Royal Household in the Reign of Queen Elizabeth." *Transactions of the American Philosophical Society,* n.s. 35 (1945): 1–89.

Wormald, Jenny. *Mary Queen of Scots: A Study in Failure.* London: George Philip, 1988.

Wrightson, Keith. *English Society, 1580–1680.* London: Hutchinson, 1982. Rpt., 1983.

Wrightson, Keith, and David Levine. *Poverty and Piety in an English Village: Terling, 1525–1700.* New York: Academic Press, 1979.

Wrigley, E. A. *Population and History.* New York: McGraw-Hill, 1969.

Wrigley, E. A., and R. S. Schofield. *The Population History of England, 1541–1871.* London: Edward Arnold, 1981.

Wyndham, Katherine S. H. "The Redistribution of Crown Land in Somerset by Gift, Sale, and Lease, 1536–1572." Ph.D. diss., University of London, 1976.

Yates, Frances A. *Astraea: The Imperial Theme in the Sixteenth Century.* London: Routledge & Kegan Paul, 1975.

INDEX

Coke, Sir Edward, 73
Colchester, 49, 57
Collen, Patrick, 167
composition, 47, 51–52. *See also* purveyance
Cooke, Sir Anthony, 29, 56
Cordell, Sir William, 142
coronation: as ceremonial dialogue, 122; of
   Elizabeth I, 18, 155; of English monarchs, 15, 17–18
cost of progresses, 4, 173; appareling,
   55–56; food, 6, 54–55; hosts and, 3, 52–
   53, 63–78, 92–93; household reform and,
   58–61; posts, 55; to queen, 52–61; repairs
   to palaces, 57; towns and, 98–106; transport, 55. *See also* Burghley; finance; purveyance
counties: composition and, 47, 51–52; purveyance and, 49–50; royal itinerary and,
   23–25, 202–3. *See also* individual names
court, royal, 11, 26; access and, 60, 63, 84,
   87, 163–64, 167; board of green cloth
   and, 41–42; Burghley and, 30; business
   of, 26–27, 36, 40; challenges of travel to,
   35–40; destinations of, 23, 38, 95; expenses of, 54–58; feeding of, 6, 10, 41–
   46, 53; on progress, 13, 19, 41, 67, 112–13;
   queen's will and, 3, 5, 19, 23, 35, 61–62,
   151, 169, 172; transport of, 45–48. *See also*
   government; household; privy council
courtiers, 5, 26, 52; advantage of progresses
   and, 39, 63; attitudes of, 11, 21, 61, 142–
   43, 148, 151, 153, 161; female sovereignty
   and, 7, 10, 61, 174; gifts from private
   hosts to, 74; gifts from towns to, 102; as
   hosts, 29–32, 53, 66–70; views of travel,
   35, 37, 40, 95. *See also* Burghley; Hatton;
   Leicester; Walsingham
Coventry, 17, 24; cost of visit, 105; Hock
   Tuesday play and, 116–20, 129–30; visit
   to, 101, 103, 123–28, 131–32, 245
Cranbrook, 101
Crane, Anthony, 60
Croft, Sir James, 102
Cromwell, Oliver, 15
crowds, 7, 55; ceremony and, 115, 122, 126–
   27, 133, 155; queen in, 1, 88, 123–25,
   130–40; royal safety in, 164–68, 173–74.
   See also citizens; popularity

Dee, Dr. John, 22
defense of the realm: Armada and, 159; cer-

emony and, 2, 154–58; gender and, 16,
   155–56, 163; navy, 156; John Smythe and,
   80. *See also* military visits
Deloney, Thomas, 122
Denmark, 15
Deptford, visits to, 156
Derby, countess of, 84
disease. *See* plague; smallpox
Doran, Susan, 7
Dover, 23–24, 88, 114; duc d'Alençon and,
   154; visit to, 21, 101, 108
Doyly, John, 166
Drake, Sir Francis, 156
Dunlop, Ian, 6

East Anglia, 2, 137, 142–43
Edinburgh, 15, 146–47; Treaty of, 145
Edward IV, king of England, 17
Edward VI, king of England, 14, 18
Egerton, Sir Thomas, 74, 76
Elizabeth I, queen of England: accidents
   and, 130–31, 165; appropriate hospitality
   and, 78, 91–92; attitudes of, 2, 137, 153,
   161; authority of, 135, 157; caution of, 24,
   33–34, 136, 145, 156; Robert Cecil and,
   67, 162; chaos of travel and, 40, 61–62,
   163; character of, 1, 11, 15, 20, 38, 58, 73,
   87, 118, 132, 140, 145, 150, 156; choices of
   destinations, 2, 23–25, 33–34, 158; church
   and, 135–44; clergy and, 27, 137; commitment to travel of, 1–4, 11, 61, 94, 148;
   compliments to hosts by, 101, 111, 115,
   124–27, 130, 132, 139, 158; coronation of,
   18, 155; courtiers and, 10, 31, 61, 67, 95;
   cultivation of popularity, 1–4, 97, 127; as
   daughter of Henry VIII, 13, 16, 18, 25,
   34, 62, 167; desire for harmony of, 2, 131,
   135, 141, 144; diet of, 45, 55, 113, 165; dis-
   like of location, 20, 31, 70–71, 154, 157;
   Robert Dudley and, 30–31, 65, 70, 133;
   enjoyment of a place, 31, 39, 65–66; excommunication of, 165; favorite hosts,
   29–32; French suitors and, 151–54; friendships of, 29–31, 70–71, 87, 94; frugality
   of, 1, 52, 81, 174–75; foreign travel and,
   13, 15; gender and, 7, 155–56, 168–72;
   gifts from private hosts, 73–74; gifts
   from towns, 101–04, 125–26; government of, 3–4, 11, 35–40, 61, 95, 128, 173;
   historians on, 52–53; health of, 19–21,
   157, 167; manipulation by, 10, 38, 135,

DATE DUE
